Emotion Experience

A special issue of the
Journal of Consciousness Studies
12.8–10 (2005)

edited by

Giovanna Colombetti
& Evan Thompson

ia

imprint-academic.com

Published in the UK by Imprint Academic
PO Box 200, Exeter EX5 5YX, UK

Published in the USA by Imprint Academic
Philosophy Documentation Center,
PO Box 7147, Charlottesville, VA 22906-7147 , USA

ISBN 1 84540 029 1 (paperback)

ISSN 1355 8250 (*Journal of Consciousness Studies*, **12**, number 8–10, 2005)

British Library Cataloguing in Publication Data
A catalogue record for this book is available from the British Library
Library of Congress Card Number: 2005923593

Printed in Great Britain by MPG Books Ltd, Bodmin, Cornwall

Cover Picture:
Le Signorine by Felice Casorati ©DACS 2005 (Detail)

Le Signorine by Felice Casorati ©DACS 2005

Contents

About Contributors

Giovanna Colombetti is a Post-Doctoral Fellow at the Cognitive Science Laboratory, University of Trento (Italy). She has studied philosophy and cognitive science in Florence, Brussels and Birmingham (UK), and did her DPhil at the School of Cognitive and Computing Sciences of the University of Sussex (UK). In 2003–2005 she was a Post-Doctoral Fellow at the Department of Philosophy, York University (Canada), where she was supervised by Evan Thompson within his 'Cognitive Science and The Embodied Mind' research project. Her research interests include emotion, embodiment, enaction, dynamical systems and consciousness.

Evan Thompson is Professor of Philosophy at the University of Toronto. From 2002 to 2005 he held a Canada Research Chair in Cognitive Science and the Embodied Mind at York University. He is the co-author of *The Embodied Mind* (MIT Press, 1991), author of *Colour Vision* (Routledge, 1995), and editor of *Between Ourselves: Second Person Issues in the Study of Consciousness* (Imprint Academic, 2001). His forthcoming book is titled *Mind In Life: Biology, Phenomenology and the Sciences of Mind*.

Louis C. Charland is Associate Professor in the Department of Philosophy at the University of Western Ontario, in London, Ontario, Canada, where he also holds a cross-appointment in Psychiatry and a joint-appointment in the Faculty of Health Sciences. Professor Charland's areas of specialization are the philosophy of emotion and the philosophy of psychiatry. In March 2003, Charland was awarded a Visiting Member Fellowship at the Institute for Advanced Study in Princeton, New Jersey, to conduct research on decision-making capacity and personal responsibility in depression. He is currently working on a book that explores nineteenth-century developments in the psychopathology of affectivity entitled, *Moral Treatment and the Passions*.

Antonio R. Damasio is Distinguished Adjunct Professor in the Department of Neurology at Iowa State University. His research focuses on the neurobiology of the mind, esspecially the understanding of the neural systems which subserve memory, language, emotion, and decision-making. His widely-read books include *Descartes' Error* (1994), *The Feeling of What Happens* (1999) and *Fundamental Feelings* (2001).

Natalie Depraz lectures in philosophy at the University of Paris IV (Sorbonne). Her research interests include Husserlian phenomenology, cognitive science and theology. Among her published books are *Transcendance et incarnation* (Vrin,

1995), *Lucidite du corps* (Vrin, 2001), and two co-edited volumes: *Alterity and Facticity* (Kluwer, 1998) and *On Becoming Aware* (Benjamins, 2003).

Ralph Ellis received his PhD in philosophy at Duquesne University in 1975. He is interested in integrating neuroscience with careful phenomenological accounts of subjective experience. His books include *Questioning Consciousness* (1995) and *Curious Emotions* (2005), and with co-editor Natika Newton the anthology, *The Cauldron of Consciousness* (2000) and the journal/year-book *Consciousness and Emotion*. He teaches at Clark Atlanta University, having previously been a social worker and a professional jazz saxophonist.

Peter Goldie is The Samuel Hall Chair and Head of Philosophy at The University of Manchester. Before that, he was Reader in Philosophy at King's College London, and prior to that a lecturer at Magdalen College Oxford.

Marc Lewis is a professor at the Department of Human Development and Applied Psychology, University of Toronto. He specializes in the study of personality development as it relates to emotion. His work is informed by developmental psychology, affective neuroscience, and a dynamic systems perspective on brain and behaviour. He has done empirical work in the area of transitions in cognitive and emotional development, and he has developed a state space grid methodology to facilitate the analysis of socioemotional behaviour over time. More recent work utilizes electrophysiological methods for identifying the neural underpinnings of emotion regulation in normal and antisocial children. His research outlining the contribution of dynamic systems theory and affective neuroscience to our understanding of child and adolescent development has appeared in several highly regarded outlets, including *Child Development*, *Behavioral and Brain Sciences*, *Journal of Abnormal Child Psychology*, and *Developmental Science*.

Jaak Panksepp, Distinguished Research Professor Emeritus at Bowling Green State University, is currently affiliated with Falk Center for Molecular Therapeutics (Northwestern University) and has recently been appointed the Bernice Gilman Baily and Joseph Baily Endowed Chair in Animal Well-Being Science at the Veterinary School of Washington State University. His work has been devoted largely to understanding the basic emotional and motivational systems of the human brain by studying homologous subcortical mechanisms in other vertebrates. In addition to neuroevolutionary psychobiological work on brain appetitive, anger and fear systems, his more recent work has focused on the nature of separation-distress (sadness) and rough-and-tumble play (social joy) in order to understand the nature of social bonding and affective consciousness, with the last few years being devoted to the study of 'laughter' like vocal processes in rodents induced by hand-play (i.e., tickling).

Jesse J. Prinz is associate professor in the Department of Philosophy at the University of North Carolina at Chapel Hill. He is the author of *Furnishing the Mind:*

Concepts and Their Perceptual Basis (MIT, 2002), *Gut Reactions: A Perceptual Theory of Emotion* (OUP, 2004), and two forthcoming books, *The Emotional Construction of Morals* (OUP) and *Beyond Human Nature* (Penguin/ Norton). He is also the editor of the forthcoming *Handbook to the Philosophy of Psychology* (OUP), and he is currently writing a book on consciousness.

James A. Russell received his PhD from UCLA and is now a Professor of Psychology at Boston College. His empirical work challenges the claim that basic emotions are revealed by innate facial signals. His theoretical work challenges both biological and social constructionist theories of emotion, suggesting instead that emotions are psychologically constructed.

Matthew Ratcliffe is a lecturer in philosophy at the University of Durham. His research interests include philosophy of mind, phenomenology and philosophy of science. He has published numerous articles, on topics including intentionality, teleology, subjectivity, delusions, emotions and folk psychology. He is currently working on intersubjectivity and feeling.

Rebecca Todd is a doctoral student in University of Toronto's programs in Developmental Science and Neuroscience.

Francisco Varela (1946–2001) held a PhD in biological science from Harvard University, and at the time of his death was Senior Researcher at the National Centre for Scientific Research in Paris. He was dedicated to progressing the science of consciousness by gathering a research community dedicated to the systematic exploration of the structure of human experience, setting out the blueprint for such a programme in a paper 'Neurophenomenology' published in the *Journal of Consciousness Studies* (1996).

Douglas F. Watt is Director of Neuropsychology at the Quincy Medical Center, Boston University School of Medicine, and has a particular research interest in the emotions. He is on the editorial board of the journal/yearbook *Consciousness & Emotion* and of the online journal *Science & Consciousness Review*.

Preface

Emotion experience permeates our conscious life. Whether subtle or over-whelming, expressed and shared, or hidden and suffocated, feelings render consciousness personally relevant. It is thus surprising that emotion experience has not occupied a more central place in the study of consciousness, and that it is discussed only in specialized journals and books, as if it were a peculiar aspect of consciousness.

This volume highlights the breadth and relevance of emotion experience, and discusses a number of issues pertaining to its investigation in science and philosophy.

What *is* an emotion experience? How does such an experience feel? It is often taken for granted that feelings are bounded experiences, like episodes of feeling fear or anger. But what exactly does such feel consist in? How does it unfold in time? In what ways do emotion experiences differ? A recurring question in the papers collected here is whether it is possible to demarcate emotion experience from other experiences. Interestingly, the replies vary considerably.

Related questions concern the possibility of unfelt emotions, the way in which they 'become' felt, the alleged 'valenced' character of feelings (do they always feel either good or bad?), and the relationship between emotion experience and imagination. Do imagined emotions feel like real ones? Are they emotions themselves? Or, when we imagine a possible course of action, do we somehow feel it? Do such feelings impinge on our decisions, and if so, how?

This volume also presents accounts of physiological mechanisms supposed to underlie emotion experience. Which neural systems are necessary for emotion experience? How do they relate to what we know about the mechanisms for bodily changes, attachment, sympathy, empathy, and decision making?

We decided to present a selection of papers addressing both emotion experience itself on its own terms and the neurophysiology of emotion experience, because we believe that phenomenological and philosophical analyses should be compared with hypotheses and research in neuroscience — and vice-versa. Both fields are important and interesting in themselves, but we also think that comparisons and cross-investigations can only benefit all researchers. This conviction is reflected in the inclusion, within the volume, of several papers that explicitly

Journal of Consciousness Studies, **12**, No. 8–10, 2005, pp. 7–8

link phenomenological considerations and accounts of underlying neurophysio-logy. Some of these accounts are explicitly 'isomorphic' in their approach; in other words, they look for structural parallels between how emotion feels and how it is implemented and regulated in the organism. Other accounts do not draw such a direct link, yet still aim to explain the character of emotion experience and its temporal unfolding by referring to neuroscience.

The collection spans various issues and disciplines, and may look diverse at first glance. Nevertheless, there are several common threads running through what are only superficially unrelated papers. This commonality gives us hope that emotion experience will be given more attention in the future, not simply as a peculiar 'hot' instance of consciousness, but as a complex, comprehensive, and far-reaching phenomenon whose study is relevant for every other aspect of our embodied lives.

Giovanna Colombetti

Evan Thompson

Jesse Prinz

Are Emotions Feelings?

The majority of emotion researchers reject the feeling theory of emotions; they deny that emotions are feelings. Some of these researchers admit that emotions have feelings as components, but they insist that emotions contain other components as well, such as cognitions. I argue for a qualified version of the feeling theory. I present evidence in support William James's conjecture that emotions are perceptions of patterned changes in the body. When such perceptions are conscious, they qualify as feelings. But the bodily perceptions constituting emotions can occur unconsciously. When that occurs, emotions are unfelt. Thus, emotions are feelings when conscious, and they are not feelings when unconscious. In the end of the paper, I briefly sketch a theory of how emotions and other perceptual states become conscious.

According to one strand in folk psychology, emotions are feelings; they are phenomenally conscious mental episodes. This little morsel of commonsense is a whipping post in philosophy. From the very first philosophical musings about the emotions to the present day it has been popular to insist that emotions are not feelings. This position is so enshrined that it might be regarded as the Fundamental Axiom of emotion research. Despite widespread disagreement about what emotions are, almost everyone seems to agree about what emotions aren't. The Fundamental Axiom is consistent with the view that emotions are felt. Even philosophers are willing to respect commonsense to some degree. Of course, we feel sad, happy, and furious. But, the Fundamental Axiom says we should not identify emotions with such feelings. On one approach, feelings are merely necessary, but not sufficient components of emotions. On another approach, feelings are contingent components. On a third approach, feelings aren't components at all; they are just ways of detecting emotions. I feel sad is like saying I feel the wind. Neither locution entails that the thing felt is a feeling.

I think the Fundamental Axiom is both right and wrong. It is a mistake to say that all emotions are feelings; emotions can be unconscious. But, when an emotion is felt, the feeling literally is the emotion, and there are no other components. I will defend this view. To do that, I will have to defend a theory of what

Correspondence: Jesse Prinz, Dept of Philosophy, Caldwell Hall, UNC, Chapel Hill, NC 27599, USA. *Email: jesse@subcortex.com*

Journal of Consciousness Studies, **12**, No. 8–10, 2005, pp. 9–25

emotions are. I will summarize and extend the evidence for an account that I have defended elsewhere (Prinz, 2004). I will also offer a theory of how emotions become felt. That theory is an instance of a more general theory of phenomenal consciousness called the AIR theory (e.g., Prinz, 2005b).

1: Standard Attitudes Towards the Feeling Theory

In attacking the view that emotions are feelings, philosophers often find themselves in the embarrassing position of attacking a straw man. It's very hard to find any defender of the feeling view in the history of philosophy. Some philosophers have said that emotions contain feelings, but few have said that emotions are feelings. Aristotle says emotions are judgments. Spinoza says emotions are judgments plus feelings of pain or pleasure. Descartes says they are judgments brought on by felt changes in the animal spirits. In the 20th century, critics of the feeling theory included Errol Bedford (1957), George Pitcher (1965), Robert Solomon (1976), Patricia Greenspan (1988), and Martha Nussbaum (2001). All of these authors take time to argue that the feeling theory is false, but all of them have difficulty identifying philosophers who take the feeling view seriously. Aristotle seems to have set the standard. Few people since him have had the courage to suppose that emotions are feelings.

There is a common thread running through most philosophical accounts. Philosophers usually presume that emotions are cognitive. A cognitive theory of the emotions is one according to which emotions essentially involve cognitions. Cognitions are usually regarded as propositional attitudes, such as beliefs or judgments, but they can also be mere conceptualizations. According to some cognitive theorists, fear involves the thought that I am in danger, and according to others it merely involves deployment of the concept *danger* without necessarily having a fully formed thought. Some cognitive philosophers, such as Descartes, admit that emotions are not merely cognitions; cognitions are just one component. But this is sufficient reason for rejecting the feeling theory. If emotions have a cognitive component, either an attitude or a concept, then they cannot be merely feelings. Concepts and attitudes are not feelings. There is a raging controversy about whether tokenings of concepts and attitudes can even be conscious, and many emotion theorists assume that emotional cognitions are generally unconscious. But suppose that concepts and feelings can be conscious. It does not follow that these mental episodes are feelings. The term feeling is usually reserved for a special class of nonconceptual mental states. If feelings are nonconceptual, and emotions have essential cognitive components, then emotions are not feelings, though they may have feelings as parts. The Fundamental Axiom is confirmed.

One might think that there is a trivial proof of the claim that emotions are feelings based on conceptual analysis. Concepts are grounded in paradigm cases, and, in ordinary language, emotions are paradigm cases of feelings. We can often use the term 'emotion' and 'feeling' interchangeably. While some languages lack a word for 'emotion,' all languages have a word for 'feeling' (Wierzbicka,

1999). In languages with no word for 'emotion,' there are still words for particular emotions, and speakers of such languages call those emotions feelings. The main semantic difference between 'feeling' and 'emotion' seems to be that the former term is broader. Some feelings are not emotions. We have some purely somatic feelings, for example: queasiness, chilliness, itchiness, and so on. But, in ordinary parlance, all emotions are feelings. Doesn't this show that the Fundamental Axiom is false?

Defenders of cognitive theories have a reply. They claim that ordinary language is not committed to the view that emotions are feelings, but merely to the view that emotions can be felt. (One might also defend the Fundamental Axiom by insisting that ordinary language is not a good guide to ontology!) When we say, 'I feel angry' we don't mean to imply that anger is a feeling. We mean rather to imply that we have a feeling of the kind that we have when we are angry. 'I feel X' does not entail 'X is a feeling'. This is confirmed by 'I feel the wind', mentioned above, or 'I feel a cold coming on', or even 'I feel uncertain about the proof'.

Cognitive theorists can block the ordinary language argument against the Fundamental Axiom, but they do need to explain the fact that we use the term 'feeling' so frequently when talking about emotions. Here there are three popular strategies. First, cognitive theorists can admit that emotions have feelings as indispensable components of emotions. Call this the Essential Part View. Spinoza and Greenspan have views like this. An emotion is a judgment plus a feeling of pleasure and pain. Stanley Schachter is associated with a related theory in psychology. For him, an emotion involves a conceptualization plus a general state of arousal. All these authors seem to underestimate the range of emotional feelings that we have. There are emotional feelings other than pleasure, pain, arousal. Disgust and sadness feel different, even though they are both forms of psychological pain. To account for the range of emotional feelings, a cognitive theorist who adopts the Essential Part View should concede that emotions have a range of different feelings as parts.

A second strategy for explaining talk of emotional feelings while maintaining the Fundamental Axiom is to argue that emotions can have feelings as parts, but these parts are optional. Call this the Contingent Part View. The contingent part view makes sense of judgments such as 'I feel sad', but they also allow us to say things like 'I am sad, but I don't feel sad'. Defenders of the Contingent Part View usually suppose that cognitions are both necessary and sufficient for emotions.

The third strategy for explaining talk of emotional feelings pushes the cognitive view even farther. This is the Non-Part View. On this strategy, feelings aren't parts of emotions at all. It just so happens that emotions often cause characteristic feelings, and these feelings can be used, with variable reliability, to determine what emotion we are currently having. One might say that feelings are symptoms of emotion. Here, 'I feel sad' is like 'I feel a cold coming on' or 'I feel sick'.

I think that defenders of the Non-Part View and Contingent Part View are right to suppose that there can be emotions without feelings. I think emotions can be unconscious. I don't think they are right, however, to suppose that feelings are merely parts of emotion when emotions are conscious. I think emotions are feelings whenever emotions are felt. To defend these views, I will defend a noncognitive theory of the emotions. For a more complete defence of that view, see Prinz (2004).

2: Emotions As Perceptions of the Body

Within the history of philosophy, there is perhaps only one prominent defender of the view that emotions are feelings. That person is none other than William James. James did not claim that emotions are a *sui generis* class of feelings. Rather, he tried to reduce emotions to a class of feelings that everyone is already committed to: feelings of changes in the body. When emotions occur, our bodies undergo various perturbations. These changes include alterations in our circulatory, respiratory, and musculoskeletal systems. Our hearts race or slow. Our breathing relaxes or becomes strained, blood vessels constrict or dilate, our facial expressions transform, and so on. Most people assume that these changes are the effects of our emotions, but James argues that this is backwards. Our bodies change, and an emotion 'just is' the feeling of that change.

This thesis has recently been resuscitated by Antonio Damasio (1994) and others (Prinz, 2004), but it is not especially popular in philosophical circles. Everyone would agree that many emotions ordinarily co-occur with bodily changes. When frightened, our muscles tense and our hair follicles stand erect. These changes prepare us for coping with dangers. When enraged, our fists clench, our extremities flush, and we lurch forward aggressively, in preparation for combat. But why identify emotions with the feelings of such changes? Why not say instead that such feelings are, at best, component parts of our emotions?

In defence of his view, James (1884) offers the following thought experiment:

> If we fancy some strong emotion, and then try to abstract from our consciousness of it all the feelings of its characteristic bodily symptoms, we find we have nothing left behind, no 'mind-stuff' out of which the emotion can be constituted, and that a cold and neutral state of intellectual perception is all that remains.... Can one fancy the state of rage and picture no ebullition of it in the chest, no flushing of the face, no dilatation of the nostrils, no clenching of the teeth, no impulse to vigorous action, but in their stead limp muscles, calm breathing, and a placid face? The present writer, for one, certainly cannot. The rage is as completely evaporated as the sensation of its so-called manifestations, and the only thing that can possibly be supposed to take its place is some cold-blooded and dispassionate judicial sentence...

Introspection suggests that, when we subtract the perceived bodily concomitants from an emotion, there is no emotion left. This gives us reason to conclude that emotions register bodily changes.

I think James's argument is compelling, but some critics are uncomfortable with arguments that depend on introspection. Therefore, we should look for convergent lines of support. Fortunately, I think the Jamesian theory explains a number of observations that are more difficult to explain on other accounts. I will focus on three bodies of evidence.

First, there is evidence that emotions co-occur with bodily changes. Every neuroimaging study of emotions shows excitation in areas of the brain associated with bodily response (e.g., Damasio *et al.*, 2000). Cingulate cortex, the insular, and even somatosensory cortex are strongly correlated with emotional states. These structures have been independently associated with interoception (Critchley *et al.* 2004).

Opponents of the Jamesian view sometimes argue that only certain emotions co-occur with bodily changes (Harré, 1986; Solomon, 1976; Griffiths, 1997). They suggest that our more phylogenetically advanced emotions, such as guilt, love, loneliness, and jealousy do not have concomitant bodily states. Weakening his own theory, James (1884: 201) entertained the suggestion that moral and aesthetic emotions are not mediated by the body. All of these alleged counter-examples are tendentious. I think that careful introspection would actually reveal that these emotions have a basis in the body. That hunch is consistent with the empirical evidence. To date, every neuroimaging study of a more advanced emotion has shown activation in exactly the same brain regions that are implicated in our more ancient emotions and, as remarked, these regions have been antecedently associated with the registration and regulation of bodily response. Shin *et al.* (2000) showed cingulate and insula activation during guilt episodes, Bartels & Zeki (2000) found the same structures come on line when subjects were viewing pictures of people they love. Jealousy is known to cause galvanic skin responses (Buss *et al.*, 1992), and loneliness is associated with heightened cortisol levels (Kiecolt-Glaser *et al.*, 1984). Aesthetic response (finding something beautiful rather than neutral) correlated with activity in anterior cingulate and orbito-frontal cortex (Kawabata & Zeki, 2004), and moral judgments engage posterior cingulate and medial frontal cortex (Greene *et al.*, 2001). I am aware of no evidence for an emotion that does not normally co-occur with bodily changes. This is predicted by the Jamesian view, and not by any theory that fails to draw a connection between emotions and the body.

The fact that emotions co-occur with bodily changes does not prove that the Jamesian view is right, however. After all, bodily responses might accompany emotions most of the time without being necessary for emotions. The correlation might be high but contingent. To establish necessity one has to show that disruption of interoceptive responses leads to diminution of emotion. The second body of evidence I will consider supports this necessity thesis. Evidence on this issue is not yet conclusive, but it is suggestive. For one thing, individuals who suffer from spinal injuries, reducing feedback from the body, sometimes report diminished emotional response (Hohmann, 1966). This is a striking finding, but it also controversial. Some researchers have noted that spinal patients generally continue to have rich, and sometimes normal, emotional lives (Chwalisz *et al.*, 1988; Cobos *et al.*, 2004). Clearly spinal cord damage does not eliminate emotions. Still, even these critics found some evidence in support of the Jamesian view. Patients with injuries very high on the cord were more likely to report a loss of emotional intensity, suggesting that the level of emotional response covaries with the amount or ease of feedback. In any case, spinal injuries may not be the best test case for the Jamesian view, because there is good evidence that the brain has other ways of gaining access to the body. For example, Montoya & Schandry (1994) have shown that spinal patients can perceive their heartbeats, and Menter *et al*. (1997) report that 35% of spinal patients suffer from gastrointestinal pain. Visceral information in spinal patients may be traveling through the vagus nerve. The vagus is implicated in heart rate, gastrointestinal function, perspiration, musculoskeletal response, and other bodily functions. If the vagus is intact in spinal patients, feedback from the body would be sufficient to support embodied emotions. To explore this possibility, Bechara (2004) investigated individuals with pathologies affecting the vagus nerve, and they found evidence for a corresponding emotional impairment. In particular, preliminary findings suggest that such individuals have impaired performance on gambling tasks that require emotionally-based decisions. In other patient populations, poor performance on such tasks has been correlated with a flat skin conductance response, suggesting that failure to engage bodily correlates of emotion leads to failures in emotional decision-making. More anecdotally, there is evidence that damage to cingulate cortex (a centre for interoception) can lead to akinetic mutism, which has been characterized as a profound deficit in emotional response (Damasio & Van Hoesen, 1983).

These findings support the conclusion that registration of bodily change does not only reliably co-occur with emotions; it is actually necessary. At this point, opponents of the registration thesis might offer a partial concession. They might admit that interoceptive states are necessary, while denying that they are sufficient. Defenders of cognitive theories, for example, might argue that emotions require judgments in addition to interoceptive states. Hybrid views of this kind are common in the literature, and the evidence presented so far does nothing to rule them out. To show that emotions are nothing but interoceptive states, the defender of the Jamesian view needs to show that judgments are only contingently associated with emotions. They need to show that interoceptive states are sufficient on their own. Several different findings support this thesis. First, drugs (such as adrenalin) that enervate the autonomic nervous system have emotional effects (Marañon, 1924). Second, false bodily feedback can influence your emotional state and affect-laden judgments (Valins, 1966; Crucian *et al*., 2000). Valins (1966) showed that subjects were more likely to make a positive emotional assessment of erotic pictures when he told them (falsely) that their hearts were racing (see also Crucian, *et al*., 2000); he thought this showed that real bodily feedback is not necessary for emotion, but, in fact, it seems to show that we make judgments about our emotional states by perceiving our bodies, even when, as in this case, those perceptions are erroneous. Third, stroke can lead to pathological laughter and crying by creating random activity in laughter and crying nuclei in the upper brainstem; when this occurs, patients report feeling happy or sad (Parvizi *et al*. 2001). Fourth, changing facial expressions and respiration influences self-reported emotions (Laird, 1984; Zajonc *et al*., 1989; Levenson *et al.*, 1990; Philippot *et al.*, 2002), and this occurs even when subjects are not aware that they are making emotional expressions, which suggests that the process is not mediated by cognitive labeling (Strack *et al.*, 1988). Fifth, seeing another individual express an emotion can cause the corresponding emotion in us (Hatfield *et al.*, 1994). Sixth, nonvocal music can have predictable emotional effects, which seem to work by eliciting patterned bodily responses (Blood & Zatorre, 2001).

Together, these findings suggest that induction of bodily change results in the subjective experience of emotions. It is conceivable that whenever emotions are elicited by direct manipulation of the body, evaluative judgments are also generated, but there is no reason to think that is the case. To presume that subjects in these various conditions are all making evaluative judgments would be *ad hoc*. Moreover, we often find ourselves in cases where our explicit judgments are actually at odds with the judgments alleged by cognitive theorists to underlie emotions. For example, a blood-curdling scream in a horror film can induce fear despite the fact that audiences know they are not in any danger.

I have, so far, presented three bodies of evidence that favour the Jamesian view. None of this evidence counts as conclusive evidence, but they provide a circumstantial case. Emotions co-occur with bodily changes, changes in the body are sufficient to induce emotions, and reduction in bodily response reduces emotional experience, suggesting that bodily registration is necessary for emotion. All these findings are predicted and explained by the Jamesian view, and none are predicted by accounts that do not strongly implicate the body in emotional response. I think this leaves us with very good empirical reasons for supposing that emotions are states of interoceptive systems (for objections and replies, see Prinz, 2004).

3. Are Emotions Feelings?

On the Jamesian view that I have been defending, an emotion is an inner state that registers a pattern of change in the body. Emotions are perceptions of bodily change. For James, this is equivalent to saying that emotions are feelings of bodily change. He rejects the Fundamental Axiom when he says that emotions are bodily feelings. But James moves a bit too quickly here. He seems to confound the claim that emotions are perceptions with the claim that emotions are feelings. Perceptions are not necessarily felt. There is such a thing as unconscious perception. The evidence that I have been describing shows that emotions are interoceptive states, but I have not argued that emotions are necessarily felt. Imagine the conscious perception of a bodily change that we call fear. What if that same perception could occur unconsciously? Should we call it unconscious fear? If so, where does this leave the Fundamental Axiom?

The issue of unconscious emotions puts us back into the arena of ordinary language. We do not seem to have a habit of referring to unconscious emotional states. Even Freud didn't think emotions could be unconscious. He thought we were often unconscious of the cause of an emotion, but the emotion itself has to be conscious. In this respect, emotion talk is like pain talk. In ordinary discourse, we rarely talk about unconscious pains. It sounds funny to say, 'That really hurt, but I didn't feel it' or 'I have a pounding headache, but fortunately it's unconscious.' That has led some people to assume that we have no unconscious pains. The term 'pain,' they say, refers to a conscious feeling. But that conclusion can be resisted. It must be recalled that commonsense does not recognize the existence of unconscious thoughts or perceptions. Unconscious states are, by definition, inaccessible to us. As a result, folk psychology does not automatically recognize their existence. Even very sophisticated philosophers had been reluctant, historically, to admit that unconscious mental states exist. Attitudes changed decisively under the pressure of evidence. Postulating unconscious mental states explains behaviour.

The most obvious demonstration of this is subliminal perception. If a stimulus is displayed briefly, followed by a mask, we have no conscious experience of it. Nevertheless, the stimulus can affect subsequent behaviour. Obviously something is going on unconsciously and, moreover, whatever is going on is the result of the fact that the stimulus was presented to our senses. Stimulus detection through a sense organ is, in essence, what perception is all about. The fact that perception is often conscious is interesting, and important, but it is not essential. What makes perceptual states qualify as perceptual is their etiology: the role of sensory transduction from the world outside the mind. So, even if we began thinking that all mentality is conscious, the case of subliminal perception is easy to digest. It is easy to get comfortable with the idea that something very much like conscious perception occurs without consciousness. When subliminal perception was discovered, we *could have* made a terminological stipulation that it is not a form of perception. We could have reserved the word 'perception' for conscious sensing, and coined a new term for the subliminal case. But we didn't go that route, because we recognized that the similarities between subliminal and conscious perception were so great that it would be useful to categorize both under the same term. The discovery of subliminal perception may have forced us to change the concept of perception by adopting a policy about whether it should be used to encompass unconscious states. Concepts co-evolve with theories in this way. But the conceptual revision was not arbitrary. For example, it is useful for science to group subliminal and superluminal cases of perception together. There is a natural psychological boundary that encompasses both. The term 'unconscious perception' sounded contradictory to many at first, but it now sounds perfectly natural (see Tallis, 2002).

Likewise, I think we should welcome talk of unconscious pains. If there are mental states the function just like pains but lack consciousness, it is useful to group them together with conscious pains. Pain carries information from nociceptors and leads to withdrawal and soothing behaviours. If there are mental episodes that play that role without awareness, we should call them unconscious pains. And the very same goes for emotions. If there are inner states that registered patterned bodily change under conditions that cause conscious emotions in us, and those inner states lead to characteristic coping behaviors, such as approach and avoidance, we should call those states unconscious emotions.

Do such states exist? Almost certainly. First of all, perceptual systems in general seem to allow unconscious perception. We can have unconscious visual states, unconscious auditory states, unconscious tactile states, and so on. It seems overwhelmingly likely, then, that we can have unconscious perceptions of the patterned bodily changes that constitute our emotions. If emotions are interoceptive states, as I argued in the last section, it seems likely that emotions can be unconscious.

Second, there is anecdotal evidence for unconscious emotions. For example, imagine being woken up by the sound of glass shattering in your living room. You might assume that burglars are breaking in and attend intensely to the sound. At the very same time, your body will undoubtedly enter into a fear pattern, but you might not experience the fear consciously because attention is consumed elsewhere. After waiting to hear if there is any more noise, you hear your cat scurrying about and you realize she must have knocked over a vase. You then notice, and only then, that your heart is racing, and your breathing is strained, and your entire body is tensed in fear. You were afraid, but you didn't realize it. Now you breathe a sigh of relief.

Third, there is some experimental evidence for unconscious emotions. In a representative study, Winkielman *et al.* (2005) subliminally presented subjects with photographs of emotional facial expressions. Subjects saw faces that were either neutral, angry, or happy, but the faces were presented too rapidly to be consciously experienced. Subjects were then given a fruity beverage and asked to pour a glass, and take a sip. They were also asked some questions about the beverage and about their feelings. Subjects who had seen the angry face and the happy face reported being in the same mood and the same level of arousal. On measures of conscious emotional feeling, they were statistically indistinguishable. But, the faces did affect their behaviour. Subjects who had seen the angry face poured less of the beverage, drank less of it, and gave it less positive ratings than subjects who had seen the smiling face. This suggests that an emotion had been induced. Emotions are known to impact behaviour in this way. So this is plausibly a case of unconscious emotions.

In sum, there are good theoretical, anecdotal, and experimental reasons for believing that emotions can be unconscious. This suggests that emotions are not always felt. When emotions are felt, the feeling is the emotion: the emotion is a conscious perception of a patterned change in the body. But emotions can go unfelt: they can be unconscious perceptions of patterned changes in the body.

The Fundamental Axiom in the philosophy of emotions says that emotions are not feelings. There is an important sense in which this Axiom is false. When emotions are felt, those feelings are the emotions. But the Axiom also has a grain of truth. Emotions can be unfelt. So there are some emotions — the unconscious ones — that are not feelings. Only some emotions are feelings. But, I would add, all emotions are feelings potentially. All emotions are perceptions of bodily states, and those perceptions can be conscious. So, there is no example of an emotion that could not, under the right conditions, be a feeling.

4: Three Objections

I have been defending the thesis that emotions are feelings, when they are consciously felt. This thesis can be challenged in various ways. Here I will briefly consider three objections. Most of these objections derive from cognitive theories of the emotions. Defenders of cognitive theories will resist the Jamesian view upon which my thesis depends.

The first objection is that we can have conscious emotions that are not feelings. I have said that, when emotions are conscious, they are feelings. The implicit argument for this conclusion goes as follows. Emotions are perceptions of bodily states; a conscious perception of a bodily state is a paradigm instance of what we call a 'feeling'; therefore, conscious emotions are feelings. Defenders of cognitive theories like to argue that we can have conscious emotions that do not qualify as feelings in this sense. Solomon (1976), for example, argues that we can have an emotion that lasts for hours across a wide range of fluctuations in our bodily states. We can be angry all afternoon, and that anger can be remain conscious, but, when this occurs, our body does not remain in any fixed state of perturbation. Therefore, we cannot identify the conscious experience of the anger with a conscious experience of a particular bodily pattern.

I have three responses. First of all, this strikes me as an empirical issue. If we are conscious of anger for an entire afternoon, then it is possible that there is a sustained bodily state throughout that temporal interval. Our body may change in many respects over the afternoon, but the pattern of, say, autonomic response may remain fixed. One can huff and scowl four hours on end. Second, it is not essential to the Jamesian view that each emotion be identified with a single bodily pattern. There may be a family of bodily states underlying anger, and we may cycle through these. Third, Solomon would need to show that there can be a conscious experience of anger without any bodily symptoms. He would have to show, for example, that one can be consciously angry in a state where one's body feels completely calm and relaxed. It is not obvious to me that we would call such a state conscious anger. Suppose that Mr. Spock, in a state of total bodily placidity, says: 'I know that you have insulted me.' I don't think we would attribute any anger to Mr. Spock, much less a conscious experience of anger. An unconscious robot could register insults, but that is not a sufficient condition for being angry. A person who claims to be angry without being in a bodily state characteristic of anger might be accused of being confused or dishonest. Try to tell someone you are furious with a calm pleasant voice. It will come across as a joke.

The second objection is that there are not enough bodily feelings to go around. If conscious emotions are conscious feelings of bodily changes, then, for every emotion that can be consciously distinguished, there must be a distinctive bodily feeling. There are an infinite number of bodily feelings, because the body is a continuous system, but there is not a distinctive bodily feeling for every emotion.

Consider guilt. Arguably, there is no set of bodily responses that distinguish guilt from other emotions. We feel pangs of guilt. When we reflect on a subject of guilt, a lump forms in our throats, and our heads hang low. All of these bodily symptoms are shared with other emotions. Most obviously, they are shared with sadness. I think the phenomenology of guilt is often just like the phenomenology of sadness. In some cases, guilt may also share its phenomenology with anxiety, or other more basic emotions. The point is that certain emotions have similar or identical phenomenology. There are many other plausible examples: indignation feels like anger, disappointment feels like sadness, awe has an element of surprise, contempt has an element of disgust, pride feels like a kind of joy, exhilaration feels like a blend of fear and joy, and jealousy feels like a blend of anger, disgust, and fear. I use the case of guilt and sadness to illustrate, but if you don't buy the intuition that these two emotions are phenomenologically alike, then pick another case. Even a single example of phenomenological overlap would seem to raise a problem for the Jamesian. If emotions are feelings, how can two distinct emotions feel alike?

I think this objection actually contains an important insight. I readily concede that there is a distinctive bodily response corresponding to every emotion. Some emotions have the same bodily realization, and therefore feel alike. I think guilt and sadness are a case of this. If so, how can they be distinguished? The answer has to do with their causal history. Sadness is a bodily state caused by a loss. Guilt is a bodily state caused by transgressing a norm. The body state may be the same, but they are occasioned by different eliciting conditions. Alternatively, one might even see guilt as a special case of sadness. When a person violates a norm, she threatens her relationships with other people; she risks being condemned by members of her community. That would be a great loss. So there is a sense in which guilt is a response to loss. As such, it is like typical cases of sadness. We might describe guilt as an emotion of transgression-loss, i.e., the loss potentially incurred by violating a norm. I am not suggesting that guilt includes a cognitive component. Guilt is not a somatic feeling of sadness *plus* a belief that the feeling is caused by a transgression. Rather, I am suggesting that guilt is a case of sadness that happens to be caused by acts of transgression, whether or not one realized the transgression is the cause. The belief that 'I have transgressed' is not a component of the emotion; it is a cause. Gordon (1988) draws a helpful analogy to sunburns and wind burns: these are physiologically alike, but we distinguish them by their causes. Guilt does not contain any judgment or perception about transgression any more than a sunburn contains the sun.

In sum, I think that guilt and sadness have different causes, but they register the same bodily states, and they share the same phenomenology. If the conscious experience of an emotion is exhausted by bodily feelings, then emotions that are somatically alike must be phenomenally alike. When we recognize that a particular feeling is guilt rather than sadness, it is not in virtue of any phenomenal difference. Rather, it is in virtue of recalling the eliciting condition. If I feel a lump in my throat after learning that my pet weasel died, I assume that the feeling is the result of that loss, and I realize that it is sadness. If I feel a lump in my throat after cheating on my wife, I assume that feeling is the result of bringing harmed to a loved-one, and I realize that the feeling is guilt. In some cases, we don't know where our feelings come from. I might have these chronic throat lumps and seek therapy. After asking me some very personal questions about my life, my therapist might conclude that the lump is a feeling of sadness or that it is a feeling of guilt. Of course, after an emotion has been identified, we may become consciously aware of the appropriate emotion label, and we may have conscious awareness of the eliciting event, but neither of these things is part of the emotion. We can have emotions without labels without any awareness of what they are called or what called them. We should not mistake an emotion for its causes and effects. The cause of an emotion determines the identity of the emotion, but those causes do not constitute the emotion, and neither do they constitute the conscious experience of the emotion. Emotions are feelings, but, like sunburns, they are individuated by their causes.

The third objection that cognitive theorists might be tempted to level against the view that I have been defending is that emotions can have intentional objects. They can be directed at things. For example, I can be angry at the government, or I can be angry that the train isn't running. Cognitive theorists like to point out that feelings cannot have intentional objects (e.g., Pitcher, 1965). Pangs, twinges, or tickles are not about anything. It doesn't make sense, in English, to say that I am panged about the government. Therefore, emotions cannot be feelings.

To reply, let me draw a distinction between an emotion, on the one hand, and an emotional attitude, on the other. I will define an emotional attitude as a propositional attitude that established a causal link between an emotion and the representation of an object or a state of affairs. In the mind, there are many causal links between representations of objects or states of affairs and mental episodes that, under many other circumstances, lack intentional objects. Consider tiredness. Being tired usually lacks an intentional object, but it can have an intentional object. I can be tired of the novel I am reading, for example. When not used metaphorically, that means there is a causal relationship between reading the novel and states of tiredness in me; the novel literally puts me to sleep. Likewise, I can be sickened by the state of the world; reading the news makes me feel ill. I can also be dazzled by the beauty of a flower; it literally takes my breath away. Things are exactly the same with the emotions. There can be causal links between emotions and mental representations of objects or states of affairs, and when certain causal links are in place, we say that the emotion has the content of those representations as its intentional object. If the right causal tie exists between thinking about the government and a feeling of anger, we say, I am angry at the government. If the right causal connections bind a feeling of anger to the news that the trains aren't running, we say I am angry that the trains aren't running. This is not merely a *façon de parler*. Like feelings of fatigue, illness, or bedazzlement, emotions can acquire intentional objects by being causally linked to mental representations. That doesn't mean emotions are anything other than bodily feelings. It's just a feature of human psychology that, *pace* Pitcher, feelings can have intentional objects. Emotions do not have particular objects intrinsically; they are not propositional attitudes. But we do have a class of attitudes — what I called emotion attitudes — that are constituted by causal links between emotions and mental representations of things.

Obviously, defenders of cognitive theories will not be fully satisfied. The debate between them and the Jamesians is old and enduring. But the burden is now on their side. I have presented a body of evidence in favour of the Jamesian view, and I argued that the evidence supports a qualified version of the feeling theory: emotions are feelings when they are conscious. I have defended this qualified feeling theory against the most obvious objections that the cognitive theorist might devise. If they are dissatisfied, the ball is in their court.

I could rest my case here, but I want to embellish the story a bit. It is one thing to argue that conscious emotions are feelings and quite another to explain how these conscious feelings arise. I have not given any explanation of how our bodily perceptions become conscious. Before closing, I want to sketch a theory of consciousness and describe how it applies to the emotions.

5: A Theory of Emotional Consciousness

Emotions have a bodily phenomenology. When we are afraid, we feel our hearts racing, our muscles tensing, our hairs standing on end, and our breath becoming more strained. Indeed, it was the bodily character of emotional experience that led William James to propose his bodily theory of the emotions in the first place. Any account of emotional consciousness should be an account of how we come to have conscious experiences of bodily changes. On this view emotions are perceptions of the body, and conscious emotions are conscious perceptions. I think that all forms of perception become conscious in exactly the same way. There is a unified theory of perceptual consciousness. I think this theory applies equally to vision, audition, olfaction, and emotion. I have made this case more fully elsewhere (Prinz, 2000; 2005a,b); here I offer only a sketch.

To keep things simple, I will restrict my comparison to vision and emotion. There are two components to a theory of phenomenal consciousness. First, there must be a theory of phenomenal qualities — the qualitative character of experience. Second, there must be a theory of how those qualities become conscious. In the case of vision, I am persuaded that the best available story goes like this. The first part was originally defended by Ray Jackendoff (1987). Vision is organized hierarchically. Low-level vision registers local edges and colour patches; each edge is represented discretely rather than being integrated into a unified whole. Intermediate-level vision binds these bits together into coherent contours, and represents whole objects from a particular vantage point. High-level vision abstracts away features of the visual signal that are not useful to recognition; it extracts invariants and represents objects in a way that is not specific to any point of view. Jackendoff's insight was that the intermediate level corresponds best to what conscious visual experiences are like. He suggested that consciousness is located there on the hierarchy. Visual qualities register objects as coherent

wholes from a point of view. But mere intermediate-level activity is not sufficient for consciousness. We can see things unconsciously. So Jackendoff's theory is incomplete on its own; he needs an account of how intermediate-level
visual states become conscious. I think the missing ingredient is attention. We
become visually conscious when intermediate-level visual representations are
modulated by attention. There is extensive evidence that withdrawal of attention
leads to the elimination of consciousness (Bisiach, 1992; Mack & Rock, 1998).
Attention works by allowing information to flow forward from perception centres to working memory centres. So consciousness arises when intermediate-level representations become available to working memory through working
memory modulation. I call this the AIR theory for 'attended intermediate-level
representations.'

   The AIR theory works for vision and, I have elsewhere argued, it can also be
applied to perception in the other senses. Since emotions are episodes in our
interoceptive sensory system, the AIR theory can plausibly be applied to emotion as well. Here, the story is entirely speculative. I propose that the systems
responsible for registering bodily change are organized hierarchically, just like
vision. Low-level interoceptive systems register local changes in the body. We
have nerve receptions distributed throughout or organs, for example, and low-
level interoceptive systems register local changes in these receptors. These low-
level systems are presumably limited in several respects. They may not integrate
a group of spatially contiguous receptors into a representation of an entire organ.
They may not integrate a sequence of temporally contiguous receptor responses
into the rhythm of the heart or the pace of breathing. These local systems, we can
presume, also lack another kind of integration: they register specific changes in
the circulatory, respiratory, digestive, musculoskeletal, and other bodily systems
without registering how these go together. Intermediate-level interoception provides integration. Adjacent receptors give rise to a representation of the heart as
an entire organ, and consecutive heartbeats become a rhythm. More importantly,
the intermediate-level that I am postulating registers patterns of bodily response;
it registers the coincident behaviour of heart, intestines, and diaphragm.
High-level interoception abstracts away from very specific patterns of bodily
change and registers patterns of patterns. It tells us that two slightly distinct body
patterns can be co-classified. This is the level of emotion recognition. Different
bodily patterns are treated as alike. High-level vision abstracts across viewpoint
specific visual images and co-classifies a thousand perspectives on a particular
object so that we can recognize that object across viewing perspectives. High-
level body perception abstracts away from the details of a specific bodily
response (e.g., the number of heartbeats per minute), and allows us to recognize
that two different patterns both qualify as states of anger, sadness, or joy. In some
cases, the high-level that I am postulating co-classifies bodily patterns that are
quite different. Two different episodes of fear can have somewhat different
bodily concomitants. Sometimes we flee in fear, and sometimes we freeze, but
we recognize both responses as the same emotion. The postulated high-level
treats both of these bodily states as instances of fear.

Intuitively, the level of emotional consciousness lies in the middle. Consider an episode of fear. The low-level is too local. Fear doesn't feel like a disconnected assortment of bodily symptoms. The bodily components are bound together into a distinctive pattern. It is difficult to focus on them in isolation, just as it is difficult to see a local edge in a contour when looking at an object. The high-level is too abstract. The phenomenal character of a freezing episode is qualitatively different from the phenomenal character of a fleeing episode. These differences are captured at the intermediate level.

Conscious experiences of emotion also require attention. Ordinarily emotions grab our attention and are consequently conscious. But, consider a case in which attention is distracted away from our emotional state. As it happens, we have already seen a case just like this. Recall the burglar. You are in bed, and you hear a window breaking in another room. You attention is completely consumed by trying to hear if there is a burglar in the house. As a result you don't notice the fact that your heart is racing a mile a minute. You are having an intense emotion, but you don't feel it because attention is focused on listening for an intruder. This case is anecdotal of course, but it supports the hypothesis that experience of emotions depends on attention. If such cases hold up to empirical scrutiny, the AIR theory will have been confirmed for emotion.

If emotions become conscious in just the same way that visual episodes become conscious, then we have a further reason for thinking that emotion is a form of perception. Paradigm cases of perception can be consciously experienced, and, if the AIR theory is right, they come to consciousness in the same way. The thesis that emotions can be feelings does not depend in any way on this theory of consciousness, but the two fit together nicely. When an emotion is consciously felt, the feeling is not separate from the emotion. The feeling is the emotion modulated by attention.

6. Conclusions

I have argued for a qualified version of the thesis that emotions are feelings. Emotions are perceptions of bodily changes, and when those perceptions are conscious, emotions are feelings. Unconscious emotions are also possible, so not all emotions are feelings. Some emotions aren't felt. If some emotions are feelings, then the Fundamental Axiom endorsed by most philosophers who have thought about the emotions is false. Most philosophers endorse cognitive theories of the emotions, and they resist the idea that emotions are feelings. They think that, at best, emotions have feelings as parts. I considered some objections that cognitive theorists might level against the feeling thesis, and I argued that the objections can be answered. Finally, I sketched a general theory of perceptual consciousness and I indicated how it might apply to emotions. If I am right, emotions become conscious in just the way other perceptual states become conscious. Emotions are unconscious when we do not attend to the changes in our bodies. Otherwise, emotions are consciously felt.

Acknowledgements

This paper benefited from the extremely helpful comments of two anonymous referees. I owe them both deep thanks. I am also indebted to Giovanna Colombetti for her patience, support, and editorial assistance.

References

Bartels, A. and Zeki, S. (2000), 'The neural basis of romantic love', *NeuroReport*, **11**, pp. 3829–34.

Bechara, A. (2004), 'The role of emotion in judgment and decision-making: Evidence from neurological patients with orbitofrontal damage', *Brain and Cognition*, 55, pp. 30–40.

Bedford, E. (1957), 'Emotions', *Proceedings of the Aristotelian Society*, 57, pp. 281–304.

Bisiach, E. (1992), 'Understanding consciousness: Clues from unilateral neglect and related disorders', in *The Neuropsychology of Consciousness*, ed. A.D. Milner & M.D. Rugg (London: Academic Press).

Blood, A.J. & Zatorre, R.J. (2001), 'Intensely pleasurable responses to music correlate with activity in brain regions implicated with reward and emotion', *Proceedings of the National Academy of Sciences,* **98**, pp. 11818–23.

Buss, D.M., Larsen, R.J., Westen, D. & Semmelroth, J. (1992), 'Sex differences in jealousy: Evolution, physiology, and psychology', *Psychological Science,* **3**, pp. 251–5.

Chwalisz, K., Diener, E. & Gallagher, D. (1988), 'Autonomic arousal feedback and emotional experience: Evidence from the spinal cord injured', *Journal of Personality and Social Psychology*, **54**, pp. 820–8.

Cobos, P., Sánchez, M., Pérez, N. & Vila, J. (2004), 'Effects of spinal cord injuries of the subjective component of emotions', *Cognition and Emotion*, **18**, pp. 281–7.

Critchley, H.D, Wiens, S., Rotshtein, P., Öhman, A. & Dolan, R.J. (2004), 'Neural systems supporting interoceptive awareness', *Nature Neuroscience*, **7**, pp. 189–95.

Crucian, G.P., Hughes, J.D., Barrett, A.M., Williamson, D.J., Bauer, R.M., Bowers, D. & Heilman, K.M. (2000), 'Emotional and physiological responses to false feedback', *Cortex*, **36**, pp. 623–47.

Damasio, A.R. (1994), *Descartes' Error: Emotion Reason and the Human Brain* (New York: Gossett/Putnam).

Damasio, A.R. & Van Hoesen, G.W. (1983), 'Emotional disturbances associated with focal lesions of the limbic frontal lobe', in *Neuropsychology of Human Emotion*, ed. K.M. Heilman and P. Satz (New York: Guilford Press).

Damasio, A.R., Grabowski, T.J., Bechara, A., Damasio, H., Ponto, L.L.B.; Parvizi, J. & Hichwa, R.D. (2000), 'Subcortical and cortical brain activity during the feeling of self-generated emotions', *Nature Neuroscience*, **3**, pp. 1049–56.

Gordon, R. (1987), *The Structure of Emotions* (Cambridge: Cambridge University Press).

Greene, J.D., Sommerville, R.B., Nystrom, L.E., Darley, J.M. & Cohen, J.D. (2001), 'An fMRI investigation of emotional engagement in moral judgment', *Science*, **293**, pp. 2105–2.

Greenspan, P. (1988), *Emotions and Reasons* (New York: Routledge).

Griffiths, P.E. (1997), *What Emotions Really Are* (Chicago, IL: University of Chicago Press).

Harré, R. (1986), 'The social constructivist viewpoint', in *The Social Construction of Emotions*, ed. R. Harré (Oxford: Blackwell).

Hatfield, E., Cacioppo, J. & Rapson, R.L. (1984), *Emotional Contagion* (New York: Cambridge University Press).

Hohmann, G.W. (1966), 'Some effects of spinal cord lesions on experienced emotional feelings', *Psychophysiology*, **3**, pp. 143–56.

Jackendoff, R. (1987), *Consciousness and the Computational Mind* (Cambridge, MA: MIT Press).

James, W. (1884), 'What is an emotion?' *Mind*, **9**, pp. 188–205.

Kawabata, H. & Zeki, S. (2004), 'Neural correlates of beauty', *Neurophysiology*, **91**, pp. 1699–705.

Kiecolt-Glaser, J.K., Ricker, D., George, J., Messick, G., Speicher, C.E., Garner, W. & Glaser, R. (1984), 'Urinary cortisol levels, cellular immunocompetency, and loneliness in psychiatric inpatients', *Psychosomatic Medicine* , **46** , pp. 15–23.

Laird, J. (1984), 'The real role of facial response in the experience of emotion: A reply to Tourangeau and Ellsworth, and others', *Journal of Personality and Social Psychology*, **47**, pp. 909–17.

Levenson, R.W., Ekman, P. & Friesen, W.V. (1990), 'Voluntary facial action generates emotion-specific autonomic nervous system activity,' *Psychophysiology, * **27**, pp. 363–84.

Mack, A. & Rock, I. (1998), *Inattentional Blindness* (Cambridge, MA: MIT Press).

Marañon, G. (1924), 'Contribution à L'Étude De L'Action Émotive De L'Adrenaline', *Revue Française d'Endocrinologie*, **2**, pp. 301–25.

Menter, R., Weitzenkamp, D., Bingley, J., Charlifue, S. & Whiteneck, G. (1997), 'Bowel management outcomes in individuals with long-term spinal cord injuries', *Spinal Cord*, **35**, pp. 608–12.

Montoya, P. & Schandry, R. (1994), 'Emotional experience and heartbeat perception in patients with spinal cord injury and control subjects', *Journal of Psychophysiology*, **8**, pp. 289–96.

Nussbaum, M.C. (2001), *Upheavals of Thought: The Intelligence of the Emotions* (Cambridge: Cambridge University Press).

Parvizi, J., Anderson, S.W., Coleman, O.M., Damasio, H. & Damasio, A.R. (2001), 'Pathological laughter and crying: A link to the cerebellum', *Brain*, **124**, pp. 1708–19

Philippot, P., Chapelle, C. & Blairy, S. (2002), 'Respiratory feedback in the generation of emotion', *Cognition and Emotion*, **16**, pp. 605–27.

Pitcher, G. (1965), 'Emotion', *Mind,* **74**, pp. 324–46.

Prinz, J.J. (2000), 'A neurofunctional theory of visual consciousness', *Consciousness and Cognition*, **9**, pp. 243–59.

Prinz, J.J. (2004), *Gut Reactions* (New York: Oxford University Press).

Prinz, J.J. (2005a), 'Emotions, embodiment, and awareness', in *Emotions: Conscious and Unconscious*, ed. P. Niedenthal, L. Feldman-Barrett, & P. Winkielman (New York: Guilford).

Prinz, J.J. (2005b), 'A neurofunctional theory of consciousness', in *Cognition and the Brain: Philosophy and Neuroscience Movement*, ed. A. Brook & K. Akins (Cambridge: Cambridge University Press).

Shin, L.M, Dougherty, D.D., Orr, S.P., Pitman, R.K., Lasko, M., Macklin, M.L., Alpert, N.M., Fischman, A.J. & Rauch, S.L. (2000), 'Activation of anterior paralimbic structures during guilt-related script-driven imagery', *Biological Psychiatry*, **48**, pp. 43–50.

Solomon, R.C. (1976), *The Passions* (New York: Doubleday).

Strack, F. Martin, L.L. & Stepper, S. (1988), 'Inhibiting and facilitating conditions of the human smile: A nonobtrusive test of the facial feedback hypothesis', *Journal of Personality and Social Psychology*, **54**, pp. 768–77.

Tallis, F. (2002), *Hidden Minds: A History of the Unconscious* (New York: Arcade Publishing).

Valins, S. (1966), 'Cognitive effects of false heart-rate feedback', *Journal of Personality and Social Psychology*, **4**, pp. 400–8.

Winkielman, P., Berridge, K.C., Wilbarger, J. (2005), 'Unconscious affective reactions to masked happy versus angry faces influence consumption behavior and judgments of value', *Personality and Social Psychology Bulletin*, **1**, pp. 121–35.

Wierzbicka, A. (1999) *Emotions Across Languages and Cultures: Diversity and Universals.* (Cambridge: Cambridge University Press).

Zajonc, R.B., Murphy, S.T., Inglehart, M. (1989), 'Feeling and facial efference: Implications of the vascular theory of emotion', *Psychological Review,* **96**, pp. 395–416.

James A. Russell

Emotion in Human Consciousness Is Built on Core Affect

This article explores the idea that Core Affect provides the emotional quality to any conscious state. Core Affect is the neurophysiological state always accessible as simply feeling good or bad, energized or enervated, even if it is not always the focus of attention. Core Affect, alone or more typically combined with other psychological processes, is found in the experiences of feeling, mood and emotion, including the subjective experiences of fear, anger and other so-called basic emotions which are commonly (but on this account, not) thought to be raw, primitive, and universal emotional qualia.

The science of consciousness must decide on its fundamental elements, just as any science must decide on its ontology. Are fear, anger, and a small number of other discrete emotional experiences — emotional qualia — to be among them? Or, are these plainly important and real events to be explained as configurations of other, more fundamental elements? To use an analogy: are discrete emotional experiences like galaxies, now established as fundamental astronomical entities, or are they more like the Big Dipper and other constellations? Constellations were once thought to be fundamental entities with important powers, but are now seen as nothing more than happenstance configurations seen from an arbitrary perspective and with no deep role to play in astronomy. Different cultures historically recognized somewhat different constellations, just as they now recognize somewhat different emotions.

Both scientists and non-scientists tend to presuppose that the subjective feelings of fear, anger, grief, jealousy, love, and so on are raw, simple, qualitatively separate and universal parts of human nature. This assumption is part of a network of concepts (a folk theory of psychology) that includes such doubtful dichotomies as mind–body, nature–nurture, and reason–emotion. Long ago, our ancestors developed the specific concepts of fear, anger, and other emotions to account for rare but dramatic events that seemed to be qualitatively different

Correspondence:
James A. Russell, Department of Psychology, Boston College, Chestnut Hill, MA 02467, USA.
Email: james.russell.1@bc.edu

Journal of Consciousness Studies, **12**, No. 8–10, 2005, pp. 26–42

from normal thinking and acting. Today, fear, anger, and other pre-scientific emotion concepts have the weight of tradition and everyday experience behind them. These concepts shape the way people view themselves and others. They frame psychological reality and the study of it. To build an adequate science of consciousness it is necessary to scrutinize carefully these assumptions embedded in the questions we ask and the answers we offer.

In this article, I discuss the subjective experience of fear, anger and so on within a broader framework that bears on any aspect of consciousness with an emotional charge (moods, emotional experiences, and so on). I elaborate on an account sketched elsewhere (Russell, 2003); my aim is to clarify that account rather than to review supporting evidence or to consider alternatives. My account offers a different way of thinking about emotional feelings than is commonly assumed. Underlying this approach to emotional feelings is a different account of emotions in general. Emotions in general (what I call prototypical emotional episodes) are psychologically rather than genetically or culturally constructed.

The idea to be explored is that the ecology of emotional life is not one of long periods of non-emotional normal life punctuated by the occasional experience of a basic emotion. Instead, emotional life consists of the continuous fluctuations in simple primitive feelings that I call Core Affect (feeling good or bad, energized or enervated) and in pervasive perception of the affective qualities of objects and events. Core Affect blends with perceptual, cognitive, and behaviour processes in forming the stream of consciousness. Occasionally, these various processes happen to form a pattern, just as stars form a constellation, that more or less resembles a script for a specific emotion. When one recognizes that pattern in oneself, that emotion is experienced. This experience overlaps imperfectly with what emotion an outside observer would see. Seemingly simple discrete emotional feelings — including the experiences of fear, anger, jealousy, and so on — are not raw, simple or universal. Instead, they are complex Gestalts that typically include the simpler, more primitive feelings of Core Affect.

Background

I shall not define 'emotion'[1] but rather replace it with 'Core Affect' – a concept better defined as the article unfolds. By consciousness, I refer to states of sentience or awareness that are subjective (i.e., private to the individual who has those states). There is something it is like to be in a conscious state (Nagel, 1974). I distinguish intentional from non-intentional conscious states, in the philosophical sense of intentional as about (or directed at) something, here called the state's Object. I distinguish primary (1st order) from secondary (2nd order) states. Secondary states are meta-experiences: they are about, depend on, or consist of primary ones. For example, hunger is primary; anticipation of hunger is

---

[1] For several reasons. 'Emotion' is a folk concept rather than a scientific one. The kind of definition appropriate therefore is a descriptive one: what in fact do everyday folk mean by the word? Descriptive definitions are an interesting and important topic (Fehr & Russell, 1984). I doubt that necessary and sufficient features can be found for 'emotion', just as classical definitions cannot be found for many folk terms.

secondary. On the account outlined here, feeling bad is primary; feeling afraid is secondary, because it typically consists of an anticipation of feeling bad, a perceived cause, a desire to do something about whatever it is that is causing the bad feeling, and so on.

I also distinguish central from peripheral conscious elements[2]. This distinction is similar to Lambie & Marcel's (2002) distinction between 'awareness' and 'phenomenal experience', respectively. I have in mind a continuum, ranging from the centre of focal attention to background to preconscious at the periphery. Or, if not a continuum, this distinction comes in at least multiple layers — I stare at a person, set against the background of a chair, which in turn is set against the background of the room, which is against the background of the entire building, set in the town, set in the province, and so on: the element focal in consciousness is understood within a context of multiple layers of background. These layers gradually fade from explicit to implicit. The most peripheral (implicit) states (phenomenal experience without awareness in Lambie & Marcel's terms) nevertheless have a phenomenology in the sense that they *can* be brought to awareness through a shift in attention. They are preconscious, as distinct from those psychological states and processes that human beings are simply not equipped to bring into awareness.

Non-emotional aspects of consciousness are beyond my scope. I shall simply assume that when awake the normal person has a single, on-going stream of consciousness. Typically included in that stream are sensations (including proprioceptive ones), percepts of external objects and events, beliefs, desires, intentions to act, and so on. These elements are linked to each other in various ways, including causal bonds. The contents of consciousness presuppose a huge background of beliefs and concepts. Although consciousness can be divided into such elements, these elements are unified in the sense that they are experienced as aspects of a single consciousness.

Core Affect

Core Affect is that neurophysiological state consciously accessible as the simplest raw (primary or non-reflective) feelings most evident in moods and emotions and emotionally charged moments. It is similar to what Thayer (1989) called *activation*, what Watson and Tellegen (1985) called *affect*, what Morris (1989) called *mood*, and what is commonly called *feeling*. The clearest examples are seen in free-floating moods when one simply feels unusually good or bad, energized or lethargic, for no known reason. Such words seem to imply, as words do, distinct categories, but the approach taken here to Core Affect is instead dimensional (Russell, 1980). Elsewhere (Russell, 2003), I summarize diverse sources of evidence supporting the concept of Core Affect.

---

[2] The primary/secondary distinction is orthogonal to the central/peripheral distinction. A primary state can be central (attending to one's hunger) or peripheral (ignoring it). A secondary state can be central (attending to the fact that one feels afraid) or peripheral (ignoring it).

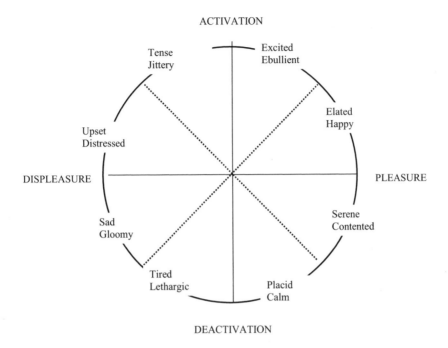

Figure 1. A descriptive model of Core Affect. Adapted from Russell (1980)

My current descriptive model of Core Affect is shown in Figure 1. The horizontal dimension, pleasure–displeasure, ranges from one extreme (e.g., agony) through a neutral point (adaptation level) to its opposite extreme (e.g., ecstasy). The vertical dimension ranges from sleep to, at the other extreme, frantic excitement, where 'frantic excitement' could be positive, negative, or neutral. One's conscious experience at a given moment, however, is not of two separate feelings, one somewhere along the horizontal dimension and another somewhere along the vertical. Rather, the conscious experience is of a single feeling that is an integral blend of the two dimensions. At a given moment, the conscious experience (the raw feeling) of Core Affect is thus describable as a single point on the map of Figure 1.

A person is always somewhere in Figure 1: Core Affect is always potentially available, although it can be focal, peripheral, or even so peripheral that it is invisible. Although, as we shall see shortly (Attributed Affect), Core Affect can come to be directed at an Object, Core Affect per se is Object-free. That is, in pure form, it is free-floating, or non-intentional in the philosophical sense. Core Affect may be rarely experienced in this pure form (perhaps the closest cases would be drug induced), but is typically experienced embedded with other elements of consciousness as one interacts with the world.

Although it is non-intentional, Core Affect is caused, and occasionally one salient event is the obvious cause (feeling delighted upon receiving a fabulous gift); such events can alter Core Affect directly or indirectly (through an evaluative process). But we often confront many events simultaneously, each contributing to Core Affect. As well, there are influences on Core Affect beyond awareness or even human ability to perceive. For instance, Core Affect is influenced by non-conscious processes, including subliminal stimuli and environmental changes we are incapable of sensing. Core Affect can be altered with drugs (stimulants, sedatives, euphoriants, dysphoriants). Relatedly, Core Affect is influenced by one's hormonal state and by bodily movement (dancing or jogging). Core Affect is greatly influenced by the other contents of consciousness – and in an interesting way: Even when we know that those contents are not real (as in films, theatre, imagination, music, and literature), Core Affect responds to *virtual reality* (Russell, 2003).

Core Affect is located not in any part of the body but in the core self. The 'core self' here is what Gallagher and Marcel (1999) called 'minimal self', what Panksepp (1998) called *SELF,* and what Damasio (1994) called *core self,* which is me here and now. Core self is irreflexive, first-order consciousness (and thus distinct from the cognitive and narrative concept of the self which is the topic of much psychological research).

Although Core Affect is an ancient and non-linguistic thing, if it were translated into language, it would be 'I feel X.' Everyday English words are used in Figure 1 to characterize some possible Xs, but the Core Affect involved is simpler than many of these words may imply. (And words in a language other than English would have slightly other implications.) Creating a scientific account out of everyday language is difficult, for everyday language and scientific language have different functions. Even the words for the horizontal dimension can be misleading: 'Feeling good' and 'feeling bad' capture, I hope, the intended generality of Core Affect, but 'good' and 'bad' here are not meant to imply any moral evaluation; and feeling bad is just as adaptive as feeling good — consider the survival benefits of pain. The words 'pleasure' and 'displeasure' could also label the horizontal dimension — provided they are freed, at least conceptually, from behavioural and sensory qualities. The prototypes in everyday thinking of 'pleasure' and 'displeasure' contain behavioural and sensory qualities as well as simply good or bad feelings. For example, the displeasure of great thirst includes searching for drink and sensations such as dryness of throat. The pleasure of then drinking includes the act of drinking and the sensory qualities of the beverage. However, other pleasures and displeasures, such as success or failure at solving a puzzle, may have no special sensations beyond the incidental. The victor in a tennis match may experience the same aches and muscle fatigue as the loser. We don't always approach pleasure or avoid pain (Parrott, 1993). The word 'pain' covers both mental anguish and physical injury, which share the displeasure of Core Affect but differ in behavioural and sensory correlates. Even with physical pain, the 'bad feeling' can be separated pharmacologically from the nociceptive sensory qualities (Melzack, 1973). And that is what I have in mind for the pleasure and displeasure of the horizontal dimension: the feeling good or bad can be separated, at least conceptually, from any accompanying behavioral or sensory qualities.

Similarly, the words 'activation' or 'arousal' labeling the vertical dimension refer here to the neurophysiological state accessible as the first-order conscious feeling of mobilization and energy. As English words, 'arousal' and 'activation' may bring to mind the situations, behavioural activities, and bodily sensations that often (and perhaps invariably in natural circumstances) accompany that simple conscious feeling, but, at least conceptually, these can all be set aside. In short, the feelings of Figure 1 cannot be reduced to behavioural, sensory, or any other more basic elements: Core Affect is an irreducible element of consciousness.

The preceding prescriptive characterization of Core Affect must also be embedded in a network of empirical hypotheses about its relation to other psychological processes. Core Affect is more than a description of elemental emotional feelings; it is a central mechanism in psychological functioning. Core Affect is a common currency for the evaluation of otherwise disparate events. Changes in Core Affect can trigger a search for their cause, typically resulting in what I call Attributed Affect, which lies at the heart of most full-blown emotions. More generally, Core Affect plays a role in reflexes, behaviour, decision making, attention, preferences, motives, attitudes, reward, and cognition (Russell, 2003). Some of these influences occur without the Core Affect being named or attributed or brought into focal attention, whereas other cannot. And many more questions can be raised. For example, are some specific behavioural changes inevitably associated with specific changes in Core Affect? Can we map out the reciprocal influences between Core Affect and attention? Which of Core Affect's influences require attention? What happens to Core Affect itself when it becomes the focus of attention? I have assumed that Core Affect remains the same, but perhaps attention reduces its intensity (Tsal *et al.*, 1994) or alters it in some other way. Could attention be required to integrate the horizontal and vertical dimensions into a single feeling (Treisman & Gelade, 1980)?

Other Emotional Events

Sometimes, Core Affect is the only emotional feeling in consciousness. Often, however, there at least appears to be more. Here I describe several others. My list is illustrative rather than exhaustive. My theme is that they all involve in some way Core Affect. For example, many are Gestalts derived from combining Core Affect with the products of non-emotional processes. Indeed, Core Affect combines with other psychological processes promiscuously, rendering them 'hot'. In everyday experience, these Gestalts can be highly salient, more salient than the Core Affect and other building blocks out of which they are constructed — just as the meaning of a perceived object can be more salient than its edges or other primitive building blocks used in the perception of that object.

Attributed Affect. Not infrequently, Core Affect, or change in Core Affect, is attributed (or misattributed) to a *specific* cause: That massage feels good. This music is calming me down. Your words are upsetting me. Attributed Affect is

therefore defined by three necessary and together sufficient elements: Core
Affect, Object, and attribution of the Core Affect to the Object. Thus, if translated into language, an Attributed Affect would be 'That Object is making me
feel X.' The attributions can presumably range from automatic to effortful, fast
to slow, or implicit to explicit and can be held with different degrees of certainty.
Because of the multiple, simultaneous, and sometimes unknown influences on
Core Affect, attributions of Core Affect to a specific cause are fallible.

Perceived Affective Quality. In the same way that a visible object enters consciousness coded for color, the object typically enters consciousness already
coded as to its affective quality: the sunset is beautiful, the path scary, the building boring. Each object or event has the ability to alter Core Affect; we apparently automatically perceive objects in terms of this ability, although, again,
fallibly.

Perceived Affective Quality and Core Affect are closely linked. They often
co-occur: a depressing story shifts Core Affect toward depression; feeling
depression leads to seeing the world as depressing. A Perceived Affective Quality logically depends on Core Affect. The dependence can be seen in
microgenesis, ontogenesis, and phylogenesis. In microgenesis, attributing current Core Affect to an Object leads to that Object's Perceived Affective Quality.
Through 'valence-tagging' (core-affect-tagging), new environmental objects
and events become associated with dimensions of Core Affect (LeDoux, 1996;
Öhman, 1999). Tasting a mango for the first time, experiencing pleasure, and
attributing the pleasure to the mango leads to the belief that mangoes are pleasant. As a result of this process, Perceived Affective Qualities develop into a distinct system. Upon encountering the next mango, one does not have to re-taste
and re-experience the pleasure; rather, even at a distance or in one's thoughts or
imagination, mangoes are simply coded as pleasant, whatever one's current Core
Affect. And during evolution, the perceived affective quality of certain objects
likely became prewired. Panksepp (2001, p. 142) used the term 'intrinisic value'
to state this hypothesis:

> a great deal of time and effort in brain evolution was devoted to the establishment of
> intrinsic values — the various feelings of goodness and badness that are internally
> experienced indicators of survival utility, elaborated with ancient regions of the
> brain shared by all mammals in remarkably homologous ways.

There is a sense, then, in which Perceived Affective Qualities are derived from
Core Affect. But because the derivation typically happened in the past, there is
also an important sense in which Perceived Affective Qualities are separate from
current Core Affect: When an Object's Affective Quality was derived earlier,
that Object simply appears in consciousness already coded as to its affective
quality, with no necessary concurrent involvement of Core Affect. I recall a
depressed patient acknowledging that the sunset was indeed particularly beautiful that evening, but also pointing out that the sunset in no way alleviated her
misery. In this sense, Perceived Affective Quality has become an autonomous
element of consciousness.

Perception of Affective Quality differs from Core Affect in a number of ways[3]. Whereas Core Affect is not necessarily attached to an Object, Perceived Affective Qualities are qualities of Objects and thus necessarily intentional. Whereas Core Affect is 'I feel X', a Perceived Affective Quality is perceived as a property of an external object: this is upsetting, that is fun, he is lovable: 'This Object is X-eliciting.' The affective quality does not, subjectively, seem to be about me, but rather it is something that lies in the external Object. We have to be taught that beauty is in the eye of the beholder. As a consequence, whereas a person has one Core Affect, he or she perceives many different objects or events at the same time, each with its affective quality. Indeed, the same object or event can have different aspects and features, and each of them may have its own affective quality. An example is the experience of deciding between two courses of action, each with distinct costs and benefits.

Mood. The term 'mood' is broad and heterogeneous. Much (but not all) of mood can be subsumed by Core Affect. That is, the most prototypical cases of mood are prolonged periods dwelling within a region of Figure 1: a prolonged Core Affect of unhappiness, especially with low arousal, is a mood of depression. To have an average Core Affect of happiness during a period of normal hassles and uplifts is to be in a happy mood. Like Core Affect, most moods are non-intentional: one simply feels depressed, agitated, chipper or whatever but not about anything (i.e., without any specific Object).

Quasi-mood. Sometimes the word 'mood' allows an Object, although of a vague sort. For example, 'anxious mood' can be a Core Affect of unpleasant arousal directed at the future; "depressive mood' (unpleasant low arousal) can be directed at everything about the self. 'Irritability' is a state in which negative Core Affect can be directed at almost any Object. Of course, vagueness and specificity form a continuum, and so mood, quasi-mood, and attributed affect fall on that continuum, as when free-floating Core Affect of unpleasant high arousal blends into an anxious mood about the future which blends into a fear of some unspecified future misfortune. In these hypothetical examples, the Core Affect stays the same, but the attributed Object varies.

Affect Regulation. We often deliberately attempt to change Core Affect in ourselves and others. I am not advocating full blown hedonism. Rather, a change in Core Affect is often an explicit goal (seeking a time and place to relax) or a means to another end (drinking coffee to keep awake while reading a boring article).

Emotion Perception. We perceive others to have specific discrete emotions: Alice is afraid, Tom jealous. Like any perception, emotion perception can be fast and automated. And like any perception, emotion perception relies on cognitive concepts — in this case, typically folk concepts such as fear, jealousy, and so on but possibly implicit concepts as well. Each such concept is a script in which specific events unfold in a temporal and causally linked sequence. These concepts

---

[3] Perceived Affective Quality differs as well from 'appraisal' taken to consist of cognitive assessment of an event for such properties as its conduciveness to fulfillment of current goals, probability of future occurrence, or availability of resources with which to cope with that event.

allow varying degrees of membership, with blurry borders separating, say, fear from not-fear. The categories of fear, jealousy and so on are therefore heterogeneous. No single feature of the script is either necessary or sufficient for the emotion. These concepts may be innate and pre-formed, as is implied by various theories of innate emotion perception via, for example, facial signalling. Evidence that all languages possess the same concepts and that children acquire words for those concepts easily would be evidence favoring such a hypothesis. In the case of emotion concepts, however, the evidence shows developmental, cultural and historical variability. Although there are great similarities across languages in emotion concepts, there are also telling differences. Various hypotheses are consistent with available evidence (Russell, 1991), but the one that most resonates with the present account is that features of the concepts are highly similar in all human beings, but that there is enough variability in patterns among those features to allow each language and culture to hone its own lexicon. For example, Tahitian (Levy 1973) includes 'mehameha', which refers to the uncanny anxious feeling one has in the presence of a ghost.

Some emotion concepts are simpler than others, but most include multiple features. In perceiving fear or mehameha, the perceiver does not require all features of the script to be observable or even present. Perception is the generation of a hypothesis that accounts for the available data and infers the rest. For example, seeing only that Alice is fleeing a bear that suddenly appeared may be sufficient for me to see her as frightened. I might see her state differently, however, as I obtain more data.

Emotional Meta-Experience. Occasionally, events in one's own life happen to line up in a way that fits one or more of the emotion scripts. For example, I see a dog; I hear it growl, think it dangerous; my Core Affect changes from calm to upset; I attribute the change in Core Affect to the dog; I feel my body become activated; I freeze and then move away from the dog, scrutinize the dog's behavior, and assess what resources are available to deal with it; I feel uncertain about what will happen next or what to do; I feel I lack the ability to control events and feel under time pressure to figure out what to do. At some point in this episode, I might recognize that what is happening to me closely resembles what happens during a fear script. Recognition means that the various elements form into a perceptual Gestalt with a specific meaning; in this case: "I'm scared." Because this Gestalt is derived from and includes many more primitive conscious elements, it is a meta-experience, a secondary consciousness. The example just narrated fits the script well, but of course other sequences can fit less well and, on occasion, one simply doesn't know if what one is experiencing is or is not a member of that emotion category.

The concept of emotional meta-experience is deliberately parallel to perception of emotion in others. Although the raw data on which they rely only partially overlap, they are both forms of perception. As in other-perception, in self- perception of emotion, resemblance is a matter of degree and not all features need be present. As in other-perception, the emotional meta-experience of being afraid does not produce the sequence of events on which the perception is based.

Rather, a sequence occurs and is then perceived (or not) to be a case of fear. Thus, an outside observer may conclude that I am frightened, even though I do not perceive myself that way, or even though I might sincerely deny that I'm frightened. During a near fatal accident it is not unusual to hear someone reporting they were too busy to feel frightened. Conversely, I might perceive myself as afraid when a more objective assessment would not. (Some phobias may develop in this way.) A perception is an interpretation of the data and is subject to influence. One can be coaxed into seeing an object as art by an artist presenting it as such. Similarly, one can be coaxed into interpreting, or re-interpreting, oneself as afraid or angry. Parents tell their children that they are not really afraid, and the women's movement coaxed women to re-interpret their depression as anger.

My claim is not that an emotional meta-experience of fear is necessary to the occurrence of fear, but rather that when one has a subjective experience of fear, that experience is an emotional meta-experience. Although emotional meta-experiences do not produce the emotions they are experiences of, they do have consequences. Emotional meta-experience plays a role in self-identity (I'm easily frightened) and in self-regulation (dogs are not really dangerous and so I shouldn't be afraid; or ghosts don't really exist and so I shouldn't feel mehameha). Thus, in emotion self-regulation, the self-perception can come to play a role in the current sequence of events, typically by steering away from its socially undesirable elements or toward rationality. As a result, common sense holds that it is very important to know what category of emotion one is feeling. A person might ask, is this really love or mere infatuation? Could I have been jealous or merely angry? The conscious experience of a discrete emotion can also be extremely salient: picture a young boy who feels frightened by the presence of another boy and who knows that boys should not feel frightened. Discrete emotions are also salient in memory. One might, for example, remember little else about an episode (a long ago vacation) except how happy it was; little about a near-accident, except how frightening it was.

The experience of mehameha or fear is not simple, universal or primitive. Because emotional meta-experiences rely on concepts that can vary historically, developmentally, culturally, and perhaps individually, there exists a large number of categories of emotional experiences. Further, each category is heterogeneous: within a given emotion category, tokens differ in many ways. Each is a Gestalt composed of somewhat different components. Thus, it would be possible but unlikely for an English speaker to have an experience very similar to a Tahitian speaker experiencing mehameha — the English speaker would have to believe in ghosts, believe in similar consequences to ghostly encounters, evaluate fear similarly, and so on.

Accounts of Emotion and Emotional Experience

Let me place the account of conscious emotional experience just outlined into a broader context. Available accounts of emotional experience appear irreconcilable; they show so little agreement that emotion experience qualifies as a mystery. LeDoux (1996) supposed emotional experience an epiphenomenon, whereas Panksepp (2001) argued forcefully for its causal efficacy. Many issues remain unresolved (and on my account are unresolvable), such as the number of discrete categories of emotional experience, which ones are basic, and so on. Here I focus on those discrete experiences that have often been offered as basic. Accounts of emotional experience are often part of a general account of emotion.

The psychology of emotional experience has been dominated by one family of accounts, which might be called the Readout Accounts (Cannon, 1927; Panksepp, 2001; Oatley and Johnson-Laird, 1987). A Readout Account is a modern and explicit version of folk psychology. Readout Accounts provide the greatest contrast with my proposal. Readout Accounts assume a small set of basic emotions as distinct causal entities. Here is one stark prototypical version: Each basic emotion has a separate neural circuit. The emotion begins when an antecedent stimulus event activates the neural circuit.[4] The neural circuit, in turn, produces both a unique subjective conscious experience of that emotion and objective observable manifestations of the emotion configured in a characteristic pattern: a telltale peripheral physiological pattern, a recognizable facial and vocal expression, an instrumental action, and perhaps other changes characteristic of that emotion. In other words, on this account, the conscious experience of a basic discrete emotion is a direct readout from that emotion's neural circuit. The readout is a simple raw feeling: a primary, primitive, irreducible conscious element, much like the conscious experience of red. Oatley and Johnson-Laird further infer that the word 'fear' for example is a semantic primitive: To know the meaning of the word 'fear', it is necessary to have the corresponding emotional experience — just as to know the meaning of the word 'red,' it is necessary to have the corresponding visual experience. Different basic emotions come with qualitatively different feelings — qualia. Implicitly, there is a discoverable number of such qualia (equal to the number of basic emotions), and sharp qualitative boundaries separate emotion from non-emotions and specific basic emotions from each other.

A variant of the Readout Account includes feedback from the observable manifestations. Basic emotions remain as causal entities and emotional experiences remain simple qualia. An antecedent event still activates a neural circuit, which again activates the same observable manifestations. But, on this variant account, the neural circuit does not directly produce the subjective emotional experience. Instead, the various manifestations produce feedback to the brain, and the perception of the feedback produces the subjective experience of the emotion. This account is often (wrongly) attributed to William James (see below), and can be found in such more modern theorists as Tomkins (1962, 1963), Damasio (1994), Laird and Bresler (1990), and Prinz (2004).

---

[4] I am not attempting to do neuroscience here; let 'activates a neural circuit' stand for whatever physical basis is ultimately found that functions in the role described here. The Readout account is a version of an ancient view now embedded in common sense. Over time, the underlying physical basis of the emotion has changed and will continue to do so. For instance, Descartes assumed that the physiological mechanism of basic emotions was imbalance among the 4 humours.

Some version of a Readout Account is implicit or explicit in much research on emotion. Nevertheless, it is not without its detractors. At the dawn of scientific psychology, the introspectionists aimed specifically at separating the basic atoms of subjective experience from compound molecules. When Wundt (1896) introspected, he found that emotional experiences such as joy, fear, anger, pride, and sorrow were compounds. Each consists of both beliefs and feelings. Wundt observed that the number of elementary feelings was large, perhaps infinitely large, but that they could be parsimoniously described in terms of three dimensions similar to those of Figure 1: pleasant-unpleasant, tension-relaxation, and excitement-inhibition. Titchner (1898) came to a similar conclusion except that he believed that the feeling component could be described in terms of a single dimension, pleasant-unpleasant. Stumpf (1899; see Reisenzein & Schonpflug, 1992) also came to a similar conclusion except that emotional experience consists of beliefs and evaluations. (Much later, Ortony, Clore, and Collins, 1988, used different methods to conclude, similarly, that emotional experience is a compound consisting of a pleasant–unpleasant valence reaction plus cognitive assessment of its eliciting event.)

William James (1890) differed from other introspectionists in many assumptions, but similarly found that emotional experiences were compounds rather than atoms. The theme of James's analysis was truly radical: there is nothing fundamental about emotion: no dedicated neural centre and no elemental emotional qualia. Instead, emotion can be completely reduced to non-emotional elements (reflexes, beliefs, somatosensory feedback, and perception of that feedback). An emotional experience includes a cold intellectual belief about the eliciting stimulus. The belief provides semantic or cognitive content to the emotional experience. For example, the belief that Jack has died occurs in the emotional experience of sadness over Jack's death. An emotional quality is added to this cold belief by sensations arising from our bodily reaction to the eliciting stimulus — the felt feedback from visceral, expressive, and behavioural reactions to the stimulus. For present purposes two points are important. First, these feedback sensations were not themselves emotional, but equivalent in kind to the sort of sensory feedback constantly generated by the body. And second, these sensations cannot be classified into some small number of distinct categories. James wrote, 'The internal shadings of emotional feeling … merge endlessly into each other. Language has discriminated some of them, as hatred, antipathy, animosity, dislike, aversion, malice, spite, vengefulness, abhorrence, etc., etc.; but in the dictionaries of synonyms we find there feelings distinguished more by their severally appropriate objective stimuli than by their conscious or subjective tone' (p. 448). Modern, neo-Jamesian theories were offered by Schachter (1964) and Mandler (1984).

More recently, Lambie & Marcel (2002) faulted the Readout Accounts for ignoring the complexity of conscious emotional experience, noting great variety even within a given category of emotion. Lambie & Marcel were not as radical as James on emotion, but did offer an expanded view by including cognitive appraisal, secondary appraisal, action readiness, and hedonic tone (the pleasure-displeasure dimension of Core Affect) along with the more traditional components listed in the Readout Account. More importantly, they expanded the description of the conscious side of emotion, with corresponding de-emphasis of its simple qualitative feel. On their account, certain of the results of the processes that constitute an emotion have a phenomenology: they exist as first-order consciousness in their own right. Attention then selects among these many components what becomes central. Attention yields differences in whether the object of attention is treated analytically or synthetically and whether one is immersed in or detached from that object. Attention can focus on the self: on bodily sensations, on urges to action, on thoughts, or on oneself as affected by the eliciting event (e.g., self as insulted or exalted). Alternatively, attention can focus on the world: how the emotion-eliciting event is menacing or hateful.

My account follows the lead of those who dissented from the Readout Accounts. My account is similar to that of James and his followers in the attempt to reduce emotion to non-emotional elements. Indeed, some of differences are merely phrasing. For example, whereas James equated 'emotion' with emotional experience, I dispense with 'emotion' as a scientific term. My major difference with James is my addition of Core Affect.

My account also follows the lead of Lambie & Marcel on consciousness, with the major difference that I dispense altogether with the discrete emotion itself as a causal entity, although I leave intact the working parts. That is, my account supposes a variety of loosely linked processes, none of which are exclusively emotional. Consider changes in the autonomic nervous system. Neural and hormonal processes operate continuously on the autonomic nervous system, not just during emotion. The same physiological arousal is produced during exercise as during flight from a frightening bear (Cannon, 1927). There are no patterns of autonomic activity unique to emotion or to a specific emotion (Cacioppo et al. 1993). On my account, there is no emotion centre in the brain[5] and no neural circuit exclusively devoted to a specific basic emotion (Posner, Russell, & Peterson, in press). To be sure, neural events occur and produce all the observable changes. But, one set of neural events produces changes in the peripheral nervous system. Separate (although potentially linked) neural events produce facial changes and, again, no one pattern of facial changes characterizes all and only cases of a specific emotion. And so on for each "manifestation" (which is now a less apt term, but refers here to the same objective observable events). Because there is no top-down organization, but largely separate neural events producing various manifestations, different cases of the 'same emotion' will have different patterns of manifestations.

Even some elements from a Readout Account are consistent with my proposal.[6] For example, my account does not deny the existence of the neural

---

[5] Of course, the brain is doing all the work. All mental and behavioural events are produced by brain events. This 'astonishing hypothesis' (Crick, 1994) is a scientific truism, but does not favour any one of the accounts described here over the others.

[6] This is a point on which I would not want to be misunderstood. Sabini & Silver (2005) explained that they do not share my view of emotion because 'We think there really is a mechanism in the brain that

circuits postulated by Panksepp (2001). Indeed, it is easy to imagine that Panksepp's RAGE circuit generates something akin to a conscious "urge to harm", which in turn is one of the features that could contribute to a self-perception of anger or some similar emotion. But I doubt a one-to-one correspondence between activation of a Panksepp circuit and the human experience of the allegedly corresponding emotion. Human anger is not simply an urge to harm: one can feel (perceive oneself to be) angry without an urge to harm (consider indignation at violence) or feel an urge to harm without feeling (perceiving oneself to be) angry (as seen vividly in some clinical cases). Human anger is more heterogeneous in its antecedents and its manifestations, and the manifestations are too loosely correlated for anger to be accounted for by a single mechanism.

Similarly, as in some Readout Accounts, 'feedback' (now a misnomer) is one of the processes on my account that contributes to the experience of a specific emotion. On my account, however, Core Affect, Perceived Affective Quality of the event to which the Core Affect is attributed, appraisal of the eliciting event, attribution of the Core Affect to the eliciting event, instrumental action, surrounding context, and so on also serve as raw data in the self-perception of an emotion. For example, although the prototype of anger is a script that includes violent aggression as one of its steps, in reality aggression is rare. Episodes without aggression can still resemble the anger script, but are not prototypical. Interestingly, some individuals report never having experienced prototypical anger, which may exist more as an ideal case than as a modal pattern. Having a goal of harm, a tentative plan for harming, or a fantasy of harm resembles the aggression component sufficiently to contribute to an overall resemblance to the anger script. Similarly, although strong change in Core Affect is a prototypical component, it is not a necessary one. In the prototype of anger, Core Affect is unpleasant high arousal. But, on rare occasions, I may perceive myself as angry but lack the high activation; imagine cold anger. I may even perceive myself as angry but lack the displeasure; imagine the feeling of enjoying revenge. More generally, during the time it takes an anger episode to unfold, Core Affect may fluctuate considerably. Because Core Affect of unpleasant activation is part of the anger script, any case lacking it is at best a peripheral case of anger — as indeed some experiences are. Resemblance to a script is a matter of degree, and no one feature is defining. In these less prototypical cases, enough of the other typical features of the emotion script are present for the case to pass some threshold as a member of the category. All this uncertainty and fuzziness would be problematic if 'anger' were used as a scientific concept, but here uncertainty and fuzziness are simply empirical facts about acts of perception.

My account follows Lambie & Marcel (2002) in faulting Readout Accounts as providing an overly simple characterization of subjective emotional experience. Lambie & Marcel broaden the topic to all that is happening in consciousness

produces desires for revenge in response to perceptions of transgression, and if so we believe this mechanism in the brain has an evolutionary history' (p. 709). It is an empirical question whether 'revenge' and 'transgression' cut nature at the joints, but I do not doubt that all desires and all perceptions are produced by the brain and that brain mechanisms have an evolutionary history.

when someone is having an emotion. (My account does replace 'having an emotion' with something like 'when the person's state fits the folk concept of an emotion.' Indeed, I suspect that Lambie & Marcel's topic could as easily be consciousness of everyday life as it is consciousness of emotion.) Lambie & Marcel point out that what happens in consciousness during different exemplars of the same emotion differ in important ways. Consider something left out of Readout Accounts altogether: what Lambie & Marcel call 'world-focused emotion experience.' They note that 'researchers have apparently overlooked it conceptually and therefore have failed to specifically look for it' (p. 223). World-focused emotion experience occurs when 'a person or animal or the world in general may be experienced as "frightening," "hateful," "empty and barren," "welcoming," or "cute," for example' (p. 223). On my analysis, such experiences certainly occur and could well be perceived as a specific emotion, either by self or another. The key to a world-focused emotion experience is that a Perceived Affective Quality becomes the focus of attention. Consider a compound experience that includes, besides the Perceived Affective Quality, a change in Core Affect and an attribution of the Core Affect to an Object as well as some individuating perceptual/cognitive features of the Object. For example, to see a home as 'welcoming' is first to see it as pleasant, but also to feel comfort and to attribute the comfort to the home, all embedded in a social context of whose home it is, who is literally welcome, and so on. Of course, the Core Affect is not necessary. One could focus entirely on the affective quality of the home and other of its features, with no contribution of actual Core Affect. Such a case might be judged a cold emotion, rather than a prototypical one. In any case, how it is judged is an empirical question.

My account resonates with Lambie & Marcel's (2002) analysis of the simple subjective feeling of fear or anger (qualia) — what they term 'categorical–emotion experience'. They describe such feelings as experiencing one's fear as fear, for example, whereas I would describe them as emotional meta-experiences. Whereas on a Readout Account, these qualia are inevitable components of each emotion, Lambie & Marcel see them as occurring only during a highly synthetic mode of attention to self, leaving many cases of fear, for example, without the categorical-emotion experience (without, in my terms, the emotional meta-experience). Having a categorical-emotion experience also requires 'possessing the relevant category' (p. 242). People can be mistaken in their categorization or in locating the cause of the emotion. I see no substantive difference between my account and theirs on emotional qualia.

Concluding Remarks

The science of consciousness is too young to expect definitive conclusions. All the accounts I have mentioned (including my own) need to be made more explicit and to undergo revision, especially through empirical testing. Another route to advancement is comparison and integration of different accounts. The standard and dominant Readout Accounts can be contrasted with a range of alternatives.

Although the alternative accounts have generally been seen as irreconcilable, they have much in common and are, I think, ready for integration. The account I have proposed provides one such integration.

The principal reason my account can reconcile seemingly irreconcilable positions is that I treat emotion concepts as folk rather than scientific terms, thus requiring rather than providing explanation. Thus, for example, questions such as 'What is an emotion?' or 'Is emotion a behaviour, a cognition, or a physiological pattern?' or 'Are there unconscious emotions?' all fall outside the science of emotion, but becomes questions about folk beliefs. Consequently, my account does not allow the commonsense assumption that persons experience a particular emotion because they have them. The subjective conscious experience of an emotion cannot be treated simply as another component of the emotion. Instead, conscious experience must be examined in its own right for the processes that produce it and for the role it plays. Another consequence is that the topic of emotional life and emotion in consciousness is expanded beyond the confines of basic emotions.

Whatever the fate of my specific proposals, the science of consciousness can benefit from the questions they raise about the status of everyday emotion concepts. These concepts are as obvious, salient and real as the Big Dipper in a clear night sky. Still, they are unwieldy tools for science. They lack clear definition and have vague boundaries. We are unsure which events lie in the concept's extension (in the set of events being referred to). Concepts that are unpacked as scripts are not necessarily illegitimate, but they are suspect. 'Sunburn' incorporates a specific cause of the burn within the concept. If the same burn can be produced without the sun, then, for scientific purposes, 'sunburn' is best replaced with a concept that leaves out the cause. Science benefits from a continual questioning of assumptions. For the science of consciousness of emotion, such questioning is particularly needed now.

References

Cacioppo, J.T., Klein, D.J., Berntson, G.G., & Hatfield, E. (1993), 'The psychophysiology of emotion', in *Handbook of Emotions*, ed. M. Lewis & J. M. Haviland (New York: Guilford).

Cannon, W.B. (1927), 'The James-Lange theory of emotion: A critical examination and an alternative theory', *American Journal of Psychology*, **39**, pp. 106–24.

Crick, F. (1994), *The Astonishing Hypothesis* (New York: Charles Scribner's Sons).

Damasio, A.R. (1994), *Descartes' Error*(New York: Avon Books, Inc).

Fehr, B. & Russell, J.A. (1984), 'Concept of emotion viewed from a prototype perspective', *Journal of Experimental Psychology: General*, **113**, pp. 464–86.

Gallagher, S. & Marcel, A.J. (1999), 'The self in contextualized action', *Journal of Consciousness Studies*, **6** (4), pp. 4–30.

James, W. (1990), *The Principles of Psychology* (New York: Dover).

Johnson-Laird, P.N., Oatley, K. (1989), 'The language of emotions: An analysis of a semantic field', *Cognition and Emotion*, **3**, pp. 81–123.

Laird, JD, & Bresler, C. (1990), 'William James and the mechanisms of. emotional experience', *Personality and Social Psychology Bulletin*, **16**, pp. 636–51.

Lambie, J.A. & Marcel, A.J. (2002), 'Consciousness and the varieties of emotion experience: A theoretical framework', *Psychological Review*, **109**, pp. 219–59.

LeDoux, J. (1996), *The Emotional Brain* (New York: Touchstone).

Mandler, G. (1975), *Mind and Emotion* (New York: Wiley).

Levy, R.I. (1973), *Tahitians* (Chicago: University of Chicago Press).

Mandler, G. (1984), *Mind and Body: Psychology of emotion and stress* (New York: Norton).

Melzack, R. (1973), *The Puzzle of Pain* (New York: Basic).

Morris, W.N. (1989), *Mood: The frame of mind* (New York: Springer-Verlag).

Nagel, T. (1974), 'What is it like to be a bat?', *Philosophical Review*, **83,** pp. 435–50.

Oatley, K. & Johnson-Laird, P.N. (1987), 'Towards a cognitive theory of emotion', *Cognition and Emotion*, **1**, pp. 29–50.

Öhman, A. (1999), 'Distinguishing unconscious from conscious emotional processes: Methodological considerations and theoretical implications', in *Handbook of Cognition and Emotion*, ed. T. Dalgleish & M. J. Power (Chichester, England: Wiley).

Ortony, A., Clore, G.L. & Collins, A. (1988), *The Cognitive Structure of Emotions* (New York: Cambridge University Press).

Panksepp, J. (1998), *Affective Neuroscience: The Foundations of Human and Animal Emotions* (New York: Oxford University Press).

Panksepp, J. (2001), 'The neuro-evolutionary cusp between emotions and cognitions', *Evolution and Cognition*, **7**, pp. 141–62.

Parrott, W.G. (1993), 'Beyond hedonism: Motives for inhibiting good moods and for maintaining bad moods', in *Handbook of mental control*, ed. D.M. Wegner & J.W. Pennebaker (Englewood Cliffs, NJ: Prentice Hall).

Posner, J., Russell, J. A., Peterson, B. (in press), 'The circumplex model of affect:An integrative approach to affective neuroscience, cognitive development, and psychopathology', *Development and Psychopathology*.

Prinz, J.J. (2004), *Gut Reactions* (New York: Oxford).

Reisenzein, R., W Schoenpflug (1992), 'Stumpf's cognitive-evaluative theory of emotion', *American Psychologist*, **47**, pp. 34–45.

Russell, J.A. (1980), 'A circumplex model of affect', *Journal of Personality and Social Psychology*, **39**, pp. 1161–78.

Russell, J.A. (1991), 'Culture and the categorization of emotion', *Psychological Bulletin*, **110**, pp. 426–50.

Russell, J.A. (2003), 'Core affect and the psychological construction of emotion', *Psychological Review*, **110**, pp. 145–72.

Sabini, J. & Silver, M. (2005), 'Ekman's basic emotions: Why not love and jealousy?', *Cognition and Emotion*, **19**, pp. 693–712.

Schachter, S. (1964), 'The interaction of cognitive and physiological determinants of emotional state', in *Advances in Experimental Social Psychology*, Vol. 1, ed. L. Festinger (New York: Academic Press).

Stumpf, C. (1899), Über den Begriff der Gemüthsbewegung [On the concept of emotion]. *Zeitschrift für Psychologie und Physiologie der Sinnesorgane*, **21**, pp. 47–99.

Thayer, R.E. (1989), *The Origin of Everyday Moods: Managing energy, tension and stress* (New York: Oxford University Press).

Titchner, E.B. (1898), *An Outline of Psychology* (New York: Macmillan).

Tomkins, S.S. (1962, 1963), *Affect, Imagery, Consciousness*, Vol. I & II (New York: Springer Publishing).

Treisman, A. and G. Gelade (1980), 'A feature integration theory of attention', *Cognitive Psychology*, **12**, pp. 97–136.

Tsal, Y., L. Shalev, *et al.* (1994), 'Attention reduces perceived brightness contrast', *Quarterly Journal of Experiemtal Psychology*, **47A**, pp. 865–93.

Watson, D. & Tellegen, A. (1985), 'Toward a consensual structure of mood', *Psychological Bulletin*, **98**, pp. 219–35.

Wellman, H.M., Harris, P. L., Banerjee, M., & Sinclair, A. (1995), 'Early understanding of emotion: Evidence from natural language', *Cognition and Emotion*, **9**, pp. 117–49.

Wundt W. (1896), *Grundrisse der Psychologie* [Outlines of psychology] (Leipzig: Engelmann).

Matthew Ratcliffe

The Feeling of Being

There has been much recent philosophical discussion concerning the relation-ship between emotion and feeling. However, everyday talk of 'feeling' is not restricted to emotional feeling and the current emphasis on emotions has led to a neglect of other kinds of feeling. These include feelings of homeliness, belong-ing, separation, unfamiliarity, power, control, being part of something, being at one with nature and 'being there'. Such feelings are perhaps not 'emotional'. However, I suggest here that they do form a distinctive group; all of them are ways of 'finding ourselves in the world'. Indeed, our sense that there is a world and that we are 'in it' is, I suggest, constituted by feeling. I offer an analysis of what such 'existential feelings' consist of, showing how they can be both 'bodily feelings' and, at the same time, part of the structure of intentionality.

Emotions and Feelings

One of the central questions addressed by recent philosophical work on emotion is that of how emotions can be complicated cognitive states and, at the same time, incorporate feelings as a major constituent. The problem is exemplified by the contrasting views of James and Solomon. James claims that emotions are feelings of certain bodily changes that are reflexively triggered during percep-tion; '*the bodily changes follow directly the* PERCEPTION *of the exciting fact, and [...] our feeling of the same changes as they occur* IS *the emotion*' (1884, p. 190). Solomon objects that emotions play a significant role in structuring our experiences of the world, whereas feelings are just perceptions of internal body states. Emotions, he argues, are not feelings but constitutive judgements. They shape the ways in which parts of the world and the world as a whole appear to us. Mere feelings 'no more constitute or define the emotion than an army of fleas constitutes a homeless dog.' (1976/1993, p. 97). Solomon not only dismisses an identification of emotion and feeling but goes further to deny even that bodily feelings play an essential *part* in emotional experience. Nussbaum offers a simi-lar view, suggesting that the term 'feeling' is ambiguous. It does not always refer to perception of body state and, in some uses, is interchangeable with terms such

Correspondence:
Email: m.j.ratcliffe@durham.ac.uk

Journal of Consciousness Studies, **12**, No. 8–10, 2005, pp. 43–60

as 'perception' and 'judgement'. She suggests that this is the case with emotional feelings. Bodily feelings are incidental to emotion and the 'feelings' that really matter could just as well be called judgements or beliefs (2001, p. 60).

Most recent philosophical accounts *do* accept that bodily feelings make an important contribution to the experience of emotion. Nevertheless, they continue to assume the distinction made by Solomon and others between bodily feelings and intentional states. Thus the problem can be construed as that of showing how something apparently trivial and self-directed is a major constituent of something important and world-directed. The conception of 'bodily feeling' routinely adopted by philosophers working on emotion is epitomised by the following passage from Ben-Ze'ev:

> ....unlike higher levels of awareness, such as those found in perception, memory, and thinking, the feeling dimension has no significant cognitive content. It expresses our own state, but is not in itself directed at this state or at any other object. Since this dimension is a mode of consciousness, one cannot be unconscious of it; there are no unfelt feelings. (2004, p. 253)

Ben-Ze'ev, like many others, makes three assumptions about bodily feelings, which I will challenge here:

(1) Bodily feelings do not have intentionality.
(2) Bodily feelings are expressions or perceptions of bodily states. In other words, when one has a bodily feeling, one has an awareness of one's body being a certain way.
(3) One is always conscious of bodily feelings.

In contrast to these assumptions, I will argue that:

(1) Bodily feelings are part of the structure of intentionality. They contribute to how one's body and / or aspects of the world are experienced.
(2) There is a distinction between the location of a feeling and what that feeling is *of*.[1] A feeling can be *in* the body but *of* something outside the body. One is not always aware *of* the body, even though that is where the feeling occurs.
(3) A bodily feeling need not be an object of consciousness. Feelings are often that *through* which one is conscious of something else.

Hence bodily feelings are more complicated than much of the recent work on emotions might indicate. Indeed, I will suggest that the commonplace assumption that all bodily feelings are perceptions of body states, coupled with a restriction of discussion to the issue of how these states are integrated into *emotional* experience, has led to the neglect of a group of philosophically important phenomena, which I will call *existential feelings*. These are not to be found on a standard list of 'emotions', alongside fear, anger, happiness, disgust, sadness, grief, guilt, jealousy, joy and envy. Nevertheless, they make a considerable contribution to the structure of experience, thought and action.

---

[1] By the 'location' of a feeling, I mean the phenomenological, rather than physiological, location. That is, the part of one's body where one takes the feeling to be occurring. As I hope will become clear, having a sense of where a feeling is occurring does not require that the feeling itself be an *object* of experience.

Existential Feelings

Everyday use of the term 'feeling' is not restricted to talk of emotions. It is also employed to articulate various ways of experiencing one's relationship with the world that would not ordinarily be regarded as 'emotions' or 'emotional'. Consider the following list:

The feeling of being: 'complete', 'flawed and diminished', 'unworthy', 'humble', 'separate and in limitation', 'at home', 'a fraud', 'slightly lost, 'overwhelmed', 'abandoned', 'stared at', 'torn', 'disconnected from the world', 'invulnerable', 'unloved', 'watched', 'empty', 'in control', 'powerful', 'completely helpless', 'part of the real world again', 'trapped and weighed down', 'part of a larger machine', 'at one with life', 'at one with nature', 'there', 'familiar', 'real'.[2]

What are we to make of these? Most, if not all, do not seem to be descriptions of one's inner states or of features of the world but of one's relationship with the world. The world can sometimes appear unfamiliar, unreal, distant or close. It can be something that one feels apart from or at one with. One can feel in control of one's situation as a whole or overwhelmed by it. One can feel like a participant in the world or like a detached, estranged observer, staring at objects that do not feel quite 'there'. Such relationships structure all experiences. Whenever one has a specific experience of oneself, another person or an inanimate object being a certain way, the experience has, as a background, a more general sense of one's relationship with the world. This relationship does not simply consist in an experience of being an entity that occupies a spatial and temporal location, alongside a host of other entities. Ways of finding oneself in a world are presupposed spaces of experiential possibility, which shape the various ways in which things can be experienced. For example, if one's sense of the world is tainted by a 'feeling of unreality', this will affect how all objects of perception appear. They are distant, removed, not quite 'there'.

There are many ways in which one can find oneself in a world and they are usually described as 'feelings', rather than 'emotions', 'moods' or 'thoughts'. The world can *feel* strange, familiar, unreal, homely, alienating or intangible. Of course, some of the 'feelings' I listed earlier may incorporate various other ingredients and might also be directed towards certain situations *in* the world, rather than being general, all-encompassing, world-orientations. For example, the feeling of being a 'fraud' perhaps involves an appraisal of one's status, abilities and conduct in a specific context of practice. In addition to a 'feeling', this appraisal might consist of intricate, intertwined narratives concerning one's relationships with others and one's abilities. And certain other 'feelings' are clearly not just 'ways of finding oneself in the world'. Take, for example, 'the feeling of being a true American', which incorporates interpretations of nationality and nationhood, or 'the feeling of being rejected by God', which is a specifically theistic interpretation or expression of one's predicament. The term 'feeling' is also

---

[2] All of these examples were obtained by typing 'the feeling of being' into the Internet search engine Google on 12th February 2005 and selecting from the first fifty hits.

employed to describe what it is like to be in quite specific situations. Think of 'the feeling of being on Brighton beach on a hot summer day'.[3] So Nussbaum (2001) is right to note that 'feeling' has diverse uses. Even so, I suggest that certain uses of the term pick out a distinctive category of phenomena, which consist of 'ways of finding oneself in the world'. They form a recognisable group in virtue of two shared characteristics. First of all, they are not directed at specific objects or situations but are background orientations through which experience as a whole is structured. Second, they are all *feelings*, in the sense that they are bodily states which influence one's awareness. As they constitute the basic structure of 'being there', a 'hold on things' that functions as a presupposed context for all intellectual and practical activity, I refer to them as 'existential feelings'.

The part played by existential feelings in our experience is different from that played by most of those states that are commonly referred to as 'emotions'. Whereas emotions are usually directed towards specific objects, events or situations, existential feelings embrace the world as a whole. Furthermore, although emotions might structure the ways in which objects are experienced, they do not constitute our sense of the *being* of those objects. For example, an escaped lion in one's garden might appear as a *frightening lion* but the emotion directed towards it does not exhaust the sense of its existence, of *there being a lion there*.[4] Existential feeling, in contrast, is a background which comprises the very sense of 'being' or 'reality' that attaches to world experience. Specifically directed emotions presuppose this background and so, whatever such emotions turn out to consist of, existential feelings are a more fundamental feature of world-experience. The distinction between 'emotions' and 'existential feelings' is, however, likely to be blurred. Some of those states commonly termed 'emotions' perhaps accord with my description of 'existential feeling'. For example, extreme grief may well be a relationship with the world as a whole, a sense of loss that structures all experience.

Much of the language used to convey existential feeling is metaphorical and the metaphors employed generally incorporate references to bodily relationships with things. For example, the world can feel 'overbearing', 'overwhelming' or 'suffocating'. One can feel 'trapped' in a situation, 'invulnerable' or 'part of something greater', and the world as a whole can be 'distant' or 'close'. This kind of language is, I suggest, no accident. The feelings that such descriptions express are indeed *bodily* or at least have bodily feelings at their core. But they are, at the same time, ways in which the world appears or ways in which one relates to the world as a whole. In what follows, I will show how, despite the pervasive tendency in philosophy to conceive of feelings as reports of internal states, certain bodily feelings are inextricable from the structure of world experience.

---

[3] Again, these three examples were obtained from the first fifty hits I got, having used Google to search for 'the feeling of being'.

[4] See, for example, the essays by de Sousa, Solomon and Roberts in Solomon ed. (2004) for the view that emotions shape experience of objects and situations. Solomon refers to them as constitutive judgements, Roberts prefers the term 'construal' and de Sousa claims that emotions are perceptual structures.

The Feel of Things

Goldie (2000, 2002) addresses the question of how 'feeling' can be integrated into the world-directedness of emotion and suggests that emotional feelings fall into two categories. There are 'bodily feelings', which lack intentionality or 'borrow' it from the intentional states that they arise in conjunction with, and there are also 'feelings towards'. These are ways of experiencing things in the world that cannot be analysed into a feeling component *and* an intentional component, as the 'feeling towards' is inextricable from the intentionality of the emotion. As Goldie puts it, 'feeling towards is unreflective emotional engagement with the world beyond the body; it is not a consciousness of oneself, either of one's bodily condition or of oneself *as* experiencing an emotion' (2002, p.241).

Drawing on this, one might propose that existential feelings are 'feelings towards' the world as a whole, rather than 'bodily feelings'. However, although I think Goldie is right to recognise that certain feelings are inextricable from experience of the world and have a directedness towards things, I suggest that he is mistaken in claiming that there are two distinct kinds of feeling, one of which is merely bodily and lacks intentionality. Goldie himself notes that, in some cases, bodily feelings and feelings towards arise as seemingly inseparable constituents of experience; 'the bodily feeling is thoroughly infused with the intentionality of emotion; and, in turn, the feeling towards is infused with a bodily characterization' (2000, pp. 56-57). However, in maintaining that bodily feelings do not themselves have intentionality, whereas feelings towards do, he retains a distinction between kinds of feeling. They may well be blended together in experience but there are still two different ingredients going into the blender. In what follows, I will suggest that Goldie's distinction is a case of double-counting; bodily feelings just are feelings towards. Some are feelings towards the body or parts of it and others are feelings towards things outside the body. An account of how this can be so will serve to clarify the nature of 'existential feeling', showing how 'bodily' feeling can contribute to experience as a whole.

If one were to model one's general conception of intentionality on the visual modality, considered in abstract isolation from proprioception and the other senses, a distinction between perceiving things in the world and having bodily feelings might well seem plausible. When one perceives an extremely desirable object X and has a bodily feeling Y, one has two distinct perceptions, the perception of X in the world and the perception of Y in the body. However, a different story is to be told if touch is taken as a starting point for phenomenological exploration and a more general account of bodily feelings is modelled on this modality. In the case of touch, bodily feeling and experience of the world are inextricable.

Consider picking up a glass of cold water. It feels cold. But what is the 'it'? The glass of water is what feels cold, rather than one's hand. Awareness is not directed towards one's own hand but towards the glass, which is felt to be smooth, round and cool. Now consider picking up a snowball in one's bare hand.

Again, the snow feels cold. One's hand begins as a vehicle of perception, *through* which the snow is perceived, rather than as an object *of* perception. But when the snowball is held for more than a few seconds, the object of perception shifts. The feeling of cold, soft, wet snow becomes an unpleasant, dull ache in one's hand. It is not the snow but the hand that is felt now. The feeling is not experienced as changing location; it is and always was in the hand. However, as it changes in intensity and perhaps quality, there is a shift in what it is a feeling *of*. Are there then two feelings, one *in* the hand and another *of* the glass, hand or snowball? There are not. There is just the feeling in one's hand. Does one need to interpret that feeling in order to determine whether it is a feeling *of* a hand or *of* an object external to one's body? It seems not. A sense of the smooth, cool object as distinct from one's body is *part of* the feeling of touch. To touch is to experience a relation between one's body and an object it comes into contact with. Yet which side of the relation, if either, is the object of experience depends on the quality of the feeling and on what one is attending to at the time. One's body can be a conspicuous object of awareness or an invisible context of tactile activity. For example, compare the activity of typing onto a keyboard, where one's hands disappear into the background, to that of trying to assemble a small, delicate device, such as a watch, with one's bare hands. In the latter case, the hands are far more conspicuous and are themselves *felt* as clumsy and indelicate.

The tactile feel of something is not alone sufficient for experiencing it as an identifiable kind of object. The feeling of cold, accompanied by a smooth, curved surface, does not amount to perception of a glass.[5] But tactile feeling does at least incorporate a sense of self and other. As one holds the snowball, the experience has, as part of its structure, a sense of the hand and not the snowball as one's own.

I want to draw two points from the example. First of all, a differentiation between self and non-self is integrated into the feeling of touch. This may not be sufficient to determine a specific intentional object but it is part of the *structure* of intentionality. Second, the bodily location of a feeling does not determine what it is a feeling *of*.[6] These related points can be generalised to encompass various other, non-tactile bodily feelings. Commonplace philosophical divisions between bodily feelings and intentionality assume that where X is located is also what X is a feeling of. However, although the body or part of it is sometimes the object that is felt, one can be aware of a feeling *as* something occurring in one's body or *as* a way in which the world appears. Feelings of the body and feelings towards objects in the world are two sides of the same coin, although one or the

---

[5] Tactile feelings should be distinguished from feelings of hot and cold, given that one can lose one's sense of touch whilst retaining an ability to detect hot and cold (Gallagher, 2005, Chapter 2). It is possible that both kinds of feeling incorporate a differentiation between self and non-self. However, it may be that the differentiation is not intrinsic to a feeling of hot or cold and that touch is required in order to experientially discriminate between one's hand feeling cold and an object feeling cold.

[6] There is a great deal more to be said concerning the phenomenology of touch. For example, touching oneself is different from touching another person and both are very different from picking up a glass of water. There are also distinctions to be drawn between active and passive touch and between various ways of touching. For further discussion of such issues, see Merleau-Ponty (1962, pp. 315–17).

other will usually be foregrounded in experience. As Drummond (2004, p.115) remarks:

> ..I must emphasize that we must be careful not to distinguish these different kinds of feelings too sharply; they are intertwined with one another in complex and various ways. Indeed, they are the same feelings considered in two different relations, once in relation to the body and once in relation to the object.

I suggest that existential feelings are feelings in the body, which are experienced as one's relationship with the world as a whole. This relationship can be quite different, depending, in part, on which side of it is foregrounded. When one feels 'at home' in the world, 'absorbed' in it or 'at one with life', the body often drifts into the background. It is that *through* which things are experienced. But it can also enter the foreground in a number of ways. Consider the sudden realisation that one is being watched by another, an experiential transformation that is vividly conveyed by Sartre's various descriptions. Before one becomes alert to the other, one is absorbed in a set of projects and not aware of oneself as an object at all. There is just a consciousness of the world. However, a rustle in the leaves, a creak on the stair or a pair of eyes pointing in one's direction can trigger an affective transformation that Sartre calls 'shame'. This is a change in how one's body feels; it ceases to be an invisible locus of projects and is suddenly *felt as an object*. This feeling, Sartre claims constitutes our most basic sense that there are others. One can only feel oneself to be an object if one is an object *for* another. So to experience oneself as an object is to recognise that there are others. Sartre is quite explicit in stating that a felt, bodily re-orientation is involved:

> ….the Other is the indispensable mediator between myself and me. I am ashamed of myself as I *appear* to the Other. [….] …this comparison is not encountered in us as the result of a concrete psychic operation. Shame is an immediate shudder which runs through me from head to foot without any discursive preparation. [….]…shame is shame of *oneself before the Other*; these two structures are inseparable. (1989, p. 222)

His account illustrates one kind of shift that can take place between unreflective absorption in the world and self-objectifying estrangement from one's projects.[7] However, it is important not to over-simplify existential feelings. Experience is not just a matter of disappearing into one's projects or becoming aware of oneself as a thing. As the range of feelings listed earlier serves to illustrate, there are many ways in which one can disappear into one's world or become aware of oneself as an object. Being at one with nature is not the same as feeling like part of a greater machine or feeling at home in a familiar environment. And the body as an object surveyed by another is not the defamiliarised, alienated body that sometimes stares back at one after gazing in the mirror for too long. Neither is it the injured or debilitated body that becomes an object of experience when it won't do what you want it to do. Furthermore, the body, in so far as it feels rather than is

---

[7] Although I do not explicitly address the nature of intersubjectivity here, I am assuming throughout that ways of finding ourselves in a world are also ways of finding ourselves in a social world *with others*. For a complementary discussion of intersubjectivity and feeling, see Ratcliffe (in press).

felt, cannot be experienced in its entirety as an object. The feeling body is 'how we find ourselves in the world', a background to all experience of objects, as opposed to an object of experience. As Merleau-Ponty (1962, p. 92) observes:

> In so far as it sees or touches the world, my body can [...] be neither seen nor touched. What prevents its ever being an object, ever being 'completely constituted', is that it is that by which there are objects. It is neither tangible nor visible in so far as it is that which sees and touches.

In tactile sensation, one's hand can be the object that is felt or it can be a transparent vehicle through which something in the world is felt. So too, the feeling body more generally is a framework through which world-experience is structured. Even when one is not explicitly aware of the body, it still functions as a structure-giving background to all experience. For example, one can have a sense of 'up', 'down', 'left' and 'right' without being explicitly aware of one's bodily position.

There is every reason to suspect that the body states involved in what I have called existential feelings will be many and diverse, able to facilitate a range of ways in which we find ourselves in the world. Consider proprioception, construed broadly as one's explicit and implicit sense of body states, unmediated by other perceptual modalities such as vision and touch. Proprioception has a complicated structure and its role is not restricted to an awareness *of* body states. Gallagher (2005) discusses a considerable body of evidence suggesting that proprioception contributes to the structure of world experience in a variety of ways. A range of body states comprise the implicit and explicit sense one has of one's body and this proprioceptive sense also contributes to the working of the other perceptual modalities in numerous ways. As Gallagher puts it, 'perceiving subjects move through a space that is already pragmatically organized by the construction, the very shape, of the body' (2005, p.140).

Gallagher's account of how the body is integrated into experience is based around a distinction he draws between 'body schema' and 'body image', arrived at by clarifying and distinguishing various historical uses of these terms. He employs the distinction to make clear the body's dual role as an object of experience and a tacit background that shapes experience. Gallagher refers to the body schema as prenoetic, meaning that it shapes experience without itself being an object of awareness or part of the structure of awareness. The body image, in contrast, is an awareness of one's body, which might not be at the centre of one's attention but is still accessible through phenomenological reflection. The 'existential feelings' that I have listed are perhaps best understood at the level of the body image. They are ordinarily part of the background structure of experience, constituting ways of finding oneself in a world that shape more specific experiences. Nevertheless, they are phenomenologically available, as is evident from the various, usually metaphorical descriptions employed to communicate them. So they are part of the structure of experience, rather than an experientially inaccessible contributor to that structure. However, there may be a thin line between noetic and prenoetic aspects of existential feeling. For example, the role of feeling in constituting our sense of reality, which I will discuss now, is perhaps something that is hidden beneath everyday experience and can only be made phenomenologically explicit through reflection upon highly unusual states of oneself or others.

The Feeling of Reality

So far, I have claimed that certain 'feelings' constitute ways of finding ourselves in the world. In support of this claim, I have appealed to everyday talk of feelings and also to the fact that bodily feelings need not have the body as their object. This is perhaps enough to show that 'existential feelings' are at least a *possible* ingredient of experience. However, further work is needed in order to make a convincing case for their existence. In this section, I will discuss work in phenomenology, neurophysiology and psychopathology, which supports the case for existential feelings. This work suggests that feeling is responsible for the 'sense of reality' incorporated into experience of the world as a whole, other people and even oneself. So, when someone says that things 'don't feel real' or that she feels 'part of the real world again', such talk can be taken literally. The quality of reality is also something that varies in intensity, allowing objects of experience, including oneself, to take on an 'unreal' aspect.

The feeling of reality is generally ignored by recent work on emotion and feeling. However, it is a theme in the work of certain phenomenologists, such as the early Heidegger, who claims that experience presupposes an 'attunement' [Befindlichkeit] (1962, p.172), a feeling of belonging to a world that is taken for granted in everyday life.[8] According to Heidegger, it is 'mood' that attunes one to the world and gives things their taken for granted meaning. He also claims that everyday attunement can be disrupted and that it collapses completely in the mood of 'anxiety'. Given that attunement underlies the very sense of Being-in-the-world, anxiety presents 'the nothing'. Although Heidegger does not explicitly discuss the role of the body in experience, he does emphasise that our relationship with the world ordinarily consists of practical dwelling, rather than detached contemplation. And his description of anxiety appears to incorporate an implicit sense of its bodily nature, of how one's sense of reality incorporates a practical, bodily orientation:

> The receding of beings as a whole that closes in on us in anxiety oppresses us. We can get no hold on things. In the slipping away of beings only this 'no hold on things' comes over us and remains. Anxiety reveals the nothing. (1978, p. 101)

The everyday, taken-for-granted sense that things 'are' and that we are 'in' the world is not a matter of perceiving our bodily locatedness amongst things but of a 'hold on things'. And to lose this hold is to lose the sense of 'being there'. Experience is no longer nested in a cosy world of projects, purposes and familiar

---

[8] 'Attunement' is the term employed by Stambaugh in her 1996 translation of *Being and Time*. Macquarrie and Robinson (1962) translate 'Befindlichkeit' rather misleadingly as 'state of mind'. It is misleading because Befindlichkeit is a way of finding oneself in the world, rather than a perception of one's internal mental states.

activities. All that is left is apprehension of a total loss of relatedness, an absence of the usual practical orientation through which things are experienced as meaningful.

Heidegger's conception of 'mood' closely approximates what I have called 'existential feeling'; 'mood' for Heidegger is responsible for a sense of Being-in-the-world. However, Heidegger explicitly focuses on only a few kinds of 'mood'. For example, there is fear (1962, p.179), boredom (1978, p.99) and anxiety (1962, pp. 228-235; 1978, pp. 100-108). But existential feelings are more varied than this. In everyday life, we might feel close to the world, distant from it, part of it, estranged from it, helpless before it, in control of 'things', at one with nature, at one with life, part of a greater whole, part of a machine, slightly lost, overwhelmed, conspicuous or inconspicuous. And the world might feel familiar, unfamiliar, intangible, unreal, threatening, safe, fascinating, empty, imbued with significance, dreamlike, surreal, alien or warming. Is every one of these a mode of everyday attunement? And 'anxiety', as described by Heidegger, is arguably not a single, distinct kind of feeling but something that accommodates a host of different experiential structures. As Glas (2003, p.238) notes, one form of anxiety is a feeling of disconnectedness from the world:

> What prevails is a tormenting feeling of distance, the awareness of an unbridgeable gap. This feeling can amount to the awareness that one lives in a vacuum and is about to suffocate, or that one lives in an unreal world in which things [are not] what they seem to be and in which attempts to connect fail as if there were a glassy wall between the person and the surrounding world.

This might look like a fairly accurate description of Heidegger's 'anxiety revealing the nothing'. However, Glas distinguishes this feeling of disconnectedness from anxiety concerning meaningless, anxiety in the face of death and anxiety before existence itself, all of which might appear to fit Heidegger's conception.

Phenomenologists such as Heidegger give rich descriptions of experience that provide support for a category of 'existential feelings'. However, it would be a mistake to understand such accounts as relating exclusively to the familiar inventory of moods and emotions. To do so would be to pass over the variety of existential feelings that are incorporated into everyday language but not into lists of emotional states. There are many ways in which one can find oneself in the world and a pervasive emphasis on 'emotions' and 'moods', coupled with the assumption that feelings are 'mere' reports of body states, has led to neglect of these experiential phenomena.

The claim that feeling constitutes one's relationship with the world and even the sense of 'reality' itself finds further support from neuroscience. For example, Damasio (1995) discusses what he calls 'background feelings', which are unremarkable, everyday perceptions of body states that tacitly structure experience. Damasio claims that they comprise 'the feeling of life itself, the sense of being' (1995, p.150) and presents an explicit neurophysiological theory of how a changing background of body states shapes perception and thought. Damasio calls this background our 'image of the body landscape' (1995, pp. 150–1). The way he employs the term 'image' suggests that, although he recognises the importance of feelings, he fails to distinguish between a feeling as something that is perceived and a feeling as something that structures the perception of something else (Gallagher, 2005, pp.135-137; Sass, 2004, p.134).[9] Damasio christens his more general account of feeling and emotion the 'somatic marker hypothesis'. According to this account, certain body states are associated with or 'mark' perceptions of particular entities or kinds of entity. Feelings of these states structure experience, thought and action. Again, Damasio interprets feeling as *the perception of a certain state of the body*' (2003, p.86). He thus omits the possibility that the body need not be the object of perception and that feelings can manifest themselves through the manner in which another object of perception, or the world in general, is perceived. However, Damasio still provides a neurophysiological theory of how certain bodily feelings act as a structuring background for experience and thought. Hence the claim that feelings *do* function in such a way is supplemented by a specific account of *how* they might do so.

Although Heideggerian phenomenology and Damasio's account of emotion both provide some support for my claim that there is a distinctive category of existential feeling, some of the most compelling evidence, in my view, comes from work in psychopathology.[10] Descriptions of various unusual and pathological experiences illustrate how the structure of intentionality can be altered in many different ways, changing the ways in which objects are experienced. We may think of intentionality as a space of possibilities for the experience of objects. Objects are not just experientially presented as 'there' or 'not there', 'existent' or 'nonexistent'. They are familiar, unfamiliar, real, surreal, dreamlike, anticipated, unanticipated, close, distant, estranged, significant, separate from oneself, experienced in their particularity or as unobtrusive members of a category, contextualised relative to one's purposes, and so forth. This possibility space is presupposed by the structure of specific experiences and various transformations of it reshape world experience as a whole. It is a 'way of finding oneself in the world', rather than an intentional object or internal state of the person.

Psychopathological case studies not only illustrate how the structure of experience can be altered but also how that alteration is related to changed bodily feeling. For example, Sass (1994) attempts to describe the experiential changes that occur in some cases of schizophrenia, focusing on the well known autobiographical account of Schreber in his *Memoirs of my Nervous Illness*. Drawing on Schreber's elaborate descriptions of his own experiences, Sass argues that schizophrenic delusions are not a matter of mistaking the unreal for the real. Such an interpretation presupposes that the usual space of experiential possibilities remains intact. Instead, Sass suggests, it is the whole structure of experience

---

[9] Recalling Gallagher's (2005) distinction between 'body image' and 'body schema', it should be noted that Gallagher's use of the term 'image' is more encompassing. A feeling can be a constituent of the 'body image' without being an object of perception, so long as it remains phenomenologically accessible. Thus feelings could be part of an experiential background, through which experience of foreground objects is structured.

[10] See Ratcliffe (2002) for a discussion of similarities between Heidegger's phenomenological descriptions and Damasio's neurophysiological account, and of how these two very different perspectives might be brought together.

that is transformed. It is not that schizophrenic persons claim reality for their delusions but, rather, that their entire experience is structured by a sense of unreality (1994, pp. 32-33). Schizophrenic patients, according to Sass, experience 'unworlding'; it is the form of the real that is warped, as opposed to the specific contents of the real (2004, pp. 136-141). The result is a kind of solipsistic experiential realm, where the sense of 'an object independent of me' has been removed from the space of experiential possibilities. He also makes clear the inextricability of experiential transformation and changes in bodily affect, observing that schizophrenic subjects manifest significantly altered affect:

> …many schizophrenic patients seem neither to feel nor to evoke a natural sense of emotional rapport. Both the affective response and the affective expression of these patients frequently seems odd, incongruent, inadequate, or otherwise off-the-mark. (2004, p.128)

Sass suggests that schizophrenia involves a general diminution of background bodily feelings, accompanied by exaggeration of certain, more specific affective responses. So it is not just a loss of the feelings that comprise our hold on things but also a transformation. Stanghellini (2004) also emphasises the role played by changes in feeling and observes how a schizophrenic person will sometimes talk of her 'deanimated body' or 'disembodied spirit' (p.19). He suggests that distortions of feeling, resulting in a sense of disembodiment, are a source of altered experience. The background of feeling through which oneself, other people and the world as a whole are ordinarily experienced breaks down. Stanghellini's discussion includes several accounts provided by schizophrenic patients, in which they report various changes in the 'feeling' of things, such as 'I cannot feel my *being* anymore' and 'I feel disconnected from myself' (2004, pp. 123-126). A further role that changed affect might play in schizophrenia is proposed by Gallagher (2005, chapter 8). He suggests that the temporal structure of experience is disturbed by anomalous feelings and that this can lead to a lack of the usual sense of anticipation and familiarity that precedes one's own thoughts or actions. The result is that these thoughts and activities are experienced as alien.

Stanghellini (2004, pp.39-40) appeals to the Heideggerian conception of mood, in order to convey the kinds of affective states that structure schizophrenic experience, and Sass prefers 'emotion' and 'affect' to 'feeling', given that:

> The term 'feeling' has a more subjective focus: unlike emotion, it refers not so much to an attitude toward the world as to a state of or within the self, one that does not elicit any action tendency or sense of urgency. (2004, p.133)

However, I suspect that the supposed 'subjective focus' of 'feeling' is a symptom of its philosophical neglect and misinterpretation, rather than of connotations that attach to the term in everyday life, and I suggest that the term 'feeling' is preferable to 'mood' or 'affect', given that we *do* refer to ways of finding ourselves in the world as 'feelings'. The term 'emotion' might invoke the usual list of states, such as anger, fear, happiness, sadness, shame, guilt, regret and so forth. And 'mood' might make one think of misery, elation, boredom or just of 'good' and 'bad' moods. But 'belonging', 'familiarity', 'completeness', 'estrangement', 'distance', 'separation' and 'homeliness' are usually referred to as feelings. One can speak of the 'feeling of being' or the 'feeling of reality', whereas the 'emotion' of being or reality sounds peculiar at best. And some 'moods' seem to be fairly superficial subjective states. For example, one might say 'I'm sorry; I'm just in a bit of a bad mood today', indicating that it is possible to assign a mood to oneself, without it enveloping one's whole relationship with the world. Such moods are states that one experiences when one is already *in* a world. Granted, certain other 'moods' do seem to be more basic ways of finding oneself *in* a world, as suggested by Heidegger. However, the term 'feeling' is less constraining, encompassing these moods plus a host of other ways of relating to the world. Hence I suggest that it be retained. The everyday phenomena that relate most clearly to pathological experience are a group of 'feelings', which are inadvertently neglected when characteristically 'emotional' feelings and 'moods' are taken as the focus of attention.

Changed existential feeling may underlie a host of other pathological experiences. Consider the Capgras delusion, for example. Sufferers of this condition maintain that certain familiars, usually spouses or other family members, have been replaced by impostors, a conviction which is impervious to all contrary evidence. In conjunction with this, they report an absence of the feeling of familiarity normally associated with visual recognition of these people. Many patients also report a more general sense of unfamiliarity or unreality attached to all their experience (Ratcliffe, 2004, pp. 31-36). Central to most recent explanations of this condition is the observation that subjects suffer a diminution of the affective response that is ordinarily associated with visual perception of close friends and relatives. This response, it seems, does not just accompany visual recognition but contributes to it. Without a background feeling of familiarity, family members appear strange and 'not known'. The altered experience, perhaps in conjunction with a reasoning impairment, is interpreted in terms of an impostor.[11]

Another delusion, which is often explained in a similar way, is the Cotard delusion. Sufferers claim that they are dead, damned, disembodied, nonexistent or that they have been effaced from the universe. Such claims all express a common experience of self-nihilation, a sense that one has been extricated from reality or that reality more generally is absent from experience. One proposed explanation is that global diminution of bodily affect manifests itself experientially as an absence of the sense of reality. The relationship between self and world, which ordinarily comprises a taken-for-granted experiential orientation through which things are encountered as 'real', has broken down and the feeling of being is itself absent from experience (Gerrans, 2000; Ratcliffe, 2004).[12]

---

[11] See Stone & Young (1997) for a two factor explanation, incorporating altered experience and a reasoning bias. See Maher (1999) for an explanation in terms of altered experience alone.

[12] Another kind of altered experience that might be explicable in terms of existential feeling is that typical of autism, which Hobson (2002) explains in terms of the absence of normal affective responsiveness to others. This responsiveness is the basis of early infant intersubjectivity and also shapes the development of intersubjective ability. Autistic experience is perhaps a different way of finding

A further question to be addressed is that of which specific affective responses are involved in various psychopathologies and whether the same kinds of affect contribute to all 'existential feelings'. However, the answer will not have a bearing on whether or not 'existential feelings' comprise an illuminating category of phenomena. The category I am attempting to make explicit here is a phenomenological, rather than a biological, category. If the underlying biology is diverse, this does not impinge upon the common experiential role that unites existential feelings. They are bodily feelings that are not felt as the objects of perception but as world-orientations, ways of being integrated into the world as a whole.

Philosophical Orientations

Although existential feelings seldom feature as objects of philosophical enquiry, I will conclude by tentatively suggesting that an appreciation of their existence and role might serve to further our understanding of the nature of philosophical thought. Sass (1994) compares the experiential predicament of Schreber to the philosophical stance of Wittgenstein and suggests that philosophy and madness have much in common. Certain philosophical preoccupations are symptomatic of the philosopher's lack of affective rootedness in reality and Wittgenstein's work is concerned with the diagnosis and cure of problems that arise from the philosopher's artificial detachment from everyday social experience:

> Wittgenstein's characterization [of philosophy as a sickness] can almost be taken literally: the sicknesses of the understanding he examined in his later work, sicknesses bound up with the philosopher's predilection for abstraction and alienation – for detachment from body, world, and community – have a great deal in common with the symptoms displayed by Schreber and many other mental patients with schizophrenia or related forms of illness. (Sass, 1994, p. x)

Such a diagnosis, though it may be accurate in certain cases, does not apply to all philosophical thought. Philosophies and philosophers are far too varied to be guided by the same world-estranging existential feeling. However, different philosophies may well have their source in a range of different existential feelings or 'ways of finding oneself in the world'. This is a view expressed in several of William James's works. Although James never explicitly retracts his 1884 claim that emotions are bodily feelings, he also indicates in his later works that feelings or emotions underlie our sense of reality and of the various experiential worlds that we take for granted[13]. For example, in *The Varieties of Religious Experience*, he suggests that the core of religious and metaphysical dispositions consists in feeling. His description of the experiential predicament of the 'sick soul' prior to religious conversion is strikingly similar to descriptions of altered experience in schizophrenia; 'a thick veil alters the tone and look of everything' and 'I weep false tears. I have unreal hands: the things I see are not real things' (1902, p.152).

---

oneself in the world, bereft of the complex of feelings towards others that structure everyday experience of oneself and one's relations with the social world.

[13] Ratcliffe (2005) suggests that James does indeed maintain that emotions are bodily feelings *and* that bodily feelings are central to the structure of world experience.

Religious conversion, James suggests, takes the form of an affective reorienta-
tion that alters the structure of one's relationship with reality. This structure is
not an explicit object of contemplation but that through which experience and
thought are moulded. Similarly, a substantial element of one's philosophical
position comes ready-made in the way that one finds oneself in a world:

> … in the metaphysical and religious sphere, articulate reasons are cogent for us only
> when our inarticulate feelings of reality have already been impressed in favour of
> the same conclusion. (1902, p.74)

Elsewhere, James suggests that different philosophical outlooks owe much to
bodily, affective dispositions:

> Pretend what we may, the whole man within us is at work when we form our philo-
> sophical opinions – Intellect, will, taste, and passion co-operate just as they do in
> practical affairs… (1956, p.92)

The sense of a coherent philosophical position is, he claims, constituted by a
'strong feeling of ease, peace, rest', and a feeling of 'relief' structures the transition from puzzlement to comprehension (1956, p.63). So philosophy is not just a
matter of trading arguments or aligning one's position with reason and evidence:

> … the philosophy which is so important in each of us is not a technical matter; it is
> our more or less dumb sense of what life honestly and deeply means. It is only partly
> got from books; it is our individual way of just seeing and feeling the total push and
> pressure of the cosmos. (1981, p.7)

Philosophies, according to James, are the outcome of various 'temperaments'.
World-orientations differ from person to person. Some are caught up in the
world, fascinated by it. Others feel distant from it, estranged, lacking in connection. Philosophers feel at home in the world in different ways and to different
extents. And the way in which a philosopher finds herself in a world is a background of sense through which her position and her arguments are formed. James
states that rationalism and empiricism have their source in different philosophical temperaments (1981, p.8) or relationships with the world, which are bodily
and felt, as opposed to abstract products of reason decoupled from one's sense of
being there.[14] He adds that one's sense of a view's implausibility or absurdity seldom has its source in a process of rational deliberation.

   In contrast to Sass, James does not see philosophy in general as akin to a kind
of madness, a reflection of pathological experiencing, entangled with a desire to
be reintegrated with the world. Indeed, a philosophical view is often not an expli-
cation of one's existential predicament at all but a retreat from it into a realm of
cosy abstraction that has little bearing on the realities of experience:

> …..it is far less an account of this actual world than a clear addition built upon it, a
> classic sanctuary in which the rationalist fancy may take refuge from the intolerably
> confused and gothic character which mere facts present. It is no *explanation* of our

---

[14] More recently, van Fraassen (2002) has suggested that empiricism is a stance, rather than a specific
   philosophical position or set of beliefs. It is an attitude or presupposed philosophical orientation,
   which is sculpted not by reason alone but by one's emotional attitudes.

concrete universe, it is another thing altogether, a substitute for it, a remedy, a way
of escape. (1981, p.14)

So James suggests that philosophy is sometimes a forgetting of existential feeling, rather than an expression or symptom of it. One hides in a realm of abstrac-
tions, playing with abstract arguments and unreal doubts, divorced from the
world of actual experience. This raises questions concerning what it even means
to think about experience and whether one can lose sight of the very problems
one is claiming to address, by reflecting on frameworks of abstract concepts,
rather than on experience itself. These concerns could perhaps be directed at
philosophical approaches that take experience to be comprised of 'representations of objects', 'qualitative feels' and the like, generated in brains that just happen to reside in bodies. Such approaches pass over structures of world
experience that are presupposed by all experiential objects, abstracting the
objects of experience from the space of possibilities through which they appear.

Questions also arise concerning what it is to *hold* a philosophical position. Is it
enough to linguistically assent to a set of propositions or must one *feel* a sense of
conviction with respect to it? And what is it to doubt a claim? As Hookway
(2002, p. 255-6) notes, 'felt doubt' has a kind of immediacy that distinguishes it
from various examples of philosophical doubt. Reflecting on the classic example
of Cartesian doubt, can one really doubt the existence of the world or of one's
body? One can think of one's body as an object, or of the world as a collection of
objects, and then think 'it is not the case that X exists'. But can one genuinely
conceive of one's disembodied existence, as a Cartesian mental substance or a
brain in a vat, when all of one's experience is structured by a tacit background of
feeling?[15] And can the reality of the world be doubted, given that the sense of 'reality' does not consist in an object being presented to consciousness but in a presupposed possibility space through which things can appear in certain ways?
Can one, in a detached, indifferent manner, doubt the sense of reality itself or of
one's bodily being in the world? I suggest not. One can doubt the existence of an
object but the structure of one's experience of body and world does not just consist in experiencing objects. It is that through which objects are experienced as
real or unreal. Hence doubting the existence of 'world as object' does not add up
to genuine doubt concerning the world's existence.

Conclusion

To summarise, talk of feelings in philosophy is usually restricted to the role that
they play in emotions. Emotions, for the most part, are ways in which specific
objects, events or situations are perceived, evaluated or felt. But all specific
intentional states presuppose general structures of intentionality, ways of finding
oneself in the world that determine the space of experiential possibilities. These
ways of finding oneself in the world are what I call 'existential feelings'. A distinction can be drawn between the location of a feeling and what it is a feeling of.

---

[15] Young & Leafhead (1996, p.149) remark that certain delusions 'are interesting with respect to the
question of what it means to say that one exists' and relate this to Cartesian doubt.

Thus accounts of bodily feeling which assume that what is felt must be the body are mistaken. Existential feelings are bodily feelings that constitute the structure of one's relationship with the world as a whole. They are thus a phenomenologically important but neglected category.

I began this paper by contrasting the views of Solomon and James on the relationship between feeling and emotion. James maintains that emotions are bodily feelings, whereas Solomon claims that they are judgements. In his more recent work, Solomon acknowledges that the body plays an important role in emotional experience:

> I am now coming to appreciate that accounting for the feelings (not just sensations) in emotion is not a secondary concern and not independent of appreciating the essential role of the body in emotional experience. (2003, p.189)

He attempts to account for the role of body in emotional judgements by invoking '*judgments of the body*' (2003, p.191). These are integrated into perception and action, for example in the bodily judgement that a fast approaching ball is catchable. What people call 'feeling', Solomon claims, can be understood as a kind of bodily judgement. According to Solomon, emotional judgements in general are not an outcome of deliberation but are 'prereflectively constitutive of experience' (2003, p.95); they are structures of intelligibility through which the objects of experience appear. Construed as such, they resemble what I have been calling existential feelings more so than they do those states that are generally referred to as emotions. A pre-reflective bodily judgement or set of bodily judgements could just as well be termed an experience-structuring feeling and here we return to James. James not only states that emotions are bodily feelings. In his later work, he also suggests that feelings constitute our sense of reality, our presupposed relationship with the world. So it seems as though James and Solomon have been talking about the Morning Star and the Evening Star; a unitary phenomenon has been miscast as two quite different things[16]. Furthermore, when they refer to those phenomena that structure our relationship with the world as a whole, they are not identifying specifically directed emotions like fear or anger but existential feelings, which are presupposed by focused emotions and constitute our sense of being.[17]

References

Ben-Ze'ev, A. (2004), 'Emotion as a subtle mental mode', in Solomon (2004).

Damasio, A. (1995), *Descartes Error: Emotion, Reason and the Human Brain* (London: Picador).

Damasio, A. (2003), *Looking for Spinoza: Joy, Sorrow and the Feeling Brain* (London: Heinemann).

Drummond, J. (2004), '"Cognitive impenetrability" and the complex intentionality of the emotions', *Journal of Consciousness Studies*, **11** (10–11), pp.109–26.

Gallagher, S. (2005), *How the Body Shapes the Mind* (Oxford: Clarendon Press).

---

[16] As Greenspan remarks, 'Affect evaluates! Emotional affect or feeling is itself evaluative – and the result can be summed up in a proposition. I think we can have it both ways. That is, about emotions as feelings or judgments' (2004, p. 132).

[17] I am grateful to my wife Beth, an audience at the National University of Ireland Galway, Giovanna Colombetti and two anonymous referees for helpful comments on a previous version of this paper.

Gerrans, P. (2000), 'Refining the explanation of Cotard's Delusion', in *Pathologies of Belief*, ed. M. Coltheart. & M. Davies (Oxford: Blackwell).

Glas, G. (2003), 'Anxiety: Animal reactions and the embodiment of meaning', in *Nature and Narrative: An Introduction to the New Philosophy of Psychiatry*, ed. B. Fulford, K. Morris, J. Sadler & G. Stanghellini (Oxford: Oxford University Press).

Goldie, P. (2000), *The Emotions: A Philosophical Exploration* (Oxford: Clarendon Press).

Goldie, P. (2002), 'Emotions, feelings and intentionality', *Phenomenology and the Cognitive Sciences*, **1**, pp. 235–54.

Greenspan, P. (2004), 'Emotions, rationality, and mind / body', in Solomon (2004).

Heidegger, M. (1962), *Being and Time*, trans. J. Macquarrie and E. Robinson (Oxford: Blackwell).

Heidegger, M. (1996), *Being and Time*, trans. J. Stambaugh (New York: State University of New York Press).

Heidegger, M. (1978), 'What is metaphysics?', in his *Basic Writings*, ed. and trans. D.F. Krell, (London: Routledge).

Hobson, P. (2002), The *Cradle of Thought: Exploring the Origins of Thinking* (London: Macmillan).

Hookway, C. (2002), 'Emotions and epistemic evaluations', in *The Cognitive Basis of Science*, ed. P. Carruthers, S. Stich & M. Siegal (Cambridge: Cambridge University Press).

James, W. (1884), 'What is an emotion?', *Mind*, **9**, pp. 188–205.

James, W. (1902), *The Varieties of Religious Experience: A Study in Human Nature* (New York: Longmans, Green and Co.).

James, W. (1956), *The Will to Believe and Other Essays in Popular Philosophy* (New York: Dover Publications).

James, W. (1981), *Pragmatism* (Indianapolis: Hackett).

Maher, B. (1999), 'Anomalous experience in everyday life: Its significance for psychopathology', *The Monist*, **82**, pp. 547–70.

Merleau-Ponty, M. (1962), *Phenomenology of Perception*, trans. Smith, C. (London: Routledge).

Nussbaum, M. (2001), *Upheavals of Thought: The Intelligence of Emotions* (Cambridge: Cambridge University Press).

Ratcliffe, M. (2002), 'Heidegger's attunement and the neuropsychology of emotion', *Phenomenology and the Cognitive Sciences*, **1**, pp. 287–312.

Ratcliffe, M. (2004), 'Interpreting delusions', *Phenomenology and the Cognitive Sciences*, **3**, pp. 25–48.

Ratcliffe, M. (2005), 'William James on emotion and intentionality', *International Journal of Philosophical Studies*, **13**, pp. 179–202.

Ratcliffe, M. (in press), 'Folk psychology and the biological basis of intersubjectivity', in *Philosophy, Biology and Life (Royal Institute of Philosophy Supplements)*, ed. A. O'Hear (Cambridge: Cambridge University Press).

Sartre, J.P. (1989), *Being and Nothingness*, trans. H.E. Barnes (London: Routledge).

Sass, L. (1994), *The Paradoxes of Delusion: Wittgenstein, Schreber, and the Schizophrenic Mind* (Ithaca: Cornell University Press).

Sass, L. (2004), 'Affectivity in Schizophrenia: A Phenomenological View', *Journal of Consciousness Studies*, **11** (10–11), pp. 127–47.

Schreber, D.P. (2000), *Memoirs of my Nervous Illness* (New York: New York Review of Books).

Solomon, R. (1993), *The Passions: Emotions and the Meaning of Life* (Indianapolis: Hackett).

Solomon, R. (2003), *Not Passion's Slave: Emotions and Choice* (Oxford: Oxford University Press).

Solomon, R. ed. (2004), *Thinking about Feeling: Contemporary Philosophers on Emotions* (Oxford: Oxford University Press).

Stanghellini, G. (2004), *Disembodied Spirits and Deanimated Bodies: The Psychopathology of Common Sense* (Oxford: Oxford University Press).

Stone, T. & Young, A (1997), 'Delusion and brain injury: The philosophy and psychology of belief', *Mind & Language*, **12**, pp. 327–64.

Van Fraassen, B. (2002), *The Empirical Stance* (New Haven: Yale University Press).

Young, A. & Leafhead, K. (1996), 'Betwixt life and death: Case studies in the Cotard Delusion', in *Method in Madness: Case Studies in Cognitive Neuropsychiatry*, ed. P. Halligan & J. Marshall (Hove: Psychology Press).

Francisco J. Varela and Natalie Depraz

At the Source of Time

Valence and the constitutional dynamics of affect[*]

The Question, the Background: How Affect Originarily Shapes Time

This paper represents a step in the analysis of the key, but much-neglected role of affect and emotions as the originary source of the living present, as a foundational dimension of the moment-to-moment emergence of consciousness. In a more general sense, we may express the question in the following terms: there seems to be a growing consensus from various sources — philosophical, empirical and clinical — that emotions cannot be seen as a mere 'coloration' of the cognitive agent, understood as a formal or un-affected self, but are immanent and inextricable from every mental act. How can this be borne out, beyond just announcing it? Specifically, what is the role of affect-emotion in the self-movement of the flow, of the temporal stream of consciousness?

Affect and the constitution of time: a new approach

The hypothesis developed here is that the key to address this question effectively has to be searched for in the dynamics of what we will hereinafter call the *fold*: the detailed transition from the pre-reflexive to the reflexive (or synonymously: pre-noetic/noetic, pre-egological/egological, pre-attentive/attentive). The hither side of the fold is pre-noetic; its far side intentional content (Fig. 1). The fold, in our analysis, has a double axis: one based on the emergence of reflection itself, leading to cognitive content; the other based on self-affection and leading to basic predispositions and a specific palette of emotions. In the sense taken here, the fold, beyond the specific three-part structure of the living present, includes in its immediate description, what can be called a short-term (working or performative) memory of the habitual lived body. When iterated this micro-

Correspondence:
Natalie Depraz, Departement de Philosophie, Université de Paris IV (Sorbonne) and Collège International de Philosophie, Paris, France. *Email: frj@ccr.jussieu.fr*

* This paper was originally published in *Arob@se. Journal de lettre et de sciences humain* **4**(1–2) (2000), special issue on *Ipseity and Alterity*, edited by Shaun Gallagher.

Journal of Consciousness Studies, **12**, No. 8–10, 2005, pp. 61–81

temporality forms the basis of a narrative- or macro-temporality which we do not address in this text. What we propose in this text is a detailed and layered description of such an embodied *temporal dynamics*, which can be found at work in all instances of ordinary, daily life.

Furthermore, we will see that the temporal unfolding of self-affection is from the very start traversed by alterity. This is rooted in the fact that self-affection is always an affection including an other, even if it is, as it is the case here, a self-alterity.[1] The most immediate manifestation of this irrevocable alterity will appear in the basic disposition to which affective valence gives rise (Section III).

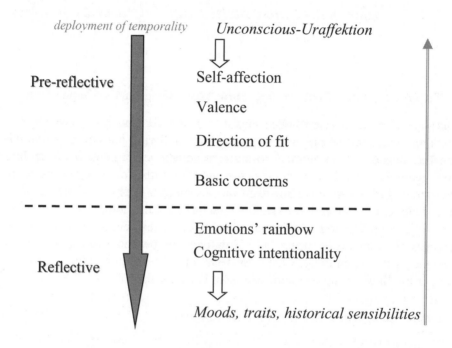

Figure 1: The fold and a summary of the main propositions in this text

In other words, the thrust of the analysis will lead us to consider that such an originally *'altered' affect* is at the very core of temporality, and is even, perhaps, its antecedent. This means that our exploration here departs from the generally accepted view in the phenomenological tradition, since we do not base our analysis on an original temporality that would, itself, structure affect. In this regard we enter into the controversy between Max Scheler and Martin Heidegger with regard to the primacy of time or affect, and our analysis supports Scheler's position. The basic ground for their difference concerns the essential part *values* play in our experience in general (and in temporality in particularly). If Heidegger put

---

[1] Ricœur (1990) shows quite well how consciousness is always already shaped by alterity; Depraz (1995) traces back the genesis of intersubjective experience in a self-alterity constituting the egoic consciousness itself (see in particular chapter 5).

time at the origin of our being, he obviously had in mind the idea of a necessary and primary neutrality of experience. On the contrary, along with Scheler we find that values and evaluating primordially constitute our experience.[2]

However, the present proposal attempts to move even further along from these classical descriptions by means of a double methodological gesture: on the one hand, a re-enacted phenomenological analysis that will reveal the role of valence; on the other hand, recent empirical work concerning affective life will reinforce this view. Our claim is that this encounter is of benefit for both methodological approaches, and in any case provides a fresh mobilization and descriptive precision to phenomenology. We will come back later to the question raised by this interdisciplinary methodology.[3]

The constitutive role of emotions for the experience of time

Before we embark on the analysis proper, a word of background is necessary to situate our analysis. As is well-known among those familiar with the history of phenomenology, the topic of the possible constitutional role of affect and the pre-reflexive realm occupies an important place in the 'genetic turn' in phenomenology (around 1920). This turn opened new paths of exploration concerning affection and drive-intentionality (*Triebintentionalität*) as well as the role of the lived body (*Leib, la chair*). Husserlian scholars group these topics generically under the term *passivity* — life and affect.[4]

This genetic orientation goes well beyond the classical Husserlian thought as stated in Husserl's *Lessons* of 1905. These earlier analyses deploy basically a static phenomenology of time in which one distinguishes two main traits:

(1) The accent is primarily placed on the description of *past* consciousness. The main discovery pertains to the immediacy of the past, of retentional experience and its close links with the living present. As a consequence (a) future consciousness is mostly understood as *symmetrical* to the past, relegated to the role of adjunct to the just past, or simply omitted. Husserl only indicates

[2] Stikkers (1997) explains well Scheler's criticism, and shows how Heidegger's neutralizing of temporal experience leads him to put aside values at the very core of such an experience.

[3] Our orientation — both thematic and methodological — was already announced in a previous inquiry concerning the living present in Varela (1999). In that paper Varela's strategy was to employ the resources from a dynamical view of the basis of temporality to illuminate the static and the genetic analysis of time in the Husserlian tradition. One result was a revised diagram of time which suggested that retention and protention do not appear as symmetrical end points of a flow of time, as has been traditionally assumed. Rather, protention appears as essentially linked to affect and as having its own, unique generative manifestation. The latter point is the focus of this paper. This paper constitutes the first in a triptych. Here we are concerned with introducing the notion of valence and basic dispositions. A second article will be devoted to the deployment, from that basis, of the full spectrum of specific emotions in human life, manifest in the intersubjective and active life of individuals. Finally, we will re-examine anew the constitution of time, giving the future, expectations and protentions, a central role.

[4] This brief presentation of background here is mostly based on Husserl (1966). For unpublished material we have profited from texts in *Alter* No. 2, *Temporalité et affectivité*, Paris, 1994, and A. Montavont (1999). Concerning drive-intentionality and *Leib*, see also, Nam-In Lee (1993), and recently, I. Yamaguchi (1997).

the need to extend to the future the layered description accomplished for the just past. (b) The accent is put on our own *self*-understanding by means of the diverse forms of the past, that is, on seeking a reference point for stabilizing one's identity with the renewed reflection of every moment giving a base to our temporal being. Later, in his *First Philosophy* (1923-24), Husserl will yoke the structure of retention to that of reflection *in statu nascendi,* related to remembrance and full-fledged reflection.

(2) The conception of time that emerges is predominantly *formal*: it makes methodical abstraction of any reference to an embodied and affective individual. The just past of a sound, is described with no grounding on the uniqueness of the sensory modality and its accompanying emotional tonality. (a) Thus the experience of the lived present remains disembodied and unspecific. It is a bodiless subject with no incarnated habitus in its phylogenetic past, with no roots in the social community in which it has grown, untraversed by recollections that would inhabit it. This is the criticism that Merleau-Ponty addressed to Husserl early on in *Phénoménologie de la perception*. When listening to a piece of music in concert, I am situated in a place (other listeners, the uncomfortable seat) as well as in a rich background (memories of other concerts, affinities for the composer). The present is thus a multilayered, dense domain that is individual, that is, carnal and intersubjective. (b) The emotional component is relegated to a secondary place, a mere accompaniment, without a constitutional role. In contrast, should one give affect-emotions a central place it follows that the source of time will be intimately linked to passivity, letting-go rather than a retentional holding. More than a return to a retentional self-knowledge, what we confront here is an opening towards an awakening which is the emotional *space* itself, a space which contains the source of the protentive future.

Self-affection and salience: A return to the constitutional analysis

Following the genetic turn, and in contrast to this earlier analysis, the role of affect-emotion appears more sharply. For us here, a main insight to recover from Husserl's analysis is that affect is primarily manifested (at the fold) as *salience* (*mise en relief, Abhebung*), the emergence of contours of a world with its fundamental orientations. Such a saliency sticks out from a pre-given field of experience and forms a contrast that 'strikes us' and 'awakens' us Husserl says in *Experience and Judgement* (Husserl, 1954). It means that I am affected by some sense-data, attracted by some affective tendencies that enable me to orient myself passively and receptively in the space and in the world. In other words, whatever affects me I cannot experience raw, as proto-impressions or impacts (*Uraffektion*). The very first appearance is *already* pervaded by affective tendencies: some form of a pre-egoic source is already affected, a world is already sketched. Now, this is evidently an *active* dimension, a pre-reflexive consciousness in *action*, which Husserl intends with the term 'receptivity', by which passivity and activity are relativized as a naive opposition. The world is not pre-given as an autonomous 'in itself' but it touches me, it has a certain 'affective relief', it is segmented according to an 'affective perspective' (Husserl, 1954, Section 1). This fundamental discovery of genetic analysis puts us squarely on the road of the inseparability between affect and cognition, between values and living itself. This then becomes the very starting point of our study here.[5]

Further, for Husserl the affective experience is a matter of intensity or *gradation*: it has an affective 'force' (*affektive Kraft*). As he says succinctly: '... a positive affective force is the fundamental condition of all life' (1966, §35, p. 170). Such a force inherent in affectivity is also described as an originary vitality (*Lebendigkeit*) and as freshness and refreshing of experience. The very choice of the term *force* is central for us, since it is a strong clue for the dynamical or development nature of affect in its temporalization. A most evident example is the change in a mental content after it has sunk into retention (thus having already gone beyond the fold). At that point its affective force is correspondingly weakened but, as Husserl writes, 'if it diminishes till zero-point, life ceases altogether in its own vitality' and ends up in unconsciousness. But beyond the metaphorical language derived from physics this analysis is still unsatisfactory. What *is*, then, this activity, this force, this gradation, this vitality?

In fact, as we have seen, even if Husserl has left aside embodiment and affect in his early analysis of time consciousness (in curious anti-symmetry to James who makes the bodily the primary cause of emotions) his later work led him to situate affect at the very origin of the absolute temporal flow. This flow is not a mere form, but is affected by primal impressions, what he calls the original *hylè* (*Urhylè*)(Depraz, 1994). However, even at this point the Husserlian analysis remains limited, since it does not propose a renewed analysis of the living present that would indicate the *precise* role played by affect. His advance remains still abstract; we do not recuperate, in his analysis, a living present suffused with the affective.

If one were now to turn to the work done after Husserl, one could point to a few important steps, but also to their limitations. Five important authors stand out as a backdrop for our project, although their style of investigation contrasts with ours in two important aspects: their abstract nature and distance from specific accounts of lived emotions, and their total absence of relation to recent empirical work. These classical authors are: Heidegger, Merleau-Ponty, Levinas, Henry and Marion.[6] They represent in a sense the classical style that has given pheno-

---

[5] For comparative purposes, it is interesting to notice that W. James reaches a comparable conclusion expressed in his choice of 'feeling' as the best designation for mental experience altogether, which is always 'warm and intimate'. Moreover: 'All mental facts without exception ...are a feeling, a peculiarly tinged segment of the stream. This tingeing is its sensitive body, the *wie ihm zu Muthe ist*, the way it feels whilst passing' James (1890). For a thoughtful analysis of feeling and mental states in James see Natsoulas (1998).

[6] (1) For Heidegger, affect and emotional tonality (*Stimmungen*) are surely determinant in the constitution of temporality, and the orientation towards the future is also central, manifested by anxiety, the *Grundstimmung* of a being-for-death. Nevertheless, for us here, his analysis remains macroscopic: the temporal horizon remains limited to that of the human destiny in its historical finitude. (2) Merleau-Ponty presents a frontal critique of the Husserlian early formal analysis, and sees

menology a base, from which our own analysis departs in order to enlarge its scope in the two dimensions just mentioned.

Thus, in spite of all these important advances, it is necessary to continue the phenomenological investigation further. The first limitation to overcome is that the role of affect in the living present remains in general too speculative or macroscopic; we therefore still do not see how the precise and specific role of affect in temporality emerges, how the living present is grounded by emotivity. In other words, our main concern is to describe the original fluctuating move, the primal asymmetric rythmicity at the core of our experience of time.[7] Fortunately the kind of investigation proposed here is beginning to develop, as witnessed by the recent work of M. Sheets-Johnstone, whose account of the link between emotions and movements aligns perfectly with ours, although developed independently (Sheets-Johnstone, 1989; 2000). We will incorporate some of her contributions below.

Against the background just sketched, our analysis will necessarily be focussed on *a detailed level of resolution of the grain of description*. This level of analysis is rooted in self-affection as a pre-noetic ground, and is deployed into a full-fledged content where emotions are recognized in their multifarious diversity. This 'rainbow' of emotions and its intrinsic coherence is, as we said, a further topic that we will take up in a separate text. For the purpose at hand, however, we only need to point out that *under*lying the level of constitution we will be focussing on, we leave unexamined the sub-personal, archaic and unconscious *Ur-affekt* antecedents. *Over*laying it we also leave unexamined the level of moods and socio-historical time from which it is inseparable. Again, the main concern is the investigation the dynamic structuring of the living present in its affective axis and its immediate after-effect, which we call here *micro*-temporality.

---

temporality as an embodied one. However he draws no clear distinctions between spatial and emotional embodiment, and a full-fledged descriptive analysis remained a project (concerning this non-distinction see G. Mazis, 1993). Besides, both Heidegger and Merleau-Ponty still give time a primacy over affect. As for Levinas and M. Henry, both suggested that affection is at the core of manifestation. (3) The first one describes as 'diachronic' a temporality which is from the very start traversed by alterity understood as an 'hetero-affection', but the part played by bodily motricity in the intrinsic move of emotional affection remains untouched ; (4) Finally, for M. Henry, a crucial element of his analysis is also the self-affection proper to the living beings, in the emotional polarization between suffering and joy. This is the basis of a dynamics, a becoming, which Henry nevertheless refuses to call time; besides, beyond joy/suffering polarity there is no specificity for the concrete role of emotions. As we indicate below, we agree with the role Henry gives to the original joy/suffering polarity; our concern is that it remains too speculative and general. Our notion of valence therefore provides, we surmise, a step into a finer analysis of the emotional. (5) Finally, one has to mention a recent phenomenological approach, which is of great interest for us. In his latest book, *Etant donné*, J.-L. Marion engages in a description of what he calls 'l'adonné', an extreme passive subject pervaded by affect, which always radically takes us by surprise. Several aspects of this original temporality are examined (the arrival, the incident), always in the register of being surprising. But again, as we will see presently, we claim a role for a primordial valence as having multiple degrees of intensity and related to events which are not necessarily extreme, as is the case of surprise (cf. see Depraz, 1998).

[7]   To our knowledge, J. Derrida is the only one to have been sensitive to such an asymmetry at the origin of the constitution of temporality, which he sums up very early in his concept of *différance*.

Valence: Primordial (E)motion

Reconducting the analysis: two examples

The analysis we propose is initiated by concrete examples that give us an experiential leading clue; it then follows the path of a *regressive* analysis founded on a radical phenomenology. Finally, we engage in the description of eidetic invariant dimensions.[8] In a further step we will re-examine these invariants through a progressive constitutional analysis. Let us start with our two chosen case studies.

Example 1. Averting the gaze

The first example is best understood as a generic and not as a singular event, through a familiar gesture that Merleau-Ponty situates in a succinct, evocative context. The hope is that the reader will re-live through it a singular instance in her/his own lived experience.

> Se cacher les yeux pour ne pas voir un danger, c'est, dit-on ne pas croire aux choses, ne croire qu'au monde privé, mais c'est plutôt croire que ce qui est pour nous est absolument, qu'un monde que nous avons réussi à voir sans danger est sans danger, c'est donc croire au plus haut point que notre vision va aux choses mêmes. Peut-être cette expérience nous enseigne-t-elle, mieux qu'aucune autre, ce qu'est la présence perceptive du monde... elle est, en deçà de l'affirmation et de la négation, en deçà de jugement... notre expérience, plus vieille que toute opinion, d'habiter le monde par notre corps... (*Le visible et l'invisible*, p. 48).[9]

We cannot insist enough that the reader now take a moment to re-enact his/her own instance of this evocative gesture directly.

Example 2. Musical exaltation

The second example is expressed as a first description of a singular experience, captured, as it were, when passing. From the notes of one of the authors (FV):

> Today went to the concert at 11, a certain heaviness in my eyelids, and a bit of a moody blues as setting. I'm sitting leaning forward onto the edge of 2nd balcony. The musicians (sublime Italian ensemble) arrive, tune up, and settle, a short silence and then begin with the sonata of the *Musical Offering*, which I love. Instantly, within the first five or six notes of the main theme, the break in mood and feeling tone arises: suddenly my chest heaves a little, my skin becomes goose-bumpy and it is as if the body is brought into position. Almost at the same time there is a wave of beauty, of poignancy which brings sudden tears into my eyes, an intensified breathing. Without premeditation, I feel my eyes close and I lean backwards to relax my body into complete receptivity. My mental-space seems to spread out and my

---

[8] For this approach to the practice of reduction, see Casey, 1976; Ihde, 1977; Depraz, Varela, and Vermersch (2003).

[9] English translation: 'It is said that to cover one's eyes so as to not see a danger is to not believe in the things, to believe only in the private world; but this is rather to believe that what is for us is absolutely, that a world we have succeeded in seeing as without danger is without danger. It is therefore the greatest degree of our belief that our vision goes to the things themselves. Perhaps this experience teaches us better than any other what the perceptual presence of the world is: ... beneath affirmation and negation, beneath judgment... it is our experience, prior to every opinion, of inhabiting the world by our body...' (Merleau-Ponty, 1968, p. 28).

ego-center to become almost imperceptible. By the time the first variation of the musical theme starts the feeling tone is fully formed and the first waves of thought-wandering have begun, the first being a memory of another occasion when the very same music also touched me to tears. The whole thing has lasted a mere fraction of a second.

Two initial remarks are in order. It is not explicitly laid out in this text, but the study of examples such as these through the method of reduction is, practically speaking, a matter of the reiteration of successive passages separated in time, until the main traits of the experience seem to point themselves out. It is misleading to assume that a cursory consideration of an individual experience will suffice. It is only by a sustained analysis that the initial opacity of raw experiences yields to eidetic invariants.[10]

The second preliminary remark is that affect cannot be defined a priori, but it is perhaps useful to try to delimit its scope. For the purposes of this discussion only, we propose to consider in the realm of affect a constellation of the following components (see Watt, 1998). These co-occurent (not necessarily successive) components will serve as guides for the analysis in what follows:

(1) a precipitating *event*, or trigger that can be perceptual (a social event, threat, or affective expression or behavior of another in social context) or imaginary (a thought, memory, fantasy or other affect) or both;

(2) a '*feeling of evidence*' of the precipitating event's meaning, the emergence of a salience. This appraisal can be fleeting or detailed, deeply realistic and empathic, much of the meaning attribution is pre-reflexive and even unconscious.

(3) a lived manifestation of a *feeling-tone* along an intrinsic polar axis, the crucial and poorly understood 'valence' dimension of affect discussed below in detail;

(4) a *motor* embodiment, especially facial and motor changes, and differential 'readiness' activations. These typically show themselves as variants of a domain of concern as discussed below;

(5) complex *autonomic* physiological changes, with the most commonly studied being various cardio-pulmonary parameters, skin conductance, and various muscle tone manifestations.

Regressive analysis as a primordial constitution

Staying close to the micro-temporality of these examples gives us access to some initially remarkable and suggestive elements, if reduction is followed patiently into its multiple layers. The first item it is crucial to notice is the fact that the original trace of temporality appears as already inhabited by e-motivity.[11] Thus in the gaze averting evocation, there are the eyelids closing, the hands that covers the eyes, the cringe of the neck as I turn the head, the posture of the mouth with a

---

[10] For more on this methodological question see Varela and Shear (1999).

[11] The use of e-motion is very expressive for us here. We borrow this usage from Mazis (1993).

half-pronounced word that comes out as accompaniment. Or, in the musical experience, as soon as the notes are heard from the background of silence, I' m already feeling the heaves of my chest with an expansive sensation that relaxes my body back into the chair.

From tendency to salience: valence in affect

Thus, the affective force manifests as a rapid, dynamical transformation from tendency to salience, involving one's *entire* Leib *as a complex*, and this at least on two main axes. First, there is an embodied movement, that itself manifests literally as a movement already possessed by an affect-feeling force. At face value, this indicates that motion is an integral part of the constitutive dynamics we are pursuing. We can further describe the nature of this motion as distinguishing a double pole, a polarity: away from the sight in shifting one's gaze, or towards the feeling in music. At this basic level, then, there already manifests the presence of a *value* sign: towards/away.[12]

Second, the motion is inseparable from its manifestation as a basic *disposition* to which we will return below in greater detail. But for this first analysis, we consider disposition as indicative of the global Gestalt composed from a variety of feeling dimensions. The visible part is the triple effector appearance: face gestures, posture and stance, and the familiar complex of autonomic components (change of breathing and heart beat, skin sensations, and diffuse changes which configure a non-neutral tone, a 'feeling-tone' (James), a drive-intentionality (the Husserlian *Triebintentionalität*)).

Basic as it is, this observation is nonetheless of fundamental importance. The conclusion is that the emergence of the living present is rooted in and arises from *a germ or source* of motion-disposition, a *primordial fluctuation*. That this has to do with a primordial fluctuation motivates our notion here that affect *precedes* temporality: affect implicates as its very nature the tendency, a 'pulsion' and a motion that, as such, can *only* deploy itself in time and thus *as* time. This deployment manifests itself in a constellation. First the very original 'pulsional' tendency just evoked. Secondly, the tendency is followed by a corresponding shift of *attention* that manifests as the emergence of *salience*. Finally, the earliest e-motion follows, including a *motion* that embodies it. Thus, this primordial fluctuation cannot be separated from its complex or multifarious constitution, since all its moments are not a linear succession, but rather dimensions of co-arising. But it is nevertheless marked by its uniqueness in the unfolding of the living present. Thus in the musical example, the composite nature manifests already in the microtemporality given by the few early notes of the melody. Already in its arising, the interrelation between movement, tendency and feeling-disposition arise as a unit.

---

[12] To avoid misunderstandings, let us point out that this original dynamics *cannot* be properly referred to as dialectical. The value sign in question is already present in the embodiment, and does not follow an ideal formal logic. In fact, as Derrida (1991) has remarked, in the constitutional realm there is fundamental asymmetry, not a dialectical cycle.

According to our analyses, it seems that regressive analysis *cannot* proceed any further in the description of the layering of temporality; that we have reached here its limits. A finer grain is perhaps possible, but not apparent from the examples we have examined. The nature of this limitation is not one of reaching the very ground of some foundational level, but rather the limits of what is given to direct apprehension. (In contrast, the complement with a progressive analysis illuminates this pre-conscious basis quite dramatically. More on this below).

Given its central importance, it is justified to present this original germ as a *constitutional invariant*. We will designate it under the term *valence*, that is, the primordial constitution of self-affection as a dynamic polarity, as manifesting in the form of a tension that takes several forms: like-dislike, attraction-rejection, pleasure-displeasure. The choice of this word is dictated by the need for a designation that is not too encumbered by previous associations from other contexts, and yet is open to empirical description. These opposing pairs are better seen as generative, spanning a space of possibilities, a topology rather than a symbolic alternative between a plus and a minus sign (see fig. 2). Valence is value-prone and value-laden.

Is absence of valence describable? The limit of the analysis of non-valence

In the topology of valence, one should not miss the complexity implicit in the intermediate point of neutrality (ignorance or indifference), the disappearance of a primordial salience into a background. It is clear that an affective force is seen here as a force in an axis of like-dislike as a continuum bounded by extremes, but in itself a manifold. In this sense, neutrality is ambiguous: it can either mean no salience (basic ignorance, or errancy), or an active ignoring whereby the movement goes into a periphery which is pre-reflexive or even repressed into the unconscious.

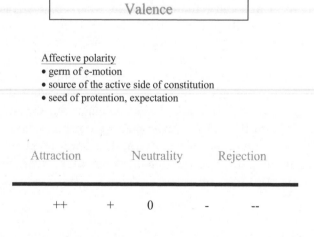

Figure 2: The basic structure of affective valence

In the context of genetic analysis, we also find this limit state of affective polarity where affect falls back onto what Husserl calls the zero-point of affect (*Nullpunkt der Affektion*). This is an ambivalent neutrality since it can fall to either side: unconscious opaqueness or pre-reflexive undifferentiation, or else active search for a place of no-pathos, of lucidity and dis-interested awareness. Consider for example Husserl's description of profound sleep:

> Le moi ne fait rien de ce qu'il pourrait faire ... il ne tient à rien de ce à quoi il tiendrait pas ailleurs... l'intérêt fait défaut... il dort, il est dénué de conscience.. il est dans le nirvana... il n'est mû par rien, c'est-à-dire que, n'étant soumis à aucune émotion liée à un intérêt, étant sans intérêt, il ne se meut, il n'agit pas, il ne fait l'expérience de rien... le moi dormant ne possède aucun intérêt... La constitution et son acquis ne sont pas perdus, mais tout cela est tombé dans la modalité de l'immersion, entendue comme absence d'intérêt... dans le 'pur' sommeil qui serait identique à l'absence de conscience caractérisant l'évanouissement total... (Husserl, 1997, p. 167).

This basic state of dis-interest can be lived as apathy or as a remarkable absence of pathos touched on by contemplative traditions in the West (Eckhart, Grégoire de Naziance) under the names of 'detachment' (*Abgeschiedenheit*) or 'dis-passion' (*a-pathia*), a heightened presence where valence has disappeared. But it is surely within the Buddhist tradition that this insight has become the very core of its phenomenology under the term of *sunyata* (openness, fullness, creative emptiness) (Varela, 2000). In its creative form, *sunyata* is openness to the condition facing us in the rich present, a full deployment of possibilities. In its obscuring form typical of ordinary life, *sunyata* is the veil of ignoring, or wandering away from the original source into categorical fixation.

But let us return to analyse further this originary constitution of emotional fluctuation stemming from the background of e-motion. How can we illuminate further the experience of valence, of motion-affect at the root of life?

Progressive analysis: The evidence from the empirical level

Animal life

In order to respond to this question one needs to turn to recapitulate the history of life from its origins. In other words we need to shift from a regressive to a *progressive* analysis of valence. It has been repeatedly said that a genetic phenomenological analysis entails a shift from conceptual categories to the roots of life itself. But this repeated invocation concerning 'life' is left unexamined beyond its evocation.[13] In fact the deep link between motion and disposition that surfaced in the regressive analysis can be found anew in the early history of animal and human life, at the very roots of what is to be endowed with movement and feeling altogether, and in the natural history of the nervous system in particular. In this sense the very ontology provided by the life sciences can serve as leading cues (*Leitfäden*) to a constitutional analysis.

---

[13] For a pioneer effort in this direction see H. Jonas (1966). For a more recent analysis where the progressive analysis is not invoked but not traced to its origins see R. Barbaras (1999).

Working through leading cues opens up a dynamic relationship between different methods of investigation. A lifeworld ontology guides the sciences, which in turn provide clues for the constitutive-phenomenological undertaking.[14] Our methodology here can also be similarly expressed in terms of "co-generativity" of the transcendental (constitutional) level of analysis and the empirical (ontological, leading-cue motivated) domains of investigation. Through *mutual constraints* both levels of analysis benefit from their respective strengths: (a) grounding of transcendental analysis derived through its empirical dimension; (b) breaking the spell of objectivism of empirical analysis derived from phenomenological insights.[15]

Life in its natural deployment has manifested a few fundamental modes of being, giving rise, correspondingly, to domains of existence open to different present-at-hand ontologies. In its most basic form, this multiplicity is grounded in the origin of life itself, that is, the transition from a chemical environment to a self-produced identity which can give a point of view that is the very origin of sense and meaning.[16]

But we will restrict ourselves here to the next fundamental level of description, corresponding to the manner in which multi-cellular individuals are harmonized together to constitute an *organism*, thus providing a second-order identity (Varela, 1991). It is here that the phenomenon of life on earth appears and is seen in its most familiar manifestation. There are fundamentally three styles of being an organism, each one grounded in the mode in which subsistence by the procurement of nourishment. First, there is the vegetal mode of being, passively feeding on light. Second, the kingdom of fungi, providing a digestive surrounding environment from which food is extracted. And finally there is the animal mode, whose manner of being in the world is centrally marked by an *active* search and pursuit of nourishment. In other words animality invents a *mode of being* which is inseparable from movement, going towards, seeking in movement.

The structural change that makes this domain possible is one and the same with the emergence of the nervous system, from the earliest animals to humans. The basic neural constitution is constant: the introduction of causal links between distant parts of an organism's composing cells, provides an active interdependence between a sensory and an effector surface, typically between a sensor and a muscle. The connecting links are a specialized class of cells, the neurons, the central components of the nervous system. This basic constitution is present already among early water invertebrates (such as *Hydra*). But once introduced, it does not fundamentally change with the diversification of animals. The only change is in the complexity of neuronal links between sensory-to-effector

[14] For a first conceptualization of this regressive/progressive phenomenological methodology, cf. E. Fink (1988); for the complementary distinction of progressive and regressive methods in termes of 'leading-cues', see A. Steinbock (1995).

[15] The idea of a mutual circulation was first evoked by Varela (1996); also see Varela (1997); and Depraz (1999).

[16] For more on this original constitution or *autopoeisis* see: Varela (1979; 1997b). See also Jonas (1966).

surfaces, or interneuron networks. This *basic neuro-logic* is always the same: the complex instauration of active links between perception-action.[17]

It follows from this foundational event in the history of life that organisms are necessarily situated, enactive, embodied agents (Varela *et al.*, 1991; Clark, 1997). This enactive character can be described as having two complementary aspects. First, animal life is an ongoing coupling of organism and context, in a permanent coping that is fundamentally mediated by sensori-motor activities. Second, the organism is constituted by emerging endogenous configurations (or self-organizing patterns) of its interneuronal activity. Thus sense and purpose originate from the sensori-motor coupling modulating an ongoing endogenous activity that the organism configures in an unceasing flow into a meaningful world.[18]

The natural history of time-space

Now, if it is true that the sensory-effector link is at the core of the being we call an animal, the next question follows immediately: What is the most basic characteristic of such a mode of constitution? The answer is simple but, we believe, essential: to constantly initiate and sustain an activity *relative* to its mode of identity, that is to say, the manifestation of its self-affection conducive to nourishment and sustaining its viability. The most elemental manifestation is a trend, a tendency, a displacement relative to the topography of the organism *necessarily* spanning the continuum that covers the choices of an action anchored in a being but inseparable from a world of significance. In this basic constitution of animal life, *space, time and affect arise together* in the only topology that the most elementary motion can have given the basic constitution of the organism's nervous system: the valence towards and away. In other words this is an original mode, the originary dynamical germ at the source of affect. Both logically and empirically, here *could* not be another more basic mode for animal-being.[19]

In brief, then, progressive analysis leads us to re-discover the central importance of valence, not only as a lived original fluctuation revealed by reduction, but also as an ancestral mode of constitution linking the very invention of space and time as motion through the motivation of the organism's identity. Stated more concisely: for progressive analysis valence is a *necessary* condition.

To regard the results of this analysis as pertinent to animality alone would be a mistake, since the same analysis can be carried into the human realm. There are, to be sure, large differences between humans and animals (as well as between animal groups themselves). But there is unchanging continuity in the grounding

[17] For an accesible presentation of these ideas from an empirical side see H. Maturana and F. Varela (1989). Such a perceptual-action scheme was already at the core of J. von Üxkühl's work, although he did not connect it to an underlying self-organizing neural network.

[18] The notion of 'structural coupling', as the keyword for the productive link between organism and world (Maturana and Varela, 1989) can be put in correpondence to Husserl's *Paarung* which also covers such an originary passive associative synthesis between ego and world.

[19] We note, in passing, that Husserl's analysis of animality (that is, drives, instinct, habitus, as phylogenetically anchored in a generative common history of the living) has resonances with the auto-poietic view of life just sketched here. See Husserl, 1995).

role of the multiple links between sensorium-motorium, a basic and invariant constitution. In the case of humans, not only is the basic sensory-motor network rigorously true, but it is now possible to point to a multiplicity of valences, which have been sedimented at the level of the brain's connectivity itself over the entire span of life. As we shall see below, we can also examine more closely the relation between this sedimentation and the role they play in proving a specific affective landscape for the living present.

Domains of Concern and Intersubjective Constitution: The Embodiment of Valence

Basic domains of concern: figures of intersubjectivity

The initial steps in the regressive analysis allowed us to identify valence and its polarity as the configuration of the initial fluctuation from the pre-egoic background, from which it emerges. This primordial quality of valence is one and the same with its inherently unstable or transient nature, a mere flutter from a pre-reflective background. As fluctuation, it is nothing but a tendency, a movement that manifests itself as a next step in an *embodied moment*, as the global intentional content of the present. The emergence of valence takes us as far as the threshold of the fold, and it is now the very crest of the fold we need to examine.

The embodiment of valence is not marked by the full appearance of an ego-center and a fully formed intentional content. Instead, we are still at the stage of an *Ur-ego*, a blurred self experienced as de-centered, but well marked by the polarity proper to valence. The central observation is that, at this stage this polarity becomes progressively more fleshed out into an embodiment, into a concern that is close to being situated and acting in the world. We will refer to this embodiment of readiness-for-action as an intersubjective *domain of concern*. This is no less than the basic structuring of our every-day posture or stance wherein the world and intraworldy beings can show up.

We return to the regressive analysis of our examples. Closing my eyes or shifting my posture to avert my gaze, is a straightforward mode of immediate coping with a worldly object, a readiness-to-hand in which fear for instance makes sense and can eventually show up as such. In contrast, letting oneself go into the early phrasing of the music manifests a space of concern with my own being, wherein wonder makes sense.

Domains of concern can thus be understand as close to the sharp distinction between categories and *existentials*, the latter term introduced by Heidegger (1927, § 9) to signify the characteristics of *Dasein* (*Seinscharakter*). Existentials can be further articulated for our purpose into three fundamental domains:

(1) Coping in everyday life;
(2) Belonging and relating in a social network;
(3) Self-identity of being.

A key point is that when examined in their proper constitution, domains of concern all have a common or invariant structuring, already anticipated above:

(a) A *feeling-tone* along an intrinsic polar axis, the crucial 'valence' dimension of affect introduced here;

(b) An embodiment as *motion*, especially facial and motor postures, which carry differential 'readiness' activations;

(c) An embodiment in a complex of *autonomic* effector changes, with the most conspicuous being cardio-pulmonary parameters including respiration, skin conductance, and various smooth muscle tone manifestations.

These three domains are not arbitrary. They correspond very clearly to the three figures of intersubjectivity that many phenomenologists have retained, with various emphasis:

(i)   The first figure refers to our capacity for spontaneous inter-action in daily life with others, in relations that are always interpersonal;

(ii) The second figure refers to the community background and those more global and multiple relations with the other;

(iii) The third figure touches on the ontological level of a basic being which remains undifferentiated and anonymous.

In fact, through these three intersubjective dispositions, we are facing three forms of alterity that Husserl, Merleau-Ponty and Heidegger have each described in privileged modes (Depraz, 1992; 1995, Chap.5.)

Domains of concern do not make sense unless marked by a primordial duality, a rough topology of *self-other*, a bare ego-center (in *status nascendi*), the origins of a 'center of gravity' of the agency in action. This self-other polarity expresses then the original fluctuation in valence as a fuller articulation from the source of self-affection into a more fully constituted relationship with world and others. Thus domains of concern have an originary structure well described by the arising of a self-other relation immanent in the shaping of a pre-reflexive level.

The proper role of this self-other polarity is that it provides a new reference, a *dual direction*, a differential between an existential tendency that may take two forms: from self-to-world or from world-to-self. This is the manifestation in the unavoidable matrix of intersubjectivity already present at this level of constitution, the inseparable presence of passivity and agency.

It is perhaps useful to think of this directionality as analogous to a direction-of-fit (conditions of satisfaction) first introduced in the analysis of speech acts (Searle, 1982). We can distinguish in any domain of concern between a self-to-others/world and a world-to-self (or self-in-public) directionality. The original valence marked by a continuum of like-dislike can now be expanded, at this level of genetic analysis, into a multiplicity of domains of concerns with their respective intersubjective direction-of-fit. As an illustration, the emotion of shame (*honte*) as exposure to the gaze of others places us in an exemplary world-to-self direction. In contrast, in its expression as tact (*pudeur*) this is inverted as a self-to world direction (Fig.3).

Let us go back once more to our two examples. Covering the eyes situates the emergence of this lived present squarely in the domain of everyday coping, and is marked by a self-to-world direction, as an agency which puts 'its trust in its own seeing'. On this basis, fear, for instance, can become established as a full-fledge emotion and cognitive content. In contrast, in letting myself go into the music I find myself predominantly concerned with my own being and where I find myself aligned with the world, that is, a world-to-self direction. Wonder as a fully developed emotion emerging during the micro temporality of this example thus appears from the background of valence embodied in concern for identity. Again we can ask the question *why* is it that every domain of concern can support or manifest a very specific and differentiated array of the emotional repertoire? Reduction can yield their nature and expose their layering, but the basis of determination of such a mode of manifestation remains hidden. We need to turn once again to the analysis of the living to illuminate the question from a complementary angle.

Domains of concerns

(E)motion is always, already embodied, situated

- coping in everyday life

- relating in language, belonging

- self-identity, being

Self-to-world   World-to-self

++   +   -   -- | --   -   +   ++

Fig. 3: Basic constitution of the domains of concern

Progressive analysis of basic dispositions in affective neuroscience

From phenomenology to the empirical: Phylogeny and ontogeny

Animal life reveals, we have said, a certain number of basic dispositions. These dispositions are not constant or universal but they do constitute the universal basis for a space of living that traverses the animal kingdom up to man. Further, from an enactive viewpoint, the arising of the living present is characterized by the concurrent participation of several functionally distinct and topographically distributed regions of the brain and their sensori-motor embodiment. This involves the complex process of relating and integrating these different components, a process at the root of temporality from the point of view of its empirical base as seen in neuroscience (Varela, 1999). The inquiry into the *phylogenetic* continuity of affect has a long history starting from Darwin's classic work on the expression of emotions (Darwin, 1882/1998). Since then there has been a considerably literature devoted to the topic (Young, 1973; de Waal, 1997). Equally important are the empirical studies on ontogenetic plasticity or developmental history. These kinds of studies make a natural bridge between animals and humans since they are in a basic sense studies of how the tactile and kinesthetic lived body is constituted in early years, and as such, centrally relevant to the specific modes affective valence takes (see specially Stern, 1985; Thelen and Smith, 1994).

The importance of basic disposition can perhaps be most clearly expressed here on the basis of the work of Jaak Panksepp (1998). He studies valence as arising from recurrent patterns common to all mammalian brains and relevant to social-biological relationships to the world, other species, and conspecifics. What is important for us is that Panksepp conjoins the expressive and motor patterns of emotions to basic networks in the midbrain-diencephalon. These networks support affective or emotional dispositions such as: attachment /social bonding, sadness/separation distress, rage, fear, play/joy, nurturance, and one prototype disposition for seeking/expectancy, clearly a key for an emotional life which touches experience in all its diversity. It thus becomes possible to associate such stable body-brain functioning to the basic invariants of dispositions and domains of concern as discussed before.

Recent research has revealed the complexity of each circuit. We illustrate this here in a simplified manner, by poiting out some of the key neuromodulators (mostly neuropeptides) of structures projecting to a complex of structures called periaquaductal gray (PAG). PAG seems to support a global value integration in which the relative activation states of all of these dispositions have a role to play. Some of the dispositions are polysemantic, and the term chosen must not be taken literally (Table 1: derived and simplified from Panksepp, 1998, by Watt 1998).

Affective Behaviour	Representative Neural Structure	Neuromodulators
Motivational 'Seeking/Exploratory'	Lateral hypothalamic to ventral thalamus, with mesolimbic and mesocortical output	DA (+), glutamate (+), many neuropeptides, opiods (+)
Rage/Anger ('Affective Attack')	Medial amygdala	Substance P (+) (ACH, glutamate (+)
Fear	Central & lateral amygdala	Glutamate, monoamines, many neuropeptides
Nurturance/Sexuality	Stria terminalis to medial cortical amygdala	Steroids (+), vasopressin, & oxytocin (+), prolactin(+)
Social Bonding, separation distress	In primates anterior cingulate/anterior thalamus	Opiods(-/+) oxytocin (-/+),prolactin (-/+) vasopressin(+)
Play	midbrain central gray	Opiods, muscarine (+), nicotine (+)

Table 1: Keys [ACH = acetylcholine; DA, dopamine;
–/+ inhibits or activates the corresponding disposition]

These basic dispositions set the background against which organisms live in everyday life. In neurobiological terms, one can say that every moment of the living present corresponds to the integration of the diffuse reticular activating system (ERTAS) modulating this complex limbic network. This interplay is the source of the self-selection of a mode of basic disposition which in turn will manifest itself as overt emotion, behavior and its mental contents. This is the basic emergent dynamics of cognition and emotions in action as seen in its organismic ground, which needs to be discussed in a broader context.

Neural correlates of affect and consciousness

It is common to read that emotion are 'limbic system functions', and that the limbic system is part of a paleocortical and archicortical evolutionary trend. Yet the limbic system cannot be neatly delineated, and its operation seems always to be Janus faced (Watt 1998).[20] On the one hand, it links downwards towards the hypothalamus and autonomic functions, on the other hand upwards to cortical cognitive functions. The point is that the microtemporality of affect we are examining here is based on the resonance of dispositions which are based on a complex, self-organizing extended network where no neat distinctions between 'higher' and 'lower' can be easily made. Neo-cortical and thalamic sensory-motor encoding inevitably carry along a valence tag that enables emotional meaning.

---

[20] As Watt (1998) notes, the borders of the 'limbic system' are vague and have changed substantially over time. Various 'extended' notions about the limbic system include a host of cortical, paralimbic, basal ganglia, thalamic and hypothalamic, basal forebrain and other subcortical systems, including even monoaminergic portions of the brainstem core (see Derryberry and Tucker, 1992).

Affect-emotions arise from an extremely extended network that can be seen in affect's composite nature. Affect links virtually every type of quality that the organism manifests. This spans the most elementary homeostatic detection of biological needs by the hypothalamic systems, to the most subtle analysis of the intentions of others in a complex social milieu using cortical modules of both verbal and nonverbal categorization. Being a *global* state recruiting many regions, affect-emotion cannot have simple neural correlates, or some specific set of structures. The neural correlates must be seen as a *dynamic pattern of arising*, with its intrinsic temporality and liability; it must be understood as relating to an interpenetrating hierarchy of biological, social and personal values. This neural architectural complexity is mirrored in affect's multi-dimensionality: patterned autonomic, endocrine, motor-executive, pain/pleasure (valence), social/signaling, and cognitive (other/self appraisal) integrations.

Thus, by their very nature the subtle modulations made possible through the limbic system, we know, will involve a complex of corporeal manifestations ancestrally established. These manifestations will include autonomic action such as respiratory, heart rate, endocrine secretion, etc., as well as the ancestral motor pattern involved in posture and movement. The feeling tone (or 'tingeing' spoken of by James) is thus intrinsically associated with the nature of these dispositions. They are a feeling grounded on the body's responsive repertoire. They also incarnate a manner of being in the world according to different modes of animality, open to historical and individual shaping. The *Leib/Körper* dimension is evident here in sedimented patterns and sub-personal predisposition's.

The cues from biological ontology are then clear: early conscious states appear to be dispositionally affective. Yet, little mention is made as yet in cognitive neuroscience of the place affect-emotion has in human consciousness as such. At best, affect is seen as another qualia, but a disadvantaged one at that compared to other better know cognitive qualities in perception or memory. As Watt (1998)[21] aptly pointed out, the point of the intersection of consciousness studies and emotion studies is 'reduced' to the problem of the neural substrates of conscious vs. unconscious emotional processes, which he calls the 'easy problem' about emotion and consciousness. Only recently has it become more clear that neat distinctions (and particularly 'oppositions') between emotion and cognition are deeply problematic, and some isolated proposals have advanced the centrality of affect to consciousness (Damasio, 1994; Schore, 1994). Our work presented does not address the 'easy' problem of seeking neural substrates for conscious vs. unconscious emotion, which is well covered elsewhere (Pankseep, 1998; LeDoux, 1996). Our focus here has been to argue that affect-emotion is not simply one among many types of aspects of lived experience; they are *generative for consciousness itself*.

---

[21] We have greatly benefited from this text for our purposes here.

Time, Affect and the Fold

In conclusion, our goal all along in this text has been to combine regressive and progressive analyses of micro-temporality at the fold's transition. This analysis points to the conclusion that affect and emotion appear as the original ground for the constitution of temporality (and thus of consciousness altogether), through the key generative layers of valence and domains of concern.

The analysis presented so far has been explicitly limited to the micro-temporality of affect of an originary ego-self, situated in a basic disposition. As we stated at the outset, it follows the unfolding of affect from its source up to the fold, but not beyond. The diagram presented as Fig.1 summarizes the main ideas of this text.

The next level of analysis should concern how emotions arise from this base, as intentionally identifiable contents deployed in the space of basic dispositions. We shall continue this analysis in a future text under the heading of the 'rainbow' of emotions, their uniqueness and their interdependencies. The 'rainbow' concerns how the diverse and changing varieties of specific emotions are expressed in the basic framework deployed here. Finally, one of the themes touched only in passing here, is the relation between the affective and the reflexive axis of temporality. This demands a separate discussion to show why the *future* dimension of temporality is not symmetrical with the past. Examining the role of affect at the source of temporality is only a preamble.

References

Barbaras, R. (1999), *Le désir et la distance* (Paris: J. Vrin).

Casey, E. (1976), *Imagining* (Indiana: Indiana University Press).

Clark, A. (1997), *Being There: Putting the Body and the Mind Together Again* (Cambridge, MA: MIT Press).

Damasio, A. (1994), *Descartes' Error: Emotion, Reason, and the Human Brain* (New York: Avon Press).

Darwin, C. (1998), *The Expression of Emotions in Animals and Man*, Third edition with notes by P. Ekman (New York: Doubleday).

Derrida, J. (1991), *Le problème de la genèse dans la philosophie de Husserl*(Paris: PUF).

Fink, E. (1988), *Sixth Cartesianische Meditation* (Dordrecht: Kluwer).

Depraz, N. (1992), Les figures de l'intersubjectivité dans les Hua XIII-XV. *Archives de philosophie*, p. 55.

Depraz, N. (1994), Temporalité et affection dans les manuscrits tardifs sur la temporalité 1929–35 de Husserl. *Alter-Revue de Phénoménologie* N°2: pp. 63-87.

Depraz N. (1995), *Transcendance et incarnation. Le statut de l'intersubjectivité comme altérité à soi chez Husserl* (Paris: Vrin).

Depraz, N. (1998), 'Can I anticipate myself? Self-affection and temporality', in *Self-awareness, Temporality and Alterity: Central Topics in Phenomenology*, ed. D. Zahavi (Dordrecht: Kluwer).

Depraz, N. (1999), 'When transcendantal genesis encounters the Naturalisation Project', in *Naturalizing Phenomenology: Current Issues in Phenomenology and Cognitive Science*, ed. J. Petitot, F.J. Varela, B. Pachoud and J.-M. Roy (Stanford, CA: Stanford University Press).

Depraz, N., Varela, F.J. and Vermersch, P. (2003), *On Becoming Aware: A Pragmatics of Experiencing* (Amsterdam and Philadelphia, PA: John Benjamins Press).

Derryberry, D. & Tucker, D.M. (1992), 'Neural mechanisms of emotion', *J. Consulting Clinical. Psychology*, **60**, pp. 329–38.

de Waal, F. (1993), *Good Natured: The Origins of Morality in Primates* (Cambridge, MA: Harvard University Press).

Heidegger, M. (1927), *Sein und Zeit*; English Translation: *Being and Time*, trans. John Macquarrie and Edward Robinson (New York: Harper and Row, 1962).

Husserl, E. (1954), *Erfahrung und Urteil, Untersuchungen zur Genealogie der Logik* (Hamburg: Glaassen & Govert).

Husserl, E. (1966), *Analysen zur passiven Synthesis*, (*Hua* XI) (Dordrecht: Kluwer).

Husserl, E. (1995), L'animal. *Alter*, n°3.

Husserl, E. (1997), Ms. A VI 14a, trans. N. Depraz in *Alter* n°5: 167 sq.

Ihde, D. (1977), *Experimental Phenomenology* (New York: Putnam's Sons).

James, W. (1890), *The Principles of Psychology* (New York: Dover).

Jonas, H. (1966), *The Phenomenon of Life* (Chicago, IL: Chicago University Press).

Lee, Nam-In. (1993), *Phänomenologie der Instinkte* (Kluwer: Dordrecht).

Mazis, G. (1993), *Emotion and Embodiment: A Fragile Ontology* (New York: Peter Lang).

Merleau-Ponty, M. (1968), *The Visible and the Invisible*, trans. A. Lingis (Evanston, IL: Northwestern University Press).

Montavont, A. (1999), *De la passivité dans la phénoménologie de Husserl* (Paris: PUF).

LeDoux, J. (1996), *The Emotional Brain: The Mysterious Underpinnings of Emotional Life* (New York: Simon and Schuster).

Maturana, H. and Varela, F.J. (1989), *The Tree of Knowledge: The Biological Basis of Human Understanding* (Boston, MA: Shambhala).

Natsoulas, T. (1998), 'On the intrinsic nature of states of consciousness: James's ubiquitous feeling aspect', *Rev.Gen.Psychology*, **2**, pp. 123–52.

Panksepp, J. (1998), *Affective Neuroscience* (Oxford: Oxford University Press).

Ricœur P. (1990), *Soi-même comme un autre* (Paris: Seuil).

Searle, J. (1982), *Intentionality* (Cambridge: Cambridge University Press).

Schore, A. (1994), *Affect Regulation and the Self: The Neurobiology of Affective Development* (Oxford: Oxford University Press).

Sheets-Johnstone, M. (1999), *The Primacy of Movement* (Amsterdam: Benjamins).

Sheets-Johnstone, M. (2000), 'Emotions and movement: A beginning analysis empirical-phenomenological analysis of their relationship', *Journal of Consciousness.Studies*, **6** (11–12), pp. 259–77.

Steinbock, A.(1995), *Home and Beyond: Generative phenomenology after Husserl* (Evanston, IL: Northwestern University Press).

Stern, D. (1985), *The Interpersonal World of the Infant* (New York: Basic Books).

Stikkers K.W. (1997), 'Value as ontological difference', in *Phenomenology of Values and Valuing*, ed. J. Hart & L. Embree (Dordrecht: Kluwer).

Thelen, E. and Smith, L. (1994), *A Dynamic Systems Approach to the Development of Cognition in Action* (Cambridge, MA: MIT Press).

Varela, F.J. (1979), *Principles of Biological Autonomy* (New York: North-Holland).

Varela, F.J. (1991), 'Organism: A meshwork of selfless selves', in *Organism and the Origin of Self*, ed. Tauber (Dordrecht: Kluwer).

Varela, F.J. (1996), 'Neurophenomenology: A methodological remedy to the hard problem', *Journal of Consciousness Studies*, **3** (4), pp. 330-350

Varela, F.J. (1997a), 'The naturalization of phenomenology as the transcendence of nature: Searching for generative mutual constraints', *Alter - Revue de Phénoménologie* n°5.

Varela, FJ.. (1997b), 'Patterns of life: Intertwining identity and cognition', *Brain Cognition*, **34**, pp. 72–87.

Varela, F.J. (1999), 'The specious present: The neurophenomenology of time consciousness, in *Naturalizing Phenomenology: Current Issues in Phenomenology and Cognitive Science*, ed. J. Petitot, F.J. Varela, B. Pachoud and J.-M. Roy (Stanford, CA: Stanford University Press).

Varela, F.J. (2000), Pour une phénoménologie de la *sunyata*. I. In: N.Depraz and J.F.Marquet (Eds.), *Gnosis, Metaphysique, Phénoménologie* (Paris: Eds. du Cerf).

Varela, F.J and Shear, J. (1999), *The View from Within: First-person Methods in the Scientific Study of Consciousness* (Exeter: Imprint Academic).

Varela, F.J., Thompson, E. and Rosch, E. (1991), *The Embodied Mind* (Cambridge, MA: MIT Press).

Watt, D.F. (1998), 'Emotion and consciousness: Implications of affective neuroscience for Extended Reticular Thalamic Activating System theories of consciousness', in ASSC Electornic Forum on Consciousness, http://www.phil.vt.edu/ASSC/.

Yamaguchi, I. (1997), *Ki als leibhaftige Vernunft* (München: Fink Verlag).

Young, P. (1973), *Emotions in Man and Animal* (Huntington, NY: R.Krieger Publishing).

Louis C. Charland

The Heat of Emotion

Valence and the Demarcation Problem

Philosophical discussions regarding the status of emotion as a scientific domain usually get framed in terms of the question whether emotion is a natural kind. That approach to the issues is wrongheaded for two reasons. First, it has led to an intractable philosophical impasse that ultimately misconstrues the character of the relevant debate in emotion science. Second, and most important, it entirely ignores **valence**, *a central feature of emotion experience, and probably the most promising criterion for demarcating emotion from cognition and other related domains. An alternate philosophical hypothesis for addressing the issues is proposed. It is that emotion is a* **naturally occurring valenced phenomenon that is variously modifiable by psychological and cultural circumstances**. *This proposal should improve the chances for collaboration between philosophical and scientific researchers interested in emotion, something that has been notoriously absent from the present 'debate', which has mostly been a philosopher's game.*

A Philosopher's Game

In a pioneering article, Amelie Rorty famously declares that emotion is not a natural class (Rorty, 1978). She does not explicitly identify any defenders of that position, nor any specific formulation. Nevertheless, since she first pronounced her thesis, philosophers of emotion have continued to repeat it 'like a mantra' (de Sousa, 1999, p. 910). In light of this, to suggest that the thesis and the debate surrounding are wrongly posed is tantamount to heresy. Yet that precisely is the aim of the present discussion.

From the point of view of emotion science, the debate over the natural kind status of emotion has really been a philosopher's game. Emotion scientists have never accepted the philosophical terms of the debate. Unlike many other philosophical contributions to the study of emotion, the philosophical debate over the

Correspondence:
Louis C. Charland, Departments of Philosophy and Psychiatry & Faculty of Health Sciences, University of Western Ontario, London Ontario Canada N6A3K7. *Email: charland@uwo.ca*

Journal of Consciousness Studies, **12**, No. 8–10, 2005, pp. 82–102

natural kind status of emotion is never cited or discussed in the relevant scientific literature. The reason is not hard to guess. On the face of it, the theoretical status of emotion does not appear to have anything to do with gold, water, tigers, and species. These of course are the most famous philosophical examples of natural kinds. Given the obvious lack of fit between these philosophical posits and the scientific domain they are meant to help illuminate, it is not surprising that the philosophical debate over the natural kind status of emotion has been ignored by emotion scientists.

In contrast, the question of the natural kind status of emotion has received some attention in philosophical circles concerned with emotion. But even here interest has been negligible. In general, the mantra that emotion is not a natural kind is simply repeated, usually with little explanation, and invariably with no citations (Charland, 2002). There is curiously little practical worry about how the philosophy of emotion or emotion science are supposed to fare without the category 'emotion'.

In the final instance, the combined philosophical and scientific picture on the natural kind status of emotion is extremely paradoxical. While philosophers question the existence of emotion, scientists instead study it. Moreover, although philosophers deny that the emotions form a distinct and unified domain, they continue to 'lump them together' as if they do (de Sousa 1999, p. 910). It is worth noting that there have been some philosophical attempts to defend the natural kind status of emotion on combined philosophical and empirical grounds (Charland, 1995a; 2002; Prinz, 2004). However, these lone initiatives appear to have had little impact on the philosophical status quo. There have been no declared converts and philosophers continue to resist treating emotion as a distinct kind, natural or otherwise.

On the whole, the philosophical debate over the natural kind status of emotion appears to have reached an impasse. No doubt, some see this as the proof that emotion 'really' is not a natural kind (Griffiths, 2004; Rorty, 2004). However, that is not an accurate interpretation of what has transpired. To be sure, the majority of philosophers who discuss this question have ruled that emotion is not a natural kind. But if there is any victory here, it is a pyrrhic victory. This is because it is a 'victory' that has somehow — incredibly — managed to steer totally clear of the relevant issues in emotion science. This is unacceptable in the current interdisciplinary climate of the philosophy of emotion today (De Sousa, 2003). The truth is that the *philosophical* debate over the natural kind status of emotion is *scientifically* miscast and misguided. No wonder emotion scientists have ignored it. The time has come to take stock and find more productive *philosophical* avenues to address the relevant scientific issues. This search will lead us to one of the most important scientific concepts at the heart of emotion experience. This is *valence*.

The Demarcation Problem

The philosophical debate over the natural kind status of emotion may only be a philosopher's game. Nevertheless, it must be conceded that there is a genuine scientific issue at stake. This is the demarcation problem for emotion. The demarcation problem can be formulated as the question how to distinguish emotion from other fields of scientific inquiry. It has certainly occupied emotion scientists of many stripes. They tend to formulate it as the question how to distinguish emotion from cognition (Lazarus, 1984a,b; 1999; Leventhal, 1984; Leventhal & Scherer, 1987; LeDoux, 1989; Zajonc, 1984a,b; Panksepp, 1998; 2003).

The argument of this paper is that formulating the scientific demarcation problem in terms of philosophical natural kinds is wrongheaded. First, it has led to an intractable impasse that ultimately misconstrues the character of the relevant debate in emotion science. Second, and most important, it almost entirely ignores the question of valence, which is probably the most important criterion for demarcating emotion from cognition and other related domains. The purpose of this discussion is to propose an alternative formulation to the traditional philosophical natural kinds approach to the demarcation problem. A new philosophical formulation based on a scientific hypothesis derived from the concept of *valence* will be suggested. For now, valence will simply be defined as the positive or negative 'charge' that is said to accompany emotions and their associated feelings. At its core, valence is an evaluative notion. It is the central normative feature in emotion. Valence is what gives emotion and its associated feelings *personal meaning* (Lazarus, 1991). It is the capacity that permits emoting organisms to care about and respond meaningfully to the world around them with *concern* (Frijda, 1986). In a powerful metaphor we will explore shortly, valence is the moving force, the *heat* of emotion.

Because of its prominence and pivotal role in emotion science, valence will be the central feature in our new strategy for addressing the demarcation problem. Philosophically, the new strategy can be formulated in terms of the following hypothesis:

> EMOTION *is a naturally occurring valenced phenomenon that is variously modifiable by psychological and cultural circumstances.*

This new hypothesis has several important qualities. First, philosophically it agrees with the old one in treating EMOTION as a *natural* kind; that is, as a naturally occurring phenomenon. But at the same time it significantly departs from it by introducing valence, and thus the idea that EMOTION is also inextricably a *normative* kind. Secondly, because of the caveat that EMOTION is '*modifiable by psychological and cultural circumstances*' our new hypothesis is more open-ended than its predecessor. The old hypothesis tends to treat natural kinds as if they are fixed and determinate entities, sometimes even with metaphysically given essences. Not so for the new hypothesis, which provides for the fact that EMOTION evolves and develops. Now this may sound like the idea that emotions are evolutionary homologies, which is the last and most promising version of the traditional philosophical natural kinds hypothesis for emotion (Charland, 2002; Elster, 1999; Griffiths, 1997). However, it should soon become evident that our new hypothesis is not restricted in this way, or to these terms. Lastly, and this will also be explained later, the use of upper-case letters in 'EMOTION" is meant to indicate that what is in question is a theoretically regimented scientific concept of a vernacular category term, not an everyday vernacular term (see e.g., Panksepp, 1998, p. 51).

In general, many modern emotion scientists consider valence 'an obvious and central feature of emotion' (Lambie & Marcel, 2002, p. 434). This makes the general lack of philosophical attention to the topic puzzling. Admittedly, the concept is sometimes employed by some philosophers of emotion (Ben-Ze'ev, 2000; Gordon, 1987). Others do not mention it at all (Goldie, 2000; Griffiths, 1997). More recently, there have been philosophical efforts to examine the concept more thoroughly (Charland, 2005; Colombetti, 2005, this volume; Prinz, 2004, pp. 162–79). However, on the whole, valence as such has been notoriously absent from contemporary philosophical discussions of the emotions, while it remains central to emotion science.

One notable exception to this rule is a devastating philosophical critique of the concept of valence that comes very close to urging us to abandon the concept entirely (Solomon, 2003a; Solomon & Stone, 2002). That critique is largely sound, but fortunately it does not spell the end of valence. Part of the reason is that it simply overlooks the *scientific* applications of the concept discussed here. It also deals primarily with the valence of emotions, which can be called *emotion valence*. But it fails to discuss the valence of feelings or affects, which will be called *affect valence*. In what follows, these two senses of valence will be distinguished. In some cases, the general term 'valence' will be used to cover general features of both, normally the general fact that each involves a normative component of evaluation.

It must be warned that the aim of this discussion is not to propose a final knock-down philosophical answer to the demarcation problem. Quite the contrary. According to our new strategy, the demarcation problem is ultimately a matter for science to settle. The primary aim of the discussion is instead to show that the traditional philosophical formulation of the demarcation problem, which is framed in terms of natural kinds, can be replaced by a new and more productive scientific approach, which is based on valence. This will require linking and assembling diverse strands of evidence regarding the nature and role of valence in emotion science. That will not be easy, since the concept of valence is both varied and variegated and its exact nature is still a matter of controversy.

It is noteworthy that philosophers typically discuss the demarcation problem as if all the relevant scientific facts are in. On that basis, some deny emotion is a natural kind (Griffiths, 1997, p. 14). Others insist instead that emotion is a natural kind (Prinz, 2004, p. 102). It is as if the theoretical status of emotion can be decided now, once and for all. A more modest strategy is to argue that the natural kind status of emotion is an empirical issue that cannot be conclusively settled in the present state of emotion science, but for which there is considerable favourable evidence (Charland, 2002). The time has come to take an even bolder step and hand the demarcation problem squarely back to science, where it belongs.

Varieties of Valence

Valence is a protean and multifaceted concept in emotion science and before we go any further it is important to distinguish two major uses of the concept. These represent, respectively, two different kinds of valence, which will be called *affect valence* and *emotion valence* (Charland, 2005).

The distinction between affect valence and emotion valence lies in the fact that affect valence is a property of individual conscious emotional feelings (often referred to as 'affect'), while emotion valence is a property of individual whole emotions. Individual emotional feelings, or 'affects', are often said to be valenced (Larsen & Deiner, 1992; Feldman *et al.*, 1999; Russell, 2003; Watson & Tellegen, 1985). This is affect valence. What is 'positive' or 'negative' in this case are individual feelings or affects. Affect valence is illustrated by the claim that feelings of joy, for example, are 'positive'; that joy is a 'positive' affect. Valence is also often considered to be an attribute of emotions (Ben Ze'ev, 2000; Gordon, 1987; Lazarus, 1991; Prinz, 2004). This is emotion valence. What is valenced in this case are individual emotions. Emotion valence is illustrated by the claim that anger, for example, is a 'negative' emotion.

The distinction between affect valence and emotion valence does not capture all cases of valence (Colombetti, 2005, this volume). Nor is it always easy to apply. For example, there are mixed cases where theories involve elements of both (Panksepp, 2001, 156, Table 2).[1] There are also attempts to define valence as an objective quality of stimuli in the world (Moors, 2001). This might be called *stimulus valence*. Nevertheless, despite these exceptions and troublesome cases, the distinction between emotion valence and affect valence is often helpful and heuristically it does mark out two important uses of the concept. These are: (1) cases where valence is primarily a property of particular feelings or subjective affects; and (2), cases where valence is primarily a property of whole emotions. To these we can maybe add (3) cases where valence is attributed to external stimuli, but in this case the notion of valence turns out to be parasitic on other, more fundamental, uses of the concept, like (1) and (2) above.

The central feature of valence in all these senses is normally theoretically expressed by the allusion to 'positive' or 'negative' charges or forces. These metaphors from chemistry and physics reflect the element of normativity that inheres in valence. More specifically, they illustrate the fact that valence is fundamentally an evaluative notion. In many scientific circles, these philosophical aspects of valence are forgotten or ignored, leaving the impression that valence

---

[1] Prinz (2004) appears to endorse a mixed theory of valence. According to him, it is individual whole emotions that are valenced (a case of emotion valence). But on his view emotions just are valenced bodily feelings (a case of affect valence). His theory is therefore ambiguous with respect to the distinction between affect valence and emotion valence drawn here.

is a straightforward explanatory concept like any other. But it is not, and these philosophical desiderata have profound implications for the sort of phenomenon valence ultimately is, which is something normative.[2]

Three Historical Vignettes

In their incisive critique of the concept of valence, Robert Solomon and Lori Stone argue that the origins of valence lie in ethics (Solomon & Stone, 2002). However, as noted previously, their analysis is restricted to *emotion valence* and they leave the modern scientific concept of *affect valence* mostly untouched, including its history. That history is in fact very different from the one they tell for emotion valence. It has more to do with science than ethics, particularly the history of physiology. A few brief historical remarks on the historical origins of affect valence are in order before we introduce its modern counterparts.

The classical origins of affect valence have yet to be systematically explored. But metaphors are revealing. Metaphorically, affect valence is the *heat* of emotion. It is the reason why emotions and their associated feelings *move* us. Indeed, in its normative character, affect valence can be compared to a kind of *force*. As such, the modern notion of affect valence is reminiscent of the 'vital heat' of the soul referred to by Aristotle and Galen. Significantly, the source of vital heat was usually traced to the heart, which for many classical authors was also considered to be the seat of the passions (Hall, 1975, p. 110). The anecdote that emotions are matters of the heart may therefore at one time have been more than simply a metaphor. It was a truth of physiology. Even today the heart remains a powerful image of the seat of emotion. At the end of his defence of the Jamesian hypothesis that emotions are indeed perceptions of bodily feelings, philosopher Jesse Prinz concludes with the claim that 'the heart pounds with significance' (Prinz, 2004, p. 245).

Another classical ancestor of the modern idea of valence is the notion of 'irritability'. That notion is associated with the work of Plato and Galen, and later Glisson, Haller and Von Helmont (Hall, 1975, pp. 141–63, 396–408; Pagel, 1967; Temkin, 1964). Irritability was thought to be a peculiar reactive power inherent in some human and animal tissue that permitted it to react to noxious stimuli. The concept went through many reiterations and was pivotal in the famous debate between vitalists and mechanists (see e.g., Whytt, 1751). The reactive capacities associated with the modern concept of valence bear much resemblance to this classical prototype. For example, in an important sense, affect valence consists in the ability of living organisms to react meaningfully to stimuli; notably, to avoid 'negative' stimuli and approach 'positive' ones. This is one of the dominant ideas associated with irritability throughout its history. It is

---

[2] Scientific research on affect valence suggests that in some respects valence exhibits systematic regularities, such as the so-called circumplex structure described by Russell (Russell, 1980). However, valence is also often strangely indeterminate in a way that seems to defy scientific explanation and philosophical understanding (Charland, 2005). In that respect, the exact character of affect valence may represent a 'mystery' rather than a 'hard problem'. It also makes the qualia in emotion very different from their standard philosophical sensory counterparts.

also a central feature of many modern accounts of affect valence, where it is
reflected in the idea that organisms are capable of meaningful 'positive' and
'negative' feelings, actions, and reactions. These are usually called 'meaningful'
because they are designed or intended to preserve the well-being of the organism
in some way.

Perhaps one of the most significant example of valence in the history of emotion is a famous thought experiment by William James. Again, affect valence
appears to be the central notion involved, even though it is not mentioned. James
asks us to imagine an emotion without its associated bodily feelings and rever-
berations. He writes:

> Can one fancy the state of rage and picture no ebullition in the chest, no flushing of
> the face, no dilation of the nostrils, no clenching of the teeth, no impulse to vigorous
> action, but in their stead limp muscles, calm breathing, and a placid face? The pres-
> ent writer, for one, certainly cannot (James, 1890, p. 452).

James then goes on to explain:

> The rage is completely evaporated as the sensation of its so-called manifestations,
> and the only thing that can possibly be supposed to take its place is some
> cold-blooded and dispassionate judicial sentence, confined entirely to the intellec-
> tual realm, to the effect that a certain person or persons merit chastisement for their
> sins (*Ibid.*).

The point of this thought experiment is to establish the conclusion that 'a purely
disembodied human emotion is a nonentity' (*Ibid.*). Stripped of its bodily dimension, an emotion like rage becomes a 'feelingless cognition'. All that is left after
we subtract bodily feeling from the emotion is cold intellectual judgment. 'Every
passion', James says, 'tells the same story' (*Ibid.*). In an important qualification,
James notes that the idea of a disembodied emotion is not a 'contradiction in the
nature of things' (*Ibid.*). His point, instead, is that 'for *us*, emotion dissociated
from all bodily feeling is inconceivable' (*Ibid.*). In other words, the idea that
emotions have a bodily feeling dimension is part of what we *mean* by 'emotion'.
It is a basic pre-theoretical datum that any viable theory of emotion we can
conceive of must accept. This is where valence comes in, particularly, affect
valence.

Now, as noted above, it is true that James never mentions the concept of
valence as such. He does mention something that comes rather close, namely, the
role of pleasure and displeasure in emotion (James, 1890, pp. 451, 468). However, he does not say that valence in this hedonic sense is necessary for emotion.
On the other hand, James clearly believes that it is the bodily feelings in emotions that *move* us. He also believes that, taken together, the various bodily feelings that accompany emotions *mean* something; they have significance and
reflect the ongoing concerns and interests of the organism that has them. So these
are not *mere* feelings (Prinz, 2004, p. 242). They are not blind irrational urges but
exhibit some intentionality and are designed to help the organism function in
relation to changing circumstances in the environment. All of this looks very
much like the idea that the bodily feelings that accompany emotions have a

distinct 'charge' or 'force' on account of which those emotions move us in the particular normative direction they do. In the words of Jesse Prinz, the bodily feelings in James' theory must be *valent* (Prinz, 2004, p. 190). Without valence and its accompanying 'charge' or 'force', we are not moved. As Prinz notes, 'emotions are motivating' (p. 128). They 'impel us to act' (p. 128). Without valence, there is no motivation to act, and no emotion. There is only intellectual judgment.

James must rely on something like this valenced conception of bodily feeling if he is to distinguish what is intellectual from what is affective in emotion. Only in this way can he explain why, and how, cognition and emotion are 'parted' as he says they are (James, 1890, p. 472). When suitably amended, the essence of his proposal is that the bodily feelings in emotion are valenced. This is a good example of how *affect valence* functions as a core ingredient in our overall conception of emotion. In the next section we explore this insight and its various manifestations in contemporary emotion science.

Valence in Emotion Science.

In modern emotion science, valence is largely responsible for the element of *personal meaning* and *concern* in emotion (Frijda, 1986; Lazarus, 1991). It is both an index and a source of *fundamental values* for the emoting organism (Damasio, 2003; Panksepp, 1998). Valence is reflected in the fact that we personally *care* about things and events in the world. Philosophically, valence is reflected in the evaluative element in emotion, which according to some philosophers is its main defining feature (Solomon, 1976; Lyons, 1980). In emotion science, that evaluative element is often referred to as *appraisal* (Arnold, 1960; Frijda, 1993; Lazarus, 1991; Scherer, 1999).

What all of these cases have in common is a core pre-theoretical sense of valence, primarily affect valence. This is the *experience* of being moved and oriented toward or away from things because of what they personally *mean* to us. Valence in this sense is inextricably *normative*. That is because it involves evaluation. It also *relational* since it is only exists in the context of the ecological encounter between an organism and its environment (de Sousa, 1987; Lazarus, 1991). Finally, as characterized, valence is *intentional*. This is because the evaluative element in valence only exists *for* an organism in relation *to* its environment. Thus the ascription of valence to the affective states of an organism requires taking the intentional stance; it requires seeing it as a creature with intentional states and goals (Dennett, 1981). All of this is inherent in the idea of what it means to *e-valuate*.

Scientific discussions devoted to the demarcation problem appear to be inspired by the pre-theoretical fact that there is something special about the normative character of emotion experience. The unifying insight revolves around the fact that emotions and their associated feelings are evaluative. That insight is best captured by saying that individual emotions involve distinct evaluative orientations to the world; each opens a particular normative window on the world.

The same can be said for emotional feelings. They point and draw our attention to or away from features in the world — although there are certainly more nuanced ways to be normatively oriented to the world than strict bivalent approach and avoidance. These pre-theoretical facts are what the various theoretical formulations of the concept of valence are meant to capture. They point to affect valence, especially, as the core notion behind valence. So the general idea behind affect valence is that, through their associated feelings, emotional states involve a special normative orientation to the world. This pre-theoretical insight is often theoretically explicated in terms of the chemical metaphor where valence is stipulated to be 'positive' or 'negative'. Consider, for example, emotional feelings. They can look inwardly to the body or outwardly to the world (Buck, 1999; Damasio, 1994; Lambie & Marcel, 2002). In other words, emotional feelings have both *interoceptive* and *exteroceptive* functions (Charland, 1995b). In both cases, the individual feelings in question can be classified as 'positive' or 'negative'. Thus you can feel 'positive' about the weather outside (exteroceptive affect) and you can feel 'negative' about your stomach ache (interoceptive affect). Of course, as we have seen, whole emotions can also be classified in terms of their 'positive' or 'negative' character. This is emotion valence. Each individual emotion in the 'positive' class is positive, and each in the 'negative' class is negative.

This general conception of valence and its metaphorical allusion to bipolar electrical 'charges' is probably the most popular one in emotion theory. There are many variations. Depending on the theory in question, the 'charge' is attributed to an emotion as a whole or to one or more of its components, which may include feelings, appraisals, or behaviours (Colombetti, 2005, this volume). But note that speaking in 'positive' and 'negative' terms like this is only *one* way to capture the pre-theoretical intuition that there is something special about the normative character of emotion: this is the special normative experience that affect valence gives emotional feelings. There are admittedly fascinating and highly technical disputes about the exact character of the alleged bipolar character of affect valence in emotion science (Russell, 1999). How to interpret the alleged bipolar character of individual emotions is also a matter of great contention (Solomon, 2003a). But these should not obscure the fact that there is widespread agreement that affect valence and emotion valence are generally considered central to emotion.

Hedonicity is probably the most popular interpretive concept for understanding the 'positive' and 'negative' character of valence. Indeed, affect valence in particular is commonly identified with hedonicity (Feldman-Barrett, 1998; Frijda, 1986; Lambie & Marcel, 2002; Watson & Tellegen, 1985; Russell & Barrett, 1999; Russell & Carroll, 1999). However, since the hedonic aspect of valence is normally present in other component features of emotion, evaluation in emotion is seldom thought to be a simple matter of pleasure or displeasure. In addition, the notion of hedonicity admits of various interpretations. It is possible to identify the positive and negative charges in emotion with pleasure and displeasure and 'good' and 'bad', respectively. This is a defining premise of hedonic psychology (Kahneman, 1999). Nonetheless, what is envisaged under the rubric of valence is seldom viewed as a simple hedonic calculus, even in hedonic theory. Still, in general, hedonicity remains the most prevalent candidate for interpreting the valenced character of emotion and emotional affect.[3] The reason for this is that it is apparently the best and only available workable concept to capture the pre-theoretical insight that emotions and their associated feelings have personal meaning. Some may want to restrict hedonicity to simple pleasure, which undoubtedly oversimplifies the special and distinct normative character of our emotional lives. But often the notion of pleasure is deployed in a careful and sophisticated manner that provides at least *one* interesting scientific insight into the mysteries of emotional meaning.

One major difficulty with the general concept of valence is that it is often implicitly present in theories even though it is not explicitly mentioned. For example, some philosophical evaluative theories of emotional judgment never mention the concept (Solomon, 1976; Lyons, 1980). However, the *pre-theoretical experience of valence* is arguably precisely what the concept of evaluation in these theories is meant to capture. The same is true of the concept of appraisal in emotion science. Even though valence in its strict sense is not mentioned, there is an underlying *pre-theoretical* element of valence that is present nonetheless. The same phenomenon is also evident in philosophical approaches that emphasize the fact that information processing in emotion has a special *affective* character (Charland, 1997). That view builds on the idea that representation in emotion is *affective representation* (Panksepp, 1982; Damasio, 1994). Again, valence in the strict sense is not mentioned. However, normativity of the relevant sort is present.

Evidently, the concept of valence is ubiquitous in large segments of emotion science and the philosophy of emotion. When it is not present as a 'positive' or 'negative' bipolar charge in the strict sense, it is nonetheless present in a more general normative pre-theoretical sense; namely, as a distinct normative orientation to the world. Note that in some theories valence is not a feature of conscious emotion experience, although it is still considered a defining attribute of emotion. Thus, in neuroscience valence is sometimes defined behaviourally, in terms of approach and avoidance, or some similar pair (Cacioppo & Bernsten, 1999; Gray, 1994; Davidson, 1992; Rolls, 1999). This sense of valence should probably be considered parasitic on the paradigmatic experiential pre-theoretical sense introduced above. The reason is that in philosophical terms the concept of valence is inextricably intentional. In other words, emotions and their associated

---

[3] Prinz (2004) claims that 'hedonic tone is equivalent to valence' (Prinz, 2004, p. 161). I prefer to say that it can productively be identified with valence, but also want to acknowledge the existence of alternative proposals where, for instance, hedonic tone and valence are sometimes distinguished for special purposes (Lambie & Marcel, 2002, p. 229). Prinz also argues that the positive and negative markers that define valence 'need not be conscious' and that 'valence markers lack intrinsic feels'. Thus, according to him, 'valence has no intrinsic phenomenology' (Prinz, 2004, pp. 176,177). In part, this means that, 'there is no feeling of unpleasantness; there are just unpleasant feelings (p. 178). These claims do not appear to be compatible with the present account, although the matter certainly deserves further study.

feelings are *about* the world, whether this be the inner world of interoception or the outer world of exteroception. Now it is impossible to non-arbitrarily describe behaviour as meaning 'approach' or 'avoidance' without importing some notion of intentionality to interpret these terms. Such descriptions require taking an intentional stance (Dennett, 1981). That is why so-called unconscious or even non-conscious valence must be parasitic on conscious valence.

We have been examining the concept of valence in emotion science. Now what about the place of valence in modern philosophy of emotion? Emotion valence, we have seen, is prevalent in some sectors of the philosophy of emotion, where the various emotions are classified as 'positive' or 'negative'. The case of affect valence is quite different. As previously noted, the concept is seldom encountered in the philosophy of emotion. This may be one reason why philosophers have not considered it in their efforts to tackle the demarcation problem. Certainly, valence as such is not mentioned in the philosophical debate over the natural kind status of emotion. The concept simply does not fall within the philosophical terms of that debate. Perhaps the reason for this is that the determination of natural kinds is seen as a purely 'scientific' matter by philosophers. The project is to 'describe' the nature of emotion, just like we scientifically describe the nature of other natural kinds, like gold or water. As we just saw, some philosophers have recently turned to biology in their efforts to explore the natural kind status of emotion (Elster, 1999; Griffiths, 1997). So perhaps the nature of emotion can be described by analogy with biological species?

But the category emotion is not a biological category like species! Nor is it like any of the other older natural kind candidates philosophers have resorted to, like gold and water. The reason is that emotion is fundamentally a *normative* notion; if it is a kind, then it is a normative kind.[4]

The suggestion made above is that this normativity ultimately springs from the *conscious experience of emotional meaning* which lies at the origins of valence. Because of its intimate association with the notion of emotional meaning, there may be aspects of how valence figures in emotion experience that fall outside the bounds of scientific understanding strictly speaking. As mentioned earlier, valence is sometimes strangely indeterminate, often eluding fixed scientific categorization due to the fact that it changes as we attempt to subjectively name and report it (Charland, 2005). However, although they are philosophically perplexing, these mysteries need not concern us here, and they do not detract

---

[4] In a short but important discussion Griffiths (2003) suggests that individual emotions should probably also be considered *normative* kinds. The basic idea Griffiths defends is that normative kinds blend description and prescription and are open-ended in a way that natural kinds are not. The full details of Griffiths proposal on the normativity of emotions are interesting and original in their own right, but they need not detain us here. What is relevant for our purposes is instead the fact that his focus is exclusively on *emotions* and not *emotion*. From the perspective of the present discussion, there are two flaws with Griffiths' normative proposal. First, it fails to countenance the possibility that, as a class, emotions might form a distinct normative kind; namely, EMOTION. Second, there is absolutely no mention of the role of valence in emotion science. Yet this is the most obvious and plausible place to locate the normative character of emotional phenomena, as will be shown in subsequent sections.

from the legitimacy and importance of the attempt to unravel the more scientifically tractable aspects of valence.

Maybe then it is because valence is inherently a normative notion that it has been excluded from the philosophical debate over the natural kind status of emotion. It simply does not fall within the scope of what the philosophical determination of natural kinds is traditionally thought to encompass. Whether this speculation is true or not, the philosophy of emotion is in trouble. The reason is that valence is a central defining feature of emotion for many leading emotion scientists (Davidson, 1992; Feldman-Barrett, 1998; Frijda, 1986; Lazarus, 1991; Lambie & Marcel, 2002; Ortony & Clore, 1987; Panksepp, 1998; Russell, 2003). The centrality of valence in these theories makes it hard to imagine what could possibly count as emotion without the normative input of valence. In this age where the philosophy of emotion is so closely allied with emotion science, the omission of the concept of valence from so many discussions of the theoretical status of emotion is unacceptable. Fortunately, the situation is changing as some leading contemporary philosophers of emotion start to explore how valence might figure in emotion (Ben Ze'ev, 2000; Prinz, 2004). However, in general, the implications of valence for the status of emotion and demarcation problem have not yet been adequately explored by philosophers. Just what those implications are will become evident once we consider recent scientific work on the place of valence in emotion science. In this theoretical environment, valence is often employed in addressing the demarcation problem.

Demarcation and Valence

It is a striking feature of the debate over the natural kind status of emotion that, while philosophers continue to deny the scientific integrity of 'emotion', scientists are busy testing and developing theories of 'emotion'. Note that the issue is most assuredly not whether a genuine scientific domain corresponds to our *vernacular* English term, 'emotion' (see e.g.,. Griffiths, 1997, p. 229). Hardly anyone believes that ordinary language is scientifically or philosophically sacrosanct anymore. The argument that nothing really corresponds to the *vernacular* term 'emotion' is therefore a red herring. There is no need to pledge allegiance to folk psychology in emotion theory, either scientifically or philosophically, and virtually no one does (Charland, 2001). We should be especially wary of the requirement that scientific emotion concepts be directly translatable into ordinary vernacular terms from English (Prinz, 2004, p. 113). Instead, the question is whether a properly *regimented* scientific or philosophical theoretical notion that is loosely based on the vernacular term 'emotion' can be successfully elaborated and eventually hold its ground in the experimental 'tribunal of experience'.

In fact, many contemporary emotion scientists actually operate according to the hypothesis that EMOTION (a scientifically regimented term) denotes a natural kind that is only imprecisely captured by 'emotion' (the vernacular term). Let us briefly consider what they have to say. The exercise is important, since it also provides crucial circumstantial evidence for our thesis that affect valence is often considered to be the key to the demarcation problem in emotion science.

A good place to start is with Jaak Panksepp's research program in 'affective neuroscience' (Panksepp, 1998). Panksepp argues that what we loosely call 'cognition' and 'emotion' correspond to two relatively distinct systems of neurobiological organization. He refers to these as the 'somatic-cognitive nervous system', which he locates on the thalamic neocortical axis, and the 'visceral-emotional nervous system', which he locates on the hypothalamic-limbic axis (Panksepp, 1998, p. 62 Fig. 4.1). The former system corresponds to the 'stream of thought' while the latter corresponds to the 'stream of feeling' (p. 62). Clearly, for Panksepp emotion and cognition constitute two distinct systems. This is his position on the demarcation problem. Note that Panksepp's claim is that both cognition and emotion are distinct *systems*. Each represents a distinct theoretical kind of neural organization. To the extent that cognition can be called a natural kind according to this account, the same probably deserves to be said of emotion. This means that Panksepp's approach to the demarcation problem is flatly incompatible with the philosophical mantra that emotion is not a natural kind. Even if emotion is not a natural kind in any strict philosophical sense, the point is that it is nonetheless a distinct unified kind that deserves to be conceptualized and studied as a separate, partly autonomous, system. Of course, there will be slippage between our everyday understanding of the terms 'cognition' and 'emotion' and their regimented scientific analogues. With respect to that question, it is important to remind ourselves that although scientific inquiry may begin by using terms and intuitions borrowed from folk psychology, there is no need to honour those terms if the facts eventually speak otherwise.

Panksepp therefore believes that emotion and cognition are distinct systems (Panksepp, 1998, pp. 318-9). He treats this as a scientific hypothesis for which he provides considerable evidence. Another subsidiary hypothesis advanced by Panksepp directly addresses the relation between affect valence and the demarcation problem. It is that specialized internal subjective affective states are generated by the hypothalamic-limbic system. According to Panksepp, those subjective states, or 'feelings', reflect fundamental values of the organism. Their affective nature derives primarily from the fact that they are valenced. Many of those valenced states arise directly out of basic emotion systems that develop naturally in the mammalian brain. Thus Panksepp is also a believer in the hypothesis that there are basic emotions that evolve during the natural development of the brain. According to him, these 'basic emotional processes emerge from homologous brain mechanisms in all mammals' (Panksepp, 1998, p. 51). At present, Panksepp believes that there are probably seven such command systems: seeking, rage, fear, panic, play, lust, and care (Panksepp, 1998, 41–58; 2001, 156). All of these emotion systems and their associated internal subjective feelings are valenced, although precise determinations of valence will vary with circumstances (Panksepp, 2001, p. 156, Table 2).

Panksepp is not the only emotion scientist to believe that the brain produces special valenced subjective feeling states. The entire area represents a significant research project in emotion science (Maclean, 1990; Damasio, 2003). The relation of these proposals to the demarcation problem is that they posit the existence of a distinct and more or less unified affective system in the brain. Panksepp refers to this system using the terminology of 'affect'. His proposal for a new 'affective neuroscience' is a perfect example of a scientific proposal that explicitly tackles the demarcation problem through the intermediary of valence.

A similar approach to valence and the demarcation problem can be found in the pioneering work of neuroscientist Antonio Damasio (Damasio, 1994; 2003). However, in a fine example of the semantic perils and complexities of emotion theory, he uses the term 'emotion' rather than the term 'affect' to circumscribe the domain he is concerned with. It is important to appreciate that the difference in terminology between Panksepp and Damasio over 'affect' and 'emotion' is of little consequence — *at least in the present context*. Both are investigating the same general evaluative domain and exploring its neurobiological basis. In fact, both agree that there are primitive basic 'emotions' in mammalian phylogeny, although they differ on exactly which and how many. Like Panksepp, Damasio also allocates a central role to subjective feelings in emotional experience (Damasio, 1994). In his recent work, he explicitly links the distinct character of emotional feelings with valence (Damasio, 2003).

Here then are two major research projects in emotion science that approach the demarcation problem from the point of view of valence. The general hypothesis behind these projects is that there exists a unified, integrated, collection of brain systems whose major task is the evaluative assessment of events in the internal and external environment. These evaluative assessments ultimately issue in subjectively experienced valenced emotional feelings. For both Panksepp and Damasio, this emotive-affective evaluative system is also responsible for planning and executing responses based on initial evaluations. As a whole, the role of the evaluative system is to rank and order events based on what they mean for the survival of the organism. This it does by indexing events according their valence and then presenting that valenced information to consciousness in the form of valenced subjective feeling states or affects. In sum, both Panksepp and Damasio allocate an absolutely central role to affect valence in the overall organization of affectivity and emotion. And both distinguish affectivity and emotion from cognition.

Terminological Obstacles

The scientific developments outlined above can be described in several ways. One way to characterize the general hypothesis involved is to frame it using the term 'emotion', as Damasio does. Following this lead, the natural kind status of emotion might be described by the thesis that humans and some other organisms might be called 'emoters' (Charland, 2001). Or, one might frame the issues in terms of affectivity, as Panksepp does. In those terms, the hypothesis of the natural kind status of emotion can be described by the thesis that humans and some animals are 'affective systems' (Charland, 1996). Exegetically, the situation is complex, since 'emotion' and 'affect' are often contrasted in philosophy and emotion science. In addition, there are cases where one wants to say that emotion is one of several systems within affectivity in general. For example, Ben Ze'ev argues that moods and emotions are distinct elements of a more general affective system (Ben Ze'ev, 2000; see also Prinz 2004, pp. 179-198). Panksepp's proposal for an affective neuroscience is similar. In his psychobiological synthesis, the basic emotions form a subsystem of a more general affective system. Still, at least in the present context, understood very generally, 'emotion' and 'affect' point toward the same overall evaluative domain. This is the fact that some of the workings of the brain are devoted primarily to the evaluative assessment of events in the internal and external environment of the emoting organism. This ultimately is the explanatory rationale behind the concept of valence. In the end, scientifically, the demarcation problem is about the nature and exclusivity of the mechanisms and processes that underlie valence; particularly and primarily, affect valence.

In general, 'emotion' is currently the term that is favoured by most emotion scientists for the general domain of inquiry we are concerned with (Charland, 2001). However, semantic pressures that develop as a result of inquiry may change this. Indeed, there exist cases when it is imperative to distinguish sharply between affect and emotion. As an example, consider the different genealogical proposals about the origins of valence proposed by James Russell and Antonio Damasio. This additional example also nicely illustrates the conceptual limits of the old philosophical natural kinds hypothesis for emotion. There is simply no way to accommodate the relevant scientific issues within that framework.

Genealogy of Valence

Psychologist James Russell argues that valence lies at the heart of a primitive experiential and scientific notion he calls 'core affect' (Russell, 2003). According to him, core affect is elaborated and incorporated into psychological constructs he calls 'emotions'. In this model, valence is above all an attribute of core affect, by which Russell means consciously experienced subjective feelings. On this model, affect comes first and emotion comes second. For Russell, then, there is a class of organisms capable of core affect. Among those organisms some go on to develop emotions. This looks very much like a natural kind hypothesis, since it asserts that there exists a distinct naturally occurring class of organism born with the capacity to experience valenced affect. In other words, 'organism capable of valenced affect' appears to be a natural kind for Russell. Now it is not easy to reformulate this hypothesis using the traditional philosophical notion of a natural kind. What then are we to do? The solution offered here is simply to abandon the traditional philosophical language of natural kinds and stick to the scientific formulations themselves.

A quite different model of the genealogy of valence is proposed by Antonio Damasio. According to him, something like the reverse of Russell's account is true. For Damasio, valence is first and above all an attribute of emotion.

According to his model, the felt valenced character of affect is a product of the subjective experience of emotion (Damasio, 2003). The two proposals are radically different. For Russell, valence is initially, and therefore primarily, an attribute of affect. For Damasio, valence is initially, and therefore primarily, an attribute of emotion. Another important difference between the two theories is that in Russell's theory there are no basic emotions and all emotions are psychological constructs, However, in Damasio's theory there are some basic emotions and not all emotions are psychological constructs. Note that both Russell and Damasio agree that the explanatory domain they are concerned with is quite distinct from cognition, or vision, or attention. Although they do not explicitly say so, what makes it distinct is the special evaluative character of valence, a shared central feature of both accounts. Yet, at the same time, these two researchers obviously disagree about the nature and origins of valence in the 'affective' or 'emotional' domain overall.

What is interesting about this example is how it fits easily into the framework for the demarcation problem suggested by valence. On the other hand, it is hard to see how to accommodate it within the natural kinds framework of philosophers. Taken together, the examples we have considered in this section suggest that it is time to abandon the philosophical natural kinds approach as a means for addressing the demarcation problem in emotion science. It grossly distorts the real character of the issues as they arise in emotion science. What the descriptive natural kinds approach omits is the central defining role of valence in affect and emotion, which is normative.

The philosophical natural kinds approach thus fails to capture what is essential to affect and emotion, namely, valence. In doing so, it makes productive collaboration between emotion science and the philosophy of emotion in this domain virtually impossible. Taken as a whole, the circumstantial evidence presented here should demonstrate two things. First, it shows that valence, especially affect valence, is a central concept in emotion science. Second, it shows that valence has no real connection to philosophical natural kinds. It is misguided philosophical imperialism to try and force the scientific issues surrounding the demarcation problem into the philosophical straightjacket of natural kinds. The philosophical pegs simply do not fit the scientific holes.

A New Philosophical Hypothesis

The accumulated exegetical evidence provided in this discussion suggests that valence is a promising concept for posing scientific questions about the demarcation of emotion. Affect valence, in particular, seems to be an ideal candidate at present. At the same time, it is hard to escape the conclusion that the philosophical debate over the natural kind status of emotion has really little to do with the demarcation problem as it arises in emotion science. This is simply not the right way to formulate the issues. An approach based on valence promises better collaboration between philosophers and scientists working in the area.

A more scientifically based approach to the demarcation problem that employs valence also offers the possibility for a new philosophical approach to demarcation as well. It suggests a new philosophical hypothesis for addressing the demarcation problem. Probably the best way to formulate that hypothesis presently is to use the term 'emotion', although other formulations in terms of affectivity also need to be explored. But recall that it is a theoretically regimented and constructed meaning and extension of the term 'emotion' that the hypothesis is meant to capture. To indicate this, we shall employ the appellation 'EMOTION' to state the hypothesis. It is important not to make too much of this term. It has been chosen here, because it is so popular in the scientific and philosophical literature under discussion. However, it is also important to appreciate that the English word 'emotion' is a relatively recent addition to Western science and philosophy (Rorty, 1982; Dixon, 2002). It is also worth keeping in mind that it has no exact equivalents in many existing natural languages (Russell, 1991; Wierzbicka, 1999). Nonetheless, it should do just fine for present purposes. There is certainly room to explore alternative formulations.

We may now state our new philosophical hypothesis:

> EMOTION is a *naturally occurring valenced phenomenon modifiable by psychological and cultural circumstances.*

The new hypothesis asserts that there exists a naturally occurring class of organisms with a capacity to develop affectively valenced states. These can be basic emotions or emotional feelings, depending on the particular theory in question. The hypothesis grants the key defining element of the original natural kinds hypothesis; namely, that there is a *natural* class of organisms capable of emotion. However, it also avoids the dangers of reductionism, which is a problem for the philosophical natural kinds approach. This is because the new hypothesis explicitly acknowledges the normative character of affectivity in EMOTION. It does this by mentioning valence. The overly descriptive scientific confines of philosophical natural kinds downplay and misconstrue the normative character of our vernacular concept of emotion and its theoretical counterpart, EMOTION. But both are normative phenomena, something the new hypothesis captures nicely but the old one does not.

The new hypothesis also includes the provision that the natural affective capacities of EMOTERS (creatures capable of EMOTION) are *modifiable by psychological and cultural circumstances*. Russell's account of the 'psychological construction' of emotion provides one way to explore this proviso. But culture also certainly plays a part in how EMOTION is shaped and manifested. It reaches deep, right into the very nature of how the nervous systems of EMOTERS is shaped and modified (Geertz, 1970a,b,c). However, at the same time, our new hypothesis is meant to avoid the rhetorical excesses of cultural relativism, since there is something naturally given in EMOTION (Geertz, 2000a,b). After all, not just any organism can evolve to become an EMOTER. As Prinz says, in the end, 'emotions depend on both nature and culture' (Prinz, 2004, p. 157). Both nature and nurture have a role to play, and the real challenge lies in sorting out the details (see e.g., Prinz, 2004, pp. 104-159). Ideological disputes aside, scientifically there is no incompatibility between nature and nurture in emotion. Our new philosophical hypothesis acknowledges this but remains open to let science settle the details.

Conclusion

Much of the argumentation in the preceding discussion has centred on establishing the case that there exists a pressing need for a new philosophical hypothesis to explore the demarcation problem as it arises in emotion science. The traditional natural kinds hypothesis with its old armchair concepts and methods will no longer do. Our new philosophical hypothesis is specially tailored to accommodate the large variety of ways in which the question of the status of emotion arises in emotion science. It appropriately focuses on valence, since it is so often in those terms that the question is framed.

Note that although our hypothesis may appear to be consistent with Prinz's proposal that 'all emotions are states of the same type', it is not tied to the same philosophical assumptions on which his theory rests (Prinz, 2004, p. 102). The philosophical natural kind terminology is not mentioned in our hypothesis, and no particular semantic theory or specific ontology is alluded to or endorsed. Prinz has proposed a very sophisticated philosophical theory of the valent character of emotions and their place in the wider affective domain – a philosopher's theory (Prinz, 2004, 160–79). He argues that 'emotions are a natural kind in a strong sense' because 'they share a common essence' (Prinz, 2004, 102). What all emotions share is the fact that they are 'embodied appraisals under the control of calibration files (*Ibid.*). Our new hypothesis is more modest. It treats the unity of emotion in more tentative terms. Prinz appears to assume that there is sufficient evidence to conclude that emotions are a natural kind in his sense at this stage of emotion science. But this seems premature and at the present time valence is scientifically compatible with other formulations of how to understand the distinct character and the 'unity' of emotion.

In sum, with rare exceptions like Prinz, modern philosophy of emotion continues to deny the unity and distinct theoretical status of emotion. But many developments in emotion science suggests otherwise. Recall the case of James, who insists that '*every* passion tells the *same* story' (James, 1890; emphasis added). Now ask yourself, 'Why?' James suggests that there may indeed be something common to all those things we call emotions. But he is wrong to focus on brute bodily feelings. Only a certain *kind* of bodily feeling can accomplish the theoretical task at hand and solve the demarcation problem. The hypothesis offered here is that valence is the missing ingredient.

It is interesting that all studied human languages appear to make a distinction between good and bad feelings (Wierzbicka, 1999). Perhaps this is because that distinction is naturally entrenched and reflected in the make-up of EMOTERS. Only science, now, can tell us whether or not this is so. This is the whole point of our new 'philosophical' hypothesis. It is no longer up to philosophy to determine the terms of this question. That intellectual game is over. But philosophy can hopefully contribute to its answer. That is a humbler role, but still a very interesting and important one, if the philosophy of emotion genuinely wants to collaborate with emotion science. It is time to put philosophical theories of emotion on hold and let science step up to the challenge.

References

Ben- Ze'ev, Aaron (2000), *The Subtlety of Emotions* (Cambridge, MA: MIT Press).

Buck, Ross (1999), 'The biological affects: a typology', *Psychological Review*, **106** (2), pp. 301–36.

Cacioppo, John. T. & Bernston, Gary G. (1999), 'The affect system: architecture and operating characteristics', *Current Directions in Psychological Science*, **8** (5), pp. 133–7.

Charland, Louis C. (2005), 'Indeterminacy of valence', in *Emotion and Consciousness*, ed. Lisa Feldman-Barrett, Paula Niedenthal & Piotr Winkielman (New York: Guilford Press).

Charland , Louis C. (2002), 'The natural kind status of emotion', *British Journal for the Philosophy of Science*, **53** (4), pp. 511–37.

Charland, Louis C. (2001), 'In defence of emotion', *Canadian Journal of Philosophy*, **31** (1), pp. 133–54.

Charland, Louis C. (1997), 'Reconciling cognitive and perceptual theories of emotion', *Philosophy of Science*, **64** (4), pp. 555–79.

Charland, Louis C. (1996), Review of 'Reason and Passion: Making Sense of Our Emotions', by Richard and Bernice Lazarus (Oxford: Oxford University Press, 1991), *Philosophical Psychology*, **9** (3), pp. 401–4.

Charland, Louis C. (1995a), 'Emotion as a natural kind: Towards a computational foundation for emotion theory, *Philosophical Psychology*, **8** (1), pp. 59–84.

Charland, Louis C. (1995b), 'Feeling and representing: computational theory and the modularity of affect', *Synthese*, **105**, pp. 273–301.

Colombetti, G. (2005), 'Appraising valence', *Journal of Consciousness Studies*, **12** (8–10), pp. 103–26.

Dalgleish, T. & M.J. Power (ed. 1999), *The Handbook of Cognition and Emotion* (Chichester and New York: John Wiley & Sons).

Damasio, Antonio (2003), *Looking for Spinoza: Joy, Sorrow, and the Human Brain* (New York: Harcourt).

Damasio, Antonio (1994), *Descartes' Error: Emotion, Reason, and the Human Brain* (New York: Putnam & Sons).

Davidson, Richard J. (1992), 'Emotion and affective style', *Psychological Science*, **3**, pp. 39–43.

Dennett, Daniel (1981), 'Intentional systems', in D. Dennett, *Brainstorms: Philosophical Essays on Mind and Psychology* (Cambridge, MA: A Bradford Book).

de Sousa, Ronald (2003), 'Emotion', *The Stanford Encyclopedia of Philosophy* (Spring 2003 Edition), Edward N. Zalta (ed.):
    URL = http://plato.stanford.edu/archives/spr2003/entries/emotion/>.

de Sousa, Ronald (1999), Review of 'What Emotions Really Are', by Paul E. Griffiths (Chicago: University of Chicago Press, 1997), *Dialogue*, **38** (4), pp. 908–11.

de Sousa, Ronald (1987), *The Rationality of Emotion* (Cambridge, MA: MIT Press).

Dixon, Thomas (2003), *From Passions to Emotions: The Creation of a Secular Psychological Category* (Cambridge: Cambridge University Press).

Ekman, Paul (1992), 'An argument for basic emotions', *Cognition and Emotion*, **6**, pp. 169–200.

Ekman, P. (1984), 'Expression and the nature of emotion', in *Approaches to Emotion*, ed. K. Scherer and P. Ekman (Hillsdale, NJ: Lawrence Erlbaum).

Ekman, Paul & Richard J. Davidson (ed. 1994), *The Nature of Emotion: Some Fundamental Question* (New York & Oxford: Oxford University Press).

Elster, Jon (1999), *Alchemies of Mind: Rationality and the Emotions* (Cambridge: Cambridge University Press).

Feldman-Barrett, Lisa, James A. Russell (1998), 'Independence and bipolarity in the structure of affect', *Journal of Personality and Social Psychology*, **17** (4), pp. 967–84.

Feldman-Barrett, Lisa, Niedenthal, Paula & Winkielman, Piotr (ed. 2005), *Emotions: Conscious and Unconscious* (New York: Guilford Press).

Frijda, Nico H. (1993), 'Appraisal and beyond: the issue of cognitive determinants of emotion', *Cognition and Emotion*, **7** (3 & 4: May/July), pp. 225–32.

Frijda, Nico (1986), *The Emotions* (Cambridge: Cambridge University Press).

Geertz, Clifford (2000), *Available Light: Anthropological Reflections on Philosophical Topics* (Princeton: Princeton University Press).

Geertz, Clifford (2000a), 'Anti anti-relativism', in Clifford Geertz, *Available Light* (Princeton: Princeton University Books).

Geertz, Clifford (2000b), 'Culture, mind, brain/ brain, mind, culture', in Clifford Geertz, *Available Light* (Princeton: Princeton University Books).

Geertz, Clifford (1970), *The Interpretation of Cultures* (New York: Basic Books).

Geertz, Clifford (1970a), 'Thick description: towards an interpretive theory of culture', in Geertz (1970).

Geertz, Clifford (1970b), 'The impact of the concept of culture on the concept of man', in Geertz (1970).

Geertz, Clifford. (1970c). 'The growth of culture and the evolution of mind', in Geertz (1970).

Gordon, Robert M. (1987), *The Structure of the Emotions* (Cambridge: Cambridge University Press).

Griffiths. Paul (1997), *What Emotions Really Are* (Chicago: University of Chicago Press).

Griffiths, Paul (2003), 'Emotion as natural and normative kinds', *Proceedings of the Philosophy of Science Association* (PSA: PSA).

Griffiths, Paul (2004), 'Is emotion a natural Kind?', in Solomon (2004).

Gray, Jeffrey, A. (1994), 'Three fundamental emotion systems', in Ekman & Davidson (1994).

Hacking, Ian (1995), *Rewriting the Soul* (Cambridge: MA: Harvard University Press).

Hall, Thomas S. (1975), *History of General Physiology* (Chicago: University of Chicago Press).

James, William (1890), *Principles of Psychology* (New York: Dover).

Johnson-Laird, Philip, N., Oatley Keith (1992), 'Basic emotions, rationality, and folk theory', *Cognition and Emotion*, **6** (3–4), pp. 201-223.

Kahneman, Daniel (1999), 'Objective happiness', in Kahneman *et al.* (1999).

Kahneman, Daniel, Diener, Ed, & Norbert Schwartz (ed. 1999), *Well-Being: The Foundations of Hedonic Psychology* (New York: Russell Sage Foundation).

Lambie, John A. & Marcel, Anthony A. (2002), 'Consciousness and the varieties of emotion experience: a theoretical framework', *Psychological Review*, **109** (2), pp. 219–59.

Larsen R.J. & and Diener E. (1992), 'Problems with the circumplex model of emotion', *Review of Personality and Social Psychology*, **13**, 25–59.

Lazarus, Richard (1999), 'The cognition-emotion debate: a bit of history', in Dalgleish and Power (1999).

Lazarus, Richard (1991), *Emotion and Adaptation* (Oxford: Oxford University Press).

Lazarus, Richard (1984a), 'Thoughts on the relation between emotion and cognition'. In Scherer & Ekman. (Eds.) *Approaches to Emotion*. (Hillsdale, NJ: Erlbaum, 1984), 247-59.

Lazarus, Richard (1984b), 'Cognition, motivation, and emotion: The doctoring of humpty dumpty', in Scherer & Ekman (1984).

LeDoux, Joseph (1996), *The Emotional Brain* (New York: Simon & Shuster).

Leventhal, Howard (1984), 'A perceptual motor theory of emotion', in Scherer & Ekman (1984).

Leventhal, H. & Scherer, K.R. (1987), 'The relationship of emotion and cognition : A functional approach to a semantic controversy', *Cognition and Emotion*, **1**, pp. 3–28.

Lyons, William (1980), *Emotion* (Cambridge: Cambridge University Press).

Maclean, Paul, (1990), *The Triune Brain in Evolution: Role in Paleocerebral Functions* (New York: Plenum).

Moors, Agnes, Houver, Jan de (2001), 'Automatic appraisal of motivational valence: motivational affective priming and simon effects', *Cognition and Emotion*, **15** (6), pp. 749–66.

Neu, Jerome (2000), *A Tear is an Intellectual Thing* (Oxford: Oxford University Press).

Ortony, Anthony, Clore, A.C. & Colins A. (1988), *The Cognitive Structure of Emotions* (New York: Cambridge University Press).

Ortony, A., & Turner T.J. (1990), 'What's basic about basic emotions?', *Psychological Review*, **97**, pp. 313–31.

Pagel, Walter (1967), 'Harvey and Glisson on irritability with a note on Van Helmont', *Bulletin of the History of Medicine*, **41**, pp. 497–514.

Panksepp, Jaak (1998), *Affective Neuroscience* (Oxford: Oxford University Press).

Panksepp, Jaak (2001), 'The Neuro-evolutionary cusp between emotions and cognitions', *Evolution and Emotion*, **7** (2), pp. 141–63.

Panksepp, Jaak (1982), 'Toward a general psychobiological theory of emotions', *Behavioral and Brain Sciences*, **5**, pp. 407–68.

Papez, J.W. (1937), 'A proposed mechanism for emotion', *Archives of Neurology and Psychiatry*, **38**, pp. 725–44.

Prinz, Jesse (2004), *Gut Reactions: A Perceptual Theory of Emotion* (Oxford : Oxford University Press).

Rolls (1999), *The Brain and Emotion* (Oxford University Press).

Rorty, Amelie (1978), 'Explaining emotions', *Journal of Philosophy*, **75** pp. 139–61.

Rorty, Amelie (1982), 'From passions and emotions to sentiments', *Philosophy*, **57**, pp. 159–72.

Rorty, Amelie (2004), 'Enough already with "Theories of Emotion"', in Solomon (2004).

Russell, James A. (1980), 'A circumplex model of affect', *Journal of Personality and Social Psychology*, **39**, pp. 1161–78.

Russell, James A. & Carroll, J.M. (1999), 'On the bipolarity of positive and negative affect', *Psychological Bulletin*, **125** (1), pp. 3–30.

Russell, James A. (1991b), 'Culture and the categorization of emotion', *Psychological Bulletin*, **110**, pp. 426–50.

Russell, James A. (2003), 'Core affect and the psychological construction of emotion', *Psychological Review*, **110** (1), pp. 145–72.

Russell , J.A., Feldman Barrett, L. (1999), 'Core affect, prototypical emotional episodes, and other things called emotion: dissecting the elephant', *Journal of Personality and Social Psychology*, **76**, pp. 805–19.

Scherer, Klaus (1999), 'Appraisal theory', in Dalgleish & Power (1999).

Scherer, K.R. (1984), 'On the nature and function of emotion: A component process approach', in Scherer & Ekman (1984).

Scherer, K.R. & Ekman, P. (ed. 1984), *Approaches to Emotion* (Hillsdale, NJ: Lawrence Erlbaum Associates).

Solomon, Robert (2003), *Not Passion's Slave* (Oxford: Oxford University Press).

Solomon, Robert (2003a), 'Against valence', in Solomon (2003).

Solomon, Robert (ed. 2004), *Think About Feeling: Contemporary Philosophers On Emotion* (Oxford: Oxford University Press).

Solomon, Robert C. and Lori D. Stone (2002), 'On "positive" and "negative" emotions', *Journal for the Theory of Social Behavior*, **32**, pp. 417–36.

Solomon, Robert (1995), 'Some notes on emotion east and west', *Philosophy East and West*, **45** (2), pp. 171–202.

Solomon, Robert C. (1976), *The Passions* (New York: Basic Books).

Temkin, Owsei (1964), 'The classical roots of Glisson's doctrine of irritation', *Bulletin of the History of Medicine*, **38**, pp. 297–328.

Watson, D. & Tellengen, A. (1985), 'Toward a consensual structure of mood', *Psychological Bulletin*, **98**, 219–35.

Wierzbicka, Anne (1999), *Emotion Across Languages and Cultures* (New York: Cambridge University Press).

Whytt, Robert (1751), *An Essay on the Vital and Other Involuntary Motions of Animals* (Edinburgh: Hamilton, Balfour & Neil).

Zachar, Peter, Bartlett S. (2001), 'Basic emotions and their biological substrates: a nominalistic interpretation', *Consciousness and Emotion*, **2**, pp. 189–221.

Zajonc, Robert, B. (1984a), 'The interaction of affect and cognition', in Scherer & Ekman. (1984).

Zajonc, Robert, B. (1984b), 'On primacy of affect', in Scherer & Ekman. (1984).

Zajonc, Robert. B. (1980), 'Feeling and thinking: preferences need no inferences', *American Psychologist*, **35**, pp. 151–76.

Giovanna Colombetti

Appraising Valence

*'Valence' is used in many different ways in emotion theory. It generally refers to
the 'positive' or 'negative' character of an emotion, as well as to the 'positive' or
'negative' character of some aspect of emotion. After reviewing these different
uses, I point to the conceptual problems that come with them. In particular, I distinguish: problems that arise from conflating the valence of an emotion with the
valence of its aspects, and problems that arise from the very idea that an emotion
(and/or its aspects) can be divided into mutually exclusive opposites. The first
group of problems does not question the classic dichotomous notion of valence,
but the second does. In order to do justice to the richness of daily emotions, emotion science needs more complex conceptual tools.*

I: Introduction

With the term 'valence' emotion theorists usually refer to the 'positive' and
'negative' character of an emotion and/or of its aspects (such as behaviour,
affect, evaluation, faces, adaptive value, etc.). The English word 'valence' was
introduced in psychology in the 1930s, but not immediately within emotion theory. Similarly, the expression 'positive and negative emotions' started to
become scientifically regimented around those years. Since then, the two expressions have gradually come together, and they are now reciprocally supporting
and mutually defining conceptual tools of contemporary emotion science.

In this paper I do two things. In the first part (sections II to V) I show that the
term 'valence' has been used in more than a half-dozen different ways since its
appearance in psychology and emotion theory, and I review and illustrate these
uses in detail. In the second part (section VI) I highlight the problems that, in my
view, go along with such uses. I distinguish problems that have to do with conflating different uses of the notion of valence, and problems that depend on the
idea that emotions and/or their aspects can be dichotomized. I conclude the discussion with an assessment of the utility of the notion of valence in emotion
theory (section VII).

Correspondence:
Giovanna Colombetti, Laboratorio di Scienze Cognitive, Università degli Studi di Trento, via
Tartarotti, 7, 38068 Rovereto, Italy. *Email: colombetti@form.unitn.it*

Journal of Consciousness Studies, **12**, No. 8–10, 2005, pp. 103–26

The first part of the paper is independent of whether one agrees with the discussion in the second part; it is, I hope, useful in itself. The process that has led 'valence' to refer to the 'positive' and 'negative' character of emotion and/or its aspects is subtle. Often the terms 'valence,' 'positive' and 'negative' appear without prior definition, on the assumption that their meaning is clear and uncontroversial. Yet what is 'positive' and 'negative' depends on one's concerns. This lack of explicitness has accumulated over the years, leading to a bundle of cross-definitions and cross-characterizations. Different meanings of 'valence' often inadvertently crop up and influence one's theory; the less aware one is of such different meanings, the more likely one is to assume and conflate them when using the word – hence the present overview.

The second part is more argumentative and builds on recent philosophical discussions of the notion of valence (Charland, 2005a; Prinz, 2004; Solomon & Stone, 2002). As I see it, some of the problems raised by the current uses of this notion do not question the idea that emotions have a positive or negative character; they just call for more terminological awareness and explicitness. Other problems, however, depend on the very idea that emotions and their aspects can be dichotomized. These problems highlight the inappropriateness of the notion of valence, and raise the question of whether this notion can be enriched, or whether it should rather be rejected.

II: From Chemistry to Psychology

The etymology of 'valence' does not refer to any polarity. The term comes from the Latin noun *valentia*, which means 'power, competence' (from the verb *valeo*, 'I am strong' or 'I am well'). In Italian, for example, the word *valenza* has kept this meaning and is used to refer to the significance or value of a situation.[1]

The English word 'valence' (or 'valency'), as well as the equivalent in other languages (*valence, valenza, valentia*, etc.), is also used in chemistry. Atoms have 'valence electrons' in their high energy levels, and these electrons are shared in the formation of compounds. Simply put, atoms with one or two valence electrons are unstable and tend to stabilize by forming compounds, whereas atoms with eight valence electrons are very stable. Atomic valence is expressed by a positive integer (1 to 8), and is thus neither positive nor negative. What is 'positive' and 'negative' is the charge of atomic components, such as electrons (negative charges) and protons (positive charges). Also, some elements attract valence electrons and as a consequence their overall charge becomes negative; other elements give up some of their valence electrons and their overall charge becomes positive.

When the English term 'valence' first appeared in psychology, it was used mainly as a synonym of 'charge.' Tolman (1932) proposed 'valence' as a translation of the German word *Aufforderungscharakter* as it appears in the works of

[1] For example: *'Il Grido' di Edward Munch ha una forte valenza emotiva* = Edward Munch's 'The Scream' has a strong emotional valence. Or: *La valenza politica di un incontro* = The political valence of a meeting.

Kurt Lewin. In illustrating both Lewin's and his own ideas, Tolman claimed that thanks to their '"invitation-characters" or "valencies" (*Aufforderungs-charaktere*)' objects exert 'attracting or repulsive forces,' which are 'stresses and strains which finally resolve themselves by causing such and such directions and turnings of behavior' (Tolman, 1932, p. 179). Lewin similarly defined *Aufforderungscharaktere* as 'imperative environmental facts' that 'determine the direction of the behaviour' (Lewin, 1935, p. 77). *Aufforderungscharaktere* can be either positive or negative. The positive ones effect approach, whereas the negative ones produce withdrawal or retreats (*ibid.*, p. 81). Notice the comment of Lewin's translators on the decision to use 'valence':

> There is no good English equivalent for *Aufforderungscharakter* as the author uses it. 'Positive *Aufforderungscharaktere*' and 'negative *Aufforderungscharaktere*' might be accurately rendered by 'attractive characters' and 'repulsive characters,' were it not desirable, for various reasons, to have a neutral term. Perhaps the most nearly accurate translation for the expression would be 'compulsive character,' but that is cumbrous and a shade too strong. In consultation with the author it has been decided to do a very little violence to an old use of the word 'valence' (see the New English Dictionary). It should be noted that, in contrast to chemical valence, which is only positive, psychological valence or a psychological valence may be either positive (attracting) or negative (repelling), and that an object or activity loses or acquires valence ... in accordance with the needs of the organism. [Translators' note]. (in Lewin, 1935, p. 77)

Auffordern in German means to invite one to do something; *Aufforderungs-charakter* thus refers to the property of inviting one to an action. An accurate translation would be 'affordance-character', where the term 'affordance' is borrowed from ecological psychology (Gibson, 1979) and refers to properties of the environment that afford or invite a certain behaviour toward it (for example, a chair affords a behaviour of sitting onto it).

What is interesting, ultimately, is that 'valence' entered Anglophone psychology via a questionable translation, and initially referred to affordance-characters rather than emotions. This use of 'valence', however, was not unambiguous and it contained the seeds of subsequent uses of the term, including its relation to emotion. First, in Lewin an affordance-character is not only a charge that induces an agent to *physically* approach or withdraw an object:

> We may at this point remark a circumstance of general importance: direction in the psychobiological field is not necessarily to be identified with physical direction, but must be defined primarily in psychological terms. ... When the child fetches a tool or applies to the experimenter for help, the action does not mean, even when it involves a physical movement in a direction opposite to the goal, a turning away from the goal but an approach to it. (1935, p. 84)

In this passage Lewin understands approach as involving an action toward a *goal-state*, irrespective of the movement's direction. This conception opens up the question of what approach and withdrawal are. As we shall see, behaviourists and cognitivists will answer differently, and thus use 'valence' in different ways.

Second, in Lewin the sign of an affordance-character often depends on the *experience* that it induces. In many of his examples, positive (negative, respectively) affordance-characters are accompanied by pleasant (unpleasant) feelings. A child who has to choose between going to a picnic or playing with his friends stands between two positive valences; a child who wants to climb a tree but is afraid of it faces something that has simultaneously a positive and a negative valence; etc. (cf. Lewin, 1935, p. 89). Here the character of experience tacitly determines the sign of the affordance-characters. As we shall see, this happens frequently in emotion theory. 'Valence' is now often used to refer to how good and bad an emotion feels; yet it often refers, at the same time, to phenomena (behaviours, goals, evaluations, etc.) tacitly assumed to feel intrinsically good or bad.

III: Object Valence, Behaviour Valence, and Emotion Valence

Charland (2005a; 2005b, this volume) has introduced a useful distinction between *emotion valence* and *affect valence*. 'Emotion valence' refers to the positive and negative character of an emotion *tout court* (the positive or negative character of fear, anger, joy, etc.), whereas 'affect valence' refers to the positive and negative character of emotion experience (how good or bad an emotion feels). In this and the following section I will adopt Charland's distinction, and I will enrich it by individuating more uses of 'valence'.

Tolman's and Lewin's notion of valence refers to the positive or negative charge of objects in the environment — let us then call it *object valence*. As we saw, Tolman and Lewin did not use 'valence' to refer to emotion. Yet current emotion theories often posit a link between object valence and emotion valence. Positive or negative emotions are said to be elicited, for example, by positive or negative environmental contingencies, stimuli, pictures, words (Cacioppo & Berntson, 1994), events (Bradley & Lang, 2000), film clips (Davidson, 1998), images, pictures and percepts (Lang *et al.*, 2000). The International Affective Picture System (IAPS, cf. Lang *et al.*, 1995) consists in a set of positive, negative and neutral pictures, aimed at eliciting emotions with the corresponding valence sign (positive pictures include happy babies, appetising food and erotica; negative ones include poisonous snakes, aimed guns and violent deaths; neutral ones involve people doing routine tasks, rental places and common household objects).

Frijda (1986) also uses 'valence' as object valence: '[e]vents, objects, and situations may possess positive and negative valence; that is, they may possess intrinsic attractiveness or aversiveness' (p. 207). Valence is for Frijda one of ten other components of what he calls 'situational meaning structure' — a set of environmental properties that define the meaning of a situation which, in turn, determines the occurrence of emotions. Other components of situational meaning structure are difficulty, urgency, seriousness, clarity, etc. (pp. 204–9); together with valence, they determine behaviour and experience. Note that on this view object valence does not directly determine emotion valence (indeed, in 1986 Frijda did not even mention 'positive and negative emotions').

Another early use of the term 'valence' is in Schneirla (1959, table on p. 30), where it refers to the direction of behaviour — let us call this *behaviour valence*. 'Positive valence' refers to approach, retaining, tolerance and acquisition; 'negative valence' refers to withdrawal, escape, refusal and aggression. Like object valence, behaviour valence was not initially used within emotion theory. At present, however, many emotion theorists relate behaviour valence and emotion valence. For example, Davidson uses 'valence' primarily to refer to approach and withdrawal, and is interested in how different brain hemispheres contribute to it. He has presented evidence that approach depends on increased activation in left prefrontal cortical regions, whereas withdrawal depends on increased activation in right prefrontal cortical ones (e.g. Davidson, 1993). In addition (and unlike Schneirla), Davidson also uses behaviour valence to determine emotion valence; he defines a positive emotion as involving approach, and a negative emotion as involving withdrawal.

It is interesting that authors who initially used 'valence' did not use 'positive and negative emotions' and also vice-versa (table 1). Arnold & Gasson (1954, p. 206) and Arnold (1960, p. 195), for example, defined positive (negative) emotions in relation to behaviours toward (against) beneficial (harmful) objects, but they never used the term 'valence.'

Authors	Use 'valence' as object or behaviour valence	Use 'positive and negative emotions'
Tolman (1932)	Yes, as object valence: positive (negative) valence refers to attractive (aversive) stimuli.	No
Lewin (1935)	"	"
Arnold & Gasson (1954)	No	Yes. Positive (negative) emotions are elicited by suitable (harmful) objects
Schneirla (1959)	Yes, as behaviour valence: positive (negative) valence refers to approach (withdrawal) behaviour	No
Arnold (1960)	No	Yes. Positive (negative) emotions involve behaviour toward (away from) objects
Frijda (1986)	Yes, as object valence: positive (negative) valence is attractiveness (aversiveness) in objects	No
Davidson (1993)	Yes, as behaviour valence: positive (negative) valence refers to approach (withdrawal) behaviour	Yes. Positive (negative) emotions involve approach (withdrawal)
Cacioppo & Bernston (1994)	Yes, as object valence: The positive (negative) valence of pictures and other stimuli	Yes
Lang *et al* (2000)	Yes, as object valence: The positive (negative) valence of pictures, images and percepts	Yes

Table 1. Early uses of 'valence' as object valence and behaviour valence, and some more recent ones. The table also indicates early definitions of 'positive and negative emotions' in relation to objects and behaviour.

IV: Affect valence

At present, valence is often used as *affect valence* (Charland, 2005a; 2005b, this volume) — it refers to how good or bad an emotion experience, or affect, feels.

Psychologists have discussed the hedonic tone of emotions — their pleasant or unpleasant feel — since Wundt's (1907) and Titchener's (1908) debate on feelings and bodily sensations (reflections on hedonic tone appeared much earlier, of course). Since then, so-called 'dimensional approaches' (e.g. Block, 1957; Russell & Mehrabian, 1977; Russell, 1980) have always posited pleasantness-unpleasantness as a fundamental dimension of emotion experience.[2] This dimension has gradually become 'the valence dimension'.[3] In this approach, hedonic tone and valence are synonyms. A different approach posits positive affect (PA) and negative affect (NA) as two separate unipolar dimensions (Bradburn, 1969). Here positive and negative affect do not coincide with pleasantness and unpleasantness, and there is no hedonic/valence dimension. For example, for Watson & Tellegen (1985) and Watson *et al.* (1988), pleasantness depends on high PA *and* low NA, and unpleasantness depends on low PA *and* high NA.[4]

In the first approach, valence is the positive-negative dimension of experience and is distinct from the dimension of arousal (or activation), and sometimes from a third or even fourth dimension. In other cases, 'valence' refers to the positive-negative character of *all* dimensions of emotion experience that one individuates. For example, according to Davitz (1969) emotion experience has four dimensions — hedonic tone, direction of behaviour, activation and competence (how good or bad one feels one is at something) — and they are all valenced. Valence cannot be decoupled from these dimensions; it is *intrinsic* in all of them.

Theories of affect valence differ in how they explain *why* an affective state feels good or bad. For Damasio (2003), for example, the valence of feelings depends on how easy and free-flowing organismic processes are. When organismic processes are optimal and non-obstructed, the accompanying feelings are positive; vice-versa, when the organism is impeded in its activity and maintenance of well-being and balance, the accompanying feelings are negative. According to Davidson (e.g. 1984), the behaviour of approach (withdrawal) is intrinsically pleasant (unpleasant); approach and approach-related positive affect depend on the left hemisphere (also responsible for fine motor control; cf. Davidson, 1984), whereas withdrawal and withdrawal-related negative affect

---

[2] These approaches developed after the so-called *semantic differential* (Osgood, 1952), originally developed to capture 'the dimensions of meaning' — the dimensions underlying 'something basic to the structuring of human judgments' (Osgood & Suci, 1955, p. 337). Osgood and colleagues individuated three such dimensions: 1) *activity* (as in sharp-dull, active-passive, fast-slow); 2) *potency* (as in strong-weak, large-small, heavy-light, hard-soft), and 3) *evaluation* (as in beautiful-ugly, nice-awful, clean-dirty, pleasant-unpleasant, delicate-rugged). The idea that meaning and experience have dimensions comes in turn from attempts to understand synesthesia (in particular whether synesthesia involves the 'parallel alignment' of two or more experiences).

[3] For example, Russell (1980) does not mention valence, but Russell & Carroll (1999) and Russell (2003) do.

[4] See Russell & Carroll (1999) for an overview of the debate between bipolar and unipolar theories, and for a defence of the former.

depend on the right hemisphere (responsible for gross withdrawal reactions). For Lambie & Marcel (2002) emotion experience depends on first-order irreflexive phenomenal experience, as well as on second-order reflexive awareness. On their view, hedonic tone can change according to attentional mode (for example, it might disappear if one attends to one's bodily sensations and feelings in a sufficiently analytic and detached manner). Drawing on this account, Charland (2005a) has proposed an explicitly 'non-intrinsic view' of affect valence, according to which affect valence is *always* constructed through the interplay of first- and second-order processes; in Charland's words, affect valence is *indeterminate*.

Although affect valence is often discussed *per se* within phenomenological analyses of emotion experience, it also often contributes more or less explicitly to other uses of valence. When emotions are called 'positive and negative' without explanation, the most plausible understanding of the expression is usually in terms of 'good and bad feelings.' Similarly, object valence, behaviour valence, and other uses of 'valence' (see next section) are often parasitic on affect valence. Table 2 lists (some of) the authors who currently use 'valence' to refer to emotion experience (pleasantness-unpleasantness, and/or positive and negative affect and/or feelings). It also indicates those who use affect valence to characterize emotion valence (*caveat*: it is not always easy to attribute these uses, so the list is not comprehensive and might not reflect the author's intentions).

Authors who use 'valence' as affect valence	Use affect valence to define emotion valence (positive emotions feel good, negative emotions feel bad)
Davitz (1969)	Yes
Tucker (1981)	No
Lang (1984; 1985)	No
Davidson (1984; 2000)	Yes
Panksepp (1998)	In part (see section V)
Russell & Carroll (1999)	No
Isen (2000)	Yes
Lambie & Marcel (2002)	No
Rozin (2003)	No
Damasio (2003)	Yes
Varela & Depraz (2005, this volume)	No

Table 2. Some authors who use valence as affect valence; and, among them, those who use affect valence to define emotion valence

V: More Valenced Phenomena, and their Relation to Emotion Valence

Other aspects of emotion are called 'valenced.' These uses further cross-define and complicate the notion of valence and its relation to emotion.

The valence of facial expressions

The 'valence' of a facial expression usually refers to the positive and negative character of the experience that the face (allegedly) expresses. What is called 'positive' and 'negative' in a face however varies according to how one views the relation between facial display and experience. It is useful to distinguish three such views:[5]

(1) The *purely categorical* approach, according to which there is a number of basic emotions expressed by typical faces. What is 'valenced,' in this view, is the whole face (Tomkins, 1962/1963, 1970; Ekman, 1999).

(2) The *componential* approach, according to which facial expressions have meaningful components, and one component can appear in the expression of different emotions. In general, eyebrow frown (produced by contracting the corrugator supercilii) is associated with unpleasant experiences, and raised lip corners (produced by contracting the zygomatic major) is associated with pleasant ones. Reinman *et al*. (2000) say that zygomatic muscle activity is a measure of positive emotion, whereas corrugator muscle activity is a measure of negative emotion. What is 'valenced' here are individual components, and they 'valence' the emotion expressed by the whole face.

(3) The *dimensional* approach, according to which facial expressions of emotion are organized along a few dimensions. Schlosberg (1941; 1952; 1954) distinguished facial expressions initially according to two dimensions (pleasantness-unpleasantness and attention-rejection) and then three (adding the level of activation). As in dimensional accounts of emotion experience, 'valence' here corresponds to the pleasantness-unpleasantness dimension.

For Davidson (e.g. 1984) facial expressions are not only an index of affect valence, but also of emotion and behaviour valence. In his view, positive facial expressions depend on neural structures in the left hemisphere that are implicated in positive emotions — namely, approach-involving emotions and associated positive affects; and negative facial expressions depend on neural structures in the right hemisphere that are implicated in negative emotions — namely, withdrawal-involving emotions and associated negative affects.

Authors who mention positive and negative facial expressions	Relation of facial valence to affect and/or emotion valence
Tomkins (1962/1963)	Faces express negative or positive affect
Ekman (1972; 1999)	Positive (negative) facial expressions express positive (negative) affects
Davidson (1984)	Positive (negative) facial expressions involve the same neural structures as positive (negative) emotions
Watson & Tellegen (1985)	Positive (negative) facial expressions express positive (negative) affects
Reinman *et al*. (2000)	Zygomatic (corrugator) activity indicates positive (negative) emotion

Table 3. Uses of 'facial valence' and their relation to emotion and/or affect valence

[5] Here I follow, in part, Smith & Scott (1997).

Evaluation valence

Emotion valence sometimes depends on *evaluation valence* – the positive or negative character of eliciting evaluations. For Ben-Ze'ev (2000) positive and negative emotions are elicited by positive and negative evaluations; a positive (negative) evaluation is an evaluation of something as good (bad). Schadenfreude is thus positive because it is elicited by a positive evaluation — that is, an evaluation of someone else's misfortunes as good. Similarly, compassion and sympathy are negative, because they are based on the evaluation of one's condition as bad. Ortony *et al.* (1988, p. 13) similarly define emotions as 'valenced reactions to events, agent, or objects, with their particular nature being determined by the way in which the eliciting situation is construed.' In their theory all emotions are elicited by an evaluation. Exactly which emotion an agent will have depends specifically on whether the evaluation is about events, actions or objects; whether these are evaluated as good or bad; and whether they are evaluated with respect to their consequences for the self or for other people. For example, A's pity for B is elicited by A's evaluation of an event as thwarting B's goals (negative valence); A's shame is elicited by A's evaluation of A's action as blameworthy (negative valence); and A's love for X is elicited by A's evaluation of X as suitable (positive valence). Emotion valence here depends on evaluation valence, and what makes an evaluation 'positive' or 'negative' depends on whether an event is evaluated as 'good' or 'bad.'

According to Lazarus (1991), a positive (negative) emotion is an emotion elicited by the evaluation that the person-environment relationship caused by the emotion is beneficial (harmful). This definition makes pity, compassion and sympathy 'positive.' Finally, Lambie & Marcel (2002, p. 243) mention 'positive and negative evaluations' as a factor that influences emotion experience. They do not specify what makes an evaluation positive or negative in the first place, but it is clear that, on their view, evaluations are 'valenced contents of emotion experience,' together with other valenced phenomena.

Authors who use valence as evaluation valence	Relation of evaluation valence to emotion and/or affect valence
Ortony *et al.* (1988)	Positive (negative) emotions are elicited by evaluations of events, objects and actions as good (bad)
Lazarus (1991)	Positive (negative) emotions are elicited by the evaluation of the emotion as socially beneficial (harmful)
Ben Ze'ev (2000)	Positive (negative) emotions are elicited by positive (negative) evaluations
Lambie & Marcel (2002)	Evaluation valence is part of the content of emotion experience

Table 4. Uses of evaluation valence and their relation to emotion and/or affect valence

Teleological uses of valence

In artificial intelligence (AI) positive and negative emotions are often defined in relation to *goals*. For Dyer (1987) positive emotions involve the attainment of a goal, and negative emotions involve the thwarting of a goal. Specific emotions differ according to how goals are attained and thwarted; whereas sadness can be seen as depending on one's goals being thwarted in general, anger depends on the presence of someone or something thwarting one's goals. According to this approach, most emotions can be called positive and negative only *a posteriori* – after a certain goal has been attained or thwarted. I call this the *teleological* use of valence, because it defines the positive or negative character of one's emotions according to the consequences of one's actions with respect to one's goals, needs or desires.

Izard (1991) chooses to define positive (negative) emotions according to whether their consequences are desirable (undesirable). Other views of valence do not explicitly mention goals and desires, but can nevertheless be seen as teleological because they define positive and negative emotions with respect to future states considered desirable or undesirable. For example, as we saw, Lazarus (1991) claims that positive (negative) emotions are elicited by the appraisal of a situation as having beneficial (harmful) social consequences. Bickhard (2000) characterizes positive emotions as diminishing uncertainty, and negative emotions as augmenting it (these examples also show that the teleological use of valence can overlap with evaluation valence). Another teleological use of 'valence' is in Rozin (2003): '[a] positive state is one that we seek or try to maintain or enhance, and a negative state is one that we seek to reduce, eliminate or avoid' (p. 840). Likewise, for Prinz (2004) '[p]ositive emotions are ones we want to sustain, and negative emotions are ones that we want to get rid of' (p. 174); valence in his view corresponds to inner positive and negative reinforcers — brain systems that make us persist in rewarding behaviours, and cease non-rewarding or punishing ones.

Authors who use valence teleologically	Relation of teleologically-used valence to emotion valence
Dyer (1987)	Positive (negative) emotions involve the realization (thwarting) of goals
Izard (1991)	Positive (negative) emotions are likely to have desirable (undesirable) consequences
Lazarus (1991)	Positive (negative) emotions are beneficial (harmful) to social relationships
Bickhard (2000)	Positive (negative) emotions diminish (augment) uncertainty
Rozin (2003)	A positive (negative) state is one that we seek to enhance (get rid of)
Prinz (2004)	A positive (negative) emotion is one that we want to sustain (get rid of)

Table 5. Teleological uses of valence and their relation to emotion valence

Valence as adaptive value-tagging

According to Panksepp (e.g. 1998; 2000; 2005, this volume), mammals share seven basic subcortical and endocrine emotional systems that encode biological values. These emotional systems are 'valenced' in the sense that they 'value-tag' objects and situations in the environment and thus regulate adaptive behaviours.

For Panksepp every basic emotional system is valenced, in the sense that, in order to guide behaviour, it attributes values to the world. Some emotional systems feel always bad (FEAR and PANIC), others feel always good (PLAY and CARE), and others feel good or bad according to the situation (SEEKING, RAGE and LUST).

Valence and norms

Finally, sometimes valence is explicitly and primarily defined in relation to norms and values. Picard (1997) thinks that an affective computer should have a sense (either hard-wired or learned) for what is morally good and bad, and this is how she defines valence (cf. p. 223). Also, scientists are becoming increasingly interested in Buddhist conceptions of mind and emotion (cf. Davidson & Harrington, 2002; Goleman, 1997; 2003), and Buddhism explicitly moralizes emotion. 'Positive and negative emotions' corresponds to a distinction between 'virtuous' and 'non-virtuous' mental factors (see Dreyfus, 2002, for an introduction to the concepts of mind and emotion in the Abidharma tradition). Negative mental factors (anger, attachment) disturb the mind and should be avoided; emotions such as loving-kindness and wishing well for other beings should be cultivated. This distinction is primarily ethical, but is at the same time intertwined with the consideration that virtuous emotions improve one's overall well-being, whereas non-virtuous ones disrupt it. Positive, virtuous emotions are wholesome, and negative, non-virtuous ones are unwholesome.

In line with this view, Davidson has investigated the health consequences of what he calls 'positive' and 'negative' *affective styles*. A positive affective style involves mainly 'positive emotions' — which for Davidson include positive affect, social engagement and extroversion. A negative affective style involves a predominance of 'negative emotions' — anxiety, depression, social disengagement and introversion. Left-prefrontal activated individuals tend to have a positive affective style, whereas right-prefrontal activated individuals tend to have a negative affective style. Davidson *et al.* (1999) have shown that, in addition, 'positive' left-activated individuals have more natural killer cells in their immune system and are less likely to become sick, whereas prototypical 'negative' right-prefrontal activated individuals have less natural killer cells and are more likely to become sick.

VI: Problems — Conflations and Dichotomies

The overview of different uses of 'valence' I have just offered is not exhaustive (for more uses see Charland, 2005a; Prinz, 2004: 167-173; Solomon & Stone, 2002). Prinz and Solomon & Stone also mention various problems raised by different uses of the expression 'positive and negative emotions.'

In my view, the problems raised by the uses of valence reviewed above can be divided into two groups. First, there are problems of *conflation* deriving from the tendency to switch back and forth between the valence sign of an emotion *tout court*, and the valence sign of different aspects of emotion. Such conflations, as we will see, induce excessive simplifications and overlook many familiar cases of emotion; because an emotion feels good, it does not follow that it is also itself positive, or that it involves positive behaviour, positive facial expressions, positive evaluations, etc. There are then deeper and more challenging problems that derive from the idea that emotion and its aspects can be *dichotomized*. Valence is typically characterized in terms of mutually exclusive poles, which logically rules out the possibility of mixtures. This characterization also oversimplifies and overlooks daily lived emotions, but in a more fundamental and worrying way. Whereas the first group of problems highlights a lack of clarity and agreement when using 'valence' that could be solved with more explicitness, the second group of problems calls into question the utility of the current notion of valence as a descriptive and explanatory tool of emotion theory.

Conflations

Conflations arise when a positive (negative) emotion is taken to necessarily have positive (negative) aspects. According to Davitz (1969), for example, positive emotions involve positive direction of behaviour ('moving toward'), positive hedonic tone ('comfort'), positive activation ('activation') and positive competence ('enhancement'). Negative-1 emotions involve negative-1 behaviour ('away'), negative-1 hedonic tone ('discomfort'), negative-1 activation ('hypoactivation') and negative-1 competence ('dissatisfaction'). Negative-2 emotions involve negative-2 behaviour ('moving against'), negative-2 hedonic tone ('tension'), negative-2 activation ('hyperactivation') and negative-2 competence ('inadequacy'). Davitz presents this taxonomy as if it exhausted all emotions. Yet one can find many examples of emotions that are not all positive, or not all negative-1 or all negative-2. Before an examination for which you are not very prepared, your state could be characterized by 'toward,' 'discomfort' and 'inadequacy'; if I am determined to leave a job that I do not like, then my emotion might be best characterized as involving 'activation,' 'enhancement' and 'away from'; and so on.

    Davidson also employs the tags 'positive' and 'negative' for several aspects of emotion *and* for emotions themselves (e.g. Davidson, 1984, 1998, 2000; Davidson *et al.*, 1990). He uses 'valence' primarily as behaviour valence, and maintains that approach depends on left prefrontal cortical regions whereas withdrawal depends on right ones. From here, however, Davidson often leaps to the claim that positive emotions *tout court* depend on the left hemisphere, and that negative emotions depend on the right one. In other words, he tends to infer the lateralization of emotion valence from the one of behaviour valence. This tendency induces him, in turn, to lateralize affect valence: left-hemisphere positive emotions feel good, whereas right-hemisphere negative emotions feel bad. He also mentions positive and negative facial expressions (e.g. Davidson, 1984), and eventually groups all positive (negative) aspects of emotion into positive (negative) personality traits dependent on left (right) hemispheric activation (the 'affective styles' mentioned above).

Davidson's view fits *prima facie* some of the classic emotions discussed in emotion theory. Fear, for example, seems to have all the characteristics of right hemispheric activation: it involves withdrawal, it feels bad, it is expressed by a negative facial expression, and it is a paradigmatic negative emotion. Similarly for contempt and sadness. Joy, on the other hand, seems to have all the characteristics of left hemispheric activation: it involves approach, it feels good, it is expressed by a positive facial expression, and it is a paradigmatic positive emotion. Similarly for pride and enthusiasm. However, there are cases that, on Davidson's own admission, the model does *not* fit. A popular counterexample is anger, which most theorists characterize as involving approach and unpleasantness. Davidson (e.g. 1994) admits that his model does not fit contentment, and post-attainment pleasant feelings in general, either. The upshot is that positive (negative) affect is only contingently related to positive (negative) behaviour, and to the general positive (negative) character of an emotion. Davidson's model does not fit all emotions conventionally discussed in emotion theory. Accordingly, one's affective style need not include either all positive or all negative traits.

The take-away message so far is that an emotion and specific behaviours, feelings, etc. need not together because they all have the same 'valence sign.' The lesson then is that emotion theorists should keep track of, and make explicit, their reasons for calling an emotion and/or its aspects 'positive' or 'negative.'

But what about the assumption that it is appropriate to dichotomize emotions and its aspects? This issue poses a more serious challenge to the current uses of the notion of valence. The major problem with Davidson's model, as I see it, is that it is not obvious that emotions such as relief, schadenfreude, jealousy, envy, contentment, etc. involve either approach or withdrawal, and always feel either good or bad. Davitz' distinction of the 'negative' part of valence into negative-1 and negative-2 does not make much progress, because it still assumes that an emotion is either comforting, discomforting *or* tense; that it leads one toward, away *or* against something; etc. In short, Davitz' tripartition still leaves no room for mixtures. I turn now to these challenging cases.

Dichotomies

The uses of valence reviewed above assume that different aspects of emotion can be dichotomized, and that the two terms of the dichotomies are mutually exclusive. 'Less positive valence' implies 'more negative valence,' which leaves no room for mixtures (typically human, but not necessarily only).

The notion of object valence implies that objects are intrinsically attractive or aversive, suitable or harmful. But attractiveness and aversiveness, and suitability and harmfulness are relational properties. They depend both on the agent's structure and concerns, as well as on the environment; the same object can be more or less appealing to the same agent depending on the context. Development and evolution make some objects more reliably attractive (aversive) than others. In short, object valence is never absolute; many environmental settings are new and unusual, and agents have different developmental histories that relate them in different ways to objects and situation (this can pose a problem for experimental settings that assume the absolute positive and negative character of stimuli). The more complex the agent, the more complex and layered its developmental history and hence the significance of its objects.

Consider next the approach-withdrawal distinction, and compare approach in love and approach in anger. The former can be understood as a movement 'toward' the source of love, and the latter is better described as a movement 'against' the object of anger (see also Davitz, 1969). The latter is a reaction to aversive stimulation, and the two senses of approach are very different. Consider also the following example. I am angry at a certain person P (a colleague of mine, say) because she has insulted me. Because I cannot punch her, I start gossiping about her at work, until she is eventually fired. The 'approach' induced by my anger consists in the exploitation of causal chains in order to have an effect on P, and these causal chains involve withdrawal from P. Or consider the case in which I seek someone's help out of fear. It does not seem possible to account for these cases with a simple bipolar dimension of behaviour whose extremes are approach and withdrawal. Approach and withdrawal are such not simply because of the direction of movement they involve (toward and away from, respectively). As Lewin (1935) already noted, they are motivational categories tangled up with shorter- and longer-term goals, intentions and desires. To characterize them as 'opposites' overlooks the fact that they often coexist, and strips them down to 'directions of behaviour' that, by themselves, cannot account for most of our motivated behaviours.

As for affect valence, philosophers have often mentioned the possibility of mixed feelings. Plato in the *Philebus* says that pleasures are rarely pure; most of the time they are mixed, that is, they contain pain (in more or less measure). While watching a comedy we feel malevolence – we laugh at the characters' misfortunes, and although we are amused, this enjoyment contains an understanding of the characters' suffering. We enjoy watching tragedies, but at the same time we are overwhelmed with sorrow. Bodily feelings can themselves be admixtures of pain and pleasure, as in the relief of scratching an itch. Prinz (2004, p. 165) notices that nostalgia feels bad because one is missing something, but at the same time involves a memory of how good it was to have that something. Or consider the mixed feeling triggered by the news that your best friend has just been offered the job you really wanted.

Psychologists usually do not discuss these cases and build their models out of alleged 'pure' cases. Some of them explain away the ambivalent nature of mixed feelings by reducing them to duck-rabbit-like attentional switches (e.g. Arnold, 1960). On this view, it is not the case that nostalgia feels bad and good at the same time. Simply, when in nostalgia you pay attention to the absence of the missed object, you feel bad; when you pay attention to how good it was to have that something, you feel good. The two affects cannot be experienced at the same time. A different view would allow true phenomenological mixtures, as in a sweet-and-sour flavour. When I taste a sweet-and-sour dish, there is a sense in which I understand why the dish is called that way. However, I do not really seem to be able to pay attention to the sourness in isolation from the sweetness, and vice versa. Perhaps mixed feelings are sweet-and-sour-like, and this is (among others) what early introspectionist studies on emotion experience were trying to assess (cf. Beebe-Centre, 1932, for an overview).

If feelings are sweet-and-sour-like – that is, irreducible to duck-rabbit-like experiences — bipolar unidimensional models of affect valence cannot account for them, because they leave no room for mixtures. A more appropriate model here could be Watson & Tellegen's (1985), according to which positive affect and negative affect are two independent dimensions. Pleasantness is characterized by low negative affect and high positive affect, and unpleasantness is characterized by high negative affect and low positive affect. In this model, mixed feelings could be characterized as containing, at the same time, high positive and high negative affect (as perhaps in *catharsis*), or low positive and low negative affect (as in *mild nostalgia*).

There are further complications. As Aristotle points out in the *Nicomachean Ethics*, there are as many pleasures as there are pleasant activities (see also Frijda, 1986; Kenny, 1963; Lambie & Marcel, 2000; Prinz, 2004; Solomon & Stone, 2002). The pleasure one takes in, say, one's friends' company feels different from the pleasure one has in eating one's favourite food; and different friends, as well as different foods, also induce different pleasures. Kenny (1963) argues that pleasure is not a separate feeling that is added or subtracted from activities, and that makes them pleasant or unpleasant accordingly. A pleasant activity is not an activity *plus* a feeling of pleasure. Rather, actions *are* pleasant or unpleasant; their peculiar pleasant feel depends on their object and, more generally, on the kind of activity they are. Similar considerations lead Lambie & Marcel (2002) to propose a notion of *multidimensional hedonic tone*. In their view, not only does every activity have its own hedonic tone; an activity might include *several* hedonic experiences. This happens because hedonicity, in their view, depends – at least in part – on how second-order attention is directed towards first-order pleasures and pains. For example, it depends on whether one's attention is immersed in the object of emotion or in one's experience (of bodily states, for example); on whether one's attention is more or less focused on the details of the experience; on whether one can change one's situation, etc.[6]

Finally, Charland's (2005a) argument for the indeterminacy of affect valence is particularly destabilizing. As we saw, he uses Lambie & Marcel's view to argue that affect valence is not an intrinsic property of emotion experience. Rather, valence is constructed through the interplay of first-order (irreflexive) phenomenology and attentional mechanisms directed to it. In this view, there is nothing fixed corresponding to affect valence, nothing objective 'already there'

[6] Many mixed feelings are likely to depend on some kind of interaction between more basic and irreflexive experiences, and higher-level reflexive ones (see Gennaro, 2000, for such an account of *catharsis*), but we should not exclude that feelings can be mixed also at the irreflexive level — perhaps as in mixed bodily feelings, such as the above-mentioned relief of scratching an itch (see Plato's *Philebus* for more examples).

that can be read out by second order attention. In other words, affect valence is an evaluative feature of emotion experience dependent on (or even arising from) second-order descriptions.[7] Charland's argument is destabilizing because it undermines attempts to justify the dichotomous positive and negative character of experience on the basis of how they 'simply' feel. How many poles or dimensions feelings have is likely to depend on the tools we (and emotion scientists) employ to investigate and report experiences.

Let us move on to 'evaluation valence.' We saw that, in the first place, there is no agreement on what makes an evaluation positive or negative, nor how evaluation valence relates to emotion valence. Second, it seems too simple to reduce appraisals in an emotion to a single evaluative dimension. As Solomon & Stone (2002) argue, '[v]irtually every emotion ... involves a multiplicity of appraisals' (p. 427), or what they call a 'multidimensional appraisal': appraisal of the situation, of oneself, moral appraisals, etc.; some of these appraisals may detect positive aspects of a situation, and others may detect negative aspects. In addition, once again: we do not seem to evaluate something as, so to say, 'good' in amount xg and therefore 'bad' in amount k-xg.' To think that this is possible is to assume that we evaluate things as 'definitely good (bad)' — not 'perfectly good (bad)' perhaps, but without anything bad (good) in it.

Whether a facial expression (or a component of it) can be appropriately labelled 'positive' or 'negative' is complicated by difficulties with interpreting faces in relation to emotion and experience, and by problems with the notion of expression itself. This topic would require a paper on its own. For present purposes it is sufficient to note that tagging a facial expression as either 'positive' or 'negative' usually relies on the following assumptions: (1) there is an underlying experience that is either positive or negative; (2) the face expresses this experience, and it is possible to unequivocally read the experience from the face; (3) the face is interpreted as the expression of an emotion by an observer. Every assumption is problematic. First, as many theorists have pointed out, there is no one-to-one relationship between experience and facial expression — between 'feeling anger' and 'expression of anger,' 'feeling fear' and 'expression of fear,' etc. (cf. Russell & Fernández-Dols, 1997). This suggests that what looks like a positive (negative) expression may not necessarily reflect a pleasant (unpleasant) feeling. Second, seeing an expression as the manifestation of an 'inner' emotional feeling is an interpretative act that can go wrong because of context effects; indeed, there is evidence that context plays a role in the tagging of facial expressions (Russell & Fehr, 1987; Fernández-Dols & Carroll, 1997). Third, facial movements depend on several factors and not all of them 'express emotions.' Fourth, it is possible to argue that, when it comes to emotion experience, others' interpretations of our expressive attempts shape our own experience (see Campbell, 1997, for an externalist view of feeling). Finally, there is always the problem that it is not evident that feelings are always either pleasant or unpleasant. Interestingly, Ekman initially thought that people typically experience

---

[7] Yet: 'perhaps not all aspects of affect valence are equally permeable to attention, some may be relatively fixed and modular' (Charland, 2005a, p. 249).

blends of emotion, and that these show up on the face (Ekman, 1982). Ekman (1972) observed that only posed expressions can be accurately defined as positive or negative; spontaneous expressions do not provide precise information in this respect. More recently, Smith & Scott (1997) have noticed that

> there is considerable evidence suggesting that it is rare for most individuals to experience strong feelings of a single isolated emotion. Instead, across a variety of emotionally evocative contexts, it is common for individuals to report the subjective experience of blends of up to four (or more) emotions. ... Although there have been attempts to describe the facial expressions characteristic of a limited number of emotional blends, ... the principles by which such blended expressions are produced have not yet been articulated. (p.235)

This passage shows nicely how the assumption that an emotion experience can be easily dichotomized influences scientific methodology. Theorists divide faces into positive and negative, and design experiments based on this idea, excluding a priori more complex possibilities.

When valence is used teleologically, the positive and negative character of an emotion is defined in relation to the consequences of one's actions with respect to one's goals, needs or desires. As we saw, for some theorists positive (negative) emotions are *caused* by the attainment (thwarting) of goals, or by certainty (uncertainty) about the future. This approach is limited, as clearly not all emotions depend on attainment or thwarting of goals and desires; often we simply enjoy, or dislike, certain activities, and are anxious, depressed or jolly irrespective of our aims. Emotions such as contentment do not seem to depend on the expectation that uncertainty will be reduced; sometimes we enjoy the thrill of the unknown. For other theorists, positive (negative) emotions somehow *involve* the desire/goal to continue (stop) a certain activity. This is, I think, an interesting definition of pleasure and displeasure. Yet one can still ask to what extent pleasures involve the desire to continue; we do not want to indulge in all pleasures for the same time, or for a very long time (the expectation of how long a pleasure will last seems to influence the pleasure one feels). I also wonder whether extreme pleasures are pure, and whether one always wants to continue them (the hedonic character of sadomasochistic feelings is an interesting case in this respect). If Plato is right and most of our pleasures contain pain, then often we will be in a situation where we want more and, at the same time, less of it. The bottom question is whether this ambivalent state can be appropriately reduced to the activity of two somewhat 'opposite' systems (e.g. reward and punishment, approach and withdrawal) that support separate phenomenological states (pleasure and displeasure), or rather is a real experiential mixture that depends on the integration (perhaps a dynamical coupling) of these systems.

Panksepp's use of 'valence' does not seem to pose particular problems if understood as 'value-tagging power' (this use is close to the etymology of 'valence'). Yet Panksepp also accepts the idea that some emotional systems feel intrinsically good or bad. For example, CARE always feels good. This is a simplification that overlooks the variety of possible cases of care; it is hard to characterize the feeling of taking care of a loved one who is terminally ill as good or bad, or even as a duck-rabbit-like state. Perhaps Panksepp would reply that more than one emotional system is at play here (CARE and FEAR, for example), which could explain the mixed hedonic tone. This possibility is interesting, but needs more analysis and discussion; once again, the hard problem is how two separate neural mechanisms can support a phenomenological mixture.

Finally, the explicitly normative characterization of valence raises complications of its own. One can mention several reasons why one should or should not have an emotion. For a consequentialist, an emotion is morally good if it brings about good consequences; despite the simple formulation, what makes a consequence 'good' is itself a complex issue, as moral philosophers know. There are also psychological and holistic reasons that make the normative connotation of 'positive' and 'negative' relative to the context. Take the common case of victims of abuse who feel guilty about it. In this context the transformation of guilt into anger might be seen as a positive event. This does not mean that a victim of abuse should feel angry forever; the point is only that, within the context of certain therapeutic practices, anger can be an emotion that one should at some point cultivate. Consider also how a holistic view of personality can justify traditionally irredeemable and sinful emotions. Goldie (2000) argues — convincingly I think – that character traits like jealousy are intertwined with other traits in such a way that one cannot just take the jealousy away from a person and obtain the same person in an 'ameliorated version.' Character is not a patchwork of separate emotional dispositions, and we cannot simply cross out the ones we do not like while remaining 'the same person.' It thus becomes possible to argue that jealousy, within the whole economy of one's character, is something one does not necessarily want to get rid of.

In addition, what exactly does it mean that one ought, or ought not, to have a certain emotion? Does it mean that one should not express it, or not feel it? In other words, what aspect of the emotion is in question? It is an old moral issue whether it is enough, for sinning, to feel a certain emotion (such as lust, greed, pride, etc.), or whether the sin consists in allowing oneself to take certain actions to indulge in it. Does virtue consist in the absence of sinful feelings, or in the fight against them? These questions relate to issues of mental health as well. What is 'negative' in a psychiatric condition, for example? To feel a certain emotion? Or to not be able to deal with it? Or not to be able to prevent certain behaviours instigated by it? According to the answer, the therapy is likely to be different. The upshot, for present purposes, is that there are several reasons why one should or should not have (or feel, or express) an emotion.

VII: Concluding Remarks

Summing up, we saw that the notion of valence does not originally and etymologically refer to a positive-negative distinction. Since its introduction in psychology (via a tentative and questionable translation) and then specifically in emotion theory, 'valence' has been linked to the tags 'positive' and 'negative' with increasing frequency. More or less inadvertently, it has been used to refer to

different aspects of emotion. At present, the ideas that there are positive and negative emotions, that emotions have positive and negative aspects, and that emotion is valenced all support one another and are interchangeable. This process of
regimentation hides many problems. One is that 'valence' often implicitly means
many different things; I have tackled this problem by disentangling its meanings.
Another problem is that these different meanings tend to be conflated; I have
shown in which sense, and claimed that this need not happen. A further, deep
problem depends on the dichotomous character of valence, which brings with it
the idea that emotion and/or its aspects can be divided into mutually exclusive
opposites; I have argued that this notion of valence (and all that comes with it) is
too simple.

Whence the allure of valence? Affect valence plays an important role in supporting other uses of valence; what makes something 'positive' or 'negative' in
an emotion often comes down, more or less explicitly, to how that something
feels. Yet it is naïve to think that affect valence can have the last word and be the
brute fact on which to build an objectively dichotomous notion of emotion. The
notion of positive or negative experience has normativity built within — it stipu-
lates that some feelings are 'good' and others are 'bad' (in this sense, the
'moralizations of valence' illustrated at the end of section V are not the only normative accounts of valence). Charland's (2005a) view that affect valence is
influenced by second-order attentional processes and is thus indeterminate
implies that how good or bad our affects feel depends on our values; in short, we
feel through our values (this I think is the idea that emotions, thanks to feelings,
are 'normative windows to the world'; see Charland, 2005b, this volume).

There might be pragmatic reasons to keep the dichotomous notion of valence.
It is evident that 'positivity' and 'negativity' are relative to the context; for
example, a behaviour of withdrawal might be called 'negative' for some reason,
but it might be adaptive or socially beneficial and hence 'positive' in some other
sense (see Solomon & Stone, 2002, for more examples). In the first part of section VI I have argued that the relativity of 'positive' and 'negative' does not
allow one to switch back and forth between the valence sign of an emotion and
the valence sign of its aspects — there is no necessity for different aspects of
emotion to go together (as in the idea that approach is necessarily pleasant)
because they have the same 'valence sign'. Yet one could still hold that *in a certain context* it is useful to distinguish positive and negative aspects of emotion; if
the context in which the notion of valence appears is clear, the definition of
valence explicit, and the relativity of the labels acknowledged, then there should
be no problem in using 'positive' and 'negative'.

I mistrust this pragmatic stance. All things considered (section VI), I believe
that when it comes to defining and characterizing emotion, the dichotomous
notion of valence is a hindrance rather than a useful tool. I find that, in practice,
most emotion theorists often keep an ironic distance from the dichotomous character of valence (and associated claims) and acknowledge that 'things in reality
are more complicated than that'; yet, at the same time, they seem to accept the
dichotomous character of valence and associated claims as an inevitable *status*

quo. My suspicion is that if reality really is more complicated than that, prag-matic irony will at some point have to yield. The view that we can call an emotion and/or its aspect 'positive' or 'negative' *at least for certain purposes* has a dan-gerous appeal, because that distinction always simplifies and distorts the normal level of complexity, no matter how carefully and ironically it is employed. Also, it reinforces and validates other simplistic descriptions. It induces one to catego-rize, isolate and circumscribe what are complex and integrated phenomena, and to overlook their temporal developments (with fluctuations in affect, behavioral dispositions, expression, evaluations, etc.).

This descriptive style is too distant from daily lived emotions, and I think this should not and need not be so. My worry is that a tool that is too simple will induce one to overlook complexity, even when one would like to acknowledge it. For example, emotion scientists have extensively investigated 'basic emotions,' and when it comes to 'more complex ones,' things tend to be kept quite simple anyway. Guilt, shame, jealousy, etc. are described as typical, univocal, discrete and static phenomena, different from other phenomena such as e.g. moods, and non-emotional states altogether (but see Ratcliffe, 2005, this volume, for a dif-ferent view). Dimensional models generally oppose the discrete emotion approach, yet they also tend to downgrade mixtures and complexities to borderline non-prototypical cases.

The difficult question, for those who believe in the possibility of a science of emotion, is: can the dichotomous notion of valence be maintained 'at bottom' and then be somewhat complexified when and if needed? In other words, can it outlast the acknowledgement of the complexities discussed above? The dilemma is evident in Solomon & Stone (2002), who announce: 'our argument is not that there is no such thing as valence or no such polarity or contrasts, but rather that there are *many* such polarities and contrasts' (p. 418), yet recognize: 'opposites depend on polarity, and polarity is just what is *not available* in even the simplest emotions ... the game of opposites has *obviously* become *quite* pointless' (p. 433, my italics), and eventually reach the compromise that emotion research should not 'dispense with such distinctions' and yet be more attentive to the phenomenological richness of emotion (*ibid.*). Can this be achieved, and how?

Here I can only hand-wave at issues that still need to be addressed and clari-fied, and at my own preferred style of investigation. We saw that some authors (including Solomon & Stone) call for 'multidimensional approaches.' This is an interesting strategy, but it needs to be clarified and spelled out in more detail to be assessed. For example: Does Lambie & Marcel's (2002) notion of 'multidi-mensional hedonic tone' eventually dispense with the bipolar pleasant-ness-unpleasantness dimension, or can it keep it and somehow build on it? This takes us back to Charland's (2005a) argument: if affect valence is indeterminate, then that dimension is entirely normative and depends entirely on how higher-order level attention turns its gaze to it. Similarly, what becomes of Rus-sell's pleasantness-unpleasantness dimension once one admits that higher-order levels of attention modify and subsume it (cf. Russell, 2003; 2005, this volume)[8]? Perhaps Varela & Depraz (2005, this volume) are right that valence is a basic organismic disposition. But what exactly do they mean when they claim that '[i]n the case of humans ... it is ... possible to point to a *multiplicity of valences*' (p. 77, my italics)? How do evolution and development impinge on that basic disposition? Does it outlast the added integration and complexity? In short, what happens to it 'at the fold'?

My preference is real complexification which, as I see it, is not affiliated with a divide-and-conquer strategy that is confident that starting from pure, simple cases can explain the complicated and mixed ones. What is at stake is the variety and richness of our experiences, including the liberty to be uniquely and originally personal (see Campbell's account of 'free-style feelings'; Campbell, 1997). Some theorists seem resigned that emotion theory will, or even should, leave us with a gap between science and daily lived emotions (see Charland, 2005b, this volume). My preference is to try to respect complexity on both sides: in phenomenological descriptions, and in accounts of underlying mechanisms. What use can we make of a science whose conceptual tools fail to capture important features of the phenomena it is meant to describe and explain? I think that, if we want science to 'eventually hold its ground in the experimental "tribunal of experience"' (*ibid.*, p. 96) we should take complexity seriously rather than ironically, and acknowledge it *by default.*[9]

References

Aristotle ([1980]), *The Nicomachean Ethics*, trans. D. Ross (Oxford: Oxford University Press).
Arnold, M.B. (1960), *Emotion and Personality. Vol.1: Psychological Aspects* (New York: Columbia University Press).
Arnold, M.B. & Gasson, J.A. (1954), 'Feelings and emotions as dynamic factors in personality integration', reprinted in *The Nature of Emotion* (1968), ed. M.B. Arnold (Penguin).
Beebe-Center, J.G. (1932), *The Psychology of Pleasantness and Unpleasantness* (New York: Van Nostrand).
Ben-Ze'ev, A. (2000), *The Subtlety of Emotions* (Cambridge, MA: MIT Press).
Bickhard, M. (2000), 'Motivation and emotion: An interactive process model', in *The Caldron of Consciousness: Affect, Motivation and Self-Organization*, eds. R.D. Ellis & N. Newton (Amsterdam: John Benjamins).
Block, J. (1957), 'Studies in the phenomenology of emotions', *Journal of Abnormal and Social Psychology,* **54**, pp. 358–63.
Bradburn, N.M. (1969), *The Structure of Psychological Well-Being* (Chicago: Aldine).
Bradley, M.M. & Lang, P.J. (2000), 'Measuring emotion: Behavior, feeling, and physiology', in *Cognitive Neuroscience of Emotion,* eds. R.D. Lane & L. Nadel (Oxford: Oxford University Press).
Cacioppo, J.T. & Berntson, G.G. (1994), 'Relationship between attitudes and evaluative space: A critical review, with emphasis on the separability of positive and negative substrates', *Psychological Bulletin,* **115**, pp. 401–23.

[8] Russell (2003) writes that mixed feelings depend on the fact that stimuli have different aspects, and so we perceive many affective qualities simultaneously; hence 'ambivalence does not occur as core affect.' Yet, he adds that perceiving many affective qualities simultaneously 'creates a single core affect' (p. 158).

[9] This work was supported by the Social Sciences and Humanities Research Council of Canada, in the form of Post-Doctoral funding through a Canada Research Chair to Evan Thompson. I earnestly thank Sue Campbell, Louis Charland and Evan Thompson for their encouragement, charity, and very helpful comments to earlier drafts of this paper.

Campbell, S. (1997), *Interpreting the Personal: Expression and the Formation of Feelings* (Ithaca NY: Cornell University Press).

Charland, L.C. (2005a), 'Emotion experience and the indeterminacy of valence', in *Emotions: Conscious and Unconscious*, eds. L.F. Barrett, P. Niedenthal & P. Winkielman (New York: Guilford Press).

Charland, L.C. (2005b), 'The heat of emotion: Valence and the demarcation problem', *Journal of Consciousness Studies*, **12** (8–10), pp. 82–102.

Damasio, A.C. (2003), *Looking for Spinoza: Joy, Sorrow, and the Feeling Brain* (Orlando: Harcourt).

Davidson, R.J. (1984), 'Affect, cognition, and hemispheric specialization', in *Emotions, Cognition, and Behavior*, eds. C.E. Izard, J. Kagan & R.B. Zajonc (Cambridge: Cambridge University Press).

Davidson, R.J. (1993), 'Cerebral asymmetry and emotion: Conceptual and methodological conundrums', *Cognition and Emotion*, **7**, pp. 115–38.

Davidson, R.J. (1994), 'Asymmetric brain function, affective style and psychopathology: The role of early experience and plasticity', *Development and Psychopathology*, **6**, pp. 741–58.

Davidson, R.J. (1998), 'Affective style and affective disorders: Perspectives from affective neuroscience', *Cognition and Emotion*, **12**, pp. 307–30.

Davidson, R.J. (2000), 'The functional neuroanatomy of affective style', in *Cognitive Neuroscience of Emotion*, eds. R.D. Lane & L. Nadel (Oxford: Oxford University Press).

Davidson, R.J. & Harrington, A. (ed. 2002), *Visions of Compassion* (Oxford: Oxford University Press).

Davidson, R.J., Ekman, P., Saron, C.D., Senulis, J.A., & Friesen, W.V. (1990), 'Approach-withdrawal and cerebral asymmetry: Emotional expression and brain physiology', *Journal of Personality and Social Psychology*, **58**, pp. 330–41.

Davidson, R.J., Coe, C. C., Dolski, I. & Donzella, B. (1999), 'Individual differences in prefrontal activation asymmetry predict natural killer cell activity at rest in response to challenge', *Brain, Behavior and Immunity*, **13**, pp. 93–108.

Davitz, J.R. (1969), *The Language of Emotion* (New York: Academic Press).

Dreyfus, G. (2002), 'Is compassion an emotion? A cross-cultural exploration of mental typologies', in *Visions of Compassion*, eds. R.J. Davidson & A. Harrington (Oxford: Oxford University Press).

Dyer, M.G. (1987), 'Emotions and their computations: Three computer models', *Cognition and Emotion*, **1**, pp. 323–47.

Ekman, P. (1972), 'Universals and cultural differences in facial expressions of emotion', in *Nebraska Symposium on Motivation 1972, Vol. 19* (Lincoln: University of Nebraska Press), pp. 207–83.

Ekman, P. (1982), *Emotion in the Human Face* (Cambridge: Cambridge University Press).

Ekman, P. (1999), 'Facial expressions', in *Handbook of Cognition and Emotion*, ed. T. Dalgeish & M. Power (New York: John Wiley & Sons).

Fernández-Dols, J.M. & Carroll, J.M. (1997), 'Is the meaning perceived in facial expression independent of its context?', in *The Psychology of Facial Expression*, ed. J.A. Russell and J.M. Fernández-Dols (Cambridge: Cambridge University Press).

Frijda, N.H. (1986), *The Emotions* (Cambridge: Cambridge University Press).

Gennaro, R.J. (2000), 'Fiction, pleasurable tragedy, and the HOT theory of consciousness', *Philosophical Papers*, **29**, pp. 107–19.

Gibson, J.J. (1979), *The Ecological Approach to Visual Perception* (Boston: Houghton Mifflin).

Goldie, P. (2000), *The Emotions: A Philosophical Exploration* (Oxford: Oxford University Press).

Goleman, D. (ed.)(1997), *Healing Emotions: Conversations with the Dalai Lama on Mindfulness, Emotions, and Health* (Boston: Shambhala).

Goleman, D. (ed.)(2003), *Destructive Emotions: How Can We Overcome Them?* (New York: Bantam).

Isen, A. (2000), 'Positive affect and decision making', in *Handbook of Emotions. Second Edition*, eds. M. Lewis & J.M. Haviland-Jones (New York: Guildford Press).

Izard, C.E. (1991), *The Psychology of Emotions* (New York: Plenum).

Kenny, A.J.P. (1963), *Action, Emotion and Will* (London: Routledge and K. Paul).

Lambie, J.A. & Marcel, A.J. (2002), 'Consciousness and the varieties of emotion experience: A theoretical framework', *Psychological Review*, **109**, pp. 219–59.

Lang, P.J. (1984), 'Cognition in Emotion', in *Emotions, Cognition, and Behavior*, eds. C.E. Izard, J. Kagan & R.B. Zajonc (Cambridge: Cambridge University Press).

Lang, P.J. (1985), 'The cognitive psychophysiology of emotion: Fear and anxiety', in *Anxiety and the Anxiety Disorders*, eds. A.H. Tuma & J.D. Maser (Hillsdale NJ: Erlbaum), pp. 131–70.

Lang, P.J., Bradley, M.M. & Cuthbert, B.N. (1995), *The International Affective Picture System (IAPS): Photographic Slides* (Gainsville: The Center for Research in Psychophysiology, University of Florida).

Lang, P.J., Davis, M. and Öhman, A. (2000), 'Fear and anxiety: Animal models and human cognitive psychophysiology', *Journal of Affective Disorders,* **61**, pp. 137–59.

Lazarus, R.S. (1991), *Emotion and Adaptation* (New York: Oxford University Press).

Lewin, K. (1935), *A Dynamic Theory of Personality: Selected Papers,* trans. D.K. Adams & K.E. Zener (New York: McGraw-Hill).

Ortony, A., Clore, G.L. & Collins, A. (1988), *The Cognitive Structure of Emotions* (Cambridge: Cambridge University Press).

Osgood, C.E. (1952), 'The nature and measurement of meaning', *Psychological Bulletin,* **49**, pp. 197–237.

Osgood, C.E. & Suci, G.J. (1955), 'Factor analysis of meaning', *Journal of Experimental Psychology,* **50**, pp. 325–38.

Panksepp, J. (1998), *Affective Neuroscience* (Oxford: Oxford University Press).

Panksepp, J. (2000), 'The neuro-evolutionary cusp between emotions and cognitions: Implications for understanding consciousness and the emergence of a unified mind science', *Consciousness and Emotion,* **1**, pp. 27–56.

Panksepp, J. (2005), 'On the embodied neural nature of core emotional affects', *Journal of Consciousness Studies*, **12** (8–10), pp. 158–84.

Picard, R.W. (1997), *Affective Computing* (Cambridge MA: MIT Press).

Plato ([1993]), *Philebus,* trans. E. Freda (Indianapolis: Hackett).

Prinz, J.J. (2004), *Gut Reactions: A Perceptual Theory of Emotion* (New York: Oxford University Press).

Ratcliffe, M. (2005), 'The feeling of being', *Journal of Consciousness Studies*, **12** (8–10), pp. 43–61.

Reinman, E.M., Lane, R.D., Ahern, G.L., Schwartz, G. & Davidson, R.J. (2000). 'Positron emission tomography in the study of emotion, anxiety, and anxiety disorders', in *Cognitive Neuroscience of Emotion,* eds. R.D. Lane & L. Nadel (Oxford: Oxford University Press).

Rozin, P. (2003), 'Introduction: Evolutionary and cultural perspectives on affect', in *Handbook of Affective Sciences,* ed. R.J. Davidson, K.R. Scherer & H.H. Goldsmith (Oxford: Oxford University Press).

Russell, J.A. (1980), 'A circumplex model of affect', *Journal of Personality and Social Psychology,* **39**, pp. 1161–78.

Russell, J.A. (2003), 'Core affect and the psychological construction of emotion', *Psychological Bulletin,* **110**, pp. 145–72.

Russell, J.A. (2005), 'Emotion in human consciousness is built on core affect', *Journal of Consciousness Studies*, **12** (8–10), pp. 26–42.

Russell, J.A. & Carroll, J.M. (1999), 'On the bipolarity of positive and negative affect', *Psychological Bulletin,* **125**, pp. 3–30.

Russell, J.A. and Fehr, B. (1987), 'Relativity in the perception of emotion of facial expressions', *Journal of Experimental Psychology: General,* **CXVI**, pp. 223-237.

Russell, J.A. & Fernández-Dols, J.M. (ed. 1997), *The Psychology of Facial Expression* (Cambridge: Cambridge University Press).

Russell, J.A. & Mehrabian, A. (1977), 'Evidence for a three factor theory of emotion', *Journal of Research in Personality,* **11**, pp. 273–94.

Schlosberg, H. (1941), 'A scale for the judgment of facial expressions', *Journal of Experimental Psychology,* **29**, pp. 497–510.

Schlosberg, H. (1952), 'The description of facial expressions in terms of two dimensions', *Journal of Experimental Psychology,* **44**, pp. 229–37.

Schlosberg, H. (1954), 'Three dimensions of emotion', *Psychological Review,* **61**, pp. 81–8.

Schneirla, T.C. (1959), 'An evolutionary and developmental theory of bi-phasic processes underlying approach and withdrawal', in *Nebraska Symposium on Motivation*, ed. M.R. Jones (Lincoln: University of Nebraska Press).

Smith, C.A. & Scott, H.S. (1997), 'A componential approach to the meaning of facial expressions', in *The Psychology of Facial Expression,* eds. J.A. Russell & J.M. Fernández-Dols (Cambridge: Cambridge University Press).

Solomon, R.C. & Stone, L.D. (2002), 'On 'positive' and 'negative' emotions', *Journal for the Theory of Social Behaviour*, **32**, pp. 417–35.

Titchener, E.B. (1908), *Lectures on the Elementary Psychology of Feeling and Attention* (New York: Macmillan).

Tolman, E.C. (1932), *Purposive Behavior in Animals and Man* (New York: Century).

Tomkins, S.S. (1962/1963), *Affect, Imagery, Consciousness* (New York: Springer).

Tomkins, S.S. (1970), 'Affect as the primary motivational system', in *Feelings and Emotions*, ed. M.B. Arnold (New York: Academic Press).

Tucker, D.M. (1981), 'Lateral brain function, emotion and conceptualization', *Psychological Bullettin*, **89**, pp. 19-46.

Varela, F.J. & Depraz, N. (2005), 'At the source of time: Valence and the constitutional dynamics of affect', *Journal of Consciousness Studies*, **12** (8–10), pp. 61–81.

Watson, D. & Tellegen, A. (1985), 'Towards a consensual structure of mood', *Psychological Bulletin*, **98**, pp. 219–35.

Watson, D., Clark, L.A. & Tellegen, A. (1988), 'Development and validation of brief measures of positive and negative affect: The PANAS scales', *Journal of Personality and Social Psychology,* **54**, pp. 1063–70.

Wundt, W. (1907), *Outlines of Psychology* (Leipzig: Englemann).

Peter Goldie

Imagination and the Distorting
Power of Emotion

In real life, emotions can distort practical reasoning, typically in ways that it is difficult to realise at the time, or to envisage and plan for in advance. This feature of real life emotional experience raises difficulties for imagining such experiences through centrally imagining, or imagining 'from the inside'. I argue instead for the important psychological role played by another kind of imagining: imagining from an external perspective. This external perspective can draw on the dramatic irony involved in imagining these typical cases, where one knows outside the scope of the imagining what one does not know as part of the content of what one imagines: namely, that the imagined emotion is distorting one's reasoning. Moreover, imagining from an external perspective allows one to evaluate the imagined events in a way that imagining from the inside does not.

I

In real life, emotions have the power to distort practical reasoning in a variety of ways. Emotions can distort practical reasoning by distorting perception. For example, when we are afraid, things can look more frightening than they in fact are. Emotions can distort practical reasoning by investing other reasons (such as beliefs and desires) with more power than authority. For example, when we are angry, we can want to do someone harm more than we ought to. And emotions can distort practical reasoning by 'skewing the epistemic landscape' of our justifications. For example, when we are sexually jealous, our beliefs about our partner's infidelities can seem to be justified when they are not.[1]

When emotions distort practical reasoning, they typically do so in ways that it is difficult either to realise at the time, or to envisage and plan for in advance. One example should suffice. You are making plans for a job interview. You

Correspondence:
Email: Peter.Goldie@Manchester.ac.uk

---

[1] For detailed discussion, see, for example, Elster (1999a, b); Pears (1984); Ross & Nisbett (1991); Zillman & Cantor (1976); Goldie (2004a, b).

know that one of the panel members is a particularly aggressive and unpleasant man, who is bound to ask endless questions which are designed to show off his own knowledge and not to test yours. Beforehand, cool calm reasoning shows you the right way forward: you plan not to let him annoy you because you are determined to get the job. However, when it comes to the heat of the actual moment you become angry, and the man's manner, his voice, his line of questioning, his whole character, put your back up much more than you expected. And suddenly, to your later chagrin, what seems to you to be more important than anything else is to make sure that this man doesn't get in the last word. Thus, in the grip of anger, you do what seems to you *at the time* to be the most important thing, but what you knew beforehand to be precisely *not* the right thing to do. Thinking about examples like this one, and others which exemplify other ways in which emotion distorts practical reasoning, led me to wondering what is going on when we deliberate and make plans in advance of an emotional experience by imagining ourselves in that situation, and whether, and in what ways, we can imagine the distorting power of emotion. And this in turn led me to thinking more generally about what exactly the role is of emotion in experiential imagination and in imagined practical reasoning.

Experiential imagining is taken paradigmatically to be imagining 'from the inside', where you imagine from the inside yourself in some situation undergoing some experience, or where you imagine from the inside someone else undergoing that experience. There has been much discussion in philosophy and in psychology about the role of this kind of imagining in explaining our ability to predict what people will think, feel and do. Sometimes called simulation, sometimes co-cognition, sometimes central imagining, sometimes empathy, sometimes putting yourself in the other's shoes, its exact nature is hotly debated, but many philosophers and psychologists emphasise its great importance.[2] One of the conclusions I draw from this paper is that the importance of this kind of experiential imagining is overemphasised, whilst another kind of experiential imagining is under-emphasised or even ignored. In this other kind of imagining, if I am trying to imagine what I will think, feel and do in the interview, I imagine the events unfolding not from the inside, but from an external perspective, where I myself am part of the content of what I imagine. And the same kind of imagining can be deployed when I am trying to imagine someone else in a similar situation. Imagining from an external perspective is, I will argue, particularly important and natural when we set out to imagine the distorting power of emotion.

I will begin with the more general line of enquiry, considering the role of emotion in experiential imagining. I will then turn to the more specific questions concerning the distorting power of emotion, and the difficulties that imagining the distorting power of emotion presents for experiential imagining from the inside.

---

[2] See, for example, Collingwood (1946), Currie & Ravenscroft (2002), Heal (1998, 2000), Wollheim (1974, 1984), Harris (2000).

II

Some kinds of psychological state have counterparts in imagination with which they share, more or less, the same character (Budd, 1989, Currie & Ravenscroft, 2002). For example, the counterpart of believing is belief-like imagining or supposing, and the counterpart of seeing is visualising or imagining seeing. Some other kinds of state do not have imaginative counterparts. Being drunk is an example. If you try to imagine being drunk, perhaps the best you can do is to imagine *that* you are drunk, and then engage in a kind of pretence in imagination, imagining behaving as if you are drunk.

What are the conceptual and psychological limitations on imaginative counterparts? Psychological limitations may well vary across individuals, as well as varying in ways that depend on the extent to which the will is involved in the imagining; for example, there may be a difference between, on the one hand, carefully trying to deploy one's experiential imagination in planning a complex series of actions, and, on the other hand, letting one's imagination have free rein, as one does when daydreaming. But, for the moment, let me leave to one side psychological limitations and consider limitations of a more conceptual variety, bearing in mind all the time that my concern at this point is with experiential imagining, rather than propositional imagining, and in particular with experiential imagining from the inside.[3] I will first focus on imagining oneself from the inside, and turn later to imagining others in this way.

I cannot experientially imagine from the inside being unconscious any more than I can in real life experience being unconscious. This is a conceptual limitation on experiential imagining and not a psychological one. Equally, it is not possible that the content of what I imagine should include something of which, in the imaginative process, I am not aware; for example, I cannot experientially imagine myself, from the inside, with someone, unperceived by me, creeping up behind me in order to surprise me.

There are other kinds of conceptual limitations that apply to real life psychological states that can equally be read across to their imaginative counterparts. Can I imagine having a false belief? I can of course imagine having a belief that I know, outside the scope what is imagined, to be false. This is just supposing. But, with the knowledge of the belief's falsity within the scope of what I imagine, the answer would seem to be no: I cannot imagine having a belief that I know, as part of what I imagine, to be false. So the conceptual limitation that applies to a real life mental state type, in this case the limitation to belief that was illuminated by Moore's Paradox (Moore, 1942), also applies to the imaginative counterpart of belief. And there are others. Maybe I cannot imagine trying to do what I know to be impossible. Maybe I cannot imagine desiring something that does not strike me in any way to be desirable: if, as Elisabeth Anscombe and others have suggested, in real life I cannot desire a saucer of mud if there is nothing desirable

---

[3]   For the distinction between propositional imagining and perceptual imagining, see Peacocke (1985).

about it for me, then the same limitation will apply to imagining desiring a saucer of mud; it is, indeed, an interesting and revealing exercise to try to do so.[4]

To the extent that each of these real life conceptual limitations is disputed or accepted, so the limitations of their imaginative counterparts ought to be disputed or accepted. But let me leave to one side the questions that arise about these particular kinds of states and their imaginative counterparts, interesting as they may be, and turn to what concerns me here — emotion. Does emotion have an imaginative counterpart, and if so, what kinds of conceptual limitations are there on imagining an emotional experience?

III

In a recent book, Greg Currie and Ian Ravenscoft have argued that emotion has no imaginative counterpart, and that, uniquely, imagination is what they call 'transparent' to emotion. This is what they say: 'emotions are peculiar states in that they are, so to speak, their own counterparts. In imagination we do not take on another's belief or desire; we take on a belief-like or a desire-like imagining that corresponds to those beliefs and desires. But when I put myself imaginatively in the position of someone being threatened, it is genuine fear I come to experience, not an imagination-based substitute for fear' (2002, p. 159). In this respect, Currie and Ravenscroft say, this unique transparency of emotion distinguishes it from, for example, pain: if I imagine feeling pain, I do not as a result actually feel pain. They suggest that this capacity, to have real emotions in response to imagined situations, evolved partly because of its role in planning: they say, 'Having a system of emotional responses poised to respond to what I imagine is a capacity we would expect to find in creatures able to choose between alternatives' (2002, p. 197). And, they add, the capacity also plays a role in our ability to predict what others will think, feel and do.

There is a lot I agree with here. I agree that our experiential imaginings can give rise to real emotions. So, for example, if someone imagines house prices falling dramatically, then, if she is a house-owner with a large mortgage, she might come actually to feel fear at what she imagines. Moreover, I welcome the thought that these emotions are not to be dismissed as what Currie used to call quasi-emotions; rather, they are real emotions that are directed towards what is imagined.

What I disagree with is the claim that emotion has no imaginative counterpart. For it seems possible for me, for example, to imagine something threatening, and to imagine feeling afraid of the threatening thing that I imagine, where the imagined fear is part of the *content* of what I imagine, and not a response *to* what I imagine.[5] I agree with Richard Wollheim here. He says the following about sexual arousal, making it clear that he believes that the same remarks apply to the

---

[4] Anscombe (1958). For discussion, see Velleman (1992) and Blackburn (2002).

[5] See Moran (1994). Currie and Ravenscroft say that the real emotion can 'occur within the scope of an imaginative project' (2002: 96). However, it is a rather misleading way of putting it, for the emotion

emotions: 'I shall use the familiar phenomenon of the erotic daydream... Let us suppose that I centrally imagine myself [that is, that I imagine myself from the inside] engaged in some sexual activity with a strange figure, or a close friend. As I do so, I centrally imagine myself becoming excited over what occurs between us. ... And as I centrally imagine myself becoming excited, so I become excited' (Wollheim, 1984, pp. 81–2). So Wollheim holds both that we can have real emotions as a result of what we imagine, and that we can have imagined emotions. If this is right, the imagined emotions, unlike the real ones, will be part of the content of what is imagined.

Why might one reject the possibility that emotions can have imaginative counterparts? After all, the possibility is not obviously open to the kind of conceptual limitations that I was canvassing earlier. One reason might be grounded in a misconception of what a real life emotional experience is, and thus in what its imaginative counterpart might be like.

A real life emotional experience involves perceptions, thoughts and feelings, typically directed towards the object of the emotion. Recognition that one is having an emotional experience is not a necessary part of every such experience. So, if an emotional experience were to have an imaginative counterpart, then we would expect it to involve *imagined* perceptions, thoughts and feelings, typically directed towards the *imagined* object. And this, I suggest, is precisely the correct picture (Goldie, 2000). If you imagine being woken up in the middle of the night by a gang of burglars breaking down your front door with axes, your imagining this — your imagined perceptions, thoughts and feelings with the right emotionally-laden content — just is your imagined fearful experience. Imagining being afraid is not something over and above the imagined fearful experience, as if there were two distinct imaginings: first, imagining a fearful thing; and then secondly, imagining feeling fear. Rather, imagining being afraid just is imagining having a fearful experience, and imagining having a fearful experience just is having imagined perceptions, thoughts and feelings, typically directed towards the imagined object. Currie and Ravenscroft, whilst rightly admitting these kinds of imaginings (2002: 96), wrongly deny that they *are* the imagined emotional experience, and thus wrongly claim that emotion is unique in not having a counterpart in imagination.[6]

There is a further reason for accepting that emotions have imaginative counterparts. In respect of some imaginative projects it is necessary that an imagined emotional experience features in imagined practical reasoning, and thus in imagined action, as it would if I were to ask you to imagine what you would decide to do, and what you would do, if you saw and heard those burglars breaking down your front door. Currie and Ravenscroft rightly emphasise the role of emotional

— the real fear about falling house prices for example — is not part of the *content* of what is imagined.

[6] It might be asked whether this kind of example generalises to all emotions (thanks to an anonymous referee for raising this). Could I not imagine from the inside having a joyful experience, not by imagining having certain perceptions, thoughts and feelings, but simply by imagining behaving in a joyful way? However, imagining behaving in a joyful way would seem to be the counterpart of pretending to be joyful, rather than the counterpart of being joyful.

response in planning, but surely in such cases the emotion has to be part of the content of what is imagined, logically and temporally prior to the imagined decision and the imagined action, for it to be able to play this role. What they call the 'generated' real life emotion (2002: 96) cannot play this role.

IV

The next question is just how these imagined emotional experiences feature in imagined practical reasoning and imagined action. Here we come back to the conceptual limitations that apply to real life psychological states, and that can be read across to their imaginative counterparts.

Real life emotion shares two features with real life perception. First, real life emotion, like real life perception, represents the world as being a certain way, and can thus be correct or incorrect. Secondly, these states, with representational content, have what John Skorupski calls 'normative impulse'[7]: we typically take the world to be the way the perception or the emotion represents it to be, unless we have reason to think otherwise; in other words, we typically take the states to be correct — we typically trust them.

Thus an untypical case in perception would be where, in the Müller-Lyer illusion, one sees the two the lines as being of different lengths whilst also believing them to be of the same length. And an untypical case in emotion would be the one discussed by David Hume, of the man suspended from a high tower in an iron cage: he is afraid he will fall whilst also believing that he is not in danger.[8] But in the typical real life case, one takes one's emotion to be 'correct': if one feels disgust at a log for example, then one also takes oneself to be correct in ascribing the property of being disgusting to the log, as well as further properties that, in turn, justify the ascription of the property of being disgusting — its being covered in crawling white maggots say (Goldie, 2004a, b).

So the same principles should be able to be read across to imagining an emotional experience, according to which it will be typical in imagination to take one's emotion to be correct: to take it that the world — the imagined world here rather than the real world of course — is the way the imagined emotion represents it to be. For example, it will be a typical case if one imagines feeling disgust towards a log and takes it that this emotion is correct — that the imagined log does have the property of being disgusting. And it will be untypical to imagine having an emotional experience but also at the same time to imagine believing that the imagined emotion is not correct. An example of an untypical case would be someone who knows that she has a disposition to fear spiders, and she imagines herself seeing a spider in the bathroom and feeling afraid of it, and also imagines believing, as part of the content of what she imagines, that there is nothing about the spider to be frightened of — it being a spider of the variety found in Britain. The typical case in imagination should thus be where the imagined

---

[7] Skorupski (2000, p. 125). Thanks to Sabine Döring here for clearing up a confusion on my part.

[8] Hume (1978, p. 148), and, for discussion, Goldie (2000, pp. 76–7).

emotion has 'normative impulse' in imagined practical reasoning, just as this is the typical case in real life, and the knowledge that the emotion is not correct should be kept out of the picture.

But how can we imagine experiencing an emotion that we know, outside the scope of our imagining, to be incorrect, whilst keeping it as a typical case, with normative impulse, inside the scope of our imagining?

V

Like alcohol or drugs, emotions in real life can distort practical reasoning, but they do so in different ways. For, unlike drink and drugs, emotional experience itself features as reason-giving in practical reasoning. My being drunk does not itself give me a reason to decide to stay at the party longer than I should, whereas my being afraid can give me a reason to run across the car park late at night. In perceiving the man over there to be threatening (he looks like a mugger to me), I take my fear to be correct and to be justified, and so I consider myself to have good reason to run, looking over my shoulder as I go.

Now let us assume that in this real life case I am a timorous sort of person, and that there really is no danger; the man is really quite harmless, and he only seems threatening to me because I am so timorous. My perception is distorted and my epistemic landscape is skewed (Goldie, 2004a). But, this being the typical case, I do not realise that my practical reasoning is being distorted by my fear: from the inside, and at the time, I consider my fear to be correct and to be justified — I consider my reasoning to be good, and I consider my reasons to be good. Of course, I might realise later that it was just silly old nervous me, but at the time it didn't seem like that. My action — my running across the car park whilst looking over my shoulder — was done for reasons, and these reasons seemed to me at the time to be good ones.

Now, let us turn to imagining myself in that situation. Can I imagine myself from the inside, reasoning about what I ought to do in this situation, and then imagine doing what I imagine deciding to do, whilst knowing, outside the scope of what I imagine, that this is not what I ought to do and that I am only reasoning like this because I am a timorous person?

Of course, it would be easy for me to make a prediction of my action here without using my imagination; all I need to know is that I am a timorous person, disposed to do things such as take harmless-looking people in car parks to be muggers. But what concerns me here is whether I can imagine the emotional experience in the right way, from the inside. Can I imagine, in the right way, the distorting power of emotion?

The question is important not only because much work is being done in philosophy and psychology on the role of this kind of imagining in prediction and planning. The question also has implications for how we ourselves go about planning what to do in emotional situations. To go back to my example at the beginning of this paper, you have a job interview coming up, and you try to imagine yourself being asked aggressive questions by that man on the interview panel whom you don't like. Can such an imaginative project result in an accurate prediction of how emotion will distort your reasoning?

There are really two questions here in one. The first question is, roughly, whether in such cases imagination is a good guide to real life without prior comparable experience. And the indications are that it is not.[9] But let me put this first question to one side here, as it is the second that interests me. The second question is whether, with prior comparable experience, I can imagine myself engaged in practical reasoning about what I ought to do, and, because of the distorting power of emotion, deciding to do what I know, outside the scope of what I imagine, to be not what I ought to do. Remember here that imagining from the inside involves more than just imagining acting in a certain way; it also involves imagining deliberating, reasoning, acting for reasons, and so on, and this practical reasoning is normative, about what I ought to do, and not just about what I will do.

I think the answer is yes, as a matter of conceptual possibility, I can do this: I can build the distorting power of the emotion into the imagined reasons that feature in the imagined practical reasoning, so that (as it typically should be) the imagined emotional experience has normative impulse. In other words, what I imagine from the inside is the emotion's power being matched by its authority (thus making the experience typical, unlike the spider example), whilst knowing, outside the scope of the imagining, that the emotion is distorting. There seems to be no conceptual barrier to this kind of imagining.[10]

However, whilst admitting the conceptual possibility of imagining from the inside the distorting power of emotion in a way that preserves the normative impulse of emotional experience, I want now to cast some doubt on the psychological facility with which this can be done, especially as part of a consciously controlled imaginative project, such as when I am using my imagination in order to plan or predict what I, or some other person, will think, feel and do. The point requires some background, and will eventually lead me to a discussion of another

[9] Consider Stanley Milgram's famous obedience experiments (Milgram, 1974). Participants were asked to be 'teachers' and to inflict punishment, which they thought to be electric shocks, on 'learners' when the learners made a mistake in some simple learning task. Before the experiment, participants were asked to predict what they would do, and what they would expect others to do. Each one said, of himself or herself, that he or she would stop inflicting the shocks very early, and the prediction of what others would do was that less than one in a thousand would choose to go the maximum of 450 volts, and that anyone who did so would be a psychopath. In fact, of the 40 subjects of Milgram's original experiment, 65 per cent of participants went to the maximum, and not one stopped before reaching 300 volts. Presumably a reasonable proportion of those attempting to make a prediction did so by trying to imagine the situation. So imagination seemed to be a bad guide to real life without prior comparable experience. Not all subjects who went to the maximum were emotionally affected; however, Milgram made it clear that many were affected. See my discussion of this in Goldie (2000).

[10] Thanks to Berys Gaut here. The point should be made, however, that knowledge gained from 'prior comparable experience' of how I engage in practical reasoning when under the influence of emotion is, in some sense, theoretical knowledge, and it remains unclear how such knowledge can be incorporated in a project of imagining from the inside. The risk is that it turns into imagining behaving in a certain way—imagining behaving in a way that is consistent with having one's practical reasoning distorted by emotion. (Thanks to an anonymous referee for raising this point.) In any event, whether or not imagining this from inside is conceptually possible, such concerns bring out further the psychological importance of the alternative, of imagining from the outside.

kind of experiential imagining of great psychological importance: imagining from an external perspective.

VI

In his seminal work on imagining, Richard Wollheim drew on a distinction which goes back to Aristotle, the distinction between two types of audience: the empathetic audience and the sympathetic audience. Observing the blinding of Gloucester in *King Lear*, the empathetic audience, as contrasted with the sympathetic audience, 'must be that part of the audience which feels what Gloucester feels, not that part which feels for Gloucester' (Wollheim, 1974, p. 66). So the empathetic audience, which observes Gloucester enduring his blinding, feels terror, and the sympathetic audience feels pity.

Now let us move the plot forward, both the plot of *King Lear*, and the plot of this paper. Gloucester is now blind and wants to die, and Edgar is telling him that he is on the edge of the cliffs of Dover, and can with one step forward thereby end his life. But in fact Edgar has merely led Gloucester up to a tiny ledge, and not to the cliffs of Dover. Here we have dramatic irony. To appreciate this dramatic irony, the audience has to be both aware of how things seem for Gloucester, and also to be aware of how things, in fact, are. Merely empathising with Gloucester, merely imagining the scene from Gloucester's perspective, cannot yield up any dramatic irony. This is a conceptual limitation on experiential imagining from the inside.

Appreciation of the two perspectives is at the heart of dramatic irony. This point is brought out by Hume in his discussion of pity. He remarks, '[H]istorians readily observe of any infant prince, who is captive in the hands of his enemies, that he is more worthy of compassion the less sensible he is of his miserable condition. As we ourselves are here acquainted with the wretched situation of the person, it gives us a lively idea and sensation of sorrow, which is the passion that generally attends it; and this idea becomes still more lively, and the sensation more violent by a contrast with that security and indifference which we observe in the person himself. A contrast of any kind never fails to affect the imagination, especially when presented by the subject; and it is on the imagination that pity entirely depends'.[11]

Whilst appreciation of both perspectives is required for appreciation of dramatic irony, consideration of these examples suggests to me that the naturally dominant perspective is external, and thus sympathetic, rather than from the inside, and thus empathetic. This, I think, is because taking up the empathetic stance requires us, so to speak, to unlearn what we know full well — to unlearn, for example, that the infant prince is in big trouble. Of course, in sympathising with him from an external perspective it is necessary for us to appreciate how it is from the little chap's point of view, but our appreciating this does not require us

---

[11] Hume (1978, p. 371). When the child feels fear when she listens to the story of Little Red Riding Hood being fooled by the wolf, her perspective is sympathetic not empathetic: she feels fear *for* the little girl in the story.

to take up that perspective in imagination, and certainly not to maintain it; after all, empathy is not the source of all knowledge of what others are thinking and feeling. It may be psychologically possible to oscillate between taking a sympathetic perspective on the infant prince and, on the other hand, imagining from the inside his experiences in his blissful ignorance, but the dramatic irony draws one towards the former kind of perspective.

Now, parallel to the examples of blinded Gloucester and the infant prince, dramatic irony — or perhaps we might call it ironic distance to remove any implication that we are just concerned with drama — is integral to the kind of cases I have been discussing, in which I imagine myself being influenced in my thoughts, feelings and actions by the distorting power of emotion. I know something outside the scope of my imagining that I do not know as part of the content of what I imagine: namely, that the imagined emotion is distorting my reasoning. My suggestion is this: awareness of the dramatic irony from outside the scope of the imagining draws one away from imagining oneself from the inside or what Wollheim calls central imagining, and towards imagining oneself from an external perspective, so that, in effect, your perspective on your imagined self is sympathetic rather than empathetic.

Imagining from an external perspective in this way is imagining from a perspective, but not from the perspective of any person in the imagined scene (Wollheim 1984; Goldie 2000). I can, for example, imagine myself from an external perspective, with, unseen by me, someone creeping up on me from behind in order to surprise me; I thus feature in the imagined scene just as does the person who is creeping up on me.[12] This kind of imagining, seeing oneself as another, is not only naturally suited to experiential imagining where dramatic irony is involved; it is also naturally suited to experiential memory where dramatic irony is involved.[13] Say I was once the victim of an outrageous confidence trick. I now ask myself: how *did* I fail to notice what it was all about; how *could* I have fallen for it? Now let me try to remember it. I think it is no easy feat to remember this experientially from the inside, ignorant of the trickery, although perhaps this is how it might come back to me in my dreams. The tendency, rather, is for me to imagine it from an external perspective, drawing on the dramatic irony, so that the trickery and my gullibility are, as such, part of what I bring to mind. 'You fool!', I say, as I run through the events in my mind. In remembering what happened in this way, my external perspective expresses my evaluative stance towards the events: with this hindsight, I evaluate what was done to me as a con-trick, and I evaluate myself as a gullible fool.

This example brings out a further fact which is implicit in imagining from an external perspective. This kind of imagining allows evaluation to be built into the perspective in a way that imagining from the inside does not. Indeed,

---

[12] My concern here is with the variety of imagining oneself from an external perspective that Wollheim (1984) calls acentral imagining, or imagining oneself from the perspective of no person within the imagined scene. There is another variety which involves imagining oneself from the perspective of another person, so that I feature peripherally, to use Wollheim's term. But see also Footnote 16.

[13] This kind of remembering is discussed in Moran (1994). For detailed discussion, see Goldie (2003).

evaluation was implicit in my earlier examples of blinded Gloucester and of the infant prince. Our feelings of pity for those two souls, from our external perspective, were guided and shaped by our thoughts that their suffering was undeserved. We might otherwise have remained indifferent, or even have felt grim satisfaction at their fate.

Let us go back to your using your imagination in planning for the job interview, bearing in mind this discussion of dramatic irony and my suggestion that when we are imagining the distorting power of emotion, in those typical cases where the imagined emotion has normative impulse, imagining from an external perspective is psychologically more natural than imagining from the inside. You know that you ought to control your temper, in spite of the aggressive and unpleasant line of questioning which you anticipate from the panel member. You also know that, when it comes to the moment, your back will go up, and you will find yourself doing just what you know you ought not to do. Accepting, as I have done, that this *could* be imagined from the inside, the dramatic irony naturally draws you towards imagining yourself in the interview from an external perspective — perhaps from a sideways-on perspective, as in the famous picture 'When did you last see your father?'[14] What you can then do is imagine yourself, as part of the content of what you imagine, doing what you know, outside the scope of what you imagine, you ought not to do, and doing it for reasons that you know, outside the scope of what you imagine, not to be good ones. You might then exclaim, 'I can just *see* myself behaving stupidly at the interview when that aggressive swine gets going!', and this exclamation expresses the external perspective, the ironic distance, and an evaluation from the advantage of this ironic distance.

This example, and the example of the remembered con-trick, reveal yet another respect in which imagining myself as another, from an external perspective, is at a psychological advantage over imagining myself from the inside: I can readily build in to the content of what I imagine certain facts about my own personality. For example, I can build in the fact that I am a cantankerous person, who is not disposed to remain calm in the face of the questioning that I might expect at this interview. This kind of fact should not typically feature as part of the content of my imagining from the inside, for it is not typical for awareness of one's personality traits to be part of one's experience; if it were (perhaps in the thought 'I am a cantankerous person'), the imagined case would turn into an untypical one, where I know, as part of what I am imagining, that my reasoning is not as it ought to be.

VII

I want to end by considering the merits of imagining others from an external perspective. So far, most of what I have said has concerned imagining oneself. But I said at the outset that imagining from the inside, under the various titles of simulation, co-cognition, empathy, or putting yourself in the other's shoes, is also

---

[14] The picture is by William Frederick Yeames. Various images of this picture can be seen on the web.

often appealed to as the paradigmatic way in which we are able to predict what others will think, feel and do.

Special difficulties arise if I am trying to imagine you from the inside if you are not relevantly similar to me. In such cases, I need to build in person-specific background facts about you in order accurately to predict what you will think, feel and do[15]: facts about your character and personality traits, and other person-specific background facts — your age, wealth and upbringing, your background emotional dispositions, your moods and state of health. But, as I have just observed in the first-personal case, these facts are not typically part of the content of your practical reasoning, so when I simulate your practical reasoning, how do I adjust for these facts? How do I make my dispositions like yours? This, I have argued elsewhere, has not such an easy answer as is often supposed (Goldie, 2002). Moreover, if you are substantially different in character from me, your motives, which I use as imagined 'inputs' to my imagined reasoning, will come to seem alien when I try to simulate your thinking, and a kind of imaginative resistance is likely to set it; as Tamar Gendler has put it, I am unwilling (but not unable) to take on a perspective on the world that I do not reflectively endorse (Gendler, 2000).

These difficulties of simulation, or imagining another from the inside, fall away if I imagine the other from an external perspective[16]. First, unlike simulation, the way the imagined events unfold can continuously and consciously depend on, or draw on, person-specific background facts about the other person. Secondly, imaginative resistance is not a problem as I am not required to take on someone else's perspective when I am imagining them from an external perspective; indeed, my external perspective can involve a negative evaluation of the other's personality and motives. Thirdly, I can readily draw on dramatic irony. Just as I can see myself behaving stupidly at that interview, for reasons that seemed to me to be good ones at the time, so I can see the other person doing the same thing for reasons that they thought to be good ones at the time. In both cases, drawing on the dramatic irony, I am experientially imagining the distorting power of emotion, but from an external perspective and not from the inside.[17]

References

Anscombe, E. (1958), *Intention* (Oxford: Blackwell).
Blackburn, S. (2002), 'How emotional is the virtuous person?', in *Understanding Emotions: Mind and Morals*, ed. P. Goldie (Aldershot: Ashgate).
Budd, M. (1989), *Wittgenstein's Philosophy of Psychology* (London: Routledge).
Collingwood, R. (1946), *The Idea of History* (Oxford: Oxford University Press).
Currie, G., & Ravenscroft, I. (2002), *Recreative Minds: Imagination in Philosophy and Psychology* (Oxford: Clarendon Press).

[15] See Heal (1998, 2000), Nichols & Stich (2003), Morton (2003).

[16] Here I might either imagine the other acentrally or peripherally — for this distinction see Footnote 12.

[17] Many thanks to all those who have commented on earlier versions of this paper, at The University of Edinburgh, at The University of Manchester, at Sussex University, and at King's College London. Special thanks to the editors, and to Rob Hopkins, Sabine Döring and Berys Gaut for detailed comments.

Elster, J. (1999a), *Strong Feelings: Emotion, Addiction, and Human Behavior* (Cambridge, MA: MIT Press).

Elster, J. (1999b), *Alchemies of the Mind: Rationality and the Emotions* (Cambridge: Cambridge University Press).

Gendler, T. (2000), 'The puzzle of imaginative resistance', *Journal of Philosophy*, **97**, pp. 55–81.

Goldie, P. (2000), *The Emotions: A Philosophical Exploration* (Oxford: Clarendon Press).

Goldie, P. (2002), 'Emotion, personality and simulation', in *Understanding Emotions: Mind and Morals*, ed. P. Goldie (Aldershot: Ashgate).

Goldie, P. (2003), 'One's remembered past: Narrative thinking, emotion, and the external perspective', *Philosophical Papers*, **32**, pp. 301–19.

Goldie, P. (2004a), 'Emotion, reason, and virtue', in *Emotion, Evolution, and Rationality*, ed. P. Cruse and D. Evans (Oxford: Oxford University Press).

Goldie, P. (2004b), 'Emotion, feeling, and knowledge of the world', in *Thinking about Feeling: Contemporary Philosophers on Emotions*, ed. R. Solomon (New York: Oxford University Press), 2004, pp. 91-106.

Harris, P. (2000), *The Work of the Imagination* (Oxford: Blackwell).

Heal, J. (1998), 'Co-cognition and off-line simulation: Two ways of understanding the simulation approach', *Mind and Language*, **13**, pp. 477–98.

Heal, J. (2000), 'Other minds, rationality and analogy', *Proceedings of the Aristotelian Society*, **supp. vol. lxxiv**, pp. 1–19.

Hume, D. (1978), *A Treatise of Human Nature*, ed. L.A. Selby-Bigge (Oxford: Oxford University Press).

Milgram, S. (1974), *Obedience to Authority: An Experimental View* (New York: Harper and Rowe).

Moore, G. E. (1942), 'A Reply to My Critics', in *The Philosophy of G. E. Moore*, ed. P.A. Schilpp (Evanston, IL: Northwestern University Press).

Moran, R. (1994), 'The expression of feeling in imagination', *The Philosophical Review*, **103**, pp. 75–106.

Morton, A. (2003), *The Importance of Being Understood* (London: Routledge).

Nichols, S., & Stich, S. (2003), *Mindreading* (Oxford: Clarendon Press).

Peacocke, C. (1985), 'Imagination, experience, and possibility: A Berkeleian view defended', in *Essays on Berkeley: A Tercentennial Celebration*, ed. J. Foster and H. Robinson (Oxford: Oxford University Press).

Pears, D. (1984), *Motivated Irrationality* (Oxford: Clarendon Press).

Ross, L. & Nisbett, R. (1991), *The Person and the Situation: Perspectives of Social Psychology* (New York: McGraw-Hill).

Skorupski, J. (2000), 'Irrealist Cognitivism', in *Normativity*, ed. J. Dancy (Oxford: Blackwell).

Velleman, D. (1992), 'The guise of the good', *Nous*, **26**, pp. 3–26.

Wollheim, R. (1974), 'Imagination and identification' in his *On Art and the Mind* (Cambridge, MA: Harvard University Press).

Wollheim, R. (1984), *The Thread of Life* (Cambridge, MA: Harvard University Press).

Zillman, D. & Cantor, J. (1976), 'Effect of timing of information about mitigating circumstances on emotional responses to provocation and retaliatory behavior', *Journal of Experimental Social Psychology*, **12**, pp. 38–55.

Ralph D. Ellis

The Roles of Imagery and Meta-emotion in Deliberate Choice and Moral Psychology

Understanding the role of emotion in reasoned, deliberate choice — particularly moral experience — requires three components: (a) Meta-emotion, allowing self-generated voluntary imagery and/or narratives that in turn trigger first-order emotions we may not already have, but would like to have for moral or other reasons. (b) Hardwired mammalian altruistic sentiments, necessary but not sufficient for moral motivation. (c) Neuropsychological grounding for what Hume called 'love of truth,' with two important effects in humans: (i) generalization of altruistic feelings beyond natural sympathy for conspecifics; and (ii) motivation to inquire into moral/political/psychological truth without automatic, a priori commitment to specific action tendencies — to avoid trivializing ethical and social choices. After deliberation, the desired behaviour is then triggered by using meta-emotion and voluntary imagery to 'pull up' and habituate the needed first-order emotions. The neuropsychological basis for Hume's 'love of truth' is traced to Panksepp's 'seeking system' in combination with some prefrontal executive capacities.

Keywords: Action-imagery, agency, choice, consciousness, determinism, embodiment, emotion, enactivism, free will, meta-emotion, motor-imagery, readiness-potential.

This paper will attempt to ground moral and other deliberate choices in the neuropsychology of imagery and meta-emotion. I hope to show that ethics has nothing to fear from the neurosciences, for the same reasons that Aquinas, in requesting permission to read the works of Ibn Rusd and Ibn Sina, urged the Pope that Christianity had nothing to fear from Arab philosophy: If one had true beliefs, Aquinas pointed out, then there would be no need to fear that any valid

Correspondence:
Ralph D. Ellis, Campus P.O. Box 1832, Clark Atlanta University, Atlanta, GA 30314, USA.
Email: ralphellis@mindspring.com

Journal of Consciousness Studies, **12**, No. 8–10, 2005, pp. 140–57

argument found in Arab philosophy would refute those beliefs; and if a given argument were invalid, one ought to be able to detect it (Copleston, 1962, pp. 11–19).

It is true that, if we ask most philosophers of mind (who do take neuroscience seriously) for a reconciliation with ethics, the response we get usually tends to be one that is disappointing from the standpoint of philosophers who specialize in ethics. The two main conciliatory strategies typically offered are (1) hardwired natural feelings such as sympathy (as in Dennett, 2003) or trust (as in fMRI images and experiments that study animal and human ability to solve the 'Prisoner's Dilemma' through cooperation: for example, see Axelrod, 1984; Rilling *et al.*, 2002); and (2) meta-emotion — i.e., having an emotion toward another emotion that can motivate us to change it, by applying our knowledge of our own psychology (again, Dennett, 2003, is an example, along with Ferrari & Koyama, 2002).

While it is obvious that mammals have natural empathy and sympathy, it is equally obvious to most moral philosophers that the first of these two strategies, relying on natural empathy and sympathy alone, misses the point of ethics. If we are naturally inclined to feel sympathy toward X, then there is no reason to tell people they *should* act altruistically toward X, since it has already been determined that they will; and if they do not feel natural sympathy toward X, then there is no reason to tell them they should act altruistically toward X, because no matter what we tell them, they cannot act in this way. For example, try telling your cat, first that it should feel altruistically toward a bird, and then that it should feel altruistically toward a sibling. In the first case, you are wasting your time because it *cannot* feel that way. In the second case, you are equally wasting your time because it is *going* to feel that way anyway. In short, you can describe the cat's feelings, but you cannot *prescribe* them.

In the Rilling *et al.* (2002) studies, the typical finding is that such-and-such social behaviour (cooperation, mutual altruism, etc.) lights up fMRI images in the nucleus accumbens, ventromedial frontal/orbitofrontal cortex, and rostral anterior cingulate — which according to Rilling *et al.* are 'brain areas that have been linked with reward processing' (p. 395). (As with most fMRI studies of emotional behaviour, however, it is useful to remember that the anterior cingulate is linked to voluntary attention to *any* object, and that ventromedial frontal and orbitofrontal cortex are linked to *any* problem solving activity!) These findings can be very useful in understanding the brain correlates of moral feeling and behaviour; but the hardwired natural feelings of 'reward' associated with cooperative behaviour are only half the picture. The other half, as I shall argue shortly, is more complicated than a straightforward hardwired emotion, and is actually hinted at by the lighting up of the anterior cingulate and orbitofrontal areas in the Rilling *et al.* findings.

The important point for now is to realize that hardwired feelings of natural sympathy or cooperativeness are too simple to account for sophisticated moral sentiment, and for behaviour that really does include (and does not just superficially resemble) ethical deliberation. And this is where the meta-emotion component of the naturalistic response comes in. We can have second-order feelings *about* how we feel at the first-order level. I can regret the fact that I enjoy staying out drinking until 4 a.m., and thus set about to re-train myself, to change my habituation in such a way that I will no longer enjoy the staying out late as much as I enjoy the image of being alert the following morning. This is merely a matter of applying my knowledge of psychological conditioning to myself, and thus adjusting the level of enjoyment I get out of different behaviours. This strategy for grounding ethics is as old as Aristotle in his *Nicomachean Ethics*, where habit development controlled by the agent serves as the foundation of moral character (see also Ellis, 1992).

But this response too strikes most moral philosophers as an inadequate grounding for ethical behaviour, because the question remains: What is to motivate me to feel the second-order regret with regard to my first-order enjoyment of staying out late more strongly than I feel the enjoyment itself? Whatever motivates the second-order regret must be caused by some natural feeling, grounded in some neurophysiological process, just as any first-order emotion would, and this raises the same problem as the one just mentioned with natural sympathy. If someone does not already feel the second-order emotion of regret, for example, then there is no point in telling them that they *should* feel the regret, since from a naturalistic standpoint they *cannot*; and in this case, it is meaningless to tell them that they *should* behave any differently from the way they are going to be caused to behave by whatever physiological processes are at work in their brains. On the other hand, if someone *does* feel the second-order regret in question, then there is no point in telling them that they *should* feel the regret (and thus change their behaviour), because it has already been naturalistically determined that they are going to feel that regret anyway. In either case — whether the naturalistic processes cause them to feel the regret and thus be able to change the behaviour, or whether they cannot feel the regret (strongly enough) and thus cannot change the behaviour, it is equally meaningless and a waste of time to tell them that they ought to act in such-and-such a way. If they were going to do X anyway, there is no point in telling them they should do X; and if they were not going to, then it is meaningless to tell them they should, since — assuming neurophysiological determinism — they cannot.

Just as with the natural sympathy strategy, the meta-emotion strategy fails to enable us to say meaningfully that anybody ought to do any behaviour X, whether X is what they are naturally motivated to do or not. If they are naturally inclined to do X, there is no point in telling them they should; and if they are not naturally inclined to do X, either by a first-order or second-order emotion, it is equally meaningless and a waste of time to tell them they should. So in the meta-emotion strategy, just as in the natural altruism strategy, the best neuroscientific accounts of moral behaviour can serve merely as *descriptions* of how we *do* behave, not as a basis for making possible any non-trivial prescriptions as to how we *should* behave.

I promised at the outset that ethics had nothing to fear from neuroscience. What is needed for an adequate moral psychology, in my view, is not only empathic feelings, plus meta-emotions, but also something else: an intellectual ability — lacking in cats and other animals without extensive prefrontal capacity — to generalize from various specific feelings of natural sympathy with specific conscious beings, to generate an appreciation of the value of *all* conscious beings and their well-being (all else being equal). This universalized feeling of appreciation of the value of conscious beings and their well-being in general can then be used to motivate (1) the needed changes in our first-order feelings toward specific conscious beings, and (2) philosophical investigation into the best ways to distribute altruistic considerations among people, given that we emotionally appreciate the value of them all. The mental skills needed to do this include the ability to produce by choice certain images which in turn can trigger the emotional inclination to make certain conscious choices (Damasio, 1994, 1999, 2003). Given the importance of orbitofrontal and anterior cingulate activity in the Rilling *et al.* studies mentioned above, it makes sense to hypothesize that a great deal more abstract reasoning and executive control of mental imagery is involved than the simple hardwired-natural-sympathy account would suggest.

To be sure, the neural substrates of the prefrontal skills at issue here are as natural as any kitten's hardwired empathic feeling toward a litter-mate. The difference is that, unlike those natural feelings by themselves, the ability to generalize from specific cases of value, combined with a natural 'love of truth' (as Hume put it in the second book of his *Treatise of Human Nature* in 1740; see also Sayre-McCord, 1994)[1] does not foreclose in advance the question as to *what* specifically is going to turn out to be the truth regarding what should be done. It leaves that question up to rational deliberation. So in this case, when someone says 'You should do X,' the generalized feeling of the value of the well-being of conscious beings, combined with the love of truth, causes us neither to automatically accept nor to automatically reject the statement. What it motivates is a rational consideration of the statement. The statement therefore is not meaningless or a waste of time, even though every step in motivating the acceptance (or rejection) of the statement, as well as the cultivation of the ability to act on the statement (through meta-emotional skills), is grounded in deterministic neurophysiology. The love of truth can be a hardwired sentiment, and is certainly conducive to survival: an animal that wants to know the truth in general, even when the truth is disturbing, is fitted for survival just as is an animal that wants to explore its environment even when not motivated by immediate hunger, as Panksepp (1998) emphasizes. But a love of truth in general is different from the love of some specific belief; the love of truth in general motivates us to seek the truth, whatever it turns out to be, and regardless of whether it conflicts with previously beloved beliefs.

In fact, it is reasonable to hypothesize that Panksepp's 'seeking' system, in interaction with the human prefrontal capacity for questioning and abstraction (Luria, 1980; Ellis, 1995) *is* the neural substrate of Hume's 'love of truth.' In mammals and many submammalian species, the essential goal of exploratory

---

[1] I am indebted to Paul Haught for convincing me of the crucial usefulness of this aspect of Hume's work for contemporary emotion studies, and especially in the present context.

behaviour, which is orchestrated by the seeking system, is to gather information ('truths') about the environment. Add to this love of exploration an ability to seek truth in abstract form — which can be supplied by the prefrontal cortex — and it seems quite predictable that a 'love of truth' would result.

The 'seeking' system is a complex emotional brain system that *endogenously* (i.e., not through secondary learning or reinforcement) motivates the animal to explore its environment. According to Panksepp, 'The extended lateral hypothalamic (LH) corridor [with ascending DA circuits and descending glutamaturgic circuits]...responds unconditionally [i.e., without any previous learning or conditioning] to homeostatic imbalances....This harmoniously operating neuroemotional system drives and energizes many mental complexities that humans experience as persistent feelings of interest, curiosity, sensation seeking, and, in the presence of a sufficiently complex cortex, the search for higher meaning' (p. 145). This 'seeking' system includes a circuit from the lateral hypothalamus to the ventral tegmental area (VTA) and heavily relies on dopamine (DA) and glutamate as neurotransmitters. While the main function of the system is emotional and motivational, as reflected in its subcortical and 'limbic' positioning, what it 'drives and energizes' can be quite complex and sophisticated, depending on the frontal and prefrontal cortex capacities of the organism in which it operates. Here, then, we have a good candidate for a neural substrate for Hume's 'love of truth.'

The power of prefrontal executive control over imagery is also important in this process, and serves the concrete purposes of meta-emotional evaluation of first-order emotions. For example, many of us have had the experience of being asked for financial help by people who have personality disturbances that render them personally obnoxious, belligerent, and insulting. In this case, mere natural sympathy does not help us get motivated to do the right thing (assuming we can determine what that is). But if we generate the right mental imagery — say, the image of some pathetic creature from *Les Miserables*, or musical imagery from Tchaikovsky's *Pathétique* Symphony — this imagery can trigger us to feel altruistic in spite of the particular individual's initially irritating manner.

Some people do not experience vivid sensory imagery as triggering their first-order feelings, but instead feel that something like a 'narrative' of a situation can pull up the feelings. It can be argued that narratives themselves are composed of combinations of imagery, including not only sensory imagery, but also proprioceptive and sensorimotor imagery (for example, see Ellis, 1995; Newton, 1996). That argument would be beyond our scope here, but Damasio (1994) uses the term 'imagery' in a broader sense when he speaks of the role of imagery in triggering feelings. So, in that sense, when I say 'imagery,' this could be taken to include complicated narratives and not just simple sensory images. The role of images and verbal phrases in 'pulling up' first-order feelings will be further discussed with the help of some of Eugene Gendlin's thinking in the concluding section of this paper.

According to Gendlin (1992b) imagery and internal narratives such as words and phrases can play a similar role in 'pulling up' the felt sense of an affective state. For example, I may form the image of a Dutch boy holding his finger in a dyke, and then notice that every time I entertain this image, the felt sense of my situation, along with its peculiar, highly specific affective tone, is felt with renewed intensity. I can then use the image or the narrative to explore the felt sense in a subtle way. Instead of lumping the felt sense in with a whole category of feeling such as 'anger' or 'sadness,' I can refer to it in its uniqueness and specificity by using the imagery to pull up the felt sense. This process will be discussed further in our concluding section.

This affinity between the role of imagery and that of narrative is also consistent with the work of Rhawn Joseph (1982) on the development of internal speech out of childhood action imagery of oneself speaking. The action commands of speech become truncated, leaving silent, internal speech. The speech imagery itself then functions like other imagery to trigger the felt sense of an intentional situation or an affective state. One can then use the speech imagery as a more refined narrative of a situation, which can then trigger more subtle feelings or felt senses at the affective level.

But in addition to the meta-emotional capacity we have been discussing, with its concomitant executive control of mental imagery and narratives, something must also initially motivate us to generate the relevant imagery or narratives in the first place, and in the case of the obnoxious but needy person (or the simply anonymous one), natural sympathy alone cannot do this job. What is needed is a combination of Hume's 'love of truth' and a meta-emotional ability to form good habits, including the habit of generating the needed imagery/narratives to trigger the needed first-order emotions at the right times — and of course reasoning skills that can open the inquiry as to what should be done, and not allow that to be foreclosed by first-order feelings.

I: The Role of Conscious Choice

Before proceeding, it is important to avoid several misunderstandings about the effects of neuroscience on agency and ethical choice. One of these has been propagated by psychologists and some philosophers of mind. Dennett (2003) and Wegner (2003), for example, argue that the feeling that our conscious choices cause us to act is illusory, and that really the feeling of making a conscious choice is a causal epiphenomenon or side-effect of the brain events that *really* cause the action, rather than the actual cause of the action. Libet *et al.* (1983; see also Libet, 1999) show that a readiness potential in the supplementary motor area (SMA) precedes the conscious experience of choice, so that when we experience ourselves as choosing to do an action, the brain actually has already initiated the action. This finding that a Readiness Potential (RP) precedes consciousness of action decisions is quickly interpreted by some philosophers to mean conscious choice is illusory.

But this conclusion is not supported by a fuller neuroscientific look at how the brain works. According to Jeannerod (1997), merely *imagining* an action requires actually sending action commands for the imaged action, while prefrontal and anterior cingulate areas inhibit the command already sent. The RP indicates that the command has been sent, not that it has been disinhibited. When we 'choose' to do the action, we disinhibit the command. Deliberately willed action requires both imaging the action (by sending the command while inhibiting it) and subsequently disinhibiting the command — although we are sometimes unconscious of this process. When we choose not to disinhibit an action command, we experience ourselves in that moment simply as deciding once and for all to do the action that the initial RP had imaged.

The readiness potential, on my account, corresponds with the earlier sending of the action command while inhibiting it, and at the subjective level this corresponds to our imaging ourselves doing the action — not actually deciding once and for all to do it. We can see this process in cats when they are considering pouncing but have not yet done so. The paws are already quivering, as if the cat were imagining the act of pouncing. The quivering paws suggest that the action command, as Jeannerod would have it, is already being sent, but is simultaneously being inhibited to facilitate the preliminary imaging of the action, prior to deciding whether to go ahead with it.

In a Jeannerod-type model of conscious choice, then, an initial action command is later disinhibited, and this disinhibition — not the RP itself — corresponds to the actual decision to act. This is because, before we can act, we must first image the action, and it is this imaging that corresponds to Libet's RP. So this account is perfectly consistent with the RP finding.

According to Jeannerod and other physiologists and psychologists who study action imagery (see Barsalou, 1987; Newton, 1996; Núñez & Freeman, 1999; Schmahmann, 1997; Schmahmann *et al.*, 2000), step (i) — imagining doing A — requires that we send an action command from brainstem to cerebellum to SMA, while at the same time inhibiting the command (Jeannerod, 1997). Step (ii) — associating a valence with A — requires that we continue sending-while-inhibiting the command, and also monitor associated positive and negative affect via emotional brain areas (hippocampus, amygdala, etc.). Step (iii) — going ahead with the action — occurs if the positive valence outweighs the negative; at this point, the gain of the RP increases, and the action command feeds forward through efferent body systems (Jeannerod, 1997).

Now the crucial question is: at which step does the RP first occur? Jeannerod's neurophysiology tells us it must occur at step (i) — the point at which the action command is initially being sent in order to imagine doing the action — not the point when we decide to go through with the action. Dennett, Wegner and many others assume that the RP is the decision to act, just because it corresponds with this initial tentative sending of the action command to the SMA, whose real purpose is only to *image* the contemplated action. So the fact that the phenomenal experience of choosing to go ahead with the action is *subsequent* to this point in time is not paradoxical or counter-intuitive at all.

We can track this whole process in terms of the timing of event related potentials (ERPs) in different brain areas. The hippocampus is activated as early as 18 ms. after the retina is stimulated by the triggering stimulus (Coles *et al.*, 1990;

Faw, 2000a). The cerebellum activates at 20 ms, indicating that a motor routine is being at least tentatively activated (Woodruf-Pak, 1997), and the cerebellum begins looping with other brain areas such as thalamus and hypothalamus, which are in reciprocal activation and inhibition relationships with the motor cortex (Haines *et al.*, 1997). All of this is prior to the consciousness of the experienced choice to do the action, which occurs at about 200ms (Libet, 1999). Meanwhile, the motor cortex is activated somewhere between 20 and 200 ms. (Damasio *et al.*, 2000), indicating that the action command is being inhibited, and it is during this time that the sensorimotor action image is being entertained. Again, there is nothing paradoxical or counterintuitive here. The RP is simply indicating that we must activate an action routine (while simultaneously inhibiting it) in order to imagine the action that we are deciding whether to do or not.

That the anterior and prefrontal cortices are involved in inhibiting action commands, as explained above, is relatively non-controversial. Still another inhibitory mechanism, proposed by Lethin (2002), is that the action command is only partially inhibited at the cortical level, and then to the extent that the partially-inhibited signal actually reaches the spinal cord, it can be further inhibited there by spinal interneurons. Even then, some of the signal might get through to the actual effector neurons in the musculature, but not enough to generate more than a trace of a movement. This would mean that the whole body is involved in subserving action imagery, and not merely the cortical map of the body. But in this case too, as in the cortical inhibition that Jeannerod says leads to action imagery, the imagery of the action requires that the action command actually be sent, but simultaneously inhibited. So here too, we would expect that the RP would accompany the preliminary imaging of the action, and not just the final decision to go through with the action.

The RP indicates that the action command has been initiated, in order to form an action image, but not that it has been disinhibited. When we 'choose' to do the action, we disinhibit the command — corresponding to Libet's 'veto power.' The 'veto power' is not an exceptional occurrence, but accompanies every willed action. When we choose not to 'veto' (disinhibit) an action command, we experience ourselves simply as deciding once and for all to do the action that the initial RP imaged.

Let me be unambiguous about the phenomenological claim here: The choice not to 'veto' the action is not a separate experience from the choice to do the action. Instead, the subjective feeling of deciding to do the action (having already imaged ourselves doing it) correlates with the disinhibition of the command. The point at which we disinhibit the command is the point at which we experience ourselves as deciding to go through with the action. The readiness potential, on my account, corresponds with the earlier sending of the action command while inhibiting it, and at the subjective level this corresponds to our imaging ourselves doing the action — not actually deciding once and for all to do it.

A Jeannerod-type model, in which an initial action command is later disinhibited, more coherently accounts for everyday experiences of responsibility and agency than the Dennett/Wegner no-conscious-choice model, in which the initial command determines the action while consciousness passively observes that a subconscious choice has been made. Responsibility must be distinguished from cases where we excuse an act resulting from a neurological condition such as a brain disease; we make this distinction because such conditions suggest passivity rather than agency (Faw, 2000b). But agency in this sense entails knowing how to (1) imagine an action by sending the action command while inhibiting it (corresponding to the RP); (2) seeing how the organism *feels* about the alternatives of disinhibiting it or not; and then (3) disinhibiting it if that is what the conscious feeling motivates. This concept of agency allows the feeling of the affective valence of imaged options to have evolved for an important purpose in choosing between the imaged alternatives, and it perfectly fits Jeannerod's story about action imagery, which when disinhibited leads to doing the previously imaged action. At the same time, it fits Libet's RP findings, when we realize that the RP corresponds to the action command prior to disinhibition. When a self isn't capable of this process, then the situation is morally similar to the case where a brain tumor causes a man to shoot people at random, thus excusing him from responsibility. This kind of question will be further pursued in the next section.

Why do philosophers and psychologists like Wegner and Dennett not accept the Jeannerod-type explanation of the RP, and instead insist that conscious choice is an illusion? I think their outlook more fundamentally arises from the conviction that any conscious experience is only another effect of the underlying physical cause, occurring in parallel with the bodily-movement effects of the underlying causal process. The argument can be schematized this way:

(a)   Physical events have necessary and sufficient physical causes.

(b)   Body movement is a physical event. Thus,

(c)   conscious choice is neither necessary nor sufficient to move our bodies (i.e., it is a causally irrelevant epiphenomenon).

The familiar Davidson (1970)-Kim (1998) picture of this paradox can be represented this way:

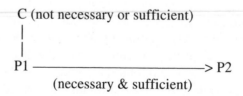

If P1 (a physical event) is necessary and sufficient for P2 (a second physical event, such as a bodily movement), then C (the conscious choice) is neither necessary nor sufficient for it, and thus cannot be a necessary or sufficient cause of it.

But neither Davidson nor Kim thinks this means the conscious choice is illusory. The reason is that they are not dualists, and thus recognize that, if C is equivalent to any P, then C has the same causal powers as that P. If C had no causal power, C would have to be non-physical! So on closer inspection, the notion that there is no mental causation actually entails dualism.

A great deal of work has been done on the neurophysiology of voluntary action and conscious choice in recent years (for example, see Núñez & Freeman, 1999; Schmahmann, 1997). A correct neuroscience does leave room for mental causation, but without violating the principle that mental processes are always grounded in physical processes that are causally-closed in Kim's (1992) sense. That is, for any given physical process in the brain, there is a physical antecedent that is necessary and sufficient to lead to it, under the given background conditions (although that same antecedent might *not* have been necessary and sufficient for that outcome *if the background conditions had been different*); and also, for any given conscious or mental event, there is a physical process that is necessary and sufficient to subserve it, under the given background conditions (although, here too, that same physical antecedent might *not* have been necessary and sufficient for that mental outcome *if the background conditions had been different*). In essence, in a self-organizing physical system, the system as a whole has the ability to rearrange the background conditions so that, if A fails to cause B under those background conditions, other background conditions can be arranged such that A *can* cause B; this is how a self-organizing system performs the continuous manipulations of background conditions to continuously find ways to maintain and enact a certain structure, or pattern of activity, across changes in the micro-components that subserve that pattern, and across exchanges of materials and energy with the environment (Ellis, 2005).

Self-organization by itself is not enough to ground an adequate moral psychology. The same kinds of objections could be raised against it that apply to the meta-emotion strategy. We must show how a conscious choice, even if it is determined neurophysiologically, can meaningfully give consideration to ethical claims and then allow a decision as to the right thing to do, at least in part because of the judged *truth* of the claims, and not merely because of some other motivation than the motivation to do the right thing.

To sum up the problems with arguments that mental causation is illusory: The argument from Libet's RP ignores the fact that the RP accompanies Jeannerod's action *imagery*, not the final choice to go through with the action by disinhibiting it. And the argument from causal closure assumes that consciousness cannot have the causal powers of a physical entity, and thus must be a non-physical kind of entity, which contradicts the first premise of the argument.

II: Contracausal Freedom *versus* Freedom from Currently External Coercion

To avoid still another confusion, we should distinguish between conscious choice, which is a modest concept, and a *contra-causal* free will, which is a radical one. For example, my friend Robert, to the chagrin of his wife, gave away his considerably lucrative inheritance to an aunt, in order to avoid allowing his daughter to grow up in snobbish 'debutante' circles. We can ask two different questions:

1. Did he do what he did 'of his own free will,' in the sense that he was not coerced by the aunt or some other factor external to himself and contrary to his will?

Suppose the answer to this question is Yes. We can then ask:

2. Was his will *contra-causally* free — i.e., free from past causal determination?

Answering Yes to the first question does not automatically decide the answer to the second one. Robert may have been caused to be the kind of person who would do what he did — in which case he was not *contra-causally* free — and yet have made his choice in a way that was free of *currently external* determining factors.

Moral responsibility is often said to entail an 'Ought implies can' principle, which might better be expressed as 'Can't implies the absence of ought.' Now philosophers like Van Inwagen (1984) argue that causal determinism would imply that the person could not have acted differently, which in turn contradicts the claim that he ought to have acted differently. If we can't act contrary to our wishes, then it isn't true that we ought to act contrary to our wishes. So determinism seems to threaten moral responsibility.

Dennett (2003), after endorsing not only causal determinism, but also Wegner's even more radical conclusion that conscious choice is illusory, tries to preserve moral responsibility nonetheless by suggesting that our wishes may be naturally altruistic. He points to the neurophysiology of empathy and bonding, subserved by oxytocin, vasopressin, etc. in mammals and having certain survival values. Given these naturally empathic sentiments to ground morality, he asks, why do we need free will, even in the modest, non-contra-causal sense?

The problem Dennett overlooks is essentially the same as what G.E. Moore (1900/1956) called the 'naturalistic fallacy.' Suppose we assume, with Dennett, that our having natural inclinations toward altruism (in situations xyz) implies that we ought to be altruistic (in situations xyz). In Moore's terms, we would be saying that an Is can then entail an Ought. But the problem is that the Ought entailed by this Is is a trivial one. It simply says 'We ought to do whatever we're naturally inclined to do' — which is morally vacuous.

For example, suppose our natural sympathy motivates us to take prisoners of war, but at the same time our natural laziness motivates us to just kill them all. Dennett's solution doesn't tell us that either course of action is better than the other, but simply that we ought to do whichever one we are more inclined to do. It then assumes that we will often be inclined to do what is right, but this assumption does not tell us what is right when we are in doubt, nor that we ought to act according to one inclination rather than another.

But if we are careful to distinguish between the modest concept of conscious choice *simpliciter* and the more radical notion of a contra-causally free will, then we lay the groundwork for a better solution to the problem of the naturalistic fallacy than the one Dennett proposes. Suppose 'I Ought to do X' means 'It would be good if I were to do X (all things considered).' And suppose that 'Good' means good for anyone (not just myself). We can get around the 'ought implies can' dilemma if some scenario such as the following occurs:

1.   I want to do whatever is best

2.   I think philosophically about whether X or Y is best

3.   If X is best, I do it, even if my natural inclination (absent step 2) were to do Y.

As long as the motive in step 1 overrides the preference for Y, I can do either X or Y, depending on which one I decide I ought to do. In concrete terms, meta-emotions — how I feel about what I feel — makes possible an Aristotelian 'rationality,' interpreted as the ability to understand our own psychology well enough to condition ourselves to prefer the valence of doing what is best over our preference for X or for Y, if doing what is best is what we previously have decided we would like to end up preferring when the occasion should arise.

How does this resolve the 'ought implies can' problem? Consider J.W., a serial bathtub murderer. Let's grant that J.W. was causally predetermined to be the kind of person he was. This presents the problem that

(1) J.W. couldn't have acted differently than to strangle women in bathtubs.

Yet,

(2) J.W. ought not to have strangled the women.

Are (1) and (2) inconsistent? No. Some people are predetermined to be the kind of people who will choose to do bad things (i.e., that they ought not to do), provided that 'I ought to do X' means 'It would be better if I were to do X.'

But then does (2) become vacuous? No. If J.W. ought not to strangle the women, then it is still meaningful to say that we ought to stop him (at least prima facie, or all else being equal). And furthermore, we *can* stop him (in fact, he is in prison now). So the 'ought implies can' neither renders the Ought vacuous, nor does it contradict causal determinism.

Does J.W. morally *deserve* punishment? If determinism is true, no. But, unfortunately in that case, we still ought to stop him, although we may feel sad for him.

The philosopher Arthur Pap (1958) tells the story of a bank robber who justified his behaviour by insisting that he really *wanted* not to want to rob the bank, but he couldn't help wanting to, because of psychological determinism. So, although he fully admitted that he had planned and premeditated the action, and wanted to do it — indeed even enjoyed doing it, and probably would do it again if given a chance — it still was not his *fault* that he wanted to do it, since there was no way he could have avoided wanting to, given determinism. In case anyone thinks this story is too far-fetched, consider the sentiment expressed in Marlene Dietrich's famous song: 'Falling in love again, what am I to do? I never wanted to, I can't help it.' The popularity of the song attests to people's empathy with the sentiment.

But the cases of Robert and J.W. answer this problem. Robert was free from external coercion, and in that sense acted freely; but this has nothing to do with whether he was contra-causally free, or whether he was predetermined to be the kind of person who would make the kind of choice he made when presented with those circumstances. Moreover, the case of J.W. shows that, even though it may not be a person's fault that he turned out to be a serial bathtub murderer (because of determinism), this does not show that J.W. should not be held responsible for choosing to obey the law, nor that he should not be punished if he fails to accept the responsibility. True, unfortunately, J.W. has been predetermined to be the kind of person who will reject that responsibility; but in general, more people will choose to accept responsibility if presented with an effective criminal justice system than not, so it does make a difference whether we offer people the proposition to accept the responsibilities we expect from them. Our offering them that choice and convincing them that they will be held responsible for it is one of the determinants (in many cases) of the person's ultimate behaviour.

III: The Role of Executive Control of Mental Imagery, Motivated by Meta-Emotion

As promised at the outset, I think we can see that ethics has nothing to fear from neuroscience, even if the latter is completely deterministic. Moral agency requires the ability to use self-generated imagery to trigger the appropriate feelings in ourselves, based on a desire to act morally. The desire to act morally in turn must be motivated somehow, and I have proposed that one likely way is that the rational capacity of the prefrontal cortex allows humans both to generalize a universal altruism from the natural mammalian feelings of altruism toward certain specific individuals; and also to generate imagery or narratives at will, even where the imagery or narrative is to be used to trigger feelings that we do not yet have, but believe we should have.

In the case of morally useful feelings that we would like to have, the use of imagery to trigger the feeling is motivated by the feeling of universalized altruism, which makes us want to do what is best on the whole, not just toward selected individuals for whom we feel natural sympathy. In response to the obnoxious but genuinely needy beggar, a universalized altruism can motivate me to generate imagery or narratives that will trigger kind feelings toward him; those kind feelings in turn will motivate me not simply to engage in 'feelgood' altruistic behaviour, but to figure out intellectually what really does seem the best thing to do — for example, give him a ride to a mental health institute rather than give him the money he thinks he needs for his next fix. Figuring this out is the role of moral philosophy, which therefore must remain a discipline completely independent from psychology, although indebted to it for an understanding of the motivation to be moral, the limits of moral capability, and the physiological substrates of the cognitive skills needed for concrete instances of moral thinking and action.

We can benefit at this point from the work of the clinical psychologist and phenomenologist Eugene Gendlin (1981/1982, 1992a, b, 1962/1998). One of Gendlin's central interests is the role that conjured imagery or verbal phrases can play in 'pulling up' feelings, as one might pull up a computer program; this process facilitates what we have been calling meta-emotion. Gendlin believes that effective use of imagery and words in such contexts can actually lead to a better understanding of the intentionality of our affective processes, and can also help them to change.

One of the main roles of imagery in relation to emotions is to allow us to explore the intentionality of the emotion, even though the image may not be what the emotion is about (Ellis, 1986, 1995, 2005). And when we generate our own fresh imagery or verbal phrases to explore the emotion, we often end up with a different and more appropriate characterization of what the emotion is about than what the initial triggering imagery might have suggested. In Gendlin's view, this way of exploring the meaning of feelings is an ordinary, everyday occurrence; some people are more prone to engage in it than others, but someone who *never* engages in it would be virtually alexithymic — unable to understand the meaning of his or her own feelings. Sundararajan (2000) tells of an alexithymic man who had murdered his father in a fit of rage. Intellectually, he acknowledged that he must have been angry, but he could not feel the rage as such. Intellectually understanding what triggered a feeling is not the same as experiencing it or understanding what it is about. The latter, in turn, requires generating our own imagery and narratives to help us to explore the meaning of the feeling, and this ability to use images and verbal phrases to trigger feelings (even ones that we are not currently feeling) is a normal human ability.

According to Gendlin, if we avoid thinking of our feelings in terms of 'stock categories' (such as 'angry' or 'hurt'), but instead find fresh imagery that is specific to the particular felt sense of the moment (for example, 'I feel like the Dutch boy holding his finger in the dyke, and then still another hole has sprung in the dyke') — then we can try out a series of such images and see which one 'pulls up' the felt sense most vividly. This does not mean that the image being used for this purpose is what the feeling is 'about'; it only means that the image can serve as an effective way to focus our attention on the unique quality of the feeling. If we then ask ourselves 'What is making me feel as if I were the Dutch boy?', we may be surprised at what comes to us: it may turn out that what is making us feel that way is not the same as what triggered the feeling in the first place — for example, failure to finish a paper on time. The triggering stimulus may only have served to call our attention to a conglomerate of intentional felt senses of our total life situation, with certain features of the life situation contributing more than others to the feeling — for example, the general way things are going at the job I work at. At this point, Gendlin believes, we have understood the felt sense more effectively than when we initially thought that we were 'angry with ourselves' for having failed to finish a paper. The intentionality of the feeling is much richer than that, and if we were to construe it too narrowly, as being 'about' the unfinished paper, we might miss the relevance of the feeling to the action it is asking for — to do something about our job situation.

For our present purposes, what is interesting about Gendlin's way of approaching the use of imagery and verbal phrases is simply the fact that we can use imagery and narratives to 'pull up' highly specific feelings in ourselves that we want to pull up at that moment, as in using a filename to open a computer program. Appropriate imagery helps us to trigger feelings that in turn will trigger appropriate actions. In organisms at our degree of complexity, there is an ability to temper and refine imagery, and to use the imagery in the service not only of understanding the intentionality of emotions, but also in the service of meta-emotions that allow us to imagine ways that we would like to feel, but are not yet feeling. In a more complicated way, a series of images and verbal phrases forming a narrative that we rehearse in our imagination can serve the same kind of purpose.

I also believe it is helpful to combine Gendlin's account with what we have learned from the neurophysiology of action and action imagery. This is discussed in detail elsewhere (Ellis, 1986; 1995; 2005), but can be sketchily summarized as follows: Emotions arise from the same areas deep in the brain as do action proclivities — the PAG, midbrain, and ventral paleocortex, which quickly activate the cerebellum to initiate action commands (Schmahmann et al., 2001). When a new stimulus is presented, the cerebellum, whose main purpose is to coordinate action, is activated much more quickly than the primary perceptual areas — as early as 20 ms. after presentation of the stimulus (Haines et al., 1997; Woodruf-Pak, 1997). If we assume that action is motivated, then a very interesting conclusion is suggested by this early cerebellar activation, especially if we also take note of the 'inattentional blindness' phenomenon (Mack & Rock, 1998), in which subjects whose attention is preoccupied fail to consciously see presented stimuli. The point is that the motivation to direct attention, as Mack & Rock suggest, is a prerequisite to being consciously aware of received information, not simply a consequence of it. Now the mechanics of the direction of attention in turn are controlled by brain processes whose motivation is to achieve the purposes of the self-organizing organism; in this sense, the act of directing attention is motivated (see Bernstein et al., 2000). Extrapolating from these kinds of observations, it is a short step to conclude that the first concern of any conscious state is to discern the action affordances of the environment. Consciousness, as Barsalou (1987) and Newton (1996) argue, must therefore include a sensorimotor imagining of how we might act relative to the world. Jeannerod, whom we discussed earlier, has shown that in order to imagine ourselves doing action X, our brains (at the subcortical and cerebellar levels) must actually send the action command X to our efferent body-moving systems, and simultaneously inhibit the signal (at the level of the SMA). The upshot is that even perceptual consciousness involves understanding ways we could act relative to objects, and these action images in turn must be motivated.

The emotional processes that motivate attention, then, are geared first of all toward action. A being must be living before it can be conscious, and to be living requires being self-organizing (Kauffman, 1993; Monod, 1971). Only self-organizing systems can act as opposed to merely reacting. The intentionality of emotion is thus addressed more toward the aims of the acting organism than toward the specific triggering stimuli that may set them off. But the aims of the organism are very general — Panksepp (1998) describes them according to seven relatively independent systems of motivation: there are separate brain systems for (1) SEEKING; (2) NURTURANCE/SEXUALITY; (3) SEPARATION DISTRESS/SOCIAL BONDING; (4) PLAY; (5) CONSUMMATORY PLEASURE; (6) RAGE; and (7) FEAR. Notice that all but the last two are things we *do* rather than things we *undergo*. They are affects endogenously motivated by our desire to engage in certain patterns of activity (for which some environmental situations might be helpful or harmful), rather than merely responses to stimuli. And it could be argued that even rage and fear presuppose that the organism previously was generally engaged in some attempted pattern of activity, and was then thwarted, or felt that it was being thwarted, in this overall pattern of activity (Ellis, 2005). This is consistent with what we know about self-organizing systems, which seek to maintain suitable patterns of activity or 'basins of attraction' across readjustments of the system's own micro-constituents and environment. So it would seem that we should understand the intentionality of emotions as being more 'about' establishing and maintaining patterns of activity appropriate to the organism's form of being than they are reactions to inputs.

Now combining this perspective with Gendlin's phenomenological observations, we can hypothesize that one of the main roles of imagery in relation to emotions is to allow us to explore the intentionality of the emotion, even though the image may not be what the emotion is about. By generating imagery or narratives that we feel will call up a particular feeling that we want to call up, for whatever reason — sometimes a moral reason motivated by generalized sympathy combined with Hume's 'love of truth' — we can trigger ourselves to perform actions that we have judged to be moral, and also train ourselves to be more likely in the future to spontaneously activate morally useful emotions.

Action presupposes action imagery, but it also presupposes some prior disposition to act on the part of the overall organism. This is where the more prefrontal aspects of moral reasoning and motivation come into play. For a human being, with its elaborate cognitive abilities grounded in prefrontal activity, *not* to recognize that the well-being of all conscious beings has value, just as does the well-being of particular conspecifics, would be somewhat like looking at a scene and missing some of the most important elements in it.

Executively-generated imagery or sequences of images forming narratives help us to understand how our organisms want to act, and help us to trigger feelings that in turn will trigger the actions. But inappropriate imagery or narratives can trigger ineffective actions, from the standpoint of the organism's self-organizational aims. In organisms at our degree of complexity, executively-generated imagery can be motivated by a combination of meta-emotions, generalized altruism, and 'love of truth'; in that case, moral deliberation, self-control, and self-conditioning become possible. Meta-emotions allow us to imagine ways that we would like to feel, but are not yet feeling. Generalized altruism can motivate some of these meta-emotions in very intelligent organisms, and the generalized love of truth motivates resistance against kneejerk, hardwired first-order feelings where those have proven not to be in line with the relevant meta-emotions. This is what gives humans an ability to function as moral agents in ways that would be impossible for lower animals, who cannot generate, refine, and control their own imagery in the ways that we can.

References

Aristotle (1962), *Nicomachean Ethics* (New York: Bobbs-Merrill).
Axelrod, R.M. (1984), *The Evolution of Cooperation* (New York: Basic Books).
Barsalou, L. (1987), 'The instability of graded structure; Implications for the nature of concepts', in *Concepts and Conceptual Development: Ecological and Intellectual Factors in Categorization*, ed. U. Neisser (New York: Cambridge University Press).
Bernstein, M., Stiehl, S. & Bickle, J. (2000), 'The effect of motivation on the stream of consciousness: Generalizing from a neurocomputational model of cingulo-frontal circuits controlling saccadic eye movements', in Ellis & Newton (2000).
Coles, M., Gratton, G. & Fabiani, M. (1990), 'Event-related brain potentials', in *Principles of Psychophysiology*, ed. M. Coles (Cambridge: Cambridge University Press).
Copleston, F. (1962), *A History of Philosophy, Vol. 2: Mediaeval Philosophy, Part II: Albert the Great to Duns Scotus* (Garden City, NY: Image/Doubleday).
Damasio, A.R. (1994), *Descartes' Error* (New York: Putnam).
Damasio, A.R. (1999), *The Feeling of What Happens* (New York: Harcourt Brace).
Damasio, A.R. (2003), *Looking for Spinoza*. (New York: Harcourt).
Damasio, A.R., Grabowski, T.J., Bechara, A., Damasio, H., Ponto, L.L. & Parvizi, J. (2000), 'Subcortical and cortical brain activity during the feeling of self-generated emotions', *Nature Neuroscience,* **3**, pp. 1049–56.
Davidson, D. (1970), 'Mental events', in *Experience and Theory,* ed. L. Foster and J. W. Swanson (Amherst: University of Massachusetts Press).
Dennett, D. (2003), *Freedom Evolves* (New York: Viking Press).
Ellis, R.D. (1986), *An Ontology of Consciousness* (Dordrecht: Kluwer/Martinus Nijhoff).
Ellis, R.D. (1992), *Coherence and Verification in Ethics* (Washington: University Press of America).
Ellis, R.D. (1995), *Questioning Consciousness: The Interplay of Imagery, Cognition and Emotion in the Human Brain* (Amsterdam: John Benjamins).
Ellis, R.D. (2005), *Curious Emotions: Roots of Consciousness and Personality in Motivated Action* (Amsterdam: John Benjamins).
Ellis, R.D. and Newton, N. (ed. 2000), *The Caldron of Consciousness* (Amsterdam: John Benjamins).
Faw, B. (2000a), 'Consciousness, motivation, and emotion: Biopsychological reflections', in Ellis & Newton (2000).
Faw, B. (2000b), 'My amygdala-orbitofrontal circuit made me do it', *Consciousness & Emotion,* **1**, pp. 167–79.
Ferrari, F. & E. Koyama. (2002), 'Meta-emotions about anger and *amae*: A cross-cultural comparison', *Consciousness & Emotion,* **3**, pp. 197–211.
Gendlin, E. (1981/1982), *Focusing* (Toronto: Bantam).
Gendlin, E. (1962/1998), *Experiencing and the Creation of Meaning* (Toronto: Collier-Macmillan).
Gendlin, E. (1992a), 'The primacy of the body, not the primacy of perception', *Man and World,* **25**, pp. 341–53.
Gendlin, E. (1992b), 'Thinking beyond patterns: Body, language, and situations', in *The Presence of Feeling in Thought,* ed. B. den Ouden and M. Moen (New York: Peter Lang).

Haines, D., Dietrich, E., Mihailoff, G.A., & McDonald, E.F. (1997), 'Cerebellar-hypothalamic axis: Basic circuits and clinical observations', in *The Cerebellum and Cognition*, ed. J. Schmahmann (New York: Academic Press).

Hume, D. (1740/1955) *Treatise of Human Nature* (New York: Bobbs-Merrill).

Jeannerod, M. (1997), *The Cognitive Neuroscience of Action* (Oxford: Blackwell).

Joseph, R. (1982), 'The neuropsychology of development: hemispheric laterality, limbic language and the origin of thought', *Journal of Clinical Psychology*, **38**, pp. 4–33.

Kauffman, S. (1993), *The Origins of Order* (Oxford: Oxford University Press).

Kim, J. (1998), *Mind in a Physical World: An Essay on the Mind-body Problem and Mental Causation* (Cambridge, MA: MIT Press).

Lethin, A. (2002), 'How do we embody intentionality?', *Journal of Consciousness Studies*, **9**(8), pp. 36–44.

Libet, B., A.G. Curtis, E.W. Wright, & D.K. Pearl. (1983), 'Time of conscious intention to act in relation to onset of cerebral activity (readiness-potential). The unconscious initiation of a freely voluntary act', *Brain*, **106**, pp. 623–42.

Libet, B. (1999), 'Do we have free will?', *Journal of Consciousness Studies*, **6** (8–9), pp. 47–58.

Mack, A. & Rock, I. (1998), *Inattentional Blindness* (Cambridge, MA: MIT/Bradford).

Monod, J. (1971), *Chance and Necessity* (New York: Random House).

Moore, G.E. (1900/1956), *Principia Ethica* (Cambridge: Cambridge University Press).

Newton, N. (1996), *Foundations of Understanding* (Amsterdam: John Benjamins).

Panksepp, J. (1998), *Affective Neuroscience* (New York: Oxford University Press).

Rilling, J., Gutman, D. Zeh, T. Pagnoni, G., Berns, G. & Kilts, C. (2002), 'A neural basis for social cooperation', *Neuron*, **35**, pp. 395–405.

Sayre-McCord, G. (1994), 'On why Hume's "General Point of View" isn't ideal — and shouldn't be', *Social Philosophy and Policy*, **11**, pp. 202–28.

Schmahmann, J. (Ed.) (1997) *The Cerebellum and Cognition* (New York: Academic Press.)

Schmahmann, J., C. Anderson, N. Newton & R. Ellis. (2001), 'The function of the cerebellum in cognition, affect and consciousness: Empirical support for the embodied mind', *Consciousness & Emotion*, **2**, pp. 273–309.

Sundararajan, L. (2000), 'Background-mood in emotional creativity: A microanalysis', *Consciousness & Emotion*, **1**, pp. 227–43.

Van Inwagen, P. (1984), *An Essay on Free Will* (Oxford: Oxford University Press).

Wegner, D. (2003), *The Illusion of Conscious Will* (Cambridge, MA: MIT).

Woodruff-Pak, D.S. (1997), 'Classical conditioning', in *The Cerebellum and Cognition*, ed. J. Schmahmann (New York: Academic Press).

Jaak Panksepp

On the Embodied Neural Nature of Core Emotional Affects

*Basic affects reflect the diversity of **satisfactions** (potential rewards/reinforcements) and **discomforts** (punishments) that are inherited tools for living from our ancestral past. Affects are neurobiologically-ingrained potentials of the nervous system, which are triggered, moulded and refined by life experiences. Cognitive, information-processing approaches and computational metaphors cannot penetrate foundational affective processes. Animal models allow us to empirically analyse the large-scale neural ensembles that generate emotional-action dynamics that are critically important for creating emotional feelings. Such approaches offer robust neuro-epistemological strategies to decode the fundamental nature of affects in all mammals, including humans, but they remain to be widely implemented. Here I summarize how we can develop a cross-species affective neuroscience that probes the neural nature of emotional affective states by studying the instinctual emotional apparatus of the mammalian body and brain. Affective feelings and emotional actions may reflect the dynamics of the primal viscero-somatic homunculus of SELF-representation.*

Overture: A Synopsis of the Affective Neuroscience Strategy

How can we ever understand how affective experience is created in the brain?

My premise is that affective experience is a deeply neurobiological process, and scholars who do not invest in the biological sciences, have little hope of shedding light on what affects really are. In my estimation, such intrinsic brain processes, shared in part by all mammals, need to be defined conjointly in terms of experiential and neural-systems characteristics. Obviously, one cannot study such psychobiological processes without fully considering the nature of human experience, but one cannot understand the neural mechanisms unless one has

Correspondence: Jaak Panksepp, Dept. of Psychology, Bowling Green State University, Bowling Green, OH 43403, USA; Center for the Study of Animal Well-Being, Dept. of Veterinary and Comparative Anatomy, Pharmacology and Physiology, Washington State University, Pullman, WA 99164-6520, USA. *Email: jpankse@bgnet.bgsu.ed* empirically compelling model systems for the brain work. Although the affective lives of the other animals can only be indirectly estimated from a study of their emotional behaviours, if we take a fully evolutionary approach, the knowledge we cull from them can be phenomenologically evaluated in our own species.

The essence of the affective neuroscience approach I have advocated is that we may comprehend the nature of affect by cross-species triangulation among three relevant lines of evidence: the behavioural, the psychological and the neuroscientific (Panksepp, 1998a). I believe the most behaviourally relevant line of evidence is the study of instinctual emotional behaviours, best done in animals who do not inhibit or regulate such behavioural outputs as much as humans. The complex cognitive aspects will continue to be best studied by human first-person self-reports, but animals' vocal signals and behavioural choices may remain essential for identifying the material substrates from which affective states first arose in brain evolution. If so, the brain mechanisms that generate affective experiences are best deciphered in animal models where the necessary physiological work can be done (Panksepp, 2005a).

My guiding premise is that there exist homologous neuro-evolutionary foundations for affective experience in all mammalian brains. Affective neuroscience seeks to reveal the causal foundations of basic human emotional feeling through a neuroscientific study of emotional operating systems in relevant animal models. The nature of such experiences in animals is an important, but secondary, issue. Establishing general principles shared by all mammals is the optimal strategy for laying a solid foundation for understanding the core affective states of humans. Thus, neuro-mechanistic insights derived from the animal work must be corroborated through human research, where first-person experiential changes can be documented (Panksepp, 1999) and clinical implications evaluated (Lane & Garfield, 2005; Panksepp, 2004).

Although the semantic and conceptual dilemmas in the field of affect science are abundant, through successive empirical iterations of this type of neuro-evolutionary strategy, lasting cross-species principles of how brain dynamics generate affect should emerge. Since this kind of approach remains to be widely implemented (Panksepp, 2005a), the aim of this essay is to highlight how progress might be facilitated. The biggest conceptual dilemma is how to *define* deep evolutionary functions of the brain, such as the affects,[1] which may be the 'ancestral voices of the genes' to use Ross Buck's felicitous phrase.

---

[1] The psychological definition of affect is largely based on the traditional Wundtian idea that all emotions have three major dimensions: i) various feelings of goodness and badness (valence), ii) levels of psychological activation (arousal) and iii) how much an emotion fills mental space (power or surgency). These are typically operationally measured with various pencil and paper self-report scales.. Obviously, the ultimate definition of an emotional affect must be strongly linked to neural properties that can not be achieved before the scientific work is reasonably well advanced. However, the general characteristics of emotional systems have been defined in neural terms, and include the following six characteristics of emotional operating systems depicted in Figure 1. Affect, in this scheme, arises from the characteristic neurodynamics of these emotional operating systems, perhaps by interacting with other brain circuits for self-representation such as those that arise from

Historical and Conceptual Perspectives

Because of the paucity of relevant discussions in neuroscience, few explicit and testable theoretical proposals concerning the nature of affect have been placed on the intellectual table. An exception would be those general neuroanatomical hypotheses arising largely from recent human brain imaging, where the likelihood of many false negatives and affect-free cognitive neuro-echoes remains large. If one carves this intellectual territory into tripartite zones, it is clear how disparate and uncoordinated present paradigms remain: 1) The traditional *behavioural neuroscience* view (i.e., that emotions are learned via reinforcement principles; Gray, 1990) suggests that affect is not a relevant question in animal research, since such experiential processes emerge in humans through our unique cortico-cognitive linguistic abilities (Rolls, 1999). 2) The traditional *cognitive neuroscience* view suggests that affects reflect the ability of neocortical processes, whether those of dorsolateral frontal cortical working-memory fields (LeDoux, 1996) or somatosensory fields of the cortex (the somatic-marker hypothesis of Damasio, 1994, 2003), to 'read out' implicit subcortical emotional information into experiential states (Lane & Garfield, 2005). 3) In stark contrast, the *affective neuroscience* view holds that raw affects arise from the neurophysiologies of a variety of sub-neocortical emotional action systems that modulate the dynamics of our core selves (MacLean, 1990; Panksepp, 1982, 1998a,b). Because of such profound ontological disagreements, the study of affect is generally ignored in basic animal research (for overview, see Panksepp, 2005a), even though it is emerging as a major theme in animal welfare studies (McMillan, 2005).

Most everyone understands what it means to feel hungry, thirsty, cold, angry, fearful, sad, happy, disgusted, lusty, and intensely interested in pursuing the many resources of our environments. This 'understanding' is psychological, reflecting our basic experiences of living in the world. We can only obtain comparable evidence in other animals by careful studies of their natural emotional and motivated behaviours (Panksepp, 1998a, 2005a), especially their emotional vocalizations that may reflect their internal affective states (Knutson *et al.*, 2002; Panksepp *et al.*, 1988, 2002). The only measures neither animals nor very young children can provide are propositional linguistic reports which require neocortical tissues far removed from, and perhaps not well connected with, brain areas that mediate emotional feelings. Thus, with respect to every measure except one, intentional verbalized feedback, we are confronted by exactly the same epistemological difficulties in studying the internal emotional experiences

---

centromedial midbrain circuits (e.g., PAG) that are strongly interconnected with medial frontal structures (for a schematic depiction, see Affective Neuroscience, Fig 3.3 (Panksepp, 1998a)). In general, it may be easier to define and study core emotional affects than sensory ones, because of the clear and measurable behavioural-action indicators evident during instinctual-emotional arousal. In any event, affects reflect relatively invisible neurodynamics of ancient brain systems that are hard to measure directly. That may require development of nove techniques where many recording probes are situated properly in the relevant circuits rather deep within the brain (Panksepp, 2000), with an attempt to reconstruct the state spaces of each basic emotion.

of all mammals. In humans we have the further problem that the relevant brain systems are inaccessible in routine research practices. But brain affective processes remain neglected in animal neuroscience, even as psychology has reclaimed affect, cautiously, as a critical mind process (Barrett *et al.*, 2005; Davidson *et al.*, 2003; Russell, 2003).

The search for a scientific understanding of basic affective feelings in behavioural neuroscience was sluggish during the past century because of the prevailing positivistic belief that such subjective states of mind either did not exist or were unknowable, and hence outside the ken of scientific inquiry. Such biases became ingrained in the psychological sciences long before modern neuroscience revealed new empirical possibilities. Affects were scientifically unknowable as long as we did not understand how the brain worked in conjunction with the body, and how the brain-body duo engaged the world. Modern neuroscience has changed all that. Neuroscience now allows us to theoretically envision the neurophysiological causes of affective experience, with abundant predictions that can be disconfirmed through rigorous investigation (Panksepp, 1998a, 2005a). With molecular advances in our understanding of the brain, such perennial problems of human and animal existence can now be scientifically clarified. But to do that we must seek to envision how large-scale neural networks establish mentality through complex interactions both inwardly and outwardly directed.

Unfortunately we still have a socio-cultural problem in brain-mind science — most psychologists are ill-prepared (even resistant) to actualize the opportunities that basic animal neuroscience is providing for a causal understanding of human emotional feelings. Conversely, many neuroscientists remain hesitant to envision how psychological processes emerge from neural dynamics, especially in other animals. To the best of our knowledge, *basic* affective feelings supervene on homologous brain systems shared by all mammals, especially the many ancient subcortical systems that remain poorly illuminated by existing brain imaging technologies (for critiques, see Panksepp, 2004a,b; Schulman & Rothman, 2004). Just as most telescopes can't see far into space, most imaging procedures focus on large, recently evolved, highly active cognitive regions of the brain rather than anatomically smaller, metabolically dimmer subcortical circuits. Only a few have used imaging technologies optimally focused on subcortical systems that animal experiments have long implicated in the genesis of emotional feelings (e.g., Damasio *et al.*, 2000) and sensory affects such as orgasms (Holstege *et al.*, 2003). In any event, neural correlates revealed by imaging only direct us to brain regions where other techniques need to be applied to ferret out causal factors. To develop comparative neuro-phenomenological perspectives and to reveal general principles of mammalian emotional systems, we do need to consider the nature of primary-process affective consciousness in other animals (Panksepp, 2003).

Abundant evidence currently affirms that other animals experience the raw biological values of existence — primary-process affective states — although they may neither cognitively dwell nor reflect on those states as we humans can.

Their experiences can be indexed by the evaluative choices they make, such as conditioned place preferences and aversions, indicating that they distinguish life-supportive and life-detracting events (Bardo & Bevins, 2000), providing a foundational understanding of human feelings (Panksepp, 1998a, 2005a).

Toward an Understanding of Affective States Within the Brain

How could spooky, hard-to-define processes such as affects (see note 1) have ever emerged in brain-mind evolution? Perhaps such internal coding of life-supporting values dramatically enhanced survival. Affects probably emerged in brain evolution to help animals anticipate various survival needs and thus prepare for them in advance. In other words, affects reflect ancestral memories — neuromental heuristics that enhance life-sustaining decision-making. Indeed, it is possible that the kinds of 'reinforcement' processes that mediate individual learning are fundamentally affective, and that there are many basic affects, not just singular forms of positive and negative valence.

In my view, emotional feelings represent only one category of affects that brains experience. Emotional affects appear to be closely linked to certain prototypical types of action readiness (e.g., rage, fear, desire, lust, distress, nurturance, playfulness) that may derive their characteristic experiential feels from brain operating systems that orchestrate such instinctual responses. Other affects, constituting the pleasures and displeasures of sensations (e.g., enticing and disgusting stimuli) and bodily homeostatic and background feelings (e.g., hunger and exhilaration), reflect how life-supportive and life-detracting stimuli create neuro-phenomenological changes that help index neuro-metabolic states of well-being. Just consider feelings of profound tiredness after vigorous physical exertions. Animals show all possible indicators of such states, except saying, 'I'm exhausted.' Fatigue arises from poorly understood brain and bodily changes, but reduction of brain dopamine activity is surely one key aspect. Since time immemorial, coca leaves have been used to alleviate fatigue in traditional cultures, and pharmacological elevation of brain dopamine increases work output in animals (Panksepp & Moskal, 2005).

Affective mentalities may be clarified by decoding the ways in which our brains were constructed through eons of evolutionary selection. For instance, brain dopamine energizes the seeking of all types of resources. Such appetitive desires are manifested in subjective feelings of exhilaration that can border on euphoria (Volkow et al., 2002), but initially such states exist without propositional contents. Early in development, the brain does not know what it is seeking—such knowledge requires experience in the world. Some say it is hard to imagine how affects could have emerged in brain dynamics as a function of evolutionary selection, but this is not so hard to conceptualize. Presumably all affects ultimately reflect various distinct neurodynamics that simultaneously code for the intrinsic behavioural and psychobiological values essential for survival.

Newborn animals must have some intrinsic capacity to anticipate life-support-ing and life-detracting events, and affects serve those functions. Learning extends and resolves them even further. Thus, hunger is a useful way to antici-pate energy needs well before body resources are dangerously depleted. Fear can keep animals out of harm's way. Separation distress can diminish the probability of becoming lost. Of course, the animal work can only illuminate basic human affects if sufficient neuro-evolutionary continuities exist to allow credible cross-species translations. While fish may have little to teach us about jealousy, mammals that show strong social attachments surely can. Each system has to be worked out on a case-by-case basis, not only with respect to individual species but also individual brain neurochemistries. With dopamine, we no longer have much doubt that circuits such as mesolimbic pathways facilitate foraging and euphoric psychic energization in all mammals. If excessively sustained, such changes degenerate into the paranoid ideation of schizophrenia and eventually depression upon drug withdrawal as organisms 'collapse' from psychic exhaustion.

If the basic emotional affects are closely associated with the instinctual emo-tional-action dynamics that all mammals exhibit spontaneously in various life-challenging situations, we have a workable strategy to understand the neuro-evolutionary sources of the kinds of feelings (primal neuro-emotional *endophenotypes*) that figure so heavily in everyday affects as well as the excesses of psychiatric disorders (Panksepp, 2004a). Cross-species neuro-ethological research may clarify how such foundational aspects of consciousness arise from the organic complexities of brains and bodies. If such foundational neurodynamics are closely related to the generation of primal experiential states, we may finally have a workable paradigm for studying the *causal* foundations of affective consciousness in animals as opposed to just the neural *correlates* of cognitive consciousness in humans. Such a *dual-aspect monism*[2] strategy pro-vides a most coherent epistemological way to proceed.

Since adult human behaviour is remarkably well regulated by higher cognitive processes, the activities of emotional action tendencies are not as easily moni-tored in our own species as in fellow animals. Contrary to William James's

---

[2] Dual-aspect monism is the view that the complexities of nature cannot be understood from a single perspective. Thus in affect science, each emotional state has several facets that go together as reflec-tive of the same process. For instance, complex emotional instinctual behaviours, such as rough-and-tumble play, are considered to have an affective facet that might be called social joy (Panksepp & Burgdorf, 2003). This reduces the need to dwell on a variety of dualistic dilemmas that could immobilize research into the brain substrates of affective processes in animals. In brain science, this 'dual-aspect theory' was first fully developed by George Henry Lewes in Chapter III of his *The Physical Basis of Mind* (1877), the third volume of his *Problems of Life and Mind*. It is more produc-tive than general mind-brain identify theories which can easily envision mentality to be epiphenomenal. If anything, we can be certain the experiential states are thoroughly neurobiological processes. Dual-aspect monism offers a clear strategy to link basic dynamic features of brain and mind, such as emotional instinctive expressions and the corresponding affective states, in empirically productive ways. If this view yielded no new predictions, it would simply be another metaphysical view. However, this strategy allows clear predictions from basic behavioural research in animals to predictions concerning brain functions that control emotional feelings in humans (Panksepp, 1999). Hence it is falsifiable.

famous conjecture (i.e., the famous James-Lange peripheral read-out theory of emotion), my premise is that it is not the peripheral bodily changes that are the main sources of our emotional feelings, but rather the central neural circuit dynamics that generate instinctual emotional actions and associated autonomic changes that support those actions. In other words, the primal emotional action networks, neural systems that James knew nothing about, may be the proximal sources of raw emotional feelings. They may directly generate affective states that are excellent brain heuristics for guiding additional learning.

Humans still have those instinctual dynamics in their brains, but adults often actively inhibit their expressions. We are adept at repressing instinctual actions — from striking out in anger to showing our grief — through higher cerebral inhibition. Just consider how well eliminative urges are regulated in humans — leading to escalating distress in various social situations. And even if inhibition of emotionality were not such an enormous problem, our experimental access to the relevant neuro-causal processes in humans remains meagre.

Despite spectacular advances in non-invasive brain imaging of higher cerebral processes, and our capacity to stimulate neocortical areas with transcranial magnetic stimulation (Nahas *et al.*, 2004; Schutter *et al.*, 2004),[3] the disentangling of brain processes that are essential for the generation of emotional feelings does require direct manipulation of subcortical causal mechanisms in ways that are ethically inconceivable in human research (and debatable in animal research). If substantive progress on such human questions could be advanced through the study of the natural emotional circuits of other mammals, it would be short sighted not to invest in models where critical evidence can be harvested. Let's remember that much of what we know about the mechanisms of memory was derived from the study of sluggish sea creatures (e.g., especially as studied by Eric Kandel and colleagues, now emulated and extended by many others).

Animal research programs seeking to understand human emotional feelings can choose to pursue neuroethological studies of natural emotional behaviours (e.g., Panksepp, 1982, 1998a), or to focus on emotional learning (e.g., LeDoux, 1996). Obviously both are important, but I favour the former since affectively rich, natural emotional behaviour patterns can be evoked by localized electrical brain stimulation (ESB). Electrical 'garbage' — brain stimulations that have no 'informational' content — applied to homologous subcortical regions yields coherent emotional behaviour patterns in all mammals. Such manipulations yield the corresponding emotional feelings in humans (Heath, 1996; Panksepp, 1985). Because this pattern of *'electrical garbage in, behavioural coherence out'* is evident across species, we can be confident that the brain stimulation is evoking natural, evolved functions of the brain. Such sub-neocortically evoked instinctual actions are also accompanied by internal states that animals find desirable or undesirable, as indicated by their behavioural choices (Panksepp,

---

[3] The author has undergone stimulation of essentially all regions of his neocortical mantle with TMS, with no elicitation of acute emotional experiences, affirming that such cerebral structures may not be critical for raw affective experiences, especially since localized stimulation of subcortical sites often yield intense affective experiences (Heath, 1996; Panksepp, 1985).

1998, 2005a). Thus, from a dual-aspect monism perspective, it seems likely that the study of the neural underpinnings of unconditioned emotional behaviours in animals is a compelling way to understand the nature of emotional affects in all mammals.

Such findings fit nicely with a naturalistic views of emotions that are resonant with more humanistic cognitive perspectives (Robinson, 2005). We humans do not learn to experience affects, but we *learn* when and how to experience them and what to do about them. The classic cognitive view that emotions always need propositional objects, must deal with the dilemma that it would be counterproductive to have ancestral memories (e.g., emotional tools for living) pre-coded for propositional contents. Why waste genetic effort on things that need to be learned, but for exceptional cases such as the smell of predators. Propositional contents must come from living in actual worlds. Raw affective feelings need not. Indeed, ancestral affective 'memories' are fine general-purpose tools for guiding subsequent learning. Since evolved emotional tools were designed to interact with cognitive structures, it is no surprise that our primitive affects come to be modulated by higher brain structures (Ochsner *et al.*, 2004).

Basic affects are cross-species gifts of nature. Since the earliest neuroscience work on such topics, it has seemed highly likely that certain core emotional feelings are 'instinctual' tools of nature rather than constructions of nurture (Panksepp, 1998). Emerging evidence continues to highlight how much our affects are dependent on our animalian emotional circuits. Just recently it has been revealed that ESB applied to nucleus accumbens can generate smiling and mirth (Okun *et al.*, 2004), and in essentially the same brain regions, we can evoke joyous playful chirping-'laughter' in rats, not unlike that seen in human children at play (Burgdorf *et al.*, 2001; Panksepp & Burgdorf, 2003). These brain areas also light-up when one is anticipating rewards with feeling of positive affect (Knutson *et al.*, 2001), just as the animal data predicted (Ikemoto and Panksepp, 1999). Although such instinctual systems are intimately related to learning processes, they were created, in raw form, by our ancestral heritage pre-dating the appearance of *H. Sapiens* on the face of the Earth.

To make progress on elucidating the nature of affective states, emotional and otherwise, one needs to consider psychological perspectives that can be linked to neuroanatomical, neurochemical and neurophysiological levels of analysis. Robust linkages to human concerns will emerge if critical underlying brain and body functions are homologous in other mammals where neural mechanisms can be studied in sufficient detail. The resulting neurochemical principles may be evaluated in human models, where one can obtain self-reported internal experiences (Panksepp, 1999; 2004b). However, before proceeding, let me pointedly highlight the continuing anti-affect sentiments in modern behavioural neuroscience.

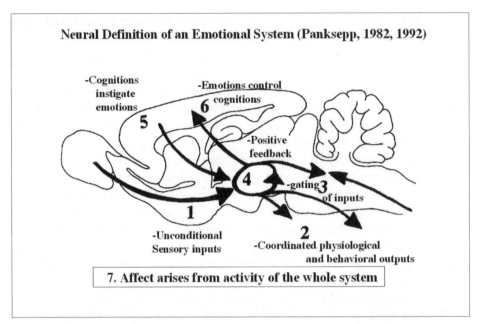

Figure 1. Neural definition of an emotional system (Panksepp, 1982, 1992).

The various neural interactions that are characteristics of all major emotional systems of the brain. (1) Various sensory stimuli can unconditionally access emotional systems; (2) emotional systems can generate instinctual motor outputs, as well as (3) modulate sensory inputs. (4) Emotional systems have positive-feedback components that can sustain emotional arousal after precipitating events have passed; also (5) these systems can be modulated by cognitive inputs and (6) can modify and channel cognitive activities. In addition, the important criterion that emotional systems create affective states is not included, but (7) it is postulated that arousal of the executive circuit for each emotion is essential for elaborating emotional feelings within the brain, perhaps by interacting with other brain circuits for self-representation such as those that exist in extended centromedial midbrain circuits (e.g. PAG) that interact with anterior cingulate and frontal cortical systems. [Adapted from Fig. 3.3 in *Affective Neuroscience* (Panksepp, 1998a), with permission from Oxford University Press.]

The Neglect of Affect and Emotions in Behavioral Neuroscience

Historically, it is easy to understand why affects and other subjective experiences were neglected in behavioural neuroscience. There are no unambiguous ways to define the evolved 'emotional' functions of the brain-mind before the relevant scientific inquiries. Good definitions of intrinsic brain functions can only follow incisive neuroscientific inquiries, but provisional definitions can be generated by the circuit properties shared by all basic emotional systems (Figure 1; see also note 1). Without intentional verbal reports of mental experiences (obviously only possible in organisms that have language), one can only proceed if one advances theoretical frameworks that lead to clear hypotheses with explicit behavioural predictions. Only after abundant research can one judiciously weigh the evidence from psychological perspectives (Knutson *et al.*, 2002; Panksepp, 2005a). Unfortunately, such theorizing has long been dismissed in behavioural neuroscience as mere speculation, and hence relevant data collection has been inordinately slow. Many have long shared profound doubts as to whether animals have any emotional experiences at all.[4]

According to our *dual-aspect monism* strategy, basic affective experience emerges from the dynamics of emotional operating systems that remain conserved among all mammalian species, leading to clear predictions about the nature of raw emotional feelings in humans. My research has aspired to provide a coherent theory of the neuro-evolutionary underpinnings of raw emotional feelings, while most of my colleagues have insisted that this topic cannot be scientifically addressed. Historically, it is understandable why modern neuro-behaviorists have little interest in understanding how animals feel, but they may be ignoring wide swaths of what is truly transpiring in brains of the animals they study. Indeed, if it were to turn out that 'reinforcement' processes were actually dependent on the affective systems of animal brains (*vide infra*), we may not fully understand the mechanisms of learning without probing the nature of neuro-affective processes.

In any event, modern behavioural neuroscience is out of step with other informed views on animal feelings (e.g., Bekoff, 2002; Grandin, 2005; MacMillian, 2005), and serious engagement on this topic is difficult unless one is willing to consider the implications of *all* the available evidence (also see Panksepp, 1998a, 2002a,b, 2005a). Thus, it is becoming increasingly important for brain researchers to discuss whether internally experienced agonies and joys, pleasures and displeasures, exist in the minds of the animals they study. If such feelings do exist and do guide their behavioural choices, we cannot understand their brains or our own, without discussing and probing such processes openly. Such subtle issues can be resolved with substantial assurance by evaluating whether conditioned place preference and place-avoidance tendencies emerge in animals experiencing apparent emotional states. If animals had no affective experiences, there would be no obvious reason for them to exhibit learned behavioral preferences. Considering the robust evidence for such affective states

[4]   For didactic purposes, let me consider the position of a most illustrious animal emotional-memory researcher, Joseph LeDoux, who has sought to understand fear-learning while attempting to 'escape from the shackles of subjectivity' (2000, p. 156). In the past, he has been consistently explicit about i) the likelihood that animals do not experience emotions, and hence ii) the supposed irrelevance of affective experience for understanding emotions in animals. Recently he changed his mind on the first aspect of this issue, while continuing to claim that such states of mind in other animals are scientifically unfathomable: In the January 4th 2005 issue of the *New York Times*, in an article entitled 'God (or Not), Physics and, of Course, Love: Scientists Take a Leap' fourteen culturally prominent thinkers were asked: 'What do you believe is true even though you cannot prove it?' LeDoux responded: 'For me, this is an easy question. I believe that animals have feelings and other states of consciousness, but neither I nor anyone else has been able to prove it. We can't even prove that other people are conscious, much less other animals. In the case of other people, though, we at least can have a little confidence since all people have brains with the same basic configurations. But as soon as we turn to other species and start asking questions about feelings and consciousness in general we are in risky territory because the hardware is different. Because I have reason to think that their feelings might be different than ours, I prefer to study emotional behaviour in rats rather than emotional feelings.' And what are those *reasons*? Animal sub-cortical 'limbic' emotional zones are organized largely the same as ours, albeit they typically have relatively less neo-cortical mass to reflect on their feelings. If affect emerges from those higher reflections, LeDoux is correct. If affects emerge from the homologous sub-neocortical limbic regions, then he is wrong.

(Panksepp, 1998a; 2005a) and the resulting novel causal predictions for human feelings (Panksepp & Harro, 2004), the century-long resistance to integrating such ideas into mainstream neuro-behavioural thinking should gradually fade. However, at present most remain true-believers of the catechisms of early 20th century behaviourism that was inspired by 19th century bio-physics and reinforced by 20th century positivism (Greenspan & Baars, 2005). It continues to be reinforced by an implicit, but rather widespread, anthropocentric neuro-dualism — the view that experiential states are only a property of massively expanded human-type neocortices.

Do Animal Have Emotional Experiences?

Perhaps it is idle anthropomorphism to conclude that other animals do have emotional feelings? Perhaps our human emotional feature detectors (cortical mirror neurons?) only coax us to envision such potential fantasy processes in the minds of other animals. But maybe affects are also essential parts of their brain realities. As every farm boy and dangerous animal trainer knows, it is important to recognize various basic emotions in other animals from their behavioural acts (Darwin, 1872) and emotional vocalizations (Leinonen et al., 2001). Such information if awfully important for staying out of harms way (Hebb, 1946).

Although it may turn out that sub-neocortical emotional neurodynamics need to be re-represented in the neocortex before affective experiences emerge (Lane & Garfield, 2005), the postulation that high-level neocortical readouts, unique to human brain expansions, are essential for core affective feelings may be as naive as the long-discarded geocentric view of the universe (Panksepp, 2005b). Does one need much better evidence for affective experience in animals than the demonstration that arthritic distress in rats increases their consumption of opioid pain-killers (Colpaert et al., 1980)? Abundant data indicate that sub-neocortical processes are critical for such effects (Ikemoto et al., 2003; Panksepp, 2005a). Opioid induced reward is elaborated low in the brain. Place preferences are obtained by putting morphine into primitive brain regions such as the Periaqueductal Gray (PAG) and the Ventral Tegmental Area (VTA), but not ten other higher brain regions that also have abundant opiate receptors (Olmstead & Franklin, 1997). The most vigorous ESB rewards and aversions are obtained from nearby subcortical regions with no robust effects from neo-cortical sites (see note 3). Self-administration of various addictive substances is achieved largely from deep medial subcortical loci (Ikemoto & Wise, 2004). The same goes for neurochemical modulation of a host of other emotional action processes such as anger-type aggression (Siegel, 2005), fearfulness (Panksepp, 1990a), sexuality (Pfaff, 1999), and maternal nurturance (Numan & Insel, 2003), even though the affective properties of such manipulations have been less consistently evaluated.

The existence of various experientially rich emotional systems in sub-neocortical regions of mammalian brains seems definitive (Panksepp, 1998a). Their precise nature is not. That will require more neuroscientists to probe the fine details of these complex systems with conceptually open-minded and methodologically hard-headed devotion. In my estimation, the best place to start is with the thorough analysis of the affects that accompany instinctual emotional behaviors, and then the re-representations of these brain functions in other brain areas, followed by a study of the more subtle affects. To my knowledge, there is little data that emotional instinctual processes are affectively vacuous, and abundant data that they are accompanied by feelings, perhaps as an integral aspect of the underlying neurodynamics (Panksepp, 2005a)

The Animalian-Emotional Sources of Basic Human Values: Toward A Taxonomy of Basic Affective Feelings

The varieties of affective feelings are enormous, and many humans are skilled in talking about the meaning of such feelings in their lives. However, at their core, raw affective experiences appear to be pre-propositional gifts of nature—cognitively impenetrable tools for living that inform us about the states of our body, the sensory aspects of the world that support or detract from our survival, and various distinct types of emotional arousal that can inundate our minds. Affects reflect the heuristic value codes that magnificently assist survival, and give 'value' to life. My *working* premise is that emotional affects reflect certain types of neurodynamics, whose hard-to-describe subjective aspects resemble the recursive-dynamic 'attractor-envelopes' of instinctual emotional actions (i.e., the large-scale neurodynamics of the respective emotional operating systems summarized below). In other words, the outward instinctual-behavioural dynamics of various emotional arousals may have class resemblances to the brain dynamics that concurrently create the experiential feelings. Just imagine the pounding feeling of anger. An empirically workable dual-aspect monism strategy may allow us to monitor affects rather directly through the large-scale network characteristics of the underling brain systems (Panksepp, 2000). However, there are other kinds of affects beside emotional ones (see note 1).

It seems reasonable to taxonomize affective experiences into at least three major varieties: 1) the homeostatic states of our body signaled by interoceptors as well as other chemical states of the body (hard to observe via external signs), 2) the great variety of exteroceptively driven affects such as taste (slightly easier to observe), and 3) the emotional affects, so evident in instinctual action dynamics. The emotional affects may be easiest to study if there are, in fact, solid predictive relationships between the brain mechanisms of emotional action dynamics and the respective feelings. It is also possible that consummatory and other bodily actions accompanying sensory affects, may provide direct read-out of the other kinds of affective processes (Berridge, 2000). In any event the dual-aspect monism strategy currently provides a robust cross-species empirical predictions for how raw emotional feelings may be created in humans (Panksepp & Harro, 2004).

There is insufficient space here for anything more than thumbnail descriptions, but the outward emotional action dynamics evident in all mammals include seven primal emotional processes: (1) SEEKING is characterized by a persistent positively-valenced exploratory inquisitiveness, with energetic forward locomotion — approach and engagement with the world—consisting of probing into the nooks and crannies of interesting objects and events (this system is critical also for most other basic emotional responses, such as the seeking of safety when threatened); (2) FEAR is characterized by bodily tenseness and a shivery negatively valenced immobility, which can burst forth into a dynamic flight pattern with chaotic-projectile movements to get out of harm's way (which may reflect recruitment of dopamine energized SEEKING urges); (3) RAGE is characterized by a vigorous casting of the body at offending objects with biting and pounding of the extremities; it is a mixture of positive and negative valence; (4) LUST is characterized by an urgent and rhythmic thrusting of the body toward receptive others, and in their absence, a craving tension with both positive and negative affective features; (5) CARE is characterized by a gentle, caressing, enveloping body dynamic accompanied by relaxed positively valenced states of the body; (6) PANIC (separation distress) is characterized by aversive crying actions, with urgent attempts at reunion, followed by weakness and a despairing body carriage as grief sets in if reunion fails; (7) PLAY is expressed in a bounding lightness of movement that has an affectively engaging dynamic poking and rhythmic quality, at times bordering on aggression. In my estimation, 'dominance' reflects the epigenetic consequence of several emotional systems, especially PLAY, in action (and should not be deemed a primary emotional system). There are many cognitive emotions that probably rely on these 'primes' for their arousal. For instance, jealousy may arise from mixed feelings of anger, separation-distress and desire, etc.

Hopefully these verbal images help us to envision the dynamic pre-propositional feelings of the various basic emotions. Perhaps a careful topographic analysis of such complex instinctual actions could eventually yield mathematical algorithms for the field-dynamics that characterize affective states. If the feelings of the basic emotions have a class similarity to the outwardly evident behavioural-instinctual action dynamics (imagine again the surging pounding feelings and behaviours of anger), then we may have an objective scientific paradigm for concurrently studying the nature of the emotional primes not only behaviourally but also as affective processes of the brain (Panksepp, 1998a). It would also provide a way to envision how the classic explanatory gap between subjective experience and objective brain events could be bridged. If this dual-aspect monism approach should prove to be misguided in specific instances, we will still have acquired important knowledge concerning the underlying brain substrates of emotional actions in other mammals, and thereby guidance for understanding comparable actions in our own species. It is a win-win research proposition, since it focuses on the spontaneous behaviours of organisms.

Emotional Action Dynamics

Only a few have attempted to objectively measure the 'force fields' of bodily emotional *dynamics* (Clynes, 1978). It is increasingly recognized that voluntary simulation of instinctual emotional action dynamics can evoke emotional feelings in humans (for a review, see Niedenthal *et al.*, 2005). One can even generate feelings by simulating emotional action dynamics mentally, without outward actions (Panksepp & Gordon, 2003), providing a methodology for imaging human emotional-action/affective states in novel ways. This also helps explain why neurologically 'locked-in' patients, with damage to ventral motor outputs of the brainstem, can still experience emotions — they retain the requisite brain emotional systems, no long expressed on the body surface. Distinct affective dynamics are also evident in emotional vocalizations (Fichtel *et al.*, 2001), which may be artistically rendered to enhance the emotional qualities of music (Clynes, 1978; Panksepp & Bernatzky, 2002).

Accumulating evidence suggests human emotional feelings are closely linked to action tendencies that are subcortically generated in both animals and humans. It is easy to communicate these bodily dynamics with selected body parts such as expressive movements of the hands (recognition of basic emotional actions is remarkably high (Panksepp, 2003, unpublished data)). Such movement dynamics can help arouse emotional feelings (Clynes, 1978). Of course, in addition to the solid foundation provided by emotional action dynamics, the full quality of each emotional feeling must also include (i) the somatic sensory-feedbacks that accompany such actions, (ii) the changes in the dynamics of neo-cortical fields, as well as (iii) the aroused autonomic and hormonal processes (Fig. 1).

An Overview of Neuroanatomical Locus of Control for Emotional Affects

A striking aspect of emotional-instinctual behaviours in animals is how they survive neo-decortication, especially if the damage is inflicted early in development. Are the animals now simply proverbial 'reflexive robots' or do they still have basic affective experiences? Most behavioural neuroscientists still subscribe to the former view, largely because they cannot envision how psychological/subjective processes have any explanatory value in their neuro-mechanistic schemes. This reflects a failure to consider the dual aspect monism view that all basic psychological processes are completely neurobiological (although typically environmentally triggered). When one takes a dual-aspect view to emotional operating systems, neither the neural nor the psychological perspectives are mechanistically privileged. They are reflections of the self-same complex network functions of the brain.

Consider the case of play — one of the biggest sources of social joy. The outward character of playfulness remains largely intact following neo-decortication, and the accompanying affective experiences seem to be sustained (Panksepp *et al.*, 1994). Such animals readily acquire various instrumental behaviours to obtain rewards (Kolb & Tees, 1990), albeit evaluations of conditioned place preferences in such animals remain regrettably scarce. As all animals mature, they become increasingly dependent on epigenetically derived functions elaborated in higher brain regions, and hence decortication is less well tolerated in older mammals. However, the critical issue here is whether the experienced dynamics of basic emotional feelings exist in such organisms, and the weight of relevant evidence suggests that affective mental contents survive radical neo-decortication.

First, emotional-instinctual behaviours can be instigated by ESB of extended neural circuits below the neocortex. As already noted, the rewarding and punishing properties of such ESB and comparable chemical stimulation of the brain derive their affective punch from subcortical systems (Heath, 1996; Panksepp, 1985). Animals self-stimulate even after surgical damage to higher neocortical regions (Huston & Borbely, 1973; 1974). Parenthetically, such findings affirm classic distinctions between brain emotional/affective and cognitive/rational processes (see next section).

Second, one could note that adult humans who lose most of their neocortical functions fall into persistent vegetative states (PVS), where the remaining expressive gestures (e.g., apparent anger) are deemed affectively vacuous (e.g., 'sham rage'). Obviously, such neurologically impaired humans cannot report on their potential affective states, but we should at least consider the possibility that they sustain some level of affective experience, especially since minimally conscious patients exhibit a great deal of brain activity that would not have been expected from their severe behavioural-communicative deficits (Schiff et al., 2005).

Just as young animals sustain coherent emotional responses following decortication, human children with brain damage that would produce unmistakable PVS symptoms in adults, exhibit emotionally rich responses as long as they are reared in loving environments (Shewmon et al., 1999). They exhibit preferences for supportive people, enjoy music and exhibit clear signs of other basic affects. Are these behaviours simply reflexive, or indicative of experiential states? This dilemma is comparable to what we routinely encounter in interpreting animal behaviour. However, to the extent that their behaviours provide critical evidence, such children do have mental lives.

As I write this essay, the neurological case of Terry Schiavo, who died several weeks after her feeding tubes were removed, should be raising the issue of whether she still had any raw affective feelings in her cognitively unconscious mind. Have her feelings been as completely erased as her cognitive abilities or have they regressed to the level of children with such brain damage (e.g., Shewmon et al., 1999)? Did she die with excruciating feelings of thirst accompanying her final passage?

If vegetative individuals like her still have any remnant of psychic distress, then death by dehydration is 'culturally' condoned cruelty, and it would be more humane for family and medical decision makers to have the option of gentle opioid euthenasia. Although such individuals are clearly cognitively unconscious, they may still have nonreflective affective feelings. Thus, we should evaluate whether such patients are capable of showing some simple conditioning and preferences for certain rewards and punishments using simple response measures such as eye movements. Although in such PVS cases surface EEGs reflect no measurable cognitive activity, might deeper brain imaging and affective conditioning studies reveal some level of felt experience even though they no longer have the wherewithal to communicate with the outside world (Schiff et al., 2005)? In the absence of additional data, it remains plausible that such pre-propositional individuals, at least those who exhibit some instinctual emotional behaviours, may have some residual emotional feelings. Their preferences, using the simplest response measures, need to be evaluated, as they have in decerebrate cats (Schlaer & Myers, 1972).

The evidence for a sub-neocortical locus of control for affect makes bottom-up approaches to raw affective experience essential to eventually understand the top-down cognitive controls related more to emotional awareness (Lane and Garfield, 2005; Panksepp, 2005b). The bottom-up views of emotional experience help clarify pre-propositional affective psychodynamics that emerge from sub-neocortical regions of the brain. In contrast, top-down views can highlight the rich cognitive tapestry of emotional experiences, where individual differences, art and creativity prevail (Barrett, et al, 2005; Robinson, 2005). While our animalian emotional circuits provide an essential infrastructure for our basic, pre-propositional affective states, higher cognitions help regulate and parse those feelings further, allowing our feelings to interpenetrate with perceptual representations of world events in a seemingly infinite number of ways. I would again emphasize that the problem of clarifying the cognitive contents of animal minds is much harder, perhaps next to impossible (Lewontin, 1998), as compared to the basic emotional contents.

Distinctions Between Cognitive and Affective Processes

There are powerful modern trends in cognitive psychology to conceptualize cognitive and emotional processes as so intertwined that there is no meaningful way to separate them (e.g., Barrett et al., 2005; Lane & Garfield, 2005). However, I suspect such conflations arise from our failure to fully consider the neuro-evolutionary evidence from other animals. From the subjective 'mind's eye' perspective, our feelings and thoughts are indeed remarkably interpenetrating, but they can be distinguished in many areas of the brain. In terms of brain evolution they probably have many distinct genetic and neural controls, as highlighted by how various sub-neocortical emotional operating systems remain remarkably intact in animals neo-decorticated during infancy (Panksepp et al., 1994). Such distinctions are also evident following various kinds of neurological damage in human where the cognitive and affective responses to the same external stimuli, such as music, can be clearly dissociated (e.g., Griffiths et al., 2004).

We can distinguish affective from cognitive processes on many other dimensions: Affects have a sub-neocortical locus of control; they arise from broad-scale *state control* functions[5] — large-scale neural ensembles in action; they are analog, less computational, and generate *intentions-in action* that guide *action-to-perception* processes, with many distinct neuropeptidergic codes. In contrast, cognitions have a neocortical locus of control; they arise from more discrete informational *channel functions*. Thus, cognitions are more digital, more computational, can generate *perception-to-action* processes that can lead to *intentions-to-act*, and are profoundly dependent on rapidly acting amino-acid transmitters. Emotional states are fundamentally evolved 'energetic' conditions of the brain-body continuum, while cognitions parse the many differences in exteroceptive space and time (see Ciompi & Panksepp, 2005; Panksepp, 2003).

This is not to suggest that our ancient emotional operating systems were not intimately linked to emerging cognitive processes in brain evolution. They surely were. Indeed, our cognitive apparatus may have been evolutionarily constructed on the solid platform of affective principles. However, raw affects do not arise *directly* from the intricacies of our higher cognitive abilities (Liotti & Panksepp, 2004), even though those abilities become decisive in our capacity to effectively and affectively navigate the world — to find 'comfort zones' where we wish to live. Much of our cognitive activity emerges in the service of maximizing our satisfactions and diminishing various discomforts. The states of the nervous system that 'reinforce' learning may be fundamentally affective.

Now that investigators have finally attempted to see which brain areas are involved in emotionally 'hot' cognitions and non-emotional 'cold' cognitions, it is clear that more ancient medial 'limbic' regions of the telencephalon are devoted to affectively rich emotional reasoning while the more recently evolved fronto-lateral areas of the brain are more involved in 'cold' types of rational deliberations (e.g., Goel & Dolan, 2004; Northoff *et al.*, 2004). It is the emotionally based reasoning that is more concerned with egocentric affective issues, while cognitions are devoted more to allocentric concerns. It is probably the case that our feeling of 'livingness' is linked more to our affective than our rational nature. Even though emotional affects can easily be repressed by cognitions as we mature, cognitive abilities do not survive after extensive damage to the brainstem substrates of attentional and emotional arousals (Parvizi & Damasio, 2001; 2003; Watt & Pincus, 2004).

The neuroscience of animal cognitions is confronted by more variety than the neuroscience of their affects. Platypuses may think with the cerebral representations of their bills (Pettigrew, et al., 1998) and star-nosed moles through their nasal tentacles (Catania & Kaas, 1997), in ways we can barely envision. But even here scientific progress can be made, especially if we recognize that most other mammals probably cogitate with perceptual images (Grandin, 2005) and that

---

[5] *State* and *channel* functions refer to the fact that all of what transpires in the brain is not information-processing. Global *states* are created by a variety of neurochemistries, from biogenic amines to peptides, that control vast regions of the brain simultaneously. Affects are presumably regulated by such neurodynamics, which can push the organism into globally distinct psychobehavioural states that are not meaningfully computable digitally; they are nonlinear large-scale analog dynamics. *Channel* functions refer to more discrete information-processing patterns where classical computational metaphors may be more effectively implemented.

much of their higher mental apparatus is devoted to finding and constructing affective comfort zones in physical and social environments (McMillian, 2005). Thus, it is understandable that in maternal behaviour, the basic emotional urge to provide care exists in lower parts of the brain (Nelson & Panksepp, 1998), while the social bonds that allow animals to selectively care for their own offspring are elaborated by higher brain functions (Keller, Meurisse & Levy, 2004). The pleasure of taste is elaborated in lower regions of the brain (Berridge, 2000) than our ability to emotionally over or under respond to qualitative shifts in taste (i.e., contrast effects: when rewards are shifted from higher to lower quality incentives).

In sum, although evolutionary divergences at higher cognitive levels are vast among species, cognitive decision-making remains tethered to affective foundations (Damasio, 1994). In this vein, a critically important neuroscientific question is how the intrinsic affective values of the nervous system help create learning.

Education of the Affects: Emotions, Learning and 'The Law of Effect'

Just as humans, other animals seek positive affect and avoid negative affect (McMillan, 2005). For most positive emotions (seeking, lust, care, play. . . and perhaps anger in certain situations) as well as for various positive environmental incentives (food, water, etc) animals must actively seek engagement with objects in the world. Thus, they need a general-purpose SEEKING system that pre-propositionally engages the world. Only through experiences with the world do such foraging 'energies' gradually get directed by learning and accruing knowledge about the world (Ikemoto & Panksepp, 1999). Animals need to avoid the major negative emotions (fear, separation distress, and anger in various situations) as well as negative sensory incentives (e.g., seek safety and avoid aversive and disgusting stimuli). They need to seek stimuli that can alleviate the distress of homeostatic imbalances (hunger, thirst, cold, etc) and the interdigitating gratifications of various social contacts (sex, nurturance, play).

Animals track optimal levels of positive affect by being 'magnetized' by positive affect supportive environmental stimuli (Cabanac, 1992). How learning is linked to these affective states-of-being has never been satisfactorily resolved, partly because of a conceptual morass concerning the scientifically unknowable nature of felt experience during the early part of the 20th century. In behavioral science, the process that supposedly mediates between the seemingly unfathomable affective nature of animals and their (our!) ability to learn is 'reinforcement,' based on Thorndike's celebrated 'law of effect.' This idea, as it was transformed from an affective to a non-affective concept, gradually led to the demise of affective thinking in all of psychology.

As initially phrased by Edward Thorndike (1874-1949), the 'law of effect' asserted that: 'Of several responses made to the same situation, those which are accompanied or closely followed by *satisfaction* to the animal will, other things being equal, be more firmly connected to the situation, so that, when it recurs, they will be more likely to recur; those which are accompanied or closely y followed by *discomfort* [annoyance] to the animal will, other things being equal, have their connections to that situation weakened, so that, when it recurs, they will be less likely to occur. The greater the *satisfaction* or *discomfort*, the greater the strengthening or weakening of this bond.' (Thorndike, 1911, p. 244, my italics).

Of course, it was hard to envision, without an in-depth knowledge of the brain, how ephemeral subjective states such as '*satisfaction*' and '*discomfort*' linked up to concrete observable behavioural changes so evident in learning. Accordingly, Hull (1884–1952), Skinner (1904–1990), and other behaviorists changed the key terms in the 'law of effect' — namely *satisfaction* and *discomfort* — into *positive* and *negative reinforcements* and *punishments*. . . which are even more theoretical concepts, but which, because of their inherent psychological ambiguity (they refer not to mental contents but what we do to animals) seemed to allow an 'escape from the shackles of subjectivity' (LeDoux, 2000, p. 156). Of course, if subjective states of the nervous system exist, and those neurodynamics are critical for understanding what animals do and how they learn, we must talk openly about such body/brain/mind entities.

As *reinforcement* concepts were taken to be real brain processes, behaviourism discarded any connection with the great diversity of affective concepts that scholars from Aristotle to Darwin had deemed essential for any coherent understanding of human and animal behaviour. However, aside from the role of excitatory amino acids, such as glutamate, that participate in all brain processes, to this day no one has given us a clear conception of what *reinforcement* really means in terms of neural functions. Still, the power of the concept has been so pervasive in psychological science that entire theories of emotion have been based on it. For instance, Jeffrey Gray (1990) framed emotion theory in terms of emotional states being created by positive and negative reinforcements. I challenged that idea by suggesting, in line with Thorndike's original view, that reinforcement is fundamentally affective — that various affective/emotional states help create behavioural change that we attribute to concepts such as reinforcement (Panksepp, 1990b). More recently Rolls (1999) has created another sophisticated reinforcement-based theory of how emotions are constructed by learning, while ignoring vast amounts of neuro-ethological evidence concerning the affective nature of the animal mind. This vast historical rift between traditional affective views of mental life and behaviouristic views of learning (with no acknowledgement of mentality) can only be healed by modern scholars considering *all* the relevant evidence, as opposed to their own favourite set of terms and findings. We need to consider how behaviour is controlled conjointly by neural and psychological causes. They reflect the same biophysical processes, but the psychological terms may be especially relevant for discussing the actions of large-scale neural networks.

When one does this, while accepting that central tenet of materialism that all aspects of mind are thoroughly biological, interesting new syntheses are possible. Lets consider brain dopamine circuits that have long been implicated in brain 'reward' processes. In fact, the ethological data suggests that this system helps energize a coherent evolutionary tool for learning, namely the foraging/SEEKING urge (Panksepp, 1981, 1986; 1992, 1998), which links up with higher associative mechanisms (Ikemoto & Panksepp, 1999). Such integrative evolutionary concepts have been consistently ignored by neuro-behaviourists, who have recently rediscovered a more limited version of the concept within a reward 'wanting' framework. This psychological construct remains carefully encased in scare quotes to alert behaviouristic readers that it is not intended to convey any experiential meaning (Berridge & Robinson, 2003; see critique in footnote #3, pp. 37–38 in Panksepp, 2005a) while concurrently allowing such mentalistic concepts to entice psychologically-oriented scholars.

However, the most puzzling behaviouristic *meme* in this field is the brain dopamine 'reward prediction error' concept, advanced on the basis of enhanced dopamine nerve cell firing in animals seeking rewards (Schulz, 1998; 2000; 2002). This concept has been applied to the study of animal behavior with inadequate consideration that arousal of brain dopamine systems contribute to natural emotive behaviour patterns and psychologically experienced states. Meanwhile, it has long been known that human drug addictions, desires and cravings ride upon the arousal of this system (Volkow *et al.*, 2002; Panksepp *et al.*, 2002). Can we really understand what dopamine does in the brain without any explicit concern for how this system helps create psychological processes that lie at the heart of our strivings to obtain rewards? Perhaps not (see Panksepp & Moskal, 2005).

It is long past time to return affective constructs back to the discussion of what 'rewards,' 'reinforcement' and 'punishers' really are. This will help fill the current void between external stimulus contingencies that lead to cognitions, and the neuro-affective functions of all mammals (Ikemoto & Panksepp, 1999). Indeed, the libidinal dopamine energized SEEKING urge may provide an essential generalized platform for the expression of many of the other basic emotional processes. For instance, it is hard to imagine predatory intent, maternal CARE and sexual LUST without SEEKING influences. It is the one system that helps animals anticipate all types of rewards.

Emotional Awareness is not the same as Emotional Affects.

Clearly, emotional systems are constituted of multi-layered hierarchical processes (Fig. 1). Animal models can clarify the pre-propositional affective mentalities of the lower substrates, while the human work is better suited to delve into the diverse cognitive-conceptual capacities of higher brain regions. The lower substrates, because of evolutionary conservation of functions, are more likely to be homologous across species, and hence more capable of empirical clarification. The many cognitive aspects of emotionality, individuated by many situational contingencies — attributions, judgments, beliefs or construals — remain the main focus of interest for most psychologists. To scientifically envision such higher emotional experiences, we must invest in new, subtle and open-ended scientific tools such as the Levels of Emotional Awareness scales (e.g., Lane & Garfield, 2005). But we also must develop new psychological paradigms — perhaps a new neuro-psychoanalysis — that aspires to link the flow of our higher mental apparatus to the ancestral emotional organic dynamics revealed by animal brain research (Panksepp, 1999; Solms & Turnbull, 2002).

Complex phenomenological theories, ungrounded by brain functions, have reigned for too long in traditional psychoanalytic and psychological theory. A new brain-mind science needs to be grounded in comparative psycho-neuro-phenomenological perspectives that can be linked to behavioral and biological variables, especially the neurochemistries for emotions clarified by neuroscience (Panksepp, 1998a; 2005a). Without a full synthesis of animal and human research, we cannot fathom the foundations of our mental apparatus.

Neuronal SELF-representations and the Neurodynamics of the Affects.

So how do organisms experience affective-emotional states within their brains? This critical question remains largely unaddressed. It must first be theoretically confronted if we are going to generate testable theories of how emotional feelings are actually generated in the brain/body. The traditional answer has been that one does not have any mental experiences until certain kinds of information interact with — are 'read out' by — higher neo-cortical mechanisms that elaborate our awareness of the world. Many still believe that affects are not experienced in the lower reaches of the brain — that all brain functions below the neocortex are experientially implicit and unconscious. Within such anthropo-centric world-views, emotional feelings cannot be understood until we figure out how the higher regions of the brain generate awareness of the world.

My own evidence-based vision of how affect emerges from the brain is rather different. To penetrate this epistemological 'brick wall' — namely what it actually means, in psycho-neurological terms, to have raw affective feelings — I think that we must entertain neuro-psychological conceptions of human and animal 'souls' through concepts such as the — 'core self' (Damasio, 1999; Gallagher & Sheard, 1999; Panksepp, 1998a). I suspect our mental lives are critically linked to primal viscero-somatic representations of the body situated in paramedian regions of the brain, and connected to associated higher limbic areas that can elaborate a variety of basic action dynamics that help constitute the organic feeling states of the basic emotions (i.e., the full activity of genetically ingrained emotional systems, as highlighted in Fig. 1). In other words, there exists a subcortical viscero-somatic homunculus, laid out in motor-action coordinates, that creates a primal representation of the body (core SELF) that can be modulated by global brain emotional networks that establish affective intentions in action, which are projected into and onto the world as prototypical affective values, helping guide cognitive intentionality (Panksepp, 1998b).

Core emotional feelings may be part and parcel of these global neurodynamics of the SELF (an acronym which can be translated as the Simple Ego-type Life Form), which finds its most coherent instantiation in brainstem regions such as the PAG and closely intermeshed paramedian diencephalic zones just above (e.g., ventral tegmental area at the hypothalamic-midbrain juncture) and just below (e.g., parabrachial regions of the brains stem). This extensive action network of the brain, extending up to medial frontal cortical regions, is modu-lated by a host of body variables, both autonomic, somatic and hormonal, as well as a variety of higher brain functions that can bring this large and coherent neural field into those action dynamics that we recognize as distinct emotional systems. The neurodynamics of such global psycho-behavioural attractors have not yet been measured objectively; at minimum, that would require accurate placement of many recording probes in carefully selected trajectories of the various emotional systems (Panksepp, 2002b).

It is within the rich neural connectivities to higher paramedian brain regions and lateral limbic cortices (e.g., insula) that higher forms of 'the self' will be found. Indeed, modern brain imaging has revealed that when we dwell self-referentially, as opposed to simply informationally, on any aspect of the world, such paramedian regions of the brain (the higher limbic zones from medial frontal, anterior cingulate regions to retrosplenial cortices toward the back of the brain) become selectively aroused; cognitive dwelling on the same stimuli leads to more lateral cortical arousal (Northoff et al., 2005). It is probably within these medial brain regions that we become aware of our emotional feel-ings — where emotional feelings and emotional cognitions are blended. These classic limbic brain regions (MacLean, 1990) are essential for us to deliberate on the deeper aspects of our emotional nature. These higher emotional regions of the brain exist in reciprocal relations to the more cognitive working memory regions that are essential for our rationality (Goel & Dolan, 2004; Liotti & Panksepp, 2004; Northoff et al., 2004).

Mental life is constructed from many global neurodynamics, and meaningful distinctions between emotional and cognitive processes within the brain should not be minimized. The lower paramedian trajectories of the basic emotional sys-tems — which converge on the more ancient periaqueductal, central gray regions of the midbrain — are essential for ancestral affective memories (Panksepp, 1998b). Those core feeling dynamics cannot cognitively reflect on themselves, but they may be experienced as cognitively unadulterated forms of pure affective livingness that may be an essential foundation for all higher mental functions. There are no principled logical or good empirical reasons to believe that experi-ences of affect cannot exist without cognitive mediation. In their basic form, affects may be cognitively blind while still being a primordial sort of mentality — neurobiologically ingrained ancestral memories that are intimately inter-twined with the genetically prescribed biological values of our bodily existence.

Perhaps many individuals lose touch with the importance and nature of such emotional values as they cognitively mature into the complex socio-cultural con-texts that mould our cognitive lives. Thereby, affects may become part of our dynamic subconscious. Still, those ancient aspects of mental life probably con-tinue to influence our emotional experiences from birth to death. Without those gifts of nature — those basic neural tools for living — we would be scarecrows in the material world, moving as the environmental winds blow (as behaviourism once envisioned), as opposed to being the deeply feeling, enactive creatures that we (and other mammals) truly are.

The failure to recognize how evolution constructed the foundational aspects of mental existence remains a continuing intellectual tragedy of 20th century behavioural science (Panksepp, 2005a). The resulting anthropocentrisms and neuro-dualisms continue to haunt us to the present day. Those cold materialistic visions still offer images of an affectively ungrounded existence, beings as intrinsically valueless as inanimate nature. But that is not a conclusion supported by functional brain research. Affective biological values — the ancestral voices of the genes — exist at the foundation of our higher cognitive apparatus. It is through the interweaving of such intrinsic value structures with cognitive processes, and our eventual capacity to reflect on them, that many special human mental capacities and behavioural abilities emerge that cannot be studied in other animals.

Recapitulation

To understand emotional feelings, where large-scale brain-mind processes are not as visible as we wish they were, theoretical perspectives that lead to concrete predictions are essential (Panksepp, 1998a). There is now abundant evidence that emotional feelings may arise substantially from the same large-scale neurodynamics that generate the various emotional-instinctual actions that all mammals, including young humans, explicitly exhibit. The emotional instincts are not affectively vacuous. Regrettably, the instinctual emotional expressions were *arbitrarily* relegated into the category of unconscious/implicit/reflexive behavioural processes long before we had neuroscientific and behavioural tools to begin to probe their neural and psychological nature. Accordingly, in behavioural neuroscience, traditional non-experiential concepts prevail to this day, even though abundant data now indicate that affective experiences are decisive for much of what animals actually do, and they may even construct those brain processes that are so important for promoting learning via that exquisitely clear *procedure*, but spooky *process*, called *reinforcement*.

Of course, all existing levels of analysis, even those that deny any mentality to animals, can contribute to a comprehensive understanding of emotionality. At present, core affective processes are best illuminated, scientifically, by studying the intrinsic emotional action-generating dynamics of animal brains. If higher cognitive emotional feelings of humans do substantially arise from instinctual action systems that are homologous in all mammals, then we may finally understand some of the more subtle aspects of human affective consciousness by studying the more primitive emotional systems of other animals. Obviously, there will be many species differences to be documented. However, granted the evolutionary continuity of the mental apparatus in all mammals (Darwin, 1872), animal neuro-ethological research can engender substantive empirical progress on such questions of ultimate human concern.

References

Bardo, M.T. & Bevins, R.A. (2000), 'Conditioned place preference: What does it add to our preclinical understanding of drug reward?', *Psychopharmacology,* 153 (1), pp. 31-43.

Barrett, L.F., Niedenthal, P.M. & Winkielman, P. (ed. 2005), *Emotion and Consciousness* (New York, Guildford Publications, Inc).

Bekoff, M. (2000), *The Smile of a Dolphin: Remarkable Accounts of Animal Emotions* (New York, Random House/Discovery Books).

Berridge, K.C. (2000), 'Measuring hedonic impact in animals and infants: Microstructure of affective taste reactivity patterns,' *Neuroscience and Biobehavioral Reviews,* **24** (2), pp. 173–98.

Berridge, K.C. & Robinson, T.E. (2003), 'Parsing reward', *Trends in Neurosciences,* **9** (9), pp. 507–13.

Burgdorf, J., Knutson, B., Panksepp, J. & Ikemoto, S. (2001), 'Nucleus accumbens amphetamine microinjections unconditionally elicit 50 kHz ultrasonic vocalizations in rats', *Behavioral Neuroscience,* **115** (4), pp. 940–4.

Cabanac, M. (1992), 'Pleasure: The common currency', Journal of Theoretical Biology, 155 (2), pp. 173–200.

Catania, K.C. & Kaas, J.H. (1997), 'Somatosensory fovea in the star-nosed mole: Behavioral use of the star in relation to innervation patterns and cortical representation', *Journal of Comparative Neurology,* **387** (2), pp. 215–33.

Ciompi, L. & Panksepp, J. (2005), 'Energetic effects of emotions on cognitions — complementary psychobiological and psychosocial findings', in *Consciousness & Emotion Book Series*, Vol 1, ed. R.D. Ellis & N. Newton, pp. 23–56 (Amsterdam: John Benjamins).

Clynes, M. (1978), *Sentics: The Touch of Emotions* (New York: Doubleday).

Colpaert, F.C., De Witte, P., Maroli, A.N., Awouters, F., Niemegeers, C.J.E. & Janssen, P.A.J. (1980), 'Self-administration of the analgesic suprofen in arthritic rats', *Life Science,* **27** (11), pp. 921–8.

Damasio, A.R. (1994), *Descartes' Error* (New York: Avon Books).

Damasio, A.R. (2003a), *Looking for Spinoza* (Orlando, FL: Harcourt Brace).

Damasio, A.R., Grabowski, T.J., Bechara, A., Damasio, H., Ponto, L.L.B., Parvizi, J. & Hichwa, R.D. (2000), 'Subcortical and cortical brain activity during the feeling of self-generated emotions', *Nature Neuroscience,* **3** (10), pp. 1049–56.

Darwin, C. (1872/1998), *The Expression of Emotions in Man and Animals*, 3rd ed. (New York: Oxford University Press).

Davidson, R.J., Scherer, K.R. & Goldsmith, H.H. (ed. 2003), *Handbook of Affective Sciences,* (New York, Oxford University Press).

Fichtel C., Hammerschmidt, K. & Jürgens U. (2001), 'On the vocal expression of emotion. A multi-parametric analysis of different states of aversion in the squirrel monkey', *Behaviour,* **138** (1), pp. 97–116.

Gallagher, S. & Shear, J., (1999), *Models of the Self* (Exeter, UK: Imprint Academic).

Goel, V., & Dolan, R. J. (2003), 'Reciprocal neural response within lateral and ventral medial prefrontal cortex during hot and cold reasoning,*Neuroimage,* **20** (4), pp. 2314–21.

Grandin, T. (2005), *Animals in Translation* (New York: Scribner).

Gray, J.A. (1990), 'Brain systems that mediate both emotion and cognition',*Cognition and Emotion,* **4** (3), pp. 269–88.

Greenspan, R.J. & Baars, B.J. (2005), 'Consciousness eclipsed: Jacques Loeb, Ivan P. Pavlov, and the rise of reductionistic biology after 1900',*Consciousness and Cognition,* **14** (1), pp. 219–30.

Griffiths, T.D., Warren, J.D., Dean, J.L. & Howard, D. (2004) ' "When the feeling's gone": A selective loss of musical emotion', *Journal of Neurology, Neurosurgery & Psychiatry,* **75** (2), pp. 344–5.

Heath, R.G. (1996), *Exploring the Mind-Body Relationship* (Baton Rouge, LA: Moran Printing, Inc).

Hebb, D.O. (1946), 'Emotion in man and animal: The intuitive processes of recognition, *Psychological Review,* **53** (2), pp. 88–106.

Holstege G., Georgiadis J.R., Paans A.M., Meiners L.C., van der Graaf F.H. & Reinders A.A. (2003) 'Brain activation during human male ejaculation', *Journal of Neuroscience,* **23** (27), pp. 9185–93.

Huston, J.P. & Borbely, A.A. (1973), 'Operant conditioning in forebrain ablated rats by use of rewarding hypothalamic stimulation', *Brain Research,* **50** (2), pp. 467–72.

Huston, J.P. & Borbely, A.A. (1974), 'The thalamic rat: General behavior, operant learning with rewarding hypothalamic stimulation, and effects of amphetamine', *Physiology & Behavior,* **12** (3), pp. 433–48.

Ikemoto, S. & Panksepp, J. (1999), 'The role of nucleus accumbens dopamine in motivated behavior, a unifying interpretation with special reference to reward-seeking', *Brain Research Reviews*, **25** (1), pp. 261–74.

Ikemoto, S. & Wise, R.A. (2004), 'Mapping of chemical trigger zones for reward', *Neuropharmacology*, **47** (Suppl 1), pp. 190–201.

Keller, M., Meurisse, M., & Levy, F. (2004), 'Mapping the neural substrates involved in maternal responsiveness and lamb olfactory memory in parturient ewes using Fos imaging', *Behavioral Neuroscience*, **118** (6), pp. 1274–84.

Knight, D.C., Smith, C.N., Cheng, D.T., Stein, E.A., & Helmstetter, F.J. (2004), 'Amygdala and hippocampal activity during acquisition and extinction of human fear conditioning', *Cognitive, Affective & Behavioral Neuroscience*, **4** (3), pp. 317–25.

Knutson, B., Adams, C.M., Fong, G.W. & Hommer, D. (2001), 'Anticipation of increasing monetary reward selective3ly recruits nucleus accumbens',*Journal of Neuroscience*, **21** (16), pp. 1–5.

Knutson, B., Burgdorf, J., Panksepp, J. (2002), 'Ultrasonic vocalizations as indices of affective states in rats', *Psychological Bulletin*, **128** (6), pp. 961–77.

Kolb, B. & Tees, C. (Eds.) (1990), *The Cerebral Cortex of the Rat* (Cambridge, MA: MIT Press).

Lane, R.D. & Garfield, D.A.S. (2005), 'Becoming aware of feelings: Integration of cognitive-developmental, neuroscientific and psychoanalytic perspectives', *Neuro-Psychoanalysis*, **7** (1), pp. 5–30.

LeDoux, J.E. (1996), *The Emotional Brain* (New York: Simon & Schuster).

LeDoux, J.E. (2000), 'Emotion circuits in the brain', *Annual Review of Neuroscience*, **23**, pp. 155–184.

Leinonen L., Linnankoski I., Laakso M.L. & Aulanko R. (1991), Vocal communication between species: man and macaque', *Language and Communication*, **11** (4), pp. 241–62.

Lewis, G.H. (1877), *The Physical Basis of Mind. With Illustrations. Being the Second Series of Problems of Life and Mind.* (London: Trübner & Co.).

Lewontin, R.C. (1998), 'The evolution of cognition: Questions we will never answer', in *Methods, Models, and Conceptual Issues: An invitation to cognitive science, Vol. 4.* (Cambridge, MA: The MIT Press).

Liotti, M. & Panksepp, J. (2004), 'Imaging human emotions and affective feelings: Implications for biological psychiatry', in *Textbook of Biological Psychiatry*, ed. J. Panksepp (Hoboken, NJ: Wiley).

MacLean, P.D. (1990), *The Triune Brain in Evolution* (New York: Plenum).

Manstead, A.S.R., Frijda, N. & Fischer, A. (ed. 2004), *Feelings and Emotions: The Amsterdam Symposium* (Cambridge: Cambridge University Press).

McMillan, F.D. (ed. 2005), *Animal Mental Health and Well-Being.* (Iowa City: Blackwell Publishing).

Murphy, F.C., Nimmo-Smith, I. & Lawrence, A.D. (2003), 'Functional neuroanatomy of emotions, A meta-analysis', *Cognitive, Affective, & Behavioral Neuroscience*, **3** (3), pp. 207–33.

Nahas, Z., Loberbaum, J.P., Kozel, F.A. & George, M.S. (2004), 'Somatic treatments in psychiatry', in *Textbook of Biological Psychiatry*, ed. J. Panksepp (Hoboken, NJ: Wiley).

Nelson, E, & Panksepp, J. (1998), 'Brain substrates of infant-mother attachment: Contributions of opioids, oxytocin, and norepinepherine'. *Neuroscience Biobehavioral Reviews*, **22**, pp. 437–52.

Numan, M. & Insel, T.R. (2003), *The neurobiology of Parental behavior* (New York: Springer).

Niedenthal, P.M., Barsalou, L.W., Ric, F. & Krauth-Gruber, S. (2005), 'Embodiment in the acquisition and use of emotion knowledge', in *Emotion and Consciousness*, ed. L.F. Barrett, P.M. Niedenthal & P. Winkielman (New York: Guildford Publications, Inc).

Northoff, G., Heinzel, A., Bermpohl, F., Niese, R., Pfennig, A., Pascual-Leone, A. & Schlaug, G. (2004), 'Reciprocal modulation and attenuation in the prefrontal cortex: an fMRI study on emotional-cognitive interaction', *Human Brain Mapping*, **21** (3), pp. 202–12.

Northoff, G., Heinzel, A., de Greck, M., Bermpohl, F. & Panksepp, J. (2005), 'Our brain and its self: The central role of cortical midline structures', in press in *Neuroimage*.

Ochsner, K.N., Cooper, R.D. Robertson, E.R., Elaine, R. *et al.,*(2004), 'For better or for worse: Neural systems supporting the cognitive down- and up-regulation of negative emotion', *NeuroImage*, **23** (2), pp. 483–99.

Okun, M.S., Bowers, D., Springer, U., Shapira, N.A., Malone, D., Rezai, A.R., Nuttin, B., Heilman. K.M., Morecraft, R.J., Rasmussen, S.A., Greenberg, B.D., Foote, K.D., & Goodman,

W.K. (2004), 'What's in a "smile?" Intra-operative observations of contralateral smiles induced by deep brain stimulation', *Neurocase*, **10** (4), pp. 271–9.

Olmstead, M.C. & Franklin, K.B.J. (1997), 'The development of a conditioned place preference to morphine: Effects of microinjections into various CNS sites', *Behavioral Neuroscience*, **111** (6), pp. 1324–34

Panksepp, J. (1981), 'Hypothalamic integration of behavior: Rewards, punishments, and related psychobiological process', in *Handbook of the Hypothalamus, Vol. 3, Part A. Behavioral studies of the hypothalamus*, ed. P.J. Morgane and J. Panksepp (New York: Marcel Dekker).

Panksepp, J. (1982), 'Toward a general psychobiological theory of emotions', *The Behavioral and Brain Sciences*, **5** (3), pp. 407–67.

Panksepp, J. (1985), 'Mood changes', in *Handbook of Clinical Neurology. Vol. 1. (45), Clinical Neuropsychology*, pp. 271–85. (Amsterdam: Elsevier Science Publishers).

Panksepp, J. (1986), 'The anatomy of emotions', in *Emotion: Theory, Research and Experience Vol. III. Biological Foundations of Emotions*, ed. R. Plutchik (Orlando: Academic Press).

Panksepp, J. (1990a), 'The psychoneurology of fear: Evolutionary perspectives and the role of animal models in understanding human anxiety', in *Handbook of Anxiety. Vol. 3, The Neurobiology of Anxiety*, ed. G.D. Burrows, M. Roth & R. Noyes, Jr. (Amsterdam: Elsevier/North-Holland Biomedical Press).

Panksepp, J. (1990b), 'Gray zones at the emotion/cognition interface', *Cognition and Emotion*, **4** (3), pp. 289–302.

Panksepp, J. (1992), 'A critical role for "affective neuroscience" in resolving what is basic about basic emotions', *Psychological Review*, **99** (3), pp. 554–60.

Panksepp, J. (1998a), *Affective Neuroscience: The foundations of human and animal emotions* (New York: Oxford University Press).

Panksepp, J. (1998b), 'The periconscious substrates of consciousness: Affective states and the evolutionary origins of the SELF', *Journal of Consciousness Studies*, **5** (5-6), pp. 566–82.

Panksepp, J. (1999), 'Emotions as viewed by psychoanalysis and neuroscience: An exercise in consilience', *Neuro-Psychoanalysis*, **1** (1), pp. 15–38.

Panksepp, J. (2002a), 'The MacLean legacy and some modern trends in emotion research', in *The Evolutionary Neuroethology of Paul MacLean*, ed. G.A. Cory & R. Gardner, Jr. (Westport, CT: Praeger).

Panksepp, J. (2000b), 'The neurodynamics of emotions: An evolutionary-neurodevelopmental view', in *Emotion, Self-Organization, and Development*, ed. M.D. Lewis & I. Granic (New York: Cambridge Univ. Press).

Panksepp, J. (2003), 'At the interface of affective, behavioral and cognitive neurosciences. Decoding the emotional feelings of the brain', *Brain and Cognition*, **52** (1), pp. 4–14.

Panksepp, J. (2004a), 'The emerging neuroscience of fear and anxiety: Therapeutic practice and clinical implications', in *Textbook of Biological Psychiatry*, ed. J. Panksepp (Hoboken, NJ: Wiley).

Panksepp, J. (2004b), 'Affective consciousness and the origins of human mind: A critical role of brain research on animal emotions', *Impuls*, **3** (3), pp. 47–6.

Panksepp, J. (2005a), 'Affective consciousness: Core emotional feelings in animals and humans', *Cognition and Consciousness*, **14** (1), pp. 30–80.

Panksepp, J. (2005b), 'On the primal nature of affective consciousness: What are the relations between emotional awareness and affective experience? Commentary on Lane & Garfield', *Neuro-Psychoanalysis*, **7** (1), pp. 40–55.

Panksepp, J. & Bernatzky, G. (2002), 'Emotional sounds and the brain; The neuro-affective foundations of musical appreciation', *Behavioural Processes*, **60** (2) pp. 133–55.

Panksepp, J. & Burgdorf, J. (2003), '"Laughing" rats and the evolutionary antecedents of human joy?', *Physiology & Behavior*, **79** (3), pp. 533–47.

Panksepp, J. & Gordon, N. (2001), 'The instinctual basis of human affect: Affective imaging of laughter and crying', *Consciousness & Emotion*, **4** (2), pp. 197–205.

Panksepp, J., & Harro, J. (2004), 'The future of neuropeptides in biological psychiatry and emotional psychopharmacology: Goals and strategies', in *Textbook of Biological Psychiatry*, ed. J. Panksepp (Hoboken, NJ: Wiley).

Panksepp, J., Knutson, B. & Burgdorf, J. (2002), 'The role of brain emotional systems in addictions: A new neuro-evolutionary perspective and new 'self-report' animal model', *Addiction*, **97** (4), pp. 459–69.

Panksepp J. & Moskal, J. (2005), 'Dopamine, pleasure and appetitive eagerness, An emotional systems overview of the trans-hypothalamic 'reward' system in the genesis of addictive urges', in *The Cognitive, Behavioral and Affective Neursociences in Psychiatric Disorders*, ed. Susan Barsch (New York: Oxford University Press).

Panksepp, J., Normansell, L., Herman, B., Bishop, P. & Crepeau, L. (1988), 'Neural and neurochemical control of the separation distress call', in *The Physiological Control of Mammalian Vocalizations*, ed. J.D. Newman (New York, Plenum Press).

Panksepp, J., Normansell, L.A., Cox, J.F. & Siviy, S. (1994), 'Effects of neonatal decortication on the social play of juvenile rats', *Physiology & Behavior,* **56** (3) pp. 429–43.

Parvizi, J., & Damasio, A. (2001), 'Consciousness and the brainstem', *Cognition*, **79** (1–2), pp. 135–60.

Parvizi, J. & Damasio, A. (2003), 'Neuroanatomical correlates of brainstem coma', *Brain*, **126** (7), pp. 1524–36.

Pfaff, D.W. (1999), *Drive: Neurobiological and molecular mechanisms of sexual behavior* (Cambridge, MA: MIT Press).

Phan, K.L., Wager, T., Taylor, S.F. & Liberzon, I. (2002), 'Functional neuroanatomy of emotion: A meta-analysis of emotion activation studies in PET and fMRI', *Neuroimage*, **16** (2), pp. 331–48.

Robinson, J. (2005), *Deeper Than Reason: Emotion and its role in literature, music and art.* (Oxford: Oxford University Press).

Rolls, E.T. (1999), *The Brain and Emotion* (Oxford: Oxford University Press).

Russell, J.A. (2003), 'Core affect and the psychological construction of emotion', *Psychological Review,* **110** (1), pp. 145–72.

Pettigrew, J.D., Manger, P.R. & Fine, S.L.B. (1998), 'The sensory world of the platypus', *Philosophical Transactions of the Royal Society of London: Biological Science,* **353** (1372), pp. 1199–210.

Schiff, N.D., Rodriguez-Moreno, D., Kamal, A., Kim, K.H.S., Giacino, J.T., Plumb, F. & Hirsch, J. (2005), 'FMRI reveals large-scale network activation in minimally conscious patients', *Neurology*, **64** (3), pp. 514–23.

Schlaer, R. & Myers, M.L. (1972), 'Operant conditioning of the pretrigeminal cat', *Brain Research,* **38** (1), pp. 222–5.

Schulman, R.G. & Rothman, D.L. (Eds.) (2004), *Brain energetics & Neuronal Activity: Applications to fMRI and medicine* (London: Wiley).

Schultz, W. (1998), 'Predictive reward signal of DA neurons', *Journal of Neurophysiology,* **80** (1), pp. 1–27.

Schultz, W. (2000), 'Multiple reward signals in the brain', *Nature Reviews Neuroscience,* **1** (3), pp. 199–207.

Schulz, W. (2002), 'Getting formal with DA reward', *Neuron,* **36** (2), pp. 241–63.

Schutter, D.J.L.G., Van Honk, J. & Panksepp, J. (2004), 'Introducing repetitive transcranial magnetic stimulation (rTMS) and its property of causal inference in investigating the brain-function relationship', *Synthese.* **141** (2), pp. 155–73.

Siegel, A. (2005), *The Neurobiology of Aggression and Rage* (Boca Raton, FL: CRC Press).

Shewmon, D.A., Holmes, D.A. & Byrne, P.A. (1999), 'Consciousness in congenitally decorticate children, pp. developmental vegetative state as self-fulfilling prophecy', *Developmental Medicine and Child Neurology,* **41** (6), pp. 364–74.

Solms, M. & Turnbull, O. (2002), *The Brain and The Inner World* (New York, Other Press).

Thorndike, E.L. (1911), *Animal Intelligence: Experimental Studies* (New York, MacMillan Co.).

Volkow, N. D., Fowler, J. S. & Wang, G-J. (2002), 'Role of dopamine in drug reinforcement and addiction in humans: results from imaging studies', *Behavioural Pharmacology*, **13** (5-6), pp. 355–66.

Watt, D.F. & Pincus, D.I. (2004), 'Neural substrates of consciousness: Implications for clinical psychiatry', in *Textbook of Biological Psychiatry*, ed. J. Panksepp (Hoboken, NJ: Wiley).

Zubieta, J.K., Ketter, T.A., Bueller, J.A., Xu, Y., Kilbourn, M.R., Young, E.A. & Koeppe, R.A. (2003), 'Regulation of human affective responses by anterior cingulate and limbic mu-opioid neurotransmission', *Archives of General Psychiatry*, **60** (11), 1145–53.

Douglas F. Watt

Social Bonds and the Nature of Empathy

Considerations stemming from a basic taxonomy of emotion suggest that the creation of social bonds is a critical domain for affective neuroscience. A critical phenomenon within this group of processes promoting attachment is empathy, a process essential to mitigation of human suffering, and for both the creation and long term stability of social bonds. Models of empathy emerging from cognitive and affective neuroscience show widespread confusion about cognitive versus affective dimensions to empathy. Human empathy probably reflects admixtures of more primitive 'affective resonance' or contagion mechanisms, melded with developmentally later-arriving emotion identification, and theory of mind/perspective taking. From these considerations, a basic model of affective empathy is generated as a gated resonance induction of the internal distress of another creature, with an intrinsic motivation to relieve the distress. It is 'gated,' in that at least four classes of hypothesized variables determine intensity of an empathic response to the suffering of another. Differential predictions of this model vs. current ones, and future tests are proposed.

'Where there are two, one cannot be wretched and one not.'

— *Euripides*

Taxonomy Must Come First: A Possible Typology of Emotion

Jaak Panksepp and I have both argued recently (Panksepp and Watt, 2003) that basic emotion typologies or taxonomies are critical to defining the problem spaces of emotion, and that our classifications schemes, if conceptually flawed, seriously impair meaningful data collection and only compound an already substantial degree of conceptual confusion. One possible typology for emotion (Panksepp, 1998; Panksepp & Watt, 2003 for some further implications) might

Correspondence:
Douglas F. Watt, Ph.D., Clinic for Cognitive Disorders, Quincy Medical Center, Boston University, School of Medicine, Quincy, MA 02169, USA.   *Email: dfwatt@brahmacom.com*

Journal of Consciousness Studies, **12**, No. 8–10, 2005, pp. 185–209

emphasize the following primary or prototype states: ***Fear, Rage, Lust, Separation Distress, Play/Social Affection, Nurturance***, and also possibly ***Disgust***. I omit '***Surprise***' from this typology, despite its appearance in many other classical typologies for emotion, as this is not a primary emotional state, more a 'cognitive or expectancy reset' mechanism involving cognitive dissonance. Additionally, the notion of a '***Seeking System***' (see Panksepp, 1998, for summary overview) centred in the VTA-to-lateral hypothalamic DA to mesolimbic-mesocortical projection tracts, falls into a special class of one, distinct from the other prototype emotional systems. Without the 'seeking system', there is no ability to instantiate *any* coherent emotional state, and in a direct sense all the prototype states simply disappear, along with virtually any motivated behaviour. This suggests that the ***Seeking System*** might provide a kind of 'central trunk line' in the brain for all emotion that the prototype emotional states may 'grab a hold of' to instantiate and organize a particular emotional state in the brain.

Even in highly cognitive creatures such as ourselves, those simple primes or prototypes remain central organizing paradigms for our more cognized emotions. Fundamental paradigms of emotion, like confrontation with a predator or powerful rival (fear), assault, or other threats to safety, free pursuit, territory or other resources (anger), the loss of mates, offspring and con-specifics (separation distress), and the comforts and joys of sex, attachment, and play all become increasingly translated and activated through complex cognitive operations that sit on the cognition-emotion border. Through human ontogenesis, these affective 'primes' are increasingly activated within, and even transformed by, this rich sea of human symbolic operations and complex meanings, as emotion is increasingly cognized. But even complex, highly cognized human emotions never lose their intrinsic grounding to these emotional primes, or else they cease to exist in the human organism. nor does emotion ever lose its fundamental reliance on the non-specific 'seeking system' that acts as a 'gain' system and modulatory control system for all the prototype states, driving organisms out there to 'mix it up' with other living things, to find essential emotional and biological supplies. Major lesions of that core system consistently create akinetic mutism and a virtually total ablation of emotion (Watt & Pincus, 2004).

In any case, this simple typology for prototype emotion does not yield a large N (only seven major primary states and 'seeking system'). However, and quite suggestively, these break down into two obvious large clusters: an *Organism Defense Cluster — Fear, Rage and Disgust* (which protects us immunologically) vs. a *Social Connection Cluster* (*Lust, Play/Affection, Nurturance and Separation Distress*). This suggests the obvious conclusion (readily supported by any introspective review of human life) that outlining fundamental processes in the brain underpinning social connection and attachment are very critical territories for affective neuroscience. However, attachment is likely to represent a large umbrella of affiliated processes that bind creatures together, involving several mammalian prototype states (such as separation distress and rough-and-tumble play), and not one simple, uni-dimensional process. In any case, the joys of love and attachment, particularly the two classical and most intense manifestations of attachment in romantic and maternal love, are among the very deepest gratifications that human beings strive to attain. Conversely, the catastrophic loss of a rewarding or deep primary attachment typically plunges us into some of the cruelest pains that human beings can ever experience. Such losses (including their symbolic variants, and cognized first cousins of separation distress found in intense guilt and shame) are far and away the most common precipitants for the induction of serious depressions.

Surprisingly in view of these considerations, the basic neural substrates of attachment, play, and social bonding are still relatively poorly charted in neuroscience, and certainly poorly charted relative to their central importance in human life. Attachment and its vicissitudes are still massively neglected in the models in psychiatry for disorders in DSM-IV. We probably know much more about visual experience and visual processing in the cognitive-sensory domain, or about fear in the emotional domain, than we do about attachment and its critical components. In a nutshell, neuroscience, outside of a few investigators such as Jaak Panksepp, has until recently (Bartels & Zeki, 2000; Bartels & Zeki, 2004) been reluctant to tackle the neural nature of love. This neglect may reflect effects of lingering behaviouristic assumptions on neuroscience yet to be fully mitigated. Indeed, the more personal, intimate and emotionally profound the experience, the less neuroscience really knows about it. Related to this has been a reluctance to consider that attachment and love are hardly uniquely human qualities (although their higher cortico-cognitive resonances likely are), and that their phylogenesis must go deep into our genetic antiquity. One of the most critical and least appreciated aspects within this large domain of social connection processes has to be the problem of empathy, one of our most critical social abilities, and essential to the mitigation of human suffering.

The Problem of Defining Empathy: Blind Men Inspecting the Elephant

The term empathy was originally translated by Titchener in 1909 from the German term '*Einfühlung*', a term from aesthetics meaning 'projecting yourself into what you observe.' There has been endless hairsplitting in various psychological literatures about the possible distinctions one might draw between the terms compassion, sympathy, and empathy. It is this author's contention that for the most part these finely nuanced distinctions offer little to empirical neuroscience, and additionally, that all terms outline a common ground of a *positively valenced supportive response to the distress of another creature*, and that defining this core process is the critical issue for neuroscience. Unfortunately, extensive literatures on empathy offer significantly different and even conflicting definitions, with conflicts typically centring on more cognitive vs. more affective emphases. One cluster of literatures emphasizes empathy as dependent upon perception of affective states, theory of mind, conscious imitation, perspective taking and the like, the other group emphasizes the centrality of affective activation in the empathizing subject. It has also been approached as an essential cross-species mammalian ability, as a more restricted higher cognitive function dependent on theory of mind, and as a conditioned/learned social behaviour. These differential concepts of empathy often lead to disparate methodologies and confusing empirical results (see Decety & Jackson, 2004; Preston & deWaal, 2002 for reviews). Empathy challenges us to develop models from the standpoint of its development in both phylogeny and ontogeny, in terms of its basic adaptive value(s), and in defining its fundamental neural mechanisms. Although much literature presents a more cognitive view of empathy, the etymology of the word suggests that the term empathy be reserved for phenomenon that extend beyond a cognitive perception of another's emotional/internal state (although those may be 'cognitive components' of empathy and critical social cognitions). Empathy, and its closest synonym 'compassion', both denote that one is 'suffering with another'. Additionally, although this is somewhat more controversial, I would argue that empathy in this core affective sense must also contain an intrinsic motivation to mitigate the distress of the other party. As Decety & Jackson (2004) emphasize, many if not most definitions of empathy involve three central components: (1) feeling what someone is feeling; (2) knowing what someone is feeling; (3) having some intent to mitigate their suffering. Although this review will emphasize a more basic affective definition of empathy, empathy shares a fundamental border with emotion identification, and with emergent higher cognitive processes involved in perspective taking, theory of mind, and many aspects of social cognition.

General Conceptual Frameworks and Organizing Hypotheses

When trying to understand processes happening within the staggering complexity of adult human brains, there is heuristic value to first developing an animal model of a target phenomenon, and testing this against the more complex process in humans. Obviously, there are many complex cognitive processes and behaviours for which this is not possible, such as the primary use of language, religious experience, meditative states, etc. However, a relatively simple animal paradigm with face validity provides an initial template for the study of empathy in humans: the response of maternal mammals to separation distress signals (and other kinds of distress and biological need states) in their infants. This animal model leads directly to several core hypotheses, although I will acknowledge that these are not universally conceded in behavioural and affective neuroscience:

(1) Based on the universal mammalian phenomenon of nurturance and maternal care, most mammals presumably have some primitive empathic capacities.

(2) Empathy appears phylogenetically coincident with the social signaling functions of emotion and with the deepening of formation of social bonds.

(3) Therefore, it seems reasonable to suspect that primitive empathic ability developed concomitant to strong attachment, that evolution in some sense carved the two processes jointly, with social bonding being

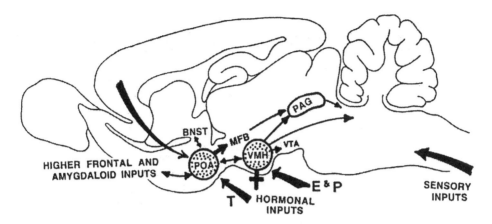

Figure 1a: Sexual Arousal Circuits

Lateral view of the rat brain summarizing two major areas that provide differential control over male and female sexual behaviours. Males contain a larger POA, and this area is essential for male sexual competence. The VMH is clearly more influential in female sexual responsivity. The systems operate, in part, by sensitizing various sensory input channels that promote copulatory reflexes. The extent to which these circuits control the affective components of sexual behaviour remains uncertain.

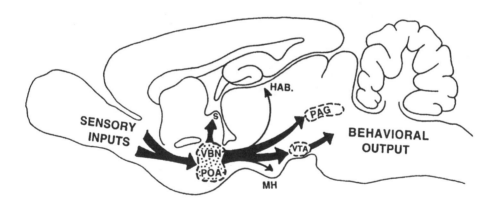

Figure 1b: Maternal Behaviour Circuits

General overview of maternal behaviour circuits in rodents. The central integrator is in the dorsal preoptic area (POA) and the ventral bed nucleus of the stria terminals (VBN), which receives various sensory cues for maternal behaviour and distributes controls into widespread brain areas, including the medial hypothalamus (MH), the ventral tegmental area (VTA), the periaqueductal gray (PAG), the habenula (HAB), and the septal area (S). The precise functions of these various areas remain to be identified.

Figure 1: Neural Systems for Sexuality and Nurturance (Panksepp, 1998)
(with permission from Oxford University Press)

critically enhanced by the ability to perceive, and relieve, the distress of a con-specific.

(4) The more complex phenomena of human empathy may reflect a 'cognized extension' of this mammalian prototype state of nurturing behaviour towards young, especially distressed young, but these critical cognitive extensions potentially allow for increasing appreciation of the internal spaces of others, and creation and extensive development of a theory of mind and perspective taking in human ontogenesis. However, these cognitive developments do not replace the largely subcortical prototype of mammalian nurturance, but rather reflect increasingly complex extensions of this process into telencephalic regions through distributed networks.

Animal Model Architectures:
Distributed Networks for Social Connection

Consistent with the above noted fundamental division in the emotion taxonomy between *organism defence* and *social connection*, animal work (summarized in three graphics here) suggests major overlap in functional networks in most mammals subserving sexual arousal, separation distress/social bonding, and for nurturance and maternal care (see Panksepp, 1998 for extended summary). The animal data on maternal care and nurturance suggest an initial hypothesis that primitive empathic ability might be organized by basic systems subserving a complex of attachment-related processes. The networks implicated in the animal work on nurturance and attachment involve preoptic areas of the hypothalamus, ventral portions of the bed nucleus of stria terminalis, and ventral septum, with likely secondary roles played by other basal forebrain, diencephalic and midbrain systems such as habenula, and other hypothalamic areas. The preoptic and ventral bed nuclei appear to be the primary organizers of maternal behaviour. Major lesions to either of these regions devastates the capacity of female mammals to care for their young. This functional network may change in phylogenesis, with more involvement of paralimbic areas, consistent with Jacksonian principles. Evidence argues that in primates and hominids the anterior cingulate and nucleus accumbens are increasingly critical for attachment and separation distress and maternal behaviour. Evidence suggests that the various prototype emotional states all have basic architectures that funnel down into different portions of periaqueductal gray and that different prototype states may reflect differential columnar activity in PAG (Watt, 2000).

Other relevant experimental results might include findings that mu opioid receptor knock-out mice are deficient in attachment behaviours, with evidence that both approach and orienting behaviour towards mother and separation distress responses are attenuated (Moles, Kieffer, & D'Amato, 2004). This suggests that the neuropeptides regulating attachment and maternal care particularly oxytocin (Uvnas-Möberg, 1998; Carter, 1998), opioids, prolactin (Panksepp, 1998) have broad relevance for regulating empathic responsiveness, but there

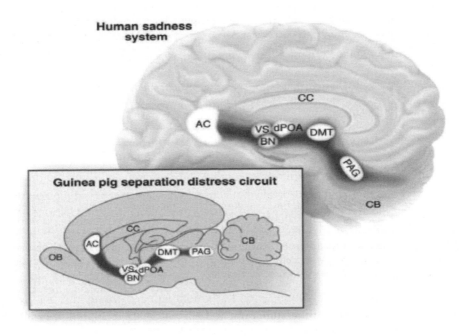

Figure 2: Human and Mammalian Separation Distress Systems
(reprinted from Panksepp, 2003 with permission of
American Association for the Advancement of Science)

has been to my knowledge no formal study of neuropeptides in human empathy. Jaak Panksepp (2004) notes three remaining major questions:

(1) Does the activation of distress circuits in young and relatively helpless animals evoke resonant activity in the same circuits of nearby adults?

(2) If such perceptually induced resonance does exist, is the evoked activity especially strong between strongly bonded individuals?

(3) Does such brain activity arouse caregiving in adults?

The default hypothesis here, suggested by the basic phenomenology of empathy, is that the questions above would be answered in the affirmative.

Empathy Functional Imaging Studies

There have been several studies of empathy or closely related phenomena using functional imaging. Unfortunately there have been different models of empathy, and different methods for testing and inducing it, making cross-study correlations and extrapolations difficult. Additionally, several basic caveats about functional imaging studies probably apply that cognitive neuroscience tends to minimize: (1) functional imaging (probably more true in fMRI than in PET) tends to minimally accent ventral brain regions (excepting cerebellum); (2) these

STUDY	METHODS	RESULTS/REGIONS OF INTEREST
Singer *et al.*, 2004	fMRI study examining neural activations associated with witnessing pain in one's significant other vs. experiencing pain one's self. No pain in self and other is the control condition.	Empathy condition shows similar but not identical activations in various limbic structures as actual pain condition, but no sensory activations in somatosensory cortex (SII) seen in pain state. Empathy state shows activation in anterior cingulate, bilateral insula extending into left lateral prefrontal cortex, bilateral occipital cortex, fusiform cortex, and lateral cerebellum.
Carr *et al.* 2003	fMRI study modeling empathy as based in putative linkages between action representation (particularly imitative components) and emotion. Measured fMRI neural activations while subjects passively viewed and also imitated affective facial expressions, including with 'fractured' stimuli (just eyes, just mouth vs. whole face).	Right anterior insular and bilateral 'mirror' areas (area 44) inferior prefrontal system activations when subjects had to imitate or observe affective facial expressions, or even part-expressions (eyes vs. mouth), but imitation generated significantly greater peaks in ROI.
Lorderbaum *et al.* 2004	fMRI comparing maternal response to standard infant cry vs. response to mother's own infant crying.	Mother's own infant cry differentially activated cerebellum (esp. vermis), anterior and posterior cingulate, preoptic area/ventral bed nucleus, septum, bilateral insula, midbrain/upper brainstem, right amygdala, and right temporal pole, hypothalamus, striatum, and thalamus.
Bartels & Zeki, 2004	Maternal love condition measured activations when mothers viewed their own child versus an age and familiarity matched acquainted child. Control for emotional valence: the same results were obtained when activity related to adult friendship was subtracted from maternal love.	Ventral/dorsal anterior cingulate cortex, frontal eye fields; fusiform cortex; bilateral insula; (ventral) lateral prefrontal cortex; occipital cortex; orbitofrontal cortex; thalamus; striatum (putamen, caudate nucleus, globus pallidus); periaqueductal gray; substantia nigra, hippocampus. Deactivations were noted in amygdala, posterior cingulate, mesial prefrontal/paracingulate, middle temporal cortex, occipitoparietal junction and temporal pole.

Meta-analysis Table for
Functional Imaging Studies of Empathy and Attachment

are correlative pictures with uncertain causal implications; (3) there is a widespread tendency in the literature to tweak p. values to yield very small hotspots, but it is very doubtful that brain really works this way, as opposed to widespread and highly distributed networks in which many structures may be variably activated or inhibited, some more so than others; (4) studies typically gloss over individual variations, often quite large. The table below summarizes the major studies and shows a broad functional overlap in many structures that we know from convergent sources are classically involved in emotional processing, especially the basal ganglia, various portions of cingulate and insula, along with various upper brainstem and basal forebrain and diencephalic regions.

Singer *et al*. (2004) found that empathy for pain in another correlates with increasing activity in the anterior portions of the insula and anterior cingulate cortex, although slightly different from regions involved in the experience of pain in one's self, and without the somatosensory components being present. The differential 'self vs. other' foci in paralimbic structures suggest that the degraded state of virtual pain in empathy isn't 'exactly' the same as actual pain experience, even after subtraction of sensory components. Of course, this study doesn't address empathy to primary emotions but the 'proto-qualia' of pain. Also notable is that this study looked at empathy activations *in a primary attachment*.

Carr *et al*. (2003) modeled empathy as based in putative linkages between action representation (particularly imitative components) and emotion. They measured with fMRI neural activations while subjects viewed affective facial expressions, including with stimuli that were 'fractured' (just eyes, just mouth vs. whole face), finding insular and inferior prefrontal system activations. One obvious question is whether the stimuli (static pictures of classic emotion faces) are evocative enough to generate real empathy, vs. just social cognition. Gallese (2003) has similarly argued that mirroring and imitation, dependent on inferior posterior prefrontal and parietal neurons, are substrates for empathy. However, it is not clear whether this truly explains empathy, and may conflate instrumental action matching (which requires mirror neurons) with the affective state induction/matching critical to empathy, which may not. Carr *et al*. also equate conscious, voluntary imitation of emotion with the emotion induction processes in empathy. These are possibly quite different, as empathy may use contagion processes, which may involve *unconscious mimicry* — see section on contagion. However, it is not established that primitive contagion processes require mirror neurons, as those mechanisms may be more primitive (Barsade, 2002), sitting 'under' systems involved in conscious imitation. All of this illustrates major continuing problems with conceptual models and definitions of empathy, esp. differing cognitive/voluntary vs. affective/involuntary emphases.

Lorderbaum *et al*. (2004) performed a functional MRI study examining maternal responses to a recording of the mother's own infant crying, comparing these responses to a recorded standard infant cry, with cerebellum (esp. vermis), anterior and posterior cingulate, preoptic area of hypothalamus, septum, midbrain, amygdala, striatum, and thalamus as regions of significant activation. Lorberbaum *et al* (2004) validates a more subcortical view of prototype emotion, as systems critical to nurturance and maternal care in mammals remain centrally active in closely related states in humans. Although this was not a study explicitly about empathy, models reviewed here suggest major relevance for understanding empathy. This is further supported in the broad overlap of regional activations between the Singer *et al.* study and this study (basal ganglia, insula, cerebellum, anterior cingulate).

A study by Bartels & Zeki (2004) reveals very similar regions of activation when activations were measured in subjects looking at their child vs. a control image of another (known) child. The study also shows a conjoint transposition of results from an earlier study (Bartels & Zeki, 2000) on romantic love with the more recent study (Bartels & Zeki, 2004) on maternal love, revealing large overlap in functional networks (and also some differences) between the two most powerful forms of human attachment. Both activate BG, ventral striatum, cingulate, insula. These are all regions activated in the Lorberbaum *et al.* (2003) study of maternal responses to infant cries, *suggesting potentially close ties between attachment and basic empathic processes*, although conjoint mechanisms remain poorly outlined.

The table above suggests a *broad distributed network of structures and pathways essential to the activation of affective positive behavioural responses to loved and valued others, particularly those in distress, either partners or offspring.* The table outlines how regions activated by the distress of significant others show major overlap with regions implicated more globally in attachment and separation distress processes in both human imaging and animal lesion work, including particularly cingulate and insula, diencephalic and basal forebrain regions such as the bed nucleus of stria terminalis and the preoptic area, midbrain reticular activating system regions such as PAG, various striatal structures (probably ventral regions particularly) and the cerebellum (perhaps particularly midline portions).

Perception → Action Model (PAM)
for Empathy from Cognitive Neuroscience

In the largest and most systematic review of empathy to date, Preston & de Waal (2002) reviewed an extraordinarily large body literature, and then presented a perception → action model (PAM) for empathy. Their model proposed that:

> the attended perception of the object's state automatically activates the subject's representations of that state; activation of these representations automatically primes or generates the associated autonomic and somatic responses. [ADD PAGE]

Although Preston and de Waal did a great service to the field in this ambitious review in bringing together into one source their coverage of an enormous body of work, along with many excellent contributed commentaries, several questions could be raised about this model. Challenges to this model might include:

(1) The model leaves out the intervening variable between perception and action of *emotion*.

(2) Does this model explain, or just restate, the basic explanatory challenge, namely that there is some kind of direct linkage between the receptive processing of, and activation of, an emotional state?

(3) What is the putative neurology and functional network(s) that might account for this linkage? Putative neural substrates were never clarified except for a 'diffuse perception-action mechanism'.

(4) The emphasis on 'representation' raises problems. Is emotional empathy dependent on cognitive 'representations' of an emotional state, or is it more a 'precognitive' process? Or potentially (and variably) both?

(5) Empathy clearly isn't automatic or 'reflexive' (Bandura, 2002), with many variables affecting its induction, so this model doesn't account for the multiple 'gating' aspects ('familiarity', cue salience, recent exposure to like trauma are findings all summarized in Preston and de Waal's review, but other variables may be intervening (see next two sections).

(6) What about empathy involving an intrinsic motivation towards reducing distress? This is totally omitted from the PAM.

(7) What about links to animal models and basic mammalian nurturance processes?

(8) What about the long intuited global relationship between empathy and attachment?

A Basic Model for Empathy:
'Gated Resonance Induction' of Another's Distress

Based in part on the above literature reviews, below is one possible model for major processing envelopes as necessary and sufficient conditions for the creation of empathy. The boxology model below emphasizes, first, receptive processing involved in appraisal and recognition of emotional states (these may be both cognitive and 'pre-cognitive'. Cognitive top-down components are presumably supplied largely by right hemisphere heteromodal systems and right somatosensory cortex (Adolphs *et al.*, 2000; Adolphs *et al.*, 2003) that process facial expressions, tones of voice, and body kinetics in terms of their affective content and meaning. There is evidence for emotion-specific contributions from various regions (insula/basal ganglia for disgust, amygdala for fear, while regionally specific contributions for recognition of sadness or separation distress and other prototype states have not yet been clearly defined). In the model, these heteromodal systems may feed into a poorly understood 'global gate' that controls relative activation of empathic states, with critical global gate variables determining the extent of 'resonance induction' for the subject, and the extent to which the 'variably degraded resonance state' is induced. This notion of resonance induction, unlike the PAM of Preston and deWaal, is not based on putative cognitive representationalist mechanisms. However, the model incorporates similar notions, in which receptive and expressive aspects of emotion are directly linked in a fashion still poorly understood. Additionally, 'resonance induction' (the mechanism implicated in contagion) may reflect a fundamental property of all the primary emotional states, as *empathic inductions appear to have basic similarities with the mutual induction of playful affection and smiling responses* between two people, and even between two members of different species. Although processes by which playfulness, smiling, sexual arousal and nurturance/tenderness are mutually and reciprocally activated in virtually any human dyad remains largely a mystery in neural terms, recognition of basic 'resonance induction' goes back at least a hundred years in psychology, and in other literatures, perhaps much longer, even thousands of years. One might note a particularly prescient intuition by McDougall in his *Introduction to Social Psychology:*

> (there is) . . a special adaptation of the receptive side of each of the principal instinctive dispositions that renders each instinct capable of being excited on the perception of the bodily expressions of the excitement of the same instinct in other persons (McDougall, 1908).

Although there isn't universal consensus on this, without some kind of affective induction and associated motivation to relieve distress, one has to assume something less than a full empathic response, only a more cognitive appreciation of the other's affective state. In human empathy, however, the motivation to relieve suffering can be expressed through an enormously large N of potential behaviors, running the gamut from direct physical rescue from life-threatening danger, to careful listening and reflecting upon the other person's emotional dynamics and history in psychotherapy, and many shades in between. In the turgid and muddy water of the real social world, many social situations presumably show highly variable admixtures of empathy, accurate cognitive perception of another's emotional state (with or without empathic induction), and distorted perception or misrepresentation of another's intentions, internal states and emotional dynamics (see section on disorders of empathy). Such admixtures surely challenge both our scientific models (which must at least initially simplify the complexity of nature), as well as our own adaptive emotional capacities, which must differentially sort out these variably helpful and hurtful responses.[1]

Critical Variables Governing Global Gate
For Activation of Empathic Responses

There are probably several if not many still poorly mapped variables that determine the intensity of an empathic response to the suffering of another. One might describe four fundamental classes of variables, some presumably genotypic (some version of 'native empathic ability'), some more phenotypic (*developed* level of empathic ability), some related to fundamental properties of the

---

[1] A study on empathy begging to be done would involve measuring neural activations in subjects attempting to formulate reasons why someone in a particular social scene might feel sadness and seeing if the accuracy or inaccuracy of this reconstruction mapped onto differential neural systems. One would speculate that various heteromodal regions classically associated with TOM would be essential, but that contributions of paralimbic regions might also appear.

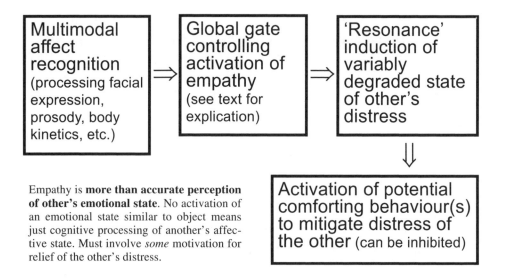

Figure 3: A Basic Model for Empathy

Many questions could be posed about each one of these boxes, their neural substrates, and any putative feedforward model such as this. For example, major questions can be raised about how much affect recognition is a conscious versus preconscious process, global gate variables for empathy induction are poorly articulated in the literature, and the links between resonance induction and behavioural activation towards comforting and relieving suffering remain a virtual mystery in neurological terms. Additionally, theory of mind processes may supplement or even replace direct perception of affect (see final section).

suffering party, and some 'state-dependent' (depending on the affective state of the empathizer). It seems very unlikely that the simple invariant/automatic PAM of Preston and de Waal can fully account for the enormous variability in our empathic responses to the manifest (and sometimes not so manifest) suffering of others; a more naturalistic model would have to model complex variables affecting empathic inductions. The model would have to centrally include both genotypic and phenotypic traits given the enormous variability in individual abilities to empathize. The animal literature well summarized by Preston and deWaal suggests that stimulus modality, familiarity with the distressed conspecific, similarity to the conspecific, and subject exposure to the same aversive event are variables, but this doesn't fully account for what we know affects empathic responses clinically and anecdotally. One might generalize from an enormous anecdotal database on empathy to hypothesize four primary classes of variables affecting empathic induction:

(1) First class of variables: native talent and developed ability. This is clearly very poorly mapped in the literature, but some evidence (Chartrand & Bargh, 1999) implicates some kind of *genomic variation in contagion/chameleon responses as a genotype* for empathy (also see Preston & de Waal, 2002). This poorly outlined genotype further

underlines the intrinsic tie of empathy to contagion (see later discussion). The phenotype would be the level of *developed ability for complex empathic responsiveness*. This presumably depends on interactions between the genotype and how empathically the person has been treated in their primary attachments, and is also poorly charted except anecdotally (Schore, 1994).

(2) Second class of variables: the degree of attachment to the object (subsumes the animal literature finding that 'familiarity' with suffering creature is an important variable). This emphasizes a likely 'proximate' mechanism for increasing empathic inductions. This is congruent with literally mountains of anecdotal data: the more we care for and love the suffering party, the more potent the resonance induction process is likely to be, *assuming that other variables don't contravene this,* such as our affective state or anger towards the other party. Imaging studies reviewed suggest that structures involved in primary attachments (Bartels & Zeki, 2000, Bartels & Zeki, 2004) have virtually total overlap with structures implicated in functional imaging studies of empathy (Singer *et al.*, 2004; Carr *et al.*, 2003) and maternal responses to infant cries (Lorderbaum *et al.*, 2004): ventral striatum, anterior cingulate, bed nucleus of stria terminalis, ventral striatum, preoptic area, and insula.

(3) Third class of variables: the degree of 'cuteness' of object, and the degree of felt potential vulnerability or helplessness of the object. This underlines the intrinsic tie of even more cognized human empathy to the mammalian prototype of nurturance: *empathy is fundamentally a protective and nurturing response to suffering in another, particularly those thought to be in need of care, and thought unable to fend for themselves*. We are far more empathically mobilized by the suffering of a small helpless creature with a rounded face and big eyes than by the suffering of a dominant, aggressive and powerful alpha male.

(4) Fourth class of variables: affective state of empathizer. In simplest terms, anger and emotional hurt towards another party tend to maximally inhibit empathy, along with many negative emotional states, particularly if they are intense. Indeed, rage transiently turns off empathic responsiveness almost completely. This reflects the basic 'gating logic' of prototype emotional states in which strongly negative states constrain activation of positives and visa versa, and empathy must come from a basically positive emotional stance towards the other party. How this 'valence gating' and reciprocal inhibition of prototype states is instantiated in the brain is unmapped (see Watt, 2000 and Bandler & Shipley, 1994 for one set of putative mechanisms). A common variation on this gating/ inhibition theme may be any version of moral judgment of the other's behaviour, with this representing a cognized expression of anger. Moral judgment is remarkably inhibiting of empathy, a point appreciated for many decades in the psychotherapy literatures. Last, but

not least, metabolic status (virtually ignored in the empathy literature) probably affects empathic induction. Simply put, we are typically lousy at empathy when tired and sleep deprived, hungry, or in pain, a point certainly not lost on virtually any overwhelmed parent!

In any case, the supposition of a 'global gate' controlling the activation of empathic responses has other predictive advantages, addressing one of Bandura's (2002) (and other commentators) chief concerns about Preston and de Waal's 'perception-action model' of empathy. It is also consistent with the multidimensional nature of virtually all affective activation, and with emotion being intrinsically 'valence-gated' (positives decreases activation thresholds for other positives and increase thresholds for negatives, and visa versa). Lastly, the model explains why the resonance state in empathy is 'variably degraded;' in situations where all of the global gate variables are largely maximized, we can experience a relatively more intense induction of the other's distress, a virtual copy as it were. Conversely, where the global gate is significantly constricted by any of those variables, one can easily predict a lesser to minimal or even absent degree of empathic activation. Additionally, it is worth noting that many of these variables also imply hidden variables/abilities in the empathizer, including reasonable affective regulation, self-non-self boundary (Decety & Jackson, 2004) and the importance of a positive emotional stance towards the suffering party.

Are Empathy and Attachment Interdigitating?

Much anecdotal clinical evidence from psychotherapy literature (Schore, 1994 for summary) suggests there is a likely massive reciprocity of attachment and empathy, and functional imaging studies just reviewed support this assumption, in terms of large overlap in activated systems and networks in empathy and attachment, although candidate shared mechanisms are still poorly plotted. However, there may be several basic functional interactions: (1) limit setting and modulation of behaviour: we can't afford to hurt the other too badly, or we lose them (they may detach and leave us); (2) basic developmental aspects linking phenotypes and genotypes of empathy: native empathic abilities are considerably strengthened (or partially eroded) by positive or negative early attachment experiences, and this long held belief in the psychological and psychotherapy literature has some support in the animal literature; (3) empathic responses when we are distressed enhance social bonding, while their absence makes attachments traumatic, chaotic and often short-lived (Schore, 1994). Empathy can also be fundamentally contrasted with common forms of 'distorted affective perception' that are basic concepts within psychodynamic theory indexing characterological pathology (e.g., concepts of 'transference', and 'projection'). These and related processes may be primary engines driving intermittent empathic failure and based in a kind of global analogical comparison between past and present, organized more in the right hemisphere (Watt, 1990).

Empathy in Psychotherapy and Psychoanalysis

The psychoanalysis and psychotherapy literatures are replete with literally many hundreds of discussions about the critical importance of empathy between therapist and patient, and the developmental literature in psychoanalysis (see Blanck & Blanck, 1979 for summary) contains literally many hundreds of references to the seriously damaging effects of early empathic failures in childhood attachments. Although reasons of space do not permit extended discussion of this vast collection of literatures, it is worth noting that empathy has been long hypothesized as a critical, *and possibly the most critical*, outcome variable from therapist side in the therapeutic interaction, in many schools of psychotherapy. The vast psychotherapy literature also emphasizes a more 'cognitive empathy', in terms of the therapist's intuition about cognitive and situational drivers for emotion, suggesting that complex cognitive operations (theory of mind, perspective taking, and emotion identification) are mixed in with more affective/empathic bridges to patients' internal distress.

Exploratory psychotherapies from the psychoanalytic tradition that centrally focus on the complex emotional currents and vicissitudes in the therapy relationship itself emphasize the pivotal importance of *empathic responses to and management of fundamentally non-empathic states.* What psychoanalysis has termed 'transference' (distorted perception of another's intentions/states based on similarity to early traumatic experiences) and projection (mis-attribution of one's own internal states to another) generate 'intermittent' empathic failures (see Langs, 1976 for overview). An empathic exchange around emotionally distorting perceptions/actions is seen as a central change agent in many psychotherapy metapsychologies, with this empathic management allowing the patient to reclaim and re-work traumatic experiences, and modify maladaptive defences and associated interpersonal distortions. In a nutshell, a large group of exploratory psychotherapies including psychoanalysis emphasize the *empathic repair of empathic failures* (Paivio & Laurent 2001). Perhaps no other literature, excepting perhaps the child development literature, underlines more categorically the centrality of empathy for creating positive personality and interpersonal dynamics than the wide ranging psychotherapy literatures. There is some evidence that mutually enhancing and reciprocal empathic failures in a dyad (what psychoanalysis termed 'transference — countertransference cycles') are generative for what Freud called the 'uncanny' ability of people to repeat the same traumatic scenarios over and over (Blanck & Blanck, 1974). Although careful operational definition of terms and empirical testing of constructs has typically not been a significant component of these literatures, such an emphasis should not go unnoticed.

Clinical Disorders of Empathy

Certainly any theory of empathy would have to account for its disorders, which can be broken down into several large clinical classes.

(1) Autistic disorders reflect a spectrum of failures (ranging from mild to catastrophic) in attachment/ empathic development, and suggests that capacities for attachment and empathy are fundamentally interdigitating in development. One suspects that theory of mind (TOM) may fail to develop secondary to failure of more basic and antecedent processes in empathy. However, the TOM literature has generally failed to consider primitive empathy/contagion as potentially precedent for TOM development.

(2) Effects of developmentally early (Anderson *et al.*, 1999) and late orbital frontal lesions (Shamay-Tsoory *et al.*, 2003) as well as the syndrome of sociopathy underline a crucial role for orbital frontal (OF) regions in empathy, although mechanisms for empathy deficit in orbital frontal lesion have not been clarified, and previous models emphasizing the OF role in internalization of interpersonal/social rules (Damasio, 1994) don't fully explain empathic deficits. Additionally, an implied component of the above model is intact affective regulation in the empathizing party, and this appears also dependent on orbital frontal function (Damasio, 1994).

(3) Massive right hemisphere insults (typically R MCA infarcts) tend to seriously blunt empathic ability (Shamay-Tsoory *et al.*, 2003) , suggesting a primary role in empathy for the right hemisphere, particularly somatosensory systems, consistent with the work of Adolphs *et al.* (2000).

(4) Milder 'intermittent' empathic failures reside in all characterological disorders, beyond sociopathy. All characterological pathologies may 'systematize' certain characteristic forms of empathic failure, depending on the particular characterological disorder. More broadly, one suspects that all maladaptive defensive operations may potentially impair cognitive and/or affective aspects of empathy.

Contagion as a Core Component Process in Empathy: A Primitive 'Precognitive' Mechanism for Emotion Induction?

Although Preston & deWaal (2002) note contagion 'on a border with empathy', an emotional empathy depends on resonance inductions, suggesting that contagion is paradigmatic. Clearly, empathy requires more than simple contagion, in that the induced state of suffering must not flood the subject, but instead has to mobilize a helpful or comforting response, suggesting that affective regulation must be relatively intact in the empathizer, as must be self-other differentiation (issues noted by Decety & Jackson, 2004). Additionally, there must be a fundamentally positive affective stance towards the sufferer, in terms of the intrinsic motivation to relieve their suffering in some fashion. Thus, empathy cannot be *reduced* to contagion, but basic contagion may function as one of its core component pieces.

Contagion is perhaps most classically reflected in fear inductions in herd behaviour, but all of the prototype emotions appear to be 'catchy,' as playful, smiling, lustful, and tender responses all facilitate and activate the same states in others in close proximity, as of course do the prototype negative emotions of fear and rage (Hatfield *et al.* , 1994). Unraveling emotional contagion would give us critical insights into how different prototype emotional states generate affective resonances in others — resonances possibly enhanced by higher cognitive abilities, but that may not depend on them entirely. We sometimes don't even have to hear the joke the other party heard to start laughing ourselves, if the other's laughter is intense or 'infectious' enough — indeed even the language we use here speaks to the centrality of the phenomenon.

Both empirical investigations and theoretical overviews of contagion (Barsade, 2002) have also suggested that it may be an critical component of empathy. Sonnby-Borgstrom (2002) compared facial mimicry reactions, as represented by EMG activity when subjects were exposed to pictures of angry or happy faces, and the degree of correspondence between facial EMG reactions and their own reported feelings. Subjects in the high-empathy group were found to have a higher degree of mimicking behaviour, while those in the low-empathy group showed inverse zygomaticus muscle reactions, 'smiling' when exposed to angry faces. Arguing for a more primitive contagion component to empathy, the author concluded that differences between the groups in empathy appeared related to differences in automatic somatic reactions to facial stimuli, rather than to differences in conscious interpretation of the emotional situation. There is evidence that primitive contagion effects extend to synchronicity of autonomic states between empathizing subject and distressed object (Levenson, 1996), as a possible 'physiological substrate' for empathy. Play and smiling responses critical to early attachment of infant and mother (Bowlby, 1977; Trevarthen & Aitken, 2001) also appear mutually inducted via contagion mechanisms.

Interestingly, the emotional contagion literature suggests two different mechanisms, paralleling the cognitive vs. affective concepts about empathy: 1) a more subconscious, automatic, 'primitive emotional contagion' (Hatfield *et al.*, 1992); 2) more conscious and cognitive process (see Gump & Kulik, 1997), with this more 'cognitive contagion' typically reflecting more conscious imitation. Most work however suggests that contagion is typically defined by the more automatic, primitive processes. This primitive contagion occurs through very fast processes based in *automatic and continuous nonverbal mimicry and feedback* (Hatfield *et al.*, 1992, 1993, 1994), including *automatic, nonconscious mimicry of the other's facial expressions* (Lundqvist & Dimberg, 1995; Dimberg, 1982), *vocal tones* (Hatfield *et al.*, 1994) and even *body language* (Chartrand & Bargh, 1999). These effects can be measured even for subliminal facial presentations (Dimberg *et al.*, 2000). These effects appear to be *transmodal* (e.g, presentation of vocal affect and not just facial affect changes facial musculatures (Hietanen *et al.*, 1998). These unconscious mimicry effects have been found even in infants as young as a few days old (Field *et al.*, 1982; Haviland & Lelwica, 1987). Indeed, one might wonder why such a central process as emotional contagion has received so little systematic attention in affective neuroscience, and one is left to ponder the effects of a possible cognitive bias (that all emotion induction is top-down and fundamentally cognitive) and/or a too 'atomistic'- individualistic image of emotion (minimizing that emotion primarily structures prototypical interactions between creatures).

The implicit assumption that conscious 'slow' imitation must be using the same neural pathways as 'fast' unconscious imitation is widespread in the empathy literature, (see method of Carr *et al.*, 2003), and contributes to the heavy emphasis on mirror neurons as paradigmatic for empathy (Gallese, 2003). However, the automatic and unconscious imitation underling contagion works on much faster time scales (Hatfield *et al.*, 1992; Dimberg *et al.*, 2000) than the conscious imitation seen in mirror neuron studies. Indeed, there may be widespread conflation of the mechanisms of contagion with notions of both mirroring and 'shared representations' (that similar actions/states across both self and other are mapped to 'pooled representations' - Decety & Jackson, 2004). However, contagion developmentally precedes such shared representations, which don't start appearing until at least 18–24 months. A tempting speculation is that contagion mechanisms form a poorly understood 'developmental ground' out of which later arriving and more cognitive 'shared representations' or 'mirroring' phenomena develop, but there is regrettably little real data on this. Additionally, conscious action matching, while potentially linked to affective state matching, can't be synonymous with it, particularly if one respects distinctions between relatively voluntary instrumental action, and relatively involuntary affective action, another distinction rarely if ever observed in the empathy literature.

Additionally, although poorly plotted in terms of neural substrates, contagion reflects induced changes in activation of core structures for emotion. For example, masked fearful and angry expressions increase, and happy expressions decrease, amygdala activity (Morris *et al.*, 1998; Whalen *et al.*, 1998). It is tempting to speculate that the balance between primitive/automatic vs. more cognitively informed contagion shifts through ontogenesis, as evidence (Field *et al.*, 1982) suggests that the more primitive and automatic contagion is gradually inhibited through ontogenesis, probably coincident with prefrontal system myelination and the development of increasing affective modulation/inhibition (Hsee *et al.*; Chemtob, 1992). However, some capacities for primitive contagion clearly remain even in adults. In this sense contagion may prime the system in a particular direction (say, fear), but based on later arriving cognitive appraisals, the system may not necessarily settle into a fear state, but may move in other directions. In this sense, the priming function of contagion is probably more powerful early in development and less so as time goes on, but still prepotent and probably underappreciated in cognitive and affective neuroscience.

Considerations from work by Adolphs (2002), suggest that these fast vs. long time scales reflect differential neural network activations, and that the short time scale activations recruit the superior colliculus and amygdala; both of them have extensive connections to PAG, and therefore (speculatively) are in a position to prime this core structure and our affective systems in a particular affective direction. There is regrettably little explicit work on the neural substrates for primitive contagion, but Barsade (2002) and others have speculated that emotion induction comes from an afferent feedback process. As many facial, postural, and vocal feedback studies have shown, once people engage in mimicking affective behavior, they then often rapidly experience the same emotion associated with the original motor outputs being mimicked. Although a candidate mechanism for contagion remains elusive, it seems reasonable to assume that the classical action categories associated with primary emotions have the ability to excite more global resonances throughout the distributed architectures underpinning each of the prototype emotional states (but this remains poorly understood and in need of future study).

In any case, these considerations suggest that *affective vocalizations, facial expressions, and affective body kinetics jointly constitute a special privileged class of stimuli for the human brain*, and that the *brain's early (short time-scale) receptive functioning prioritizes contagion responses while later responses may prioritize more cognitive processing*. It also seems quite likely that there may be differential structures/ networks activated in fear contagion vs. play contagion vs. separation distress/sadness contagion, but much of this remains to be clarified and there is no empirical work that I am aware of looking at these issues.

Remaining Questions, Hypotheses and Potential Tests

A most basic question would be 'does the brain generate the primary receptive processing categories for the basic emotions out of the same neural cloth as the primary affective behaviours, and only later, through cortical ontogenesis, develop the fine grain of receptive ability that allows us to see these primary emotional categories in all their subtlety and range?' Recent evidence shows that *both recognition of fear in others and fear conditioning require the amygdala* (Adolphs *et al.*, 2001), underlining intrinsic linkages between receptive processing/recognition, and conditioning to and activation of prototype emotional states. A key question becomes: *does a 'categorical' and 'preconscious' (pre-cognitive?) recognition of the prototype states of separation distress, anger, fear, play, etc., emerge from the same basal forebrain, diencephalic and paralimbic regions necessary for the core affective states?* If so, then cortical receptive processing and recognition of emotion (organized largely in the right hemisphere) may be a cortical-cognitive 'extension' of a more primitive receptive processing possibly invisibly embedded in the distributed subcortical emotion architectures. Although there is increasing interest on 'shared representations' (Decety & Jackson, 2004) and notions of a 'common neural code' linking action and perception as critical to empathy (as emphasized in Preston & deWaal's PAM), one has to wonder if the linkages revealed in contagion are potentially precedent for later developing cortical mirroring functions. Perhaps this primitive 'direct linkage' can be potentially accessed, even late in ontogenesis, in basic contagion phenomena, using mechanisms antecedent to and more primitive than traditional and better researched top-down activation of emotion by appraisal and cognitive processing. Contagion work in human infants (Field *et al.*, 1982) and with very short stimulus presentations (Dimberg *et al.*, 2000), and animal work showing intact affective responsiveness in decorticate 'lower' mammals (Panksepp *et al.*, 1994) all suggest the above hypotheses. This type of resonance induction may thus be a developmentally primitive induction mechanism that cognitive development largely but not totally supplants. This must be tempered with a critical caveat: Jacksonian developmental principles argue for increasing functional dependence of lower systems on dorsal cortical systems in both ontogenesis and phylogenesis. In other words, it remains to be seen whether even the most basic receptive processing of emotion in humans is, like movement, much more dependent on cortex than in other mammals.

Critical tests of proposed models would involve: (1) empirical testing and confirmation of the hypothesized four classes of variables controlling the 'global gate' for the activation of empathy; (2) clarification of relative contributions to emotional empathy from more primitive preconscious contagion type processes vs. conscious top down cognitive recognition of affective states, (3) clarification of differential networks underwriting fast, unconscious contagion (poorly mapped) versus more conscious imitation (better mapped and presumed dependent on mirror neuron areas [Gallese, 2003]); (4) clarification of mechanisms that link resonance induction of distress (whether from more cognitive vs. precognitive mechanisms) to helping/comforting behaviours (virtually totally unexplored).

Envelopes of Social Connection and the Challenge of the Cognition: Emotion Border

Empathy, play, and separation distress, have been mostly conceptualized in neuroscience as largely discrete processes. However, all of these may have been jointly selected as different threads woven into the full fabric of an increasingly social brain, different yet equally essential components of evolution's discovery of the major advantages in tying creatures together. Play and empathy both powerfully cement social bonds between affective creatures, and both may be critical to the regulation of mood. However, creating such a deeply social brain meant also increasing developmental vulnerability to loss and separation distress, deep emotional hurt, subsequent promotion of pathological defences, and increasing vulnerability to depression and low self esteem, given close links between depression and prolonged separation distress (Bowlby, 1977). In view of this, empathy may be nature's inoculation against these dangers, evolution's gift to balance the intrinsic deep emotional vulnerabilities of a highly social brain. Additionally, empathy enables the creation of 'intersubjectivity' and the increasingly social and shared nature of much of the content of human consciousness, in which individuals can have deeply shared emotional spaces, with this becoming a critical aspect of all long term attachments.

One is also left with the sense that like many phenomena on the cognition – emotion border, the concept of empathy is likely to be beset with controversies and confusion about its fundamental nature for some time to come. Indeed, the sprawling and disjointed literature on empathy resembles the blind men inspecting different portions of the elephant, defying the efforts of Preston and deWaal and many other reviewers to bring theoretical coherence to it. However, as they point out, the term is a global umbrella concept covering a large affiliated group of cognitive and affective processes and not a single unitary process. This suggests considerable complexities sitting on the vast emotion-cognition border, in terms of a continuum of affiliated and interactive processes: complex reciprocal influences between theory of mind constructions, emotion identifications, and affective resonance inductions (see graphic below). This continuum of processes on the emotion-cognition border is consistent with much evidence that the brain instantiates parallel mechanisms towards the same purposes, cutting across more ventral subcortical and more dorsal cortical systems. The later arriving cortical mechanisms supplement and modulate, rather than simply replace, the more primitive subcortical mechanisms, consistent with the seminal formulations of John Hughlings Jackson. One readily suspects that these two developmentally linked trends are largely responsible for the divisive fracturing of the empathy literature along 'cognitive *vs* affective' lines. Instead, it seems very likely that what we call 'empathy' naturalistically involves variable admixtures of more cognitive versus more affective activations.

In view of the skill of cortically intact humans in suppressing emotional displays, and how affect display prohibitions also potentially make others' feeling states anything but clear, interaction between these two major components may be adaptively essential. For example, one can find that careful cognitive analyses of another person's behaviour might reveal evidence of hidden distress and hurt, masked by defensive (or offensive!) behaviours that previously had elicited irritation or resentment. However, such additional perspective taking and review might activate an empathic response to a previously unseen hurt or emotional need, hidden completely from the empathizer's prior awareness, and this empathic response now supplants a previously irritated and judgmental position. Thus, fuller development of a complex and affectively sophisticated theory of mind, melded with more primitive resonance induction mechanisms, may allow us to empathize with suffering where it is not particularly visible. Such linkages between high-level cognitive processes and more fundamental affective contagion/resonance induction mechanisms may supply adaptive skill sets absolutely essential to the most effective therapists and parents (and much appreciated in our valued significant others and close friends!). Perhaps our most effective empathic responses cannot reflect a 'cognitive versus an affective' process but rather a potential linking of several affiliated processes:

(1) cognitive modeling of predisposing factors in the other person's personality, context/circumstances jointly determining potential activations of painful emotion in the other (a cognitively mediated awareness of

primary emotional 'drivers' and precipitators). This ability is ultimately dependent on complex, high-level conceptual knowledge of
human emotional dynamics and an '*affective* theory of mind';

(2) other cognitive abilities involved in differential identification of prototype emotions, potentially driving internal access to knowledge bases
about what typically precipitates such emotions;

(3) resonance inductions that would allow us to feel some of the other person's pain (whether perceived or inferred);

(4) an associated desire to mitigate their suffering in some fashion.

How these various processes might become linked together is unclear, but there
is considerable evidence in the literature reviewed earlier that several paralimbic
regions are likely involved, including several regions of anterior cingulate, posterior and anterior insular, and orbital frontal systems. In any case, it is likely that
such complex processes emerge from the concerted working of multiple
heteromodal, paralimbic, and subcortical systems. One also strongly suspects
that a complex and optimal developmental trajectory for the brain is required to
truly maximally develop empathy, in which the individual is both treated
empathically, and is also expected to respect other's feelings and respond
supportively to upset and pain. More primitive 'resonance induction' process also
may developmentally bootstrap more cognitive processes in theory of mind/per-
spective taking; one hypothesis emerging directly from the above considerations
would be that the failure of such bootstrapping is a critical dynamic in the cascade
of developmental failures in autism. On the other hand, successful developmental
instantiation of such adaptive operational linkages between resonance induction, a
complex, affectively attuned theory of mind, and nurturing behavior may constitute what is referred to in folk psychology as 'wisdom and emotional sensitivity'.
One suspects that this kind of complex multidimensional empathy is often times
our best adaptive response as therapists, parents, mentors and friends to other suffering human beings. Thus, the very formidable challenge for a developing neuroscience of empathy is to bring our models asymptotically closer to the real,
humbling complexity of nature — in this case, our human nature.

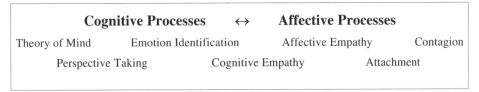

Cognitive Processes	↔	Affective Processes	
Theory of Mind	Emotion Identification	Affective Empathy	Contagion
Perspective Taking	Cognitive Empathy		Attachment

References

Adolphs, R. (2002), 'Recognizing emotion from facial expressions: Psychological and neurological mechanisms', *Behavioral and Cognitive Neuroscience Reviews* **1** (1), pp. 21–61.

Adolphs, R. (2003), 'Cognitive neuroscience of human social behavior', *Nature Reviews /Neuro-
science*, **4** (177), pp. 165–78.

Adolphs, R., Damasio, H., Tranel, D., Cooper, G. & Damasio, A.R. (2000), 'A role for somatosensory cortices in the visual recognition of emotion as revealed by three-dimensional lesion mapping', *Journal of Neuroscience*, **20**, pp. 2683–90.

Adolphs, R., Tranel, D. & Damasio, A.R. (2003), 'Dissociable neural systems for recognizing emotions', *Brain and Cognition*, **53**, pp. 61–9.

Anderson, S.W., Bechara, A., Damasio, H., Tranel, D. & Damasio, A.R.(1999), 'Impairment of social and moral behavior related to early damage in human prefrontal cortex', *Nature Neurosci.*, **2**, pp. 1032–7.

Bandura, A. (2002), 'Reflexive empathy: On predicting more than has ever been observed. Commentary, Preston & de Waal (2002) Empathy: its proximate and ultimate basis', *Behavioral and Brain Sciences*, **25** (1), pp. 24–5.

Bandler, R. & Shipley, M.T. (1994), 'Columnar organization in the midbrain periaqueductal gray: Modules for emotional expression?', *Trends Neurosci.*, **17**, pp. 379–89.

Barsade, S.G. (2002), 'The ripple effect: Emotional contagion and its influence on group behavior', *Administrative Science Quarterly*, **47**, pp. 644–75.

Bartels, A. & Zeki, S. (2000), 'The neural basis of romantic love', *NeuroReport*, **17** (11), pp. 3829–34.

Bartels, A. & Zeki, S. (2004), 'The neural correlates of maternal and romantic love', *NeuroImage*, **21** (3), p. 1155–66.

Blanck, G. & Blanck, R. (1979), *Ego Psychology 2: Psychoanalytic Developmental Psychology* (New York: Columbia University Press).

Bowlby, J. (1977), 'The making and breaking of affectional bonds: Aetiology and psychopathology in the light of attachment theory', *Br J Psychiatry*, **130**, pp. 201–10.

Carr, L., Iacoboni, M, Dubeau, M-C., Mazziotta, J.C. & Lenzi, J.L. (2003), 'Neural mechanisms of empathy in humans: A relay from neural systems for imitation to limbic areas', *PNAS*, **100** (9) pp. 5497–502.

Carter, C.S. (1998), 'Neuroendocrine perspectives on social attachment and love', *Psychoneuroendocrinology*, **8**, pp. 779–818.

Chartrand, T.L. & Bargh, J.A. (1999), 'The chameleon effect', *J. Pers. Soc. Psychol.*, **76**, pp. 893–910.

Damasio, A.R. (2003), *Looking for Spinoza: Joy, Sorrow, and the Feeling Brain* (Orlando, FL: Harcourt).

Damasio. A. (1999), *The Feeling of What Happens: Body and emotion in the making of consciousness* (New York: Harcourt Brace & Co).

Decety, J. & Jackson, P.L. (2004), 'The functional architecture of human empathy', *Behavioral and Cognitive Neuroscience Reviews*, **3** (2), *pp.* 71–100.

Dimberg, U., Thunberg, M. & Elmehed, K. (2000), 'Unconscious facial reactions to emotional facial expressions', *Psychological Science*, **11**, pp. 86–9.

Dimberg, U. (1982), 'Facial reactions to facial expressions', *Psychophysiology*, **26**, pp. 643–7.

Field, T.M., Woodson, R., Greenberg, R. & Cohen, D. (1982), 'Discrimination and imitation of facial expressions by neonates', *Science*, **218**, pp. 179–81.

Gallese, V. (2003), 'The roots of empathy: The shared manifold hypothesis and the neural basis of intersubjectivity', *Psychopathology*, **36** (4), pp. 171–80.

Gump, B.B. & Kulik, J.A. (1997), 'Stress, affiliation, and emotional contagion', *Journal of Personality and Social Psychology*, **72**, pp. 305–19.

Hatfield, E.J., Hsee, C.K., Costello, J. & Weisman, M.S. (1995), 'The impact of vocal feedback on emotional experience and expression', *Journal of Social Behavior and Personality*, **10**, pp. 293–312.

Hatfield, E., Cacioppo, J. & Rapson, R.L. (1992), 'Primitive emotional contagion', in *Review of Personality and Social Psychology: Emotion and Social Behavior*, ed. M.S. Clark, **14**, pp. 151–77 (Newbury Park, CA: Sage).

Hatfield, E., Cacioppo, J. & Rapson, R.L. (1993), 'Emotional contagion', *Current Directions in Psychological Science*, **2**, pp. 96–9.

Hatfield, E., Cacioppo, J. & Rapson, R.L. (1994), *Emotional Contagion* (New York: Cambridge University Press).

Haviland, J.M. & Lelwica, M. (1987), 'The induced affect response: 10-week-old infants' responses to three emotion expressions', *Developmental Psychology*, **23**, pp. 97–104.

Hietanen, J.K., Surakka, V. & Linnankoski, I. (1998), 'Facial electromyographic responses to vocal affect expressions', *Psychophysiology*, **35**, pp. 530–6.

Hsee, C.K., Hatfield, E. & Chemtob, C. (1992), 'Assessments of the emotional states of others: Conscious judgments versus emotional contagion', *Journal of Social and Clinical Psychology*, **11**, pp. 119–28.

Langs, Robert (1976), *The Therapeutic Interaction: A Critical Overview and Synthesis*, volume two (New York: Jason Aronson Press).

Levenson, R.W. (1996), 'Biological substrates of empathy and facial modulation of emotion', *Motivation and Emotion*, 20, pp. 185–204.

Lorderbaum, J., Kose, S., Dubno, J.R., Horwitz, A.R., Newman, J.D., Kose, R., Hamner, M.B., Bohning, D.E., Arana, G.W. & George, MS. (2004), 'A third fMRI study of healthy mothers hearing infant cries', Poster, Neuroscience.

Lundqvist, L.O., & Dimberg, U. (1995), 'Facial expressions are contagious', *Journal of Psychophysiology*, **9**, pp. 203–11.

McDougall, W. (1908), *An Introduction To Social Psychology* (Methuen).

Moles, A., Kieffer, B.L. & D'Amato, F.R. (2004), 'Deficit in attachment behavior in mice lacking the mu-opioid receptor gene', *Science*, **304** (5679), pp. 1888–9.

Morris, J.S., Friston, K.J., Buchel, C., Frith, C.D., Young, A.W., Calder, A.J. & Dolan, R.J. (1998), 'A neuromodulatory role for the human amygdala in processing emotional facial expressions', *Brain*, **121**, pp. 47–57.

Paivio, S.C. & Laurent, C. (2001), 'Empathy and emotion regulation: Reprocessing memories of childhood abuse', *J Clin Psychol.*, **57** (2), pp.213–26.

Panksepp, J. (1998), *Affective Neuroscience: The foundations of human and animal emotions* (New York: Oxford University Press).

Panksepp, J. (2003), 'Feeling the pain of social loss', *Science*, **302**, pp. 237–9.

Panksepp, J. (2004), 'Altruism and helping behaviors, neurobiology', in: *Encyclopedia of Neuroscience*, Third Edition, ed. G. Adelman & B.H. Smith (Elsevier).

Panksepp, J. & Watt, D. (2003), 'The ego is first and foremost a body ego', *Neuropsychoanalysis*, **5**, pp. 201–18.

Panksepp, J., Normansell, L.A., Cox, J.F. & Siviy, S. (1994), 'Effects of neonatal decortication on the social play of juvenile rats', *Physiology & Behavior*, **56**, pp. 429–43.

Preston, S.D. & de Waal, B.M. (2002), 'Empathy: Its ultimate and proximate bases', *Behavioral and Brain Sciences*, **25** (1), pp. 1–72.

Schore, A.N. (1994), *Affective Regulation and the Origins of the Self* (New York: Lawrence Erlbaum Associates).

Shamay-Tsoory, S.G., Tomer, R., Berger, B.D. & Aharon-Peretz, J. (2003), 'Characterization of empathy deficits following prefrontal brain damage: The role of the right ventromedial prefrontal cortex', *Journal of Cognitive Neuroscience*, **15** (3), pp. 324–37.

Shamay-Tsoory, S.G., Tomer, R., Goldsher, D. Berger, B.D. and Aharon-Peretz, J. (2004), 'Impairment in cognitive and affective empathy in patients with brain lesions: anatomical and cognitive correlates journal of clinical and experimental neuropsychology', 26 (8), pp. 1113–27.

Singer. T., Seymour, B., O'Doherty, J., Kaube, H., Dolan, RJ. & Frith, C.D. (2004), 'Empathy for pain involves the affective but not sensory components of pain', *Science*, **303** (20), pp. 1157–61.

Sonnby-Borgstrom, M. (2002), 'The facial expression says more than words: Is emotional "contagion" via facial expression the first step toward empathy?', *Lakartidningen*, **99** (13), pp. 1438–42.

Titchener, E. (1909), *Experimental Psychology of the Thought Processes* (Macmillan).

Trevarthen, C. & Aitken, K.J. (2001), 'Infant intersubjectivity: research, theory, and clinical applications', *J Child Psychology Psychiatry*, **42** (1), pp. 3–48.

Uvnas-Möberg, K. (1998), 'Oxytocin may mediate the benefits of positive social interaction and emotions', *Psychoneuroendocrinology*, **23**, pp. 819–35.

Watt, D. F. (1998), 'Affective neuroscience and extended reticular thalamic activating system theories of consciousness', Target Article, *Association For The Scientific Study of Consciousness Electronic Seminar*.

Watt, D.F. & Pincus, D.I. (2004), 'Neural substrates of consciousness: Implications for clinical psychiatry', in *Textbook of Biological Psychiatry*, ed. J. Panksepp (New York, Wiley).

Watt, D.F. (2000), 'The centrencephalon and thalamocortical integration: neglected contributions of periaqueductal gray', *Emotion and Consciousness*, **1** (1), pp. 93–116.

Whalen, P.J., Rauch, S.L., Etcoff, N.L., McInerney, S.C., Lee, M.B. & Jenike, M.A. (1998), 'Masked presentations of emotional facial expressions modulate amygdala activity without explicit knowledge', *Journal of Neuroscience*, **18**, 411–18.

Marc D. Lewis & Rebecca M. Todd

Getting Emotional

A Neural Perspective on Emotion, Intention, and Consciousness

Intentions and emotions arise together, and emotions compel us to pursue goals. However, it is not clear when emotions become objects of awareness, how emotional awareness changes with goal pursuit, or how psychological and neural processes mediate such change. We first review a psychological model of emotional episodes and propose that goal obstruction extends the duration of these episodes while increasing cognitive complexity and emotional intensity. We suggest that attention is initially focused on action plans and their obstruction, and only when this obstruction persists does focal attention come to include emotional states themselves. We then model the self-organization of neural activities that hypothetically underlie the evolution of an emotional episode. Phases of emotional awareness are argued to parallel phases of synchronization across neural systems. We suggest that prefrontal activities greatly extend intentional states while focal attention integrates emotional awareness and goal pursuit in a comprehensive sense of the self in the world.

People and cats can stare vacantly out the window and watch the world go by: until something happens. An itch needs to be scratched, a movement grabs our interest, a hunger pang reminds us of lunch, or a wish for company demands our focused attention. Thus, attention crystallizes in the moment and changes our mode of being in the world: from a watcher to a doer, a planner, or an intender. Cats will suddenly gaze from their perch at a spot on your lap, then hunch their bodies, tense their muscles, and spring to their intended place. Humans rapidly hatch a plan to snack or browse the web, thus beginning their stream of intended action by thinking about a sojourn to the kitchen or the office. For both cats and people, cognition converges rapidly to a plan in the service of intention. However, such plans are not always successful: the lap is blocked by an open newspaper, or the plan to snack is hampered by thoughts about one's waistline. That is

Correspondence:
Marc D. Lewis, University of Toronto, 252 Bloor Street West, Toronto, Ontario M5S 1V6, Canada.
Email: mlewis@oise.utoronto.ca

Journal of Consciousness Studies, **12**, No. 8–10, 2005, pp. 210–35

when things get emotional — when goals are blocked and intentions are extended in time. Or, more accurately, that is when the preconscious feelings that accompany the immediate impulse to act begin to blossom into more coherent and more compelling emotional states, and only then can these emotional states themselves become the object of focal attention — at least for humans.

In this article, we examine the progression from watching (or listening), to intending action, to extending that intention through the maze of blocked goals that characterizes real life, with particular emphasis on the emotional and subjective states that accompany this progression. We first argue that directed attention is always intentional and always emotional, as described by Walter Freeman (2000). We then review a psychological model of emotional episodes unfolding in real time, and we propose several levels of goal obstruction that extend the duration of these episodes and contribute to their complexity and intensity. We suggest that attention is focused on the obstructions to our intended actions at first, and only later, when the obstructions persist, does focal attention come to include emotional feelings themselves. We then go on to model the synchronization of neural structures proposed to underlie the evolution of an emotional episode. Like Freeman (2000) and Tucker (e.g. Tucker, Derryberry, & Luu, 2000), we view the synchronization of neural structures as a rapid self-organizing process that consolidates activity across all levels of the nervous system. However, in tracking this process of synchronization over time, we come to the conclusion that prefrontal cortical structures are among the last to come fully on board. It is these structures that mediate attention to the meaning of events in the world as well as the possibilities for acting in accordance with those events. And it is these structures that, at least on some occasions, mediate integration of awareness of external reality with awareness of emotional feelings generated in the body. We emphasize that preattentive or background emotional feeling *always* accompanies intended action, but that focal attention to emotion arises *only* when those intentions are extended over time.

Before going on, we note that we have tried to avoid the complexities involved in defining and cataloguing aspects of consciousness by confining our discussion to two kinds of cognitive states. The first is focal attention, also described as direct, deliberate, or executive attention. This state corresponds to explicit or higher-order consciousness in some accounts, or at least to a major component of explicit consciousness. The second is preattentive or background awareness, as when something is subjectively felt but not 'cognitively accessed'. With respect to affects, such as those accompanying emotions, preattentive awareness can include feelings (e.g., tightness in the chest) before they are the object of focal attention. Our use of preattentive awareness is similar to the notion of implicit consciousness in some accounts.

At the Psychological Level of Description

Emotion theorists make very specific claims about the direction of attention. The position shared by most investigators is that attention is guided by emotion toward perceptions, interpretations, memories, goals, and plans that are relevant to whatever the emotion is about. In fact the biological function of emotion is to impel appropriate behaviour, given past learning and present circumstances, by steering attention toward useful options for acting on the world and urging one to pursue them. Thus, cognition in general and attention in particular are assumed to be guided by emotional relevance. This conclusion is supported by many lines of research. Emotion has been found to cue the recall and recognition of emotionally relevant events (Bower, 1981). Emotion influences the style of information processing and the organization of thinking (Isen, 1984), partly by drawing attention to semantic forms with which it is associated (Mathews, 1990). Sad versus happy emotions differentially affect attentional style and content (Isen, 1990). Anxiety narrows attention to specific themes or percepts (Mathews, 1990). Emotion also biases judgements and attributions, assigning significance to affectively salient causes (Dodge, 1991). Critical junctures in plans are highlighted by emotion (Oatley & Johnson-Laird, 1987). Moreover, interest, one of the most ubiquitous of emotions, appears to be necessary if learning is to take place at all (Renninger, 1992).

Although conventional emotion theories are right about the influence of emotion on attention, they have generally not been successful at modelling the ebb and flow of emotional experience—or any experience for that matter—in a realistic way. This is partly because emotion theorists continue to segregate the cognitive processes giving rise to emotions from the cognitive processes following from emotions. The former are referred to as appraisals, defined as evaluations of a situation in terms of its relevance for oneself, specifically one's goals or wellbeing (e.g., Lazarus, 1968). Appraisal approaches attempt to determine the specific perceptions, evaluations, interpretations, and so forth, that are necessary and sufficient to elicit a particular emotional state. Thus, most theorists divide the emotion-cognition connection into two linear causal processes: some study cognitions (appraisals) that give rise to emotions and others study emotions that influence cognition. This approach is consistent with and perhaps demanded by the cognitivist tradition in which emotion theory grew up. Frijda (1993; Frijda & Zeelenberg, 2001) is among the few emotion theorists who have begun to emphasize reciprocal causal processes that link cognition and emotion within a single appraisal event. Other contemporary approaches specify a continuous stream of evaluative events in which appraisals and emotions are interspersed (Ellsworth, 1991; Lazarus, 1999; Parkinson, 2001; Scherer, 2001). This is a good start. But to model the flow of cognition and emotion realistically, one cannot ignore the fundamental structure of an emotional episode, triggered along with an intention to act. In such episodes (watch what happens when you look up from the page and think about going out for dinner with your best friend), appraisal, emotion, and intention arise together.

The cognitivist or computationalist theoretical framework in which emotion theory was fashioned is being replaced in many areas of psychology by attention to the properties of self-organizing dynamic systems. Emotion theorists who have taken a dynamic systems approach (Fogel, 1993; Lewis, 1995; 1996;

Scherer, 2000) view emotions as evolving wholes, rather than end-points in a cognitive computation or starting points in the production of a cognitive bias. Emotional wholes are seen as cohering in real time through the interaction of many constituent processes, and it is the synchronization of these processes, as well as the properties of the whole, that becomes the focus of investigation. However, it is extremely difficult to study the real-time interaction of such constituent processes with behavioural methods. Observational techniques cannot see them, self-report cannot access them, and experimental manipulation cannot segregate them. Thus, we believe that dynamic systems approaches to emotion will be most fruitful when they go beneath the level of behaviour and look at biological systems — most notably the brain.

Before moving to the brain in the present article, we briefly review our own psychological model of emotional processes. Lewis (2005) describes interacting elements that give rise to a global appraisal-emotion amalgam or *emotional interpretation* (EI) over the time course of what is often called an 'emotion episode'. According to this model, appraisal constituents (e.g., perceptual events, mental images) cause or activate emotional constituents (e.g., feelings, action tendencies) that reciprocally influence the direction of attention in appraisal, which simultaneously tunes the emotional response, and so forth, in a rapidly converging feedback relation linking multiple elements. This interaction of constituents soon gives rise to the consolidation and integration of appraisal *and* emotion in a stable and coherent psychological state. As sketched in Figure 1, the evolution of a self-organizing EI begins with a *trigger* phase, as positive feedback rapidly recruits new psychological components, often in response to a perturbing event or situation in the world. For example, an EI might be triggered by the refusal of one's child to perform a routine task — or by the memory or image of a child's stubborn refusal. Positive feedback continues briefly in a phase of *self-amplification*, as the psychological system becomes transformed by reciprocally augmenting changes in attention, emerging goals, and the onset of emotional sensations. During self-amplification, cognitive activities are increasingly focused on emotionally-relevant cues. One may focus on the defiant child's body language, the stubborn look of resentment on her face, and the dirt spots suggesting further rebelliousness, while anger brews and the urge to yell 'rises in one's throat'. This phase flows seamlessly into a *self-stabilizing phase*, as negative feedback consolidates relations among thoughts and images, goals and plans, feelings and intentions, and so forth. Images of the child as exasperating but lovable may consolidate, while anger becomes focused but controlled, and a plan for appropriate discipline begins to unfold. A coherent and stable appraisal and plan of action may consolidate within a few tenths of a second. As is typical of self-organizing systems, the stabilization of an EI allows for a higher level of organization or complexity, represented by the additional horizontal lines branching out from the central line in Figure 1. We can think of this organization ramifying 'inward' via the interlocking of complementary cognitive forms (e.g., images in context, associated memories, analogies, rehearsed strategies) and 'outward' via the establishment of a planned action sequence that begins to

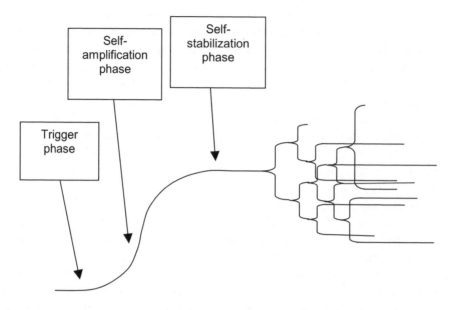

Figure 1. Sketch of a self-organizing emotional interpretation progressing in real time.

unfold as the body moves through space. The elaboration of dialogue and negotiation is a common expression of this tendency.

The phrase 'emotional interpretation' suggests only that this consolidating psychological macrostructure is both emotional and interpretive. However, we agree with Freeman that it is also fundamentally intentional. Emotions, including the interest that leads us to pick up an article and the anxiety that compels us to avoid making a harsh remark, concern improving our relations with the world through some action or change of action. Muscles tense, the tongue moves or the lips compress, hands reach, and bodies twist in new directions. Emotion theorists incorporate goal-relatedness in their portrayal of emotions, and each basic emotion can be catalogued with the class of goals to which it relates: fear and escape, anger and self-assertion, shame and hiding, desire and seeking, interest and exploration, sadness and succour. However, emotion theorists regard goals as stored representations that become activated, compared with present states, and finally deactivated when they have been attained. This conception bears the stamp of the cognitive revolution from which it sprung (e.g., Newell & Simon, 1972). In real life, however, goals emerge through a messy juxtaposition of past attainments and present opportunities, elaborated through emotional processes including physical sensations, and they tilt us forward in a continuous preoccupation with the future. That is the essence of Freeman's (2000) intentionality, and our use of the term *goal* follows suit.

Describing EIs in terms of interacting appraisal and emotional constituents, even with the addition of intentionality, is awkward at best and misleading at worst. If appraisal and emotion characterize the macrostructure that emerges from the interaction of psychological constituents, then these terms cannot properly describe the constituents themselves. Furthermore, the constituents that give rise to global states may not fit into one category or the other. They may be neither appraisal nor emotion, or they may be identifiable as a component of either or both (Colombetti & Thompson, 2005). For example, is heightened attention to a salient stimulus a constituent of emotion or appraisal? Thus, the difficulty psychologists encounter in studying constituent elements using behavioural techniques is reflected in the difficulty of classifying them. In a recent article, Lewis (2005) bypassed this difficulty by moving to a neural analysis. It is relatively easy to distinguish constituent neural systems in terms of structure and, to a lesser degree, function, and to specify the mechanisms of connection by which they interact. From this starting point, one can concretely model reciprocal causal relations among interacting constituents, leading to emergent wholes, in a manner that is appropriate for discussing processes of self-organization. One can then analyse the subjective as well as objective aspects of emotional episodes by examining these interactions in detail.

Continuing this line of reasoning, we now pose a question of relevance to the present issue, and one that may only be answerable by bridging the psychological and neural levels of description: When do emotions become the focus of attention and how does focal attention to emotions contribute to their function? This question — and related questions concerning emotion and consciousness — has been of great interest to emotional neurobiologists, Damasio (e.g., 1999), Lane (e.g. 1997; 1998) and Panksepp (e.g., 1998; 2005), and they have taken critical steps toward answering it. However, by using our model of emotion episodes, with its temporal framework and its emphasis on increasing complexity, and by integrating this model with a focus on intentional action, we can move further in this direction. In fact, our proposal for relating emotion to consciousness hinges on the pragmatics of intentional states: intentions can be short-lived or enduring, depending on how ready the world is to accommodate them. We propose that, under normal circumstances, obstructed (or diverted) intentions are the condition for background emotional awareness, whereas greater obstructions correlate with focal awareness of emotional states. Associating emotional awareness with temporality is certainly not a new idea. Öhman and colleagues (e.g., Öhman *et al.*, 2000) argue that emotion guides attention without consciousness and that the explicit awareness of emotional stimuli is precisely what takes time. Damasio (1999) distinguishes between the core consciousness that emerges transiently with emotions and the "extended consciousness" that requires additional integration over time. However, our approach links emotions with consciousness in the service of intentions or goals, especially when they become extended over time. We argue that focal awareness (or explicit consciousness) of emotions can be functional or dysfunctional, depending on the circumstances.

What happens when goals emerge? The urgings of our emotions compel us to satisfy them immediately. Even positive emotional states such as interest, attraction, and excitement are goal-related and they propel action as much as do fear and anger. In fact, intentions *are* the emotional thrust of goal pursuit. If the goal can be attained right away, action takes its course and the emotions that directed it disappear quickly, often before we know they were ever present. We swat the mosquito, shout to a friend, pick up an interesting object, kick off our shoes, or avoid the unpleasant image on page three of the newspaper. However, goals are very often elusive, their satisfaction is delayed or blocked entirely, alternate routes present themselves, and attention is taken up for an extended period with the means for attaining them. These states of extended goal pursuit stretch out intentionality (and emotion) in time, and any emotional episode lasting for at least half a second may be characterized by some degree of goal blockage. Three levels (or stages) of extended intentional states can be distinguished, and their relations to focal attention are portrayed in Figure 2. At the first level, the simple delay of a goal is usually unnoticed, and the self-stabilizing phase of an EI includes the budding of automatized plans for attaining it through well-rehearsed action (e.g., lining up to get on a bus, speeding up to change lanes, bending down to pick up a napkin). Focused attention to emotional feeling plays no part in this process, even though preattentive emotional feeling is present, propelling action plans. At the second level, many goals require directed cognitive efforts and remain out of reach until those efforts pay off. This state of affairs is pivotal in the interpersonal world, where conflicting agendas require ongoing thought, planning, and negotiation, but it is common in other domains as well. We suggest that in this condition of extended goal-blockage emotions continue to consolidate and even intensify, preattentive awareness of feeling states is enhanced, but one's focal attention is occupied by the features of the blockage and the strategies for overcoming it (e.g., preparing a response to a frustrating comment, the weight of a table that has to be moved and the positioning of one's hands), not by emotions. Finally, at the third level of goal blockage, the intensity of the emotion, or its informational value, invites the emotional feeling itself into focal attention. And this has unique consequences. It may enhance the stability and coherence of the current EI by focusing attention on one's intentional state (e.g., I'm really angry and I'm going to beat you in this match). It may thereby reduce the complexity of current cognitive elaborations (as sketched in Figure 2). One misses a loved one who is impossibly far away, fantasizes about steps toward a reunion, and only then becomes conscious of the longing. However, it can also trigger a new EI fueled by a new intention. The three-year old cannot reach the toy that has fallen through the grate. Only when he becomes aware of the intensity of his grief does his attention shift from the toy and the grate to finding his mother. The pounding music through the wall draws out a blend of anger and anxiety that becomes, itself, the focus of attention. Only then do plans to assert one's rights replace the original goal of being left alone. Thus, emotions accompany intentions and move us toward or away from the things we desire or fear; but it may be during states of obstructed and extended intentionality that emotions become the object of explicit awareness and refine present intentions or establish intentions of their own.

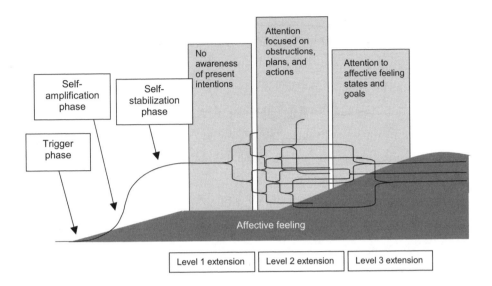

Figure 2. The evolution of an emotional interpretation in relation to attention. The stretching out of intentional states over time (through goal blockage) determines the contents of focal attention.

At the Neural Level of Description

The brain is the ultimate self-organizing system. In the cerebral cortex alone, approximately 20 billion cells, each with thousands of connections, provide a massive population of interacting units in a state of continuous flux. Despite its potential for immense noise, chaos, or disorder, this system converges rapidly to highly-ordered, synchronous states (e.g., Thompson & Varela, 2001). Each of those states taps enormous cooperativity across the elements in this system, even at relatively great distances. And this convergence, or synchronization, occurs whenever we calculate a tip or recite a poem. Corresponding with neural self-organization, but at a different level of description, the components of cognition and attention can be said to converge and form into coherent thoughts and plans. The various sensory, motor, and executive systems become linked, working memory becomes engaged, actions are selected and refined, and so forth. Some scientists have studied the parallels between neural coherence and cognitive coherence (e.g., Engel *et al.*, 2001; Skarda & Freeman, 1987; Thompson & Varela, 2001), and most studies of neural coherence indeed focus on phase synchrony, involving synchronous activation between distant groups of neurons, in the cerebral cortex (usually at the frequency range of gamma oscillations). However, as neuroscientists become increasingly interested in emotion, they have begun to examine coherence or synchrony across subcortical as well as cortical systems, with particular emphasis on the brain stem, hypothalamus, hippocampus, and amygdala (e.g., Kocsis & Vertes, 1994; Paré *et al.*, 2002). What they have discovered is that the same processes of phase synchrony at work in the

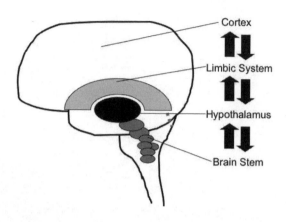

Figure 3. Vertical integration across four levels of the neuroaxis.
The sketch highlights the bidirectional flow of information
that integrates functioning over the entire brain.

cortex also take place across multiple subcortical systems. There is evidence for spontaneous coupling or synchrony at the theta frequency range across brainstem, hypothalamic, limbic, and paralimbic systems when animals are motivationally aroused, exposed to violated expectancies, or required to learn new contingencies — in other words, when they are emotional (see Lewis, 2005, for a review and synthesis).

In order to think about neural synchronization across multiple subsystems, and to establish its importance for emotion as well as cognition, we will review the functional anatomy of the major hierarchical levels of the neuroaxis. A more complete analysis would include bodily processes as well, though these go beyond the scope of the present article. We can roughly divide the brain into three levels, each more advanced and appearing later in evolution than the previous one. Figure 3 provides a rough sketch of some of the systems housed at each of these levels.

1. The brain stem and hypothalamus

The shaft of nerve tissue at the core of the brain (divided into midbrain, pons, medulla) contains sets of nuclei for programmed responses to internal and external events. These nuclei control relatively primitive, packaged response patterns (e.g., defensive and attack behaviour, vigilance, feeding, freezing, sexual behaviour, facial expressions), each highly independent and stimulus-bound, and many of which go back to our reptilian ancestors. In higher animals, the actions of many of these systems are coordinated by or synchronized with activity in the hypothalamus, which sits just above them. The hypothalamus controls the internal milieu, including the organs and vascular systems, partly through output to the autonomic nervous system via direct axonal pathways, and partly through the release of hormones into the blood. It also receives information from these systems in return, and thus functions as a central regulator of bodily responses to relevant environmental events. Brainstem systems orchestrate emotional behaviour even in the absence of higher brain systems. For example, animals without a forebrain display 'sham rage', which has the behavioural appearance of rage. Panksepp (1998) argues that there is nothing 'sham' about this rage: it exemplifies a basic emotion system functioning without cortical inhibition. He emphasizes that partially independent brainstem (and striatal) circuits can be identified for anger, fear/anxiety, love/attachment, interest/excitement, sadness, joy, and sexual desire — hence the brain stem is the seat of many basic emotions, and the behavioural propensities it orchestrates may be considered the *action tendencies* discussed by emotion theorists (e.g., Frijda, 1986). Critically, the brain stem also produces a variety of neurochemicals (e.g. dopamine, norepinephrine) that modulate activity in the cortex and virtually all other brain systems. Many of these chemicals also affect bodily systems, such that bodily responses are prepared to correspond with brain changes. At the same time, the hypothalamus produces neuropeptides that set body and brain systems into coherent goal-directed states, such as territorial aggression, scavenging for food, courting and mating, and so forth. These states are organized at a higher level than the more elementary modes of the brainstem, and their neurochemical outputs organize more comprehensive action orientations than the diffuse arousal modes elicited by brainstem neuromodulators (Panksepp, 1998).

2. The limbic system

Although the validity of the notion of a limbic system has been challenged (LeDoux, 1995), this phrase refers to a series of structures between the brainstem and the cortex thought to mediate a number of emotional and cognitive processes. Over the course of evolution, this rough semicircle of structures grew out of the diencephalon and evolved profoundly in mammals. These structures mediate learning and memory, whereas lower structures are involved in controlling perception and action according to fixed 'programs' that require no learning. The processing of sensory input and motor output is slowed down in the limbic system, so that responses can be fit more precisely to the learned aspects of situations (Tucker *et al.*, 2000). According to Tucker and colleagues, this slowdown was necessarily accompanied by the evolutionary advent of emotions, whose motivational force works by maintaining the focus of attention and action rather than by triggering some 'fixed action pattern'. Indeed, the limbic system mediates emotional states that orient attention and action to whatever is presently meaningful. For example, the amygdala (AM), a key limbic structure, is involved in tagging neutral stimuli with emotional content (LeDoux, 1995; Rolls, 1999), thereby creating chains of associations based on emotional experiences. Connections from the AM to lower (hypothalamic and brainstem) structures activate motivational response systems given current stimulus events, and connections from the AM up to the cortex entrain perception, attention, and planned action to these events. The AM requires the participation of lower structures to produce emotional states, while the converse is not true (Panksepp, 1998). Other limbic structures, including the septal and hippocampal structures, also support emotional behaviors (e.g., play, sex, nurturance) and organization of episodic memory and attention (e.g., MacLean, 1993).

3. The cerebral cortex

The layers of the cortex surround the limbic system, and the recently evolved cells that inhabit these layers are the locus of what we normally call cognition, perception, and attention. In the cortex, the time between stimulus and response appears to be greatly stretched out (Tucker et al., 2000). Inputs from the world and potential actions connect with each other through a matrix of associations, comparisons, synthesis across modalities, planning, reflection, and sometimes, but not always, volitional control. These operations take time, and emotions maintain a coherent orientation to the world during that period of time. For example, deliberate action is guided by attention to alternative plans, and anticipatory attention is constrained by emotions concerning the pursuit of particular goals. Thus, cortically mediated actions are functional, not only at the level of some phylogenetically ancient blueprint, but also at the level of a continuously refined model of the world, achieved by selecting, comparing, and pursuing particular plans while integrating the information fed back by the world. The cortex is also a key system for the cognitive control of emotional responses — often referred to as 'emotion regulation'. In particular, the prefrontal regions and related midline structures execute sophisticated perceptual and cognitive activities (including attention, monitoring, decision-making, planning, and working memory) that are recruited by (and that regulate) the emotional responses mediated by brainstem and limbic structures (Davidson & Irwin, 1999; Barbas, 1995; Bechara et al., 2000).

There are three cortical systems that are especially important for emotional processes: the anterior cingulate cortex (ACC), the orbitofrontal cortex (OFC), and the insula. All three regions are at the outskirts of the prefrontal cortex. They are phylogenetically older and closer to the limbic system and are therefore called 'paralimbic', and they appear to mediate cognitive activities relevant to emotional states (Barbas, 2000; Rolls, 1999). The ACC is found on the medial surfaces of the posterior prefrontal cortex (PFC). ACC activation has been associated with monitoring and evaluating potential actions, monitoring and resolving conflicts (as in error detection), and selective attention more generally (Carter et al., 2000; Gehring et al. 1993; van Veen et al., 2001). The executive system mediated by the (dorsal) ACC is activated in contexts requiring voluntary choice as well as directed attention and learning (Frith et al., 1991; van Veen et al., 2001). However, the more ventral regions of this complex system have been closely linked with emotional processing. OFC activity is associated with encoding and holding attention to context-specific, motivationally relevant contingencies (Rolls, 1999). Such processes are thought to extend or build onto the more basic conditioning functions of the amygdala (Cardinal *et al.*, 2002). OFC function is far more flexible than that of the AM. The OFC is responsive to changes in the hedonic tone of anticipated events (Hikosaka & Watanabe, 2000; Rolls, 1999), and it is activated when 'implicit appraisals' of motivationally relevant situations are held in mind (Schore, 1994). Its downstream connections are also integral to emotional states, and its activity has been frequently implicated in regulation of emotion through the inhibition of AM activation (Davidson *et al.*, 2000; Hariri *et al.*, 2003; Lévesque *et al.*, 2003; Ochsner *et al.*, 2002).

The OFC and ACC are highly interconnected and, as mentioned, both have been characterized as loci for the interaction of attention and emotion (Barbas, 1995; Lane *et al.*, 1998). However, each is associated with a distinct 'style' of processing. The ACC is a pivotal structure in the dorsal cortical trend, and it plays a role in integrative, holistic, and synthetic processes. It is involved in the direction of attention to potential actions, the evaluation of their utility for intended outcomes, and the selection or generation of a unitary stream of action through its connections to the motor areas (see Goldberg, 1985; Cardinal *et al.*, 2002). The ACC is implicated in the generation of intentions (no doubt in interaction with other structures, including the hippocampus), and it dispatches signals on to the motor areas for execution (as noted by Luu *et al.*, 1998, damage to this area can produce dissociation between actions and intentions). In contrast, the orbitofrontal cortices (and related areas such as ventromedial PFC) belong to the ventral cortical trend, and these structures mediate attention to the environment rather than to anticipated actions. OFC activity is stimulus-bound, reactive rather than proactive, and it processes perceptual information in great detail. It allows us to ascertain and anticipate the rewarding or punishing character of a given stimulus (see Goldberg, 1985). In general, the OFC mediates information processing in reaction to intentions that have already been established, but not the generation of intentions per se. The dorsal cortical trend has been characterized as the 'where' system, concerned with action, spatial location, and context, whereas the ventral trend has been characterized as the 'what' system, attuned to the categorical properties of objects and people. We will show how the differences in 'cognitive style' that characterize these two trends can help map out the cortical terrain in a way that contributes to our understanding of emotion and consciousness.

A final cortical structure is the insula, an 'island' of tissue tucked between the temporal lobe and prefrontal cortex, which mediates the integration of information from multiple sensory modalities, including information about the state of the whole body (Craig, 2002). Because the insula is thought to be a critical structure for the perception of emotional feelings, we review the relevant findings in some detail. The insula is responsive to autonomic arousal (Critchley *et al.*, 2001), temperature, pain, itch, sensual touch, muscular contraction and relaxation, and other distinct somatic sensations (Craig, 2002). It is densely interconnected with the amygdala, hypothalamus, OFC, and regions of the brain stem (Craig, 2002), and hence it can be readily activated by the cascade of changes initiated in emotional responses. Indeed, while it has long been associated with visceral sensations, and with the viscerally-mediated emotion of disgust, recent research suggests a role for the insula in mediating affective feeling in general (e.g., Craig, 2002; Critchley *et al.*, 2004). Increased activation in the insula has been consistently associated with the intensity of emotion experience (Lorberbaum *et al.*, 2004; Phan *et al.*, 2004), unsuppressed emotional responses (Eisenberger *et al.*, 2003; George *et al.*, 1996; Levesque *et al.*, 2003, Taylor *et al.*, 2003), autobiographical emotional memories (Damasio *et al.*, 2000; Lane *et al.*, 1997; Reiman *et al.*, 1997), interoceptive awareness (Critchley et al., 2004), and emotional awareness (Lane *et al.*, 1998). While a number of studies have found insula activation to be associated with sadness (Lévesque *et al.*, 2003; Mayberg *et al.*, 1999; Phan *et al.*, 2003), it has also been associated with a range of other emotions and experimental paradigms (e.g., Damasio *et al.*, 2000; Eisenberger *et al.*, 2003; Reiman *et al.*, 1997). Insula activation has been found to increase with the intensity of both positive and negative pictures, and it has been linked with participant reports of an image's self-relatedness (Phan *et al.*, 2003). Finally, the viscerosensory functions of the insula, and its location between the OFC and temporal lobe, place it at the root of the ventral trend — an anchor point joining the ventral cortex to the amygdala and other limbic structures. Thus, one could say that while the OFC mediates apprehension of the outside world, the insula mediates apprehension of the internal world. For this reason, Craig (2002) has dubbed the insula the sensory cortex of the limbic system.

The hierarchy of brain levels is often construed in terms of domination or control of lower levels by higher levels. Indeed, the cerebral cortex subordinates the more primitive functions of limbic system and brain stem. However, as emphasized by Tucker *et al.* (2000), there are two important caveats. First, more primitive brain systems continue to evolve, so that their functions can provide support to the higher levels of control. For example, visual systems in the cortex rely on midbrain nuclei that tune them to sudden movements, higher cognitive processes depend on cerebellar coordination, and so forth. Second, as shown in Figure 3, the downward flow of control and modulation — e.g., from cortex to limbic system to brain stem — is reciprocated by an upward flow of synaptic activation and neurochemical stimulation. The brain stem and hypothalamus entrain limbic structures by means of neuromodulators and neuropeptides, locking in perceptual biases and associations, and they also recruit cortical activities to ancient mammalian and even reptilian agendas, which we have identified as emotional *action tendencies*. Primitive agendas and requirements thus flow up the neuroaxis from its most primitive roots at the same time as executive attention, planning, and knowledge subordinate each lower level by the activities of the cortex. If not for the bottom-up flow, the brain would have no energy and no direction for its activities. If not for the top-down flow, recently evolved mechanisms for perception, action and integration would have no control over bodily states and behaviour. It is the reciprocity of these upward and downward flows that links sophisticated cognitive processes with basic motivational mechanisms.

The reciprocation of motivational and executive flows, up and down the neuroaxis, appears to be responsible for the rapid synchronization of the entire brain through a process of "vertical integration" (Tucker *et al.*, 2000). This process of synchronization is hypothesized to occur whenever a significant change in internal or external events triggers an emotion, and thus demands the initiation of a cognitive or motor response. Vertical integration is considered necessary to coordinate perception, attention, and action planning with basic action tendencies, so that the animal can behave flexibly, skilfully, and intelligently when motivated (Tucker *et al.*, 2000; cf. Buck, 1999). In recent work, Lewis (2005) identified several mechanisms of integration through which vertical integration comes about. Most important among these are reciprocal (feedback) circuits among participating structures and neuromodulatory actions that enhance particular global organizations. Both processes may depend largely on the temporal phase-locking (particularly in the theta range) of activity between neural populations up and down the neuroaxis. Moreover, phase-locking between cooperating systems is hypothesized to arise spontaneously across many independent sites, but to be modulated in a top-down fashion by the global resonance to which it gives rise. In dynamic systems theory, this top-down control of bottom-up coordination is referred to as circular causality (Haken, 1977), and it has important properties for establishing and maintaining self-organizing wholes (but see Bakker, 2005, for an alternative view). For now we wish to explore the implications of vertical integration for emotional episodes. We propose that the evolution of an EI maps on to vertical integration and corresponds with it temporally. A careful analysis of the temporal profile of this mind-brain relation may provide a valuable perspective for understanding emotional awareness.

Integrating Neural and Psychological Descriptions in Time

An EI was argued to proceed from a trigger, to a self-amplification phase, and then to a self-stabilization phase, in which the complexification of appraisal ramifies over time. What goes on in the brain over this time course? At the start of an emotional episode, brainstem systems are activated, often by the amygdala, and primitive orienting responses and action tendencies arise along with the release of particular neurochemicals to other brain and bodily systems. Positive feedback between the amygdala (or striatum) and the brain stem amplifies these activities and recruits cortical activities (through pathways directly from limbic structures as well as the hypothalamus and brain stem). These activities include sensory focusing and synthesis by posterior and temporal cortex, targeting emotionally relevant environmental events, parietal integration of sensory and somatic states, and, critically, activation of the insula where emotional feelings are synthesized based on inputs from body and brain stem. Thus, perception of the external world and the internal milieu are among the earliest cortical involvements in the self-amplification of a new EI. In this initial self-amplifying phase, activity builds on itself and the profile of change is exponential. However, as more and more neural and bodily components become recruited to the emerging

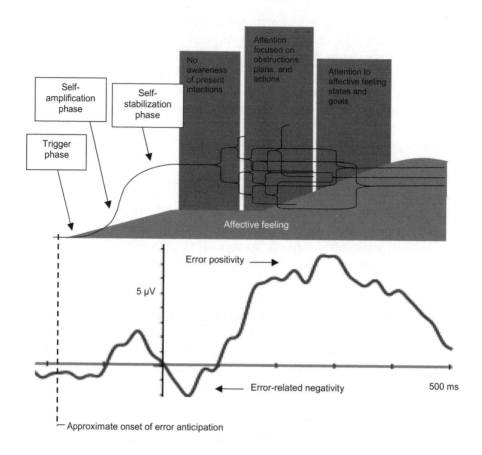

Figure 4. Comparison of the evolution of an emotional interpretation with the evolution of a
cognitive ERP. The error-related negativity does not imply explicit consciousness of the error.
The error positivity has been linked with explicit consciousness
of the error along with its emotional implications.

constellation, disparate processes settle into an ongoing resonance, characterized by negative feedback. This is the self-stabilizing phase of the EI. Now, deviations or fluctuations are damped, because many different neural subsystems
reinforce each other's ongoing activity, and functional synchronization (as well
as temporal synchronization, e.g., within the theta band) extends across brain
regions through processes of vertical integration. Thus, in the self-stabilization
phase, multiple activities across the neuroaxis contribute to a unitary emotional
state, cognitive appraisal, and intended action, hypothetically due to the synchronization of oscillations among subcortical, cortical, and paralimbic systems.
This synchronization of activities across all levels of the neuroaxis embodies the
animal's intention to *do* something about its state in the world (Freeman, 2000).
Emotions are useless without intentions to act, and intentions can be translated
into actions effectively only through the coordination of the many neural
systems that have been designed by evolution to work together in emotional
states.

How can the evolution of an EI be shown to correspond with the evolution of synchrony in the brain, and what evidence is there to estimate the time course of this process? As shown in Figure 4, we suggest that the stabilization phase of an EI corresponds with the stabilization of cortical oscillations — the tip of the iceberg of whole-brain synchronization — at a particular time point, and this shows up as an event-related potential (ERP) in scalp EEG when averaged over trials (see Makeig *et al.*, 2002). ERPs have been conceptualized as the averaging of phase-locked cortical waveforms (synchronized to a stimulus) across trials. For example, Makeig *et al.* (2002) claim that perceptual ERPs result from the compilation of alpha-band oscillations, synchronized by the triggering effect of a visual stimulus. In Figure 4, an ERP component called the error-related negativity (ERN) is shown to correspond with the onset of self-stabilization in an EI. The ERN is commonly observed after subjects have made an error of which they are implicitly aware, and it is thought to be triggered by response-monitoring cognitions that begin prior to the response itself (by about 200-300 ms), even though it is measured following that response. The ERN is followed by a second component, the error-positivity (Pe), a positive peak that hypothetically reflects additional cognitive processing of the significance of the error and its emotional concomitants (Nieuwenhuis *et al.*, 2001). Indeed, Luu and colleagues (2003) have argued that action-monitoring ERPs, including the ERN and Pe, reflect the onset of phase synchronization at the theta band, and this hypothesis is particularly interesting in light of evidence for the large-scale synchronizing properties of theta oscillations (Buzsaki, 1996; von Stein & Sarnthein, 2000).

So far, we have suggested that vertical integration parallels and in fact mediates the evolution of an EI, as multiple brain regions are recruited to a particular agenda. This results in the consolidation of an emotional state, a global appraisal, and a coherent intention to act. Now we are ready to tackle the question that is most central to our discussion: What role is played by the subjective attributes of emotion — both preattentive emotional feeling and direct attention to emotion — in this progression? We begin by examining the timetable of vertical integration more carefully. Previously we touched on Tucker *et al.*'s (2000) contention that the time between a stimulus and a response, or between an emotional perturbation and a resulting action, expands enormously as one travels up the neuroaxis from the brain stem to the cortex. In other words, action tendencies are released by brainstem nuclei immediately when neighbouring brainstem nuclei pick up coarse perceptual information, but top-down, cortically-mediated planned behaviour is initiated only after perceptual events have been thoroughly processed, outcomes have been rehearsed in working memory, and so forth. The slowing of the animal's response results, according to these authors, from (1) the evolution of sensory organs that can apprehend the world at a distance (e.g., smell, vision, and hearing), allowing time to prepare a response, and (2) the coevolution of more advanced brain structures, allowing learning, memory, response selection, and planning to intercede between the impulse and the action, given this extended preparatory period.

We propose that the slowing down of time from brain stem to cortical responding is extrapolated further in the cortex itself. It is generally accepted that the prefrontal cortex is the ultimate buffer between emotional impulses and behaviour, through the medium of executive processes including inhibitory control, working memory, and response monitoring. Mesulam (2002) describes the PFC as allowing us to be diverted from the automaticity of the 'default mode' from stimulus to response — thus mediating one of the most revered aspects of human cognition: thought itself. Residing at the apex of cortical integration, the PFC synthesizes information about the anticipated impact of events in the world with information concerning the opportunities and consequences of intentional action. Hence, the PFC allows for the greatest slowing down and stretching out of the distance between impulse and action. The PFC and related structures (e.g., the ACC) can function to delay the initiation of action almost indefinitely and to tailor it carefully once it has been initiated. Thus, from our perspective, frontocortical activities are late to get on board the wave of vertical integration and, once they do, they are capable of maintaining whole-brain synchrony for extended periods of time while actions are delayed and/or modified.

Evidence for delay in prefrontal involvement comes from the ERP literature. The appearance of a meaningful stimulus or the recognition of one's own erroneous response evokes frontal or frontocentral ERP components about 200–500 ms later, whereas posterior perceptual components appear within 50–100 ms of stimulus onset. Specifically, emotional faces and other affective stimuli have been shown to evoke emotion-sensitive activity in the occipital and temporal visual cortices as early as 80 or 90 ms after stimulus onset (Batty & Taylor, 2003; Pizzagalli et al., 2003; Rolls, 2000), while OFC, ACC and other prefrontal activity tends to come on line somewhat later. MEG and ERP studies have generally found OFC and ACC activation beginning at 220 ms (Schnider et al., 2002; Streit et al., 1999). However, frontal activation associated with conscious recognition or evaluation of a stimulus may occur considerably later (Schnider et al., 2002; Dehaene et al., 2003). There is evidence that ACC systems become activated within 200-300 ms when emotional judgements need to be made (e.g., in the frontal N2 response). In a recent ERP study by Tucker et al. (2003), participants were presented with positive vs. negative adjectives, and had to endorse the words (yes or no) as either describing or not describing themselves or a friend. Results showed an initial main effect of word valence (good vs. bad) at frontal midline scalp sites between 304 and 332 ms after stimulus onset. Source localization indicated a cortical generator for this scalp difference in the vicinity of the right dorsal ACC. A main effect of endorsement (yes/no) was found about 100 ms later, at frontopolar sites, peaking at 436 ms. This activity was modeled with a cortical generator in the region of the right OFC. Imaging data also suggest a delay between the perceptual processing of stimuli and frontocortical mediation in preparation for a response. In a study by Cunningham et al. (2004), white participants viewed images of both black and white faces, which were presented for either 30 ms or 525 ms time-periods. During the short (implicit) presentation condition, amygdala activation was greater for black than white faces, presumably indexing anxiety. In contrast, when faces were viewed for longer, there was increased frontal activation and the difference in amygdalar response was reduced, suggesting reappraisal and self-regulation. Furthermore, Ochsner *et al.* (2002) found that both ACC and right OFC activation corresponded with amygdala deactivation when subjects were asked to reappraise (more positively) their interpretations of disturbing images. These data are consistent with a role for the PFC in response regulation — or emotion regulation as it is often called — more generally (see also Davidson & Irwin, 1999; Hariri *et al.*, 2003; Lévesque *et al.*, 2003). Moreover, frontal activities may become integrated with other neural changes more slowly, even after initial activations are observed, and they may maintain their organization longer than other cortical activities, reflecting their enmeshment with memory constellations that change more slowly than perceptual events. As noted by Streit *et al.* (1999) such ventral prefrontal areas as the OFC may first become activated in relation to the initial encoding of events, as indicated by single-cell findings of early OFC activation, but then repeated iterations of information processing may entrain the OFC with other frontal regions in explicit processes involving working memory and elaboration of associations. In fact, the complexification of interpretations, strategies, and plans presumably mediated by the PFC may last a great deal longer than the perceptual gestalt with which they are associated. This 'slowing down' goes well beyond the evolution of our sensory systems and parallels instead the evolutionary developments of language and thought that permit extended planning.

Thus, the slowing down and stretching out of intentional states may set the occasion for a final phase of vertical integration, incorporating the PFC in an extended sequence of iterative processes. Furthermore, this phase may parallel the complexification that builds up in a self-stabilizing EI, once appraisals have consolidated but goals are not yet attained, and more articulated and focused cognitive activities are required to attain them. Although Freeman (2000) may be right in ascribing intentional action to all animals, we suggest that the slow-down of planned action through frontocortical processes elaborates intentionality in a uniquely human way: from a momentary surge — exemplified by the pouncing of a cat onto a mouse or onto its owner's lap — to a rich and articulated psychological preoccupation with a particular future state — characteristic of human consciousness.

Emotional Awareness and Intentionality: Toward a Neuropsychological Timeline

Emotional feeling serves its earliest function in the self-amplification phase of an EI, when intentionality first emerges. At the psychological level, it drives our attention to focus on particular aspects of situations and it initiates our compulsion to reorient the stream of action toward the targets of that attention. But affective feeling may feed back directly to neural changes as well. Here we refer to Panksepp's (2005) radical proposal that neural function and phenomenology are two features of the same unitary process. In Panksepp's view, affective feeling initiated by the brain stem directly signals other information-processing systems in the brain to attend to the situation associated with the affect (e.g., the excitement of *seeking* tunes perceptual systems to novel vistas to be explored). He states that 'an emotive system for resource acquisition is an intrinsic part of the nervous system, and...it entails an affective feel — an invigorated positive feeling of engagement with tasks...The affect would be a good way to encode the importance of arousal of a brain system that motivates such behavioral richness' (p. 26). However, during the initial phase of an EI, affective feeling remains largely preattentive. While it initiates attentional focusing and other cognitive activities, it is not yet the focus of these activities. The research reviewed earlier suggests that the insula may be involved in affective feeling at this level, though Panksepp argues that the outputs of brainstem activity are all that are necessary for implicit affective feeling. We suggest that the proximity of the insula to the limbic system, and its direct connections to both amygdala and brain stem, make it a likely organ of affective feeling even in the early phases of an EI. Research concerning the role of the insula in unsuppressed emotional responses (Eisenberger *et al.*, 2003; George *et al.*, 1996; Lévesque *et al.*, 2003, Taylor *et al.*, 2003) also suggests that higher cognitive processes are not necessary for the emotional feelings mediated by the insula, and may at times suppress them. Indeed the insula has been proposed as a key mediator of Damasio's (1994) somatic markers (Craig, 2002), which operate largely at a preattentive level of awareness.

We described three levels of goal blockage that increasingly extend the duration of a self-stabilizing EI, enhance its complexity, and stretch out intentionality over time. At the first level, an expectable and unremarkable delay in goal satisfaction requires no explicit planning or decision-making. Background awareness of emotional feeling, mediated by the insula, is enough to maintain attention to the task at hand and to direct perceptual and cognitive activities toward achieving the desired outcome. Vertical integration has by now recruited coordinated activities across the neuroaxis, including the posterior cortex, but prefrontal cortical systems are not yet committed to the new intentional state, and may in fact maintain some pattern of activity that remains from a prior EI. One frequently remains engaged in an intricate conversation while speeding up or slowing down in order to change lanes. Gabriel *et al.* (2002) discuss the role of the posterior cingulate cortex in automatized routines that have already been well-learned. This region of the action-oriented cingulate may be responsible for small modifications in the execution of automatized routines, but it is not involved in challenging situations that require explicit attention and new learning (Gabriel *et al.*, 2002).

At the second level of goal obstruction, deliberate cognitive efforts are required to attain goals that cannot be achieved on the fly. There is ample evidence to indicate that the dorsal ACC often becomes involved at this level. Both neuroimaging and electrophysiological methods implicate the ACC in response selection and performance monitoring. For example, ACC activation is commonly associated with the 'inhibitory N2', a negative ERP peak 200–400 ms after a visual stimulus, which taps successful performance on tasks requiring one to make difficult choices, inhibit prepotent actions, or overcome misleading cues. The ACC is also assumed to underlie the error related negativity (ERN, e.g., Luu *et al.*, 2003; van Veen & Carter, 2002), which taps error monitoring, as depicted in Figure 4. Both the inhibitory N2 and the ERN peak about 200-400 ms following the initiating event (cognitive registration of anticipated error in the case of the ERN). And because the ERN is thought to precede explicit consciousness *of the error,* we may tentatively conclude that early ACC involvement directs focal attention to the stream of action rather than to internal cognitive or emotional events. The role of the ACC in explicit, volitional consciousness has been well documented (Allman *et al.*, 2001; Bechara & Naqvi, 2004; Dehaene *et al.*, 2003; Lane *et al.*, 1997). Moreover, a number of studies have demonstrated little ACC activity when subjects are viewing emotional pictures passively but pronounced ACC activity when they are making judgements about those pictures (Hariri *et al.*, 2003; Lane *et al.*, 1998, and Taylor *et al.*, 2003). We have suggested that the kind of attention mediated by the ACC is integrative and holistic, focused on action and its anticipated consequences. Thus, recent perceptual information about the obstructive features of the world should serve as a springboard to the 'aiming' of intended action mediated by the ACC. Yet the question remains: what is the content of consciousness at this level of goal obstruction? We propose that the obstructions themselves are at least implicit in consciousness, but the means for overriding them occupy focal attention more centrally. That is, one's attention is focused on the actions one is about to undertake and on the changes in the world that are likely to result from them. The beam of attention is focused on the objects of intentionality. An extended stay at this level of deliberate goal pursuit probably involves a great deal of entrainment among dorsal and lateral prefrontal systems, as attention moves back and forth from the specifics of the obstructions to the strategies needed to overcome them. However, neither explicit awareness of the blocked goal itself nor of the emotion arising from it need play any part in this process. Only implicit awareness of affect is necessary to continue to guide attention, planning, and action.

The third level of goal obstruction is designated by changes in the internal milieu rather than changes in the world, but it follows upon the failure (either actual or anticipated) of intended actions to achieve desired outcomes. If one's goal is to escape an impending threat, then the continued failure to reach a safe haven amplifies feelings of fear and anxiety until they cannot be ignored. If one's goal is a sexual exploit, then the delay in achieving it generates a level of excitement that can flood one's awareness and interfere with conversation. If one wishes to defeat an opponent in tennis, then every point lost increases frustration and anger until awareness of these emotions becomes insistent and focal. Or, when anger turns to sadness, because defeat seems inevitable, the awareness of a sense of bleak deflation may suddenly occupy focal attention and cause one to give up. In all these examples, it is either intensity or unexpected change in emotional feeling that brings it into focal awareness.

At this final phase of an EI, vertical integration may in a certain sense be complete. Now, cingulate and prefrontal processes may finally be fully coordinated with limbic and brainstem activities. This state of affairs does not necessarily take a long time to evolve. It does not take long to realize one's fear when an approaching stranger refuses to look away. But to pinpoint the time course of explicit emotional awareness, we can look again to the ERP waveform shown in Figure 4. The Pe peaks about 300–500 ms following the ERN — that is, about 800 ms following the first cognitive perturbation in the sequence. Because the Pe is associated with explicit awareness of the emotional significance of events (Nieuwenhuis *et al.*, 2001), and because its cortical generator is apparently in the ventral region of the ACC (van Veen & Carter, 2002), one may speculate that dorsal-ventral integration is completed within this time frame. Now attention to actions, mediated by the dorsal ACC, becomes integrated with attention to emotional contingencies in the environment, mediated by the ventral PFC (including the OFC), and with attention to emotional feelings themselves, mediated by the insula through its connections to the ventral PFC. Indeed, the OFC and other ventral prefrontal structures must be crucial arbiters of emotional awareness. As reviewed earlier, these areas are thought to process context-specific, motivationally relevant contingencies in the world, to mediate explicit emotional appraisals, and to support a system of emotional working memory that extends the perception of emotional states over time (e.g., Rolls, 1999; Schore, 1994). Damage to these systems has been associated with unrestrained actions, freed up from the anxiety generated by the anticipation of negative consequences (Bechara *et al.*, 2000; Blair *et al.*, 2001; Damasio, 1994). What we are proposing is that ventral prefrontal activation tunes attention to how things are, not just how we would like them to be. Now the insula's map of the internal milieu, intensely coloured by emotional feeling states, is made fully available to prefrontal processes mediating appraisal. As well, the neuromodulators and neuropeptides that enhance the activity of specific circuits in all parts of the brain now constrain focal attention mediated by the PFC toward those aspects of the world that match primitive motivational agendas. The prefrontal cortex can now be said to be captured by messages about one's emotional state.

One could argue that the emotional responses needed to make prudent decisions and maintain appropriate behaviour need not be the focus of direct attention. Indeed, the appraisal and regulatory activities mediated by the ventral PFC may not require focal attention to function smoothly. However, we do not claim that the stimulus-bound, reactive 'cognitive style' of the ventral trend is sufficient for focal attention to emotional states. Its role in cognitive processes, characterized by preoccupation with the details of experience, would be inadequate for a gist-like sense of the self in the world. Instead, we are proposing that the integration (or synchronization) of activity in ventral prefrontal structures *with* that of dorsal prefrontal systems mediates comprehensive awareness of emotional states. The stimulus-bound processing of the ventral trend should be sufficient to perceive the emotion-relevant properties of the outside world as well as the bodily concomitants of emotional states mediated by insular activity.

However, the synchronization of these processes with dorsal and lateral prefrontal systems, mediating working memory, response selection, and planning, should be necessary for a comprehensive awareness of the inner world, the outer world, and the generation of intended actions designed to adjust the relation between the two.

What does emotional awareness buy us? One possibility is that the extended integration of an explicit emotional consciousness catalyses awareness of intentions themselves. When we are pursuing goals, adjusting our actions to compensate for the obstructions in our way, we are not aware of the goals — only of the obstructions and our efforts to overcome them. However, explicit emotional awareness may compel us to include, in our appraisal of our actions in the world, an appraisal of what is propelling those actions. That would be the best way to make sense of the feelings we experience. The integration we have modeled among dorsal and ventral systems would permit awareness to bump up and down between what we are doing and how we are feeling, such that a global gestalt of ourselves *as* intentional beings can finally emerge. We further suggest that explicit awareness of one's intentional state may scale back the ramifications of cognitive complexity that have emerged in a stable EI. One may continue to strive for the same goal, but with renewed focus, vigor, and concentration. Or, one may abandon the present intention because it is unattainable or less relevant than was previously assumed. With focal attention to one's feelings and intentions dominating consciousness, there are now opportunities to engage volitional processes and aim them in a novel direction. Whether explicit consciousness of emotion is an evolutionary adaptation that contributes to perspective-taking and volition, or whether it is a byproduct of the evolution of our wonderfully complex cognitive capacities, we are lucky to have it. It not only enriches our sense of ourselves as emotional and volitional beings but it also allows us to look up from the details of the world to the gist of our movement through it.

References

Allman, J., Hakeem, A., Erwin, J.M., Nimchinsky, E. & Hof, P. (2001), 'The anterior cingulate cortex: The evolution of an interface between emotion and cognition', in *Unity of Knowledge: The Convergence of Natural and Human Science*, ed. A. R. Damasio and A. Harrington, *Annals of the New York Academy of Sciences*, **935** (New York: New York Academy of Sciences).

Bakker, B. (2005), 'The concept of circular causality should be discarded', *Behavioural and Brain Sciences*, **28**, pp. 137–8.

Barbas, H. (1995), 'Anatomic basis of cognitive-emotional interactions in the primate prefrontal cortex', *Neuroscience & Biobehavioral Reviews*, **19**, pp. 449–510.

Batty, M., & Taylor, M. J. (2003), 'Early processing of the six basic facial emotional expressions', *Cognitive Brain Research*, **17**, pp. 613–20.

Bechara, A., Damasio, H., & Damasio, A.R. (2000), 'Emotion, decision making and the orbitofrontal cortex', *Cerebral Cortex*, **10**, pp. 295–307.

Bechara, A., & Naqvi, N. (2004), 'Listening to your heart: Interoceptive awareness as a gateway to feeling', *Nature Neuroscience*, **7** (2), pp. 102–3.

Blair, R.J.R., Colledge, E., & Mitchell, D.G.V. (2001), 'Somatic markers and response reversal: Is there orbitofrontal cortex dysfunction in boys with psychopathic tendencies?', *Journal of Abnormal Child Psychology*, **29**, pp. 499–511.

Bower, G.H. (1981), 'Mood and memory', *American Psychologist,* **36**, pp. 129–48.

Buck, R. (1999), 'The biological affects: A typology', *Psychological Review*, **106**, pp. 301–36.

Buzsaki, G. (1996), 'The hippocampal-neocortical dialogue', *Cerebral Cortex*, **6**, pp. 81–92.

Cardinal, R.N., Parkinson, J.A., Hall, J., & Everitt, B.J. (2002), 'Emotion and motivation: the role of the amygdala, ventral striatum, and prefrontal cortex', *Neuroscience and Biobehavioral Reviews*, **26**, pp. 321–52.

Carter, C.S., MacDonald, A.M., III, Botvinick, M.M., Ross, L.L., Stenger, V.A., Noll, D. & Cohen, J.D. (2000), 'Parsing executive processes: Strategic vs. evaluative functions of the anterior cingulate cortex', *Proceedings of the National Academy of Sciences*, **97**, pp. 1944–8.

Critchley, H.D., Mathias, C.J., & Dolan, R.J. (2001), 'Neuroanatomical basis for first-and second-order representations of bodily states', *Nature Neuroscience*, **4**, pp. 207–12.

Critchley, H.D., Wiens, S., Rotshtein, P., Öhman, A. & Dolan, R.J. (2004), 'Neural systems supporting interoceptive awareness', *Nature Neuroscience,* **7**, pp. 189–95.

Colombetti, G. & Thompson, E. (2005), 'Enacting emotional interpretations with feeling', *Behavioural and Brain Sciences*, **28**, pp. 137–8.

Craig, A. D. (2002), 'How do you feel? Interoception: The sense of the physiological condition of the body', *Nature Reviews Neuroscience*, **3**, pp. 655–66.

Cunningham, W.A., Johnson, M.K., Raye, C.L., Gatenby, J.C., Gore, J.C., & Banaji, M.R. (2004), 'Separable neural components in the processing of black and white faces', *Psychological Science*, **15**, pp. 806–13.

Damasio, A.R. (1994), *Descartes' Error: Emotion, Reason and the Human Brain* (New York: Avon Books).

Damasio, A.R. (1999), *The Feeling of What Happens: Body and Emotion in the Making of Consciousness* (Fort Worth, TX: Harcourt College Publishers).

Damasio, A.R., Grabowski, T. J., Bechara, A., Damasio, H., Ponto, L. L. B., Parvizi, J., & Hichwa, R. D. (2000), 'Subcortical and cortical brain activity during the feeling of self-generated emotions', *Nature Neuroscience,* **3**, pp. 1049–56.

Davidson, R.J., & Irwin, W. (1999), 'The functional neuroanatomy of emotion and affective style', *Trends in Cognitive Sciences*, **3**, pp. 11–21.

Davidson, R.J., Jackson, D.C. & Kalin, N.H. (2000), 'Emotion, plasticity, context, and regulation: Perspectives from affective neuroscience', *Psychological Bulletin Special: Psychology in the 21st Century*, **126**, pp. 890–909.

Dehaene, S., Sergent, C. & Changeux, J.-P. (2003), 'A neuronal network model linking subjective reports and objective physiological data during conscious perception', *Proceedings of the New York Academy of Sciences,* **100**, pp. 8520–5.

Dodge, K. A. (1991), 'Emotion and social information processing', in *The Development of Emotion Regulation and Dysregulation,* ed. J. Garber and K.A. Dodge (Cambridge: Cambridge University Press).

Eisenberger, N.I., Lieberman, M.D., & Williams, K.D. (2003), 'Does rejection hurt? An fMRI study of social exclusion', *Science*, **302**, pp. 290–2.

Ellsworth, P.C. (1991), 'Some implications of cognitive appraisal theories of emotion', in *International Review of Studies on Emotion*, ed. K.T. Strongman (Chichester, England: Wiley).

Engel, A.K., Fries, P. & Singer, W. (2001), 'Dynamic predictions: Oscillations and synchrony in top-down processing', *Nature Reviews Neuroscience*, **2**, pp. 704–16.

Fogel, A. (1993), *Developing Through Relationships: Origins of Communication, Self, and Culture* (Chicago: University of Chicago Press).

Freeman, W.J. (2000), 'Emotion is essential to all intentional behaviours', in *Emotion, Development and Self-organization: Dynamic Systems Approaches to Emotional Development*, ed. M. D. Lewis and I. Granic (New York: Cambridge University Press).

Frijda, N.H. (1986), *The Emotions* (Cambridge: Cambridge University Press).

Frijda, N.H. (1993), 'The place of appraisal in emotion', *Cognition and Emotion*, **7**, pp. 357–87.

Frijda, N.H. & Zeelenberg, M. (2001), 'Appraisal: What is the dependent?' in *Appraisal Processes in Emotion: Theory, Methods, Research*, ed. K.R. Scherer, A. Schorr, and T. Johnstone (New York: Oxford University Press).

Frith, C.D., Friston, K., Liddle, P.F. & Frackowiak, R.S. (1991), 'Willed action and the prefrontal cortex in man: A study with PET', *Proceedings of the Royal Society of London: Series B, Biological Science*, **244**, pp. 241–6.

Gabriel, M., Burhans, L., Talk, A. & Scalf, P. (2002), 'Cingulate cortex', in *Encyclopedia of the Human Brain, Vol. 1*, ed. V.S. Ramachandran (San Diego, CA: Academic Press).

Gehring, W.J., Goss, B., Coles, M.G.H., Meyer, D.E. & Donchin, E. (1993), 'A neural system for error detection and compensation', *Psychological Science*, **4**, pp. 385–90.

George, M.S., Ketter, T.A., Priti, I.P., Herscovitch, P. & Post, R.M. (1996), 'Gender differences in regional cerebral blood flow during transient self-induced sadness or happiness', *Biological Psychiatry*, **40**, pp. 859–71.

Goldberg, G. (1985), 'Supplementary motor area structure and function: Review and hypotheses', *Behavioral and Brain Sciences*, **8**, pp. 567–616.

Haken, H. (1977), *Synergetics — An Introduction: Nonequilibrium Phase Transitions and Self-Organization in Physics, Chemistry and Biology* (Berlin: Springer-Verlag).

Hariri, A.R., Mattay, V.S., Tessitore, A., Fera, F. & Weinberger, D.R. (2003), 'Neocortical modulation of the amygdala response to fearful stimuli', *Biological Psychiatry*, **53**, pp. 494–501.

Hikosaka, K. & Watanabe, M. (2000), 'Delay activity of orbital and lateral prefrontal neurons of the monkey varying with different rewards', *Cerebral Cortex*, **10**, pp. 263–71.

Isen, A.M. (1984), 'Toward understanding the role of affect in cognition', in *Handbook of Social Cognition*, ed. R.S. Wyer and T.K. Srull (Hillsdale, NJ: Erlbaum).

Isen, A.M. (1990), 'The influence of positive and negative affect on cognitive organization: Some implications for development', *Psychological and Biological Processes in the Development of Emotion*, ed. N. Stein, B. Leventhal, and T. Trabasso (Hillsdale, NJ: Erlbaum).

Kawasaki, H., Adolphs, R., Kaufman, O., Damasio, H., Damasio, A.R., Granner, M., Bakken, H., Hori, T. & Howard M.A. (2001), 'Single-unit responses to emotional visual stimuli recorded in human ventral prefrontal cortex', *Nature Neuroscience*, **4**, pp. 15–16.

Kocsis, B. & Vertes, R.P. (1994), 'Characterization of neurons of the supramammillary nucleus and mammillary body that discharge rhythmically with the hippocampal theta rhythm in the rat', *Journal of Neuroscience*, **14**, pp. 7040–52.

Lane, R.D., Reiman, E.M., Ahern, G.L., Schwartz, G.E. & Davidson, R.J. (1997), 'Neuroanatomical correlates of happiness, sadness, & disgust', *American Journal of Psychiatry*, **154**, pp. 926–33.

Lane, R.D., Reiman, E.M., Axelrod, B., Yun, L., Holmes, A. & Schwartz, G.E. (1998), 'Neural correlates of levels of emotional awareness: Evidence of an interaction between emotion and attention in the anterior cingulate cortex', *Journal of Cognitive Neuroscience,* **10,** pp. 525–35.

Lazarus, R.S. (1968), 'Emotions and adaptation: Conceptual and empirical relations', in *Nebraska Symposium on Motivation*, **16**, ed. W.J. Arnold (Lincoln, NE: University of Nebraska Press).

Lazarus, R.S. (1999), 'The cognition-emotion debate: A bit of history', in *Handbook of Cognition and Emotion*, ed. T. Dalgleish and M. Power (Chichester, England: Wiley).

LeDoux, J. E. (1995), 'In search of an emotional system in the brain: Leaping from fear to emotion and consciousness', in *The Cognitive Neurosciences,* ed. M.S. Gazzaniga (Cambridge, MA: MIT Press).

Lévesque, J., Eugène, F., Joanette, Y., Paquette, V., Mensour, B., Beaudoin, G., Leroux, J.-M., Bourgouin, P. & Beauregard, M. (2003), 'Neural circuitry underlying voluntary suppression of sadness', *Biological Psychiatry*, **53**, pp. 502–10.

Lewis, M.D. (1995), 'Cognition-emotion feedback and the self-organization of developmental paths', *Human Development*, **38**, pp. 71–102.

Lewis, M.D. (1996), 'Self-organising cognitive appraisals', *Cognition and Emotion,* **10,** pp. 1-25.

Lewis, M.D. (2005), 'Linking emotion theory and neurobiology through dynamic systems modeling', *Behavioral and Brain Sciences*, **28**, pp. 105–31.

Lorberbaum, J.P., Kose, S., Johnson, M.R., Arana, G.W., Sullivan, L.K., Hamner, M.B., Ballenger, J.C., Lydiard, R.B., Brodrick, P.S., Bohning, D.E. & George, M.S. (2004), 'Neural correlates of speech anticipatory anxiety in generalized social phobia', *Neuroreport,* **15**, pp. 2701–5.

Luu, P., Tucker, D.M., & Derryberry, D. (1998), 'Anxiety and the motivational basis of working memory', *Cognitive Therapy and Research,* **22** (6) pp. 577–94.

Luu, P., Tucker, D.M., Derryberry, D., Reed, M., & Poulsen, C. (2003), 'Activity in human medial frontal cortex in emotional evaluation and error monitoring', *Psychological Science*, **14**, pp. 47–53.

MacLean, P.D. (1993), 'Perspectives on cingulate cortex in the limbic system', in *Neurobiology of Cingulate Cortex and Limbic Thalamus: A Comprehensive Handbook*, ed. B.A. Vogt and M. Gabriel (Boston: Brikhauser).

Makeig, S., Westerfield, M., Jung, T.-P., Enghoff, S., Townsend, J., Courchesne, E. & Sejnowski, T.J. (2002), 'Dynamic brain sources of visual evoked responses', *Science*, **295**, pp. 690–4.

Mathews, A. (1990), 'Why worry? The cognitive function of anxiety', *Behaviour Research and Therapy*, **28**, pp. 455–68.

Mayberg, H.S., Liotti, M., Brannan, S.K., McGinnis, S., Mahurin, R.K., Jerabek, P.A., Silva, J.A., Tekell, J.L., Martin, C.C., Lancaster, J.L. & Fox, P.T. (1999) 'Reciprocal limbic-cortical function and negative mood: Converging PET findings in depression and normal sadness', *American Journal of Psychiatry*, **156** (5), 675–82.

Mesulam, M. (2002), 'The human frontal lobes: Transcending the default mode through contingent encoding', in *Principles of Frontal Lobe Function*, ed. D.T. Stuss and R.T. Knight (New York: Oxford University Press).

Newell, A. & Simon, H.A. (1972), *Human Problem Solving* (Englewood Cliffs, NJ: Prentice-Hall).

Nieuwenhuis, S., Ridderinkhof, K.R., Blom, J., Band, G.P.H. & Kok, A. (2001), 'Error-related brain potentials are differentially related to awareness of response errors: Evidence from an antisaccade task', *Psychophysiology*, **38**, pp. 752–60.

Oatley, K. & Johnson-Laird, P.N. (1987), 'Towards a cognitive theory of emotions', *Cognition and Emotion*, **1**, pp. 29–50.

Ochsner, K.N., Bunge, S.A., Gross, J.J. & Gabrieli, J.D.E. (2002), 'Rethinking feelings: An fMRI study of the cognitive regulation of emotion', *Journal of Cognitive Neuroscience*, **14**, pp. 1215–29.

Öhman, A., Flykt, A. & Lundqvist, D. (2000), 'Unconscious emotion: Evolutionary perspectives, psychophysiological data, and neurophysiological mechanisms', in *Cognitive Neuroscience of Emotion*, ed. R. Lane and L. Nadel (Oxford: Oxford University Press).

Panksepp, J. (1998), *Affective Neuroscience: The Foundations of Human and Animal Emotions* (New York: Oxford University Press).

Panksepp, J. (2005), 'Affective consciousness: Core emotional feelings in humans and animals', *Consciousness and Cognition*, **14**, pp. 30–80.

Paré, D., Collins, D. R. & Pelletier, J. G. (2002), 'Amygdala oscillations and the consolidation of emotional memories', *Trends in Cognitive Sciences*, **6**, pp. 306–14.

Parkinson, B. (2001), 'Putting appraisal in context', in *Appraisal Processes in Emotion: Theory, Methods, Research*, ed. K.R. Scherer, A. Schorr, and T. Johnstone (New York: Oxford University Press).

Phan, K.L., Taylor, S.P., Welsch, R.C., Ho S.-H., Britton, J.C., & Liberzon, I. (2004), 'Neural correlates of individual ratings of emotional salience: a trial-related fMRI study', *Neuroimage*, **21**, pp. 768–80.

Pizzagalli, D.A., Regard, M. & Lehmann, D. (1999), 'Rapid emotional face processing in the human right and left brain hemispheres: An ERP study', *NeuroReport*, **10**, pp. 2691–8

Reiman, E.M., Lane, R.D., Ahern, G.L. & Schwartz, G.E. (1997), 'Neuroanatomical correlates of externally and internally generated human emotion', *American Journal of Psychiatry*, **154**, pp. 918–25.

Renninger, K.A., Hidi, S. & Krapp, A. (1992), *The Role of Interest in Learning and Development* (Hillsdale, NJ: Erlbaum).

Rolls, E.T. (1999), *The Brain and Emotion* (Oxford: Oxford University Press).

Rolls, E.T. (2000), 'The orbitofrontal cortex and reward', *Cerebral Cortex*, 10, 284–94.

Scherer, K.R. (2000), 'Emotions as episodes of subsystem synchronization driven by nonlinear appraisal processes', in *Emotion, Development, and Self-organization: Dynamic Systems Approaches to Emotional Development*, ed. M.D. Lewis and I. Granic (New York: Cambridge University Press).

Scherer, K.R. (2001), 'Appraisal considered as a process of multilevel sequential checking', in *Appraisal Processes in Emotion: Theory, Methods, Research*, ed. K.R. Scherer, A. Schorr, and T. Johnstone (New York: Oxford University Press).

Schore, A.N. (1994), *Affect Regulation and the Origin of the Self: The Neurobiology of Emotional Development* (Hillsdale, NJ: Erlbaum).

Schnider, A., Valenza, N., Morand, S. & Michel, C.M. (2002), 'Early cortical distinction between memories that pertain to ongoing reality and memories that don't', *Cerebral Cortex*, **12**, pp. 54–61.

Skarda, C.A. & Freeman, W.J. (1987), 'How brains make chaos in order to make sense of the world', *Behavioral and Brain Sciences*, **10**, pp. 161–95.

Streit, M., Ioannides, A.A., Liu, L., Wölwer, W., Dammers, J., Gross, J., Gaebel, W., Müller-Gärtner, H.W. (1999), 'Neurophysiological correlates of the recognition of facial expressions of emotion as revealed by magnetoencephalography', *Cognitive Brain Research*, **7**, pp. 481–91.

Taylor, S.F., Phan, K.L., Decker, L.R. & Liberzon, I. (2003), 'Subjective rating of emotionally salient stimuli modulates neural activity', *Neuroimage*, **18**, pp. 650–9.

Thompson, E. & Varela, F.J. (2001), 'Radical embodiment: Neural dynamics and consciousness', *Trends in Cognitive Sciences*, **5**, pp. 418–25.

Tucker, D.M., Derryberry, D. & Luu, P. (2000), 'Anatomy and physiology of human emotion: Vertical integration of brainstem, limbic, and cortical systems', in *The Neuropsychology of Emotion*, ed. J.C. Borod (London: Oxford University Press).

Tucker, D.M., Luu, P., Desmond Jr., R.E., Hartry-Speiser, A., Davey, C. & Flaisch, T. (2003), 'Corticolimbic mechanisms in emotional decisions', *Emotion*, **3**, pp. 127–49.

van Veen, V., Cohen, J.D., Botvinick, M.M., Stenger, V.A. & Carter, C.S. (2001), 'Anterior cingulate cortex, conflict monitoring, and levels of processing', *Neuroimage*, **14**, pp. 1302–8.

von Stein, A. & Sarnthein, J. (2000), 'Different frequencies for different scales of cortical integration: From local gamma to long range alpha/theta synchronization', *International Journal of Psychophysiology,* **38**, pp. 301–13.

David Rudrauf and Antonio Damasio

A Conjecture Regarding the Biological Mechanism of Subjectivity and Feeling

In this article we present a conjecture regarding the biology of subjectivity and feeling, based on biophysical and phenomenological considerations. We propose that feeling, as a subjective phenomenon, would come to life as a process of resistance to variance hypothesized to occur during the unfolding of cognition and behaviours in the wakeful and emoting individual. After showing how the notion of affect, when considered from a biological standpoint, suggests an underlying process of resistance to variance, we discuss how vigilance, emotional arousal and attentional behaviours reflect a dynamics of controlled over-excitation related to cognitive integration and control. This can be described as a form of resistance to variance. We discuss how such a dynamics objectively creates an internal state of tension and affectedness in the system that could be associated with subjective states. Such a dynamics is shaped by the system's need to cope with its own inertia, to engage in intentional behaviours, attend, preserve coherence, grapple with divergent cognitive, emotional and motivational tendencies, and delayed auto-perturbations of the brain-body system. More generally, it is related to the need to respect the hierarchy of the various influences which affect its internal dynamics and organization.

1: Introduction

This article is part of the contemporary effort to solve the hard-problem and close the so-called explanatory gap in the study of consciousness, i.e. the effort to understand consciousness as a biophysical phenomenon. We present a conjecture regarding the biology of subjectivity and feeling[1]. This conjecture is based

Correspondence:
Email: *david_rudrauf@hotmail.com*

---

[1] This paper is a condensed version of a text to be published in Rudrauf & Damasio (2005).

Journal of Consciousness Studies, **12**, No. 8–10, 2005, pp. 236–62

on simple phenomenological intuitions and general biological and neurocognitive observations, which suggest the existence of a certain type of mechanisms at the core of the biology of subjectivity and feeling. We do not claim to account for every aspect of the problem with this theory. However, we think that it can provide an understanding of why and how we are sentient entities, i.e. why and how being the biological systems that we are makes us feeling subjects.

1. Why Feeling?

Given the difficulty of the problem and the epistemological obstacles faced by those who try to solve it, it seems reasonable to begin exploring the fundamental relationships of consciousness with the biophysical field in which we exist, by isolating something characteristic and 'simple' about it, something which captures the core experience of being. This should be accomplished before trying to account for the most complex and subtle meta-representational and symbolic aspects of consciousness. At the same time, the need for simplification must not lead to select phenomena of interest that lose critical properties.

Proposed explanations of consciousness are often attributed by neuroscientists and cognitive scientists to the extraordinary informational and representational ability of the brain, its capacity to discriminate, bind, and integrate specific, exteroceptive and/or interoceptive information through neural connectivity, mapping and interactions (Varela, 1995; Logothetis, 1998; Edelman, 1999; Zeki & Bartels, 1999; Tononi & Edelman, 2000; Dehaene & Naccache, 2001; Crick & Koch, 2003).

Although of importance, the type of neural computation and neurodynamical phenomena brought to the fore in these approaches is somewhat disembodied and selfless. Consciousness is indissociable from the pervasive class of phenomena that we refer to as a 'feeling subject'. Such an embodied sentient entity is the core of consciousness and is hardly explained by these approaches. It cannot be reduced to the simple notion of sensory integration and discrimination.

Some would perhaps immediately see in such a perspective the spectrum of unsolvable and ill-posed philosophical problems and would discard the notion of 'feeling subject' as an illusory and naïve byproduct of 'language', and thus irrelevant for science. We believe that would be an error. The notion of feeling subject is a recurrent idea that is virtually impossible to avoid while thinking about consciousness. Although it may appear vague, it refers to an intuitively basic phenomenon: if asked 'what is it that feels in your body?', most people would spontaneously answer 'me, as a subject'. Thus pragmatism and parsimony call for coping with this phenomenon precisely as one would with any other natural phenomenon. Somehow, trying to account for consciousness without reference to subjectivity and feeling is like trying to account for blood circulation without reference to heart contractions.

Subjectivity and feeling themselves appear indissociable. On the one hand, subjectivity exists, as a first person experience, only as an ongoing feeling. On the other, feeling does not seem conceivable without the notion of subjectivity: it explicitly requires considering the general problem of what makes a system capable of being a subject of sensory experiences, of sensory experiences of itself in particular. Consequently, at a certain level of approximation, accounting for feeling, subjectivity and core consciousness is the same thing (Damasio, 1999).

These phenomena are difficult to grasp and characterize, and yet are relatively limited from a biological standpoint. As suggested by neuropsychology, core consciousness is independent from autobiographical memory (Damasio, 1999). It does not necessarily involve explicit metarepresentational abilities. It is likely to be related to basic mechanisms of vigilance and attention, to be present before we can even speak (infants in all likelihood feel various sensations and emotions), and probably in other species (as suggested by the similarity of brain organization and behaviours, and by basic principles of evolutionary continuity).

2. Does It Feel Like Something to Be a Pattern in Space and Time?

Science describes phenomena as patterns in space and time, submitted to internal and external constraints, formulated as laws. As biological entities, we can potentially be entirely described as a set of complex, multiscale, spatial and temporal patterns, more or less deterministic. In keeping with the way science describes the world, solving the so-called hard-problem requires to figure out how subjectivity and feeling are, *per se*, patterns in space and time, an objective behaviour; which is the same thing as to understand them in a mechanical framework. If a solution to this problem exists, below the words 'me, as a feeling subject', there must be something concrete, some phenomenology based on the implementation of some type of biophysical mechanisms, some patterns in space and time, trackable in our objective being, which feel like feeling, so to speak. If by the end a difference remains between feeling and the corresponding biological phenomena it would have to be accounted for by a difference in point of view or referential. That is to say, such differences are the effect of seeing the same thing from different angles: being oneself the events observed or observing the events without being them. Two general practical and empirical principles can guide us in this research.

The first one is a principle of isomorphism. If one is really describing the same thing from two different points of views or referentials, the isolated biological phenomena must show a high degree of isomorphism with subjectivity and feeling, and conversely. Rigorously, at the limit of a full isomorphism the condition of isomorphism is a fully sufficient condition because it implies that the described phenomena are indistinguishable, i.e. identical in all respects. In other words, there would be no explanatory gap.

In practice, we won't achieve such a full isomorphism, but the research for maximizing isomorphism, through the progressive definition of mutual constraints between the different levels of observation, is still a satisfying heuristics which could reveal how they are related (Varela, 1996). A practical condition can be expressed using an optical metaphor: we look for a point of view on the biology of the system such that the feeling subject would be 'visible' through the isolated biological mechanisms, in spite of the deforming lens that the situation of external observation constitutes. Obviously, the isolated phenomena would also have to show an actual empirical relationship with subjectivity and feeling, as assessed by experimental science.

The goal is certainly not to 'reduce' the subjective domain to the objective domain, in the sense of the reduction of something complex and global to a simpler local substrate, such as the release of a hormone. Such a reductionism or elementarism would represent a mismatch between levels of organization, and thus would not satisfy the heuristics of strong isomorphism. The problem is to understand and model one 'complex' level of the phenomenology — the subjective phenomenology — in the framework of another 'complex' phenomenological level — the description of an embodied being undergoing multiscale biophysical transformations.

The second guiding principle is a principle of 'induction'. Based on evolutionary considerations, heuristic principles and empirical observations, it is reasonable to believe that the ability to feel is so central in the biology and behaviour of higher animals that the understanding of how subjectivity and feeling are implemented, and what they really are, should follow from a proper analysis of the biological and neurophysiologic characteristics of such animals. At the limit, a full knowledge of these characteristics should make these phenomena perfectly transparent. Because feeling implies the presence of subjectivity, specific occasions of feeling should contain all the information required to understand subjectivity as a biological mechanism. We also believe that general biological principles might contain relevant information about the biological roots of these phenomena and that the resulting explanatory model will connect subjectivity and feeling with general principles of chemistry and physics.

3. Working Definitions

In this section, we provide working definitions of certain abstract terms and concepts that are used in the article. These definitions are qualitative and generic, because the putative phenomena to which they are meant to refer are not yet well understood or circumscribed from a technical standpoint. However they will prove useful to deal with our problem.

Grappling: The condition or dynamical pattern of a physical system involved in overcoming the impediments that its own mechanics or embodiment generate relatively to the continuation of the behaviour it is engaged in, or the production of new behaviours. These impediments possess a certain form of inertia relative to the action or reaction of the system to its own perturbed state. Grappling is particularly intense at the level of neurocognitive behaviours, e.g. sensory integration, attention, decision-making, executive control and affect. Behaviourally, grappling may be reflected in slower execution of certain tasks, increased difficulty in executing those tasks, and increased arousal.

Inertia: A dynamical property associated with neurocognitive perturbations and compensations or neurocognitive processes in general. It is reflected by the energy and time taken by a neurocognitive system to control internal perturbations and direct behaviour. In our framework, inertia emerges at the level of large-scale systems, i.e. the brain and the organism as an autonomous system, including multiple parallel convergent-divergent multistep connections. This architecture allows mass effects of global waves of distributed changes that could not be controlled by simple fast local mechanisms. As such these changes possess an inertia.

Variance: Local or large-scale changes in the internal state of the system propagating through connected domains within the system's functional architecture. Variance influences the behaviour as well as the biomechanical and cognitive dynamical structure of the system. This influence depends on the internal state of the system. It can be modulated by the brain and can lead to phenomena of resonance due to the recursive organization of the system. It can also represent a form of inertia in relation to the system's intentional endeavour.

Perturbations: Internal instance of variance affecting endogenous processes through functional connectivity.

Divergence: Changes in the state and allocation of resources of a system related to a loss of control over perturbations, which disorganize the behaviour of the system in a way that can lead to potentially harmful phenomena.

Over-excitation or overflow: Neurophysiological perturbations propagating along functional pathways that jeopardize the capabilities of adaptation and compensation of the system. The development of seizures can be taken as a pathological and dramatic example of overflow.

Resistance: The ensemble of intensive, compensatory neurophysiological and neurocognitive processes which operate in vigilance, attention, motivation, decision-making, affect and intentional behaviours. These processes allow a neurocognitive system to grapple with the inertia of its own variance (as well as relative invariance) during the process of cognition, by maintaining impeding perturbations under adaptive limits. It enables a steady state of conflict shaping the instantaneous potential of influence of incoming perturbations. Resistance to variance allows for a specific focus on functional perturbations, and integration of these perturbations as information by other functions coupled to the process.

Tension: The internal neurocognitive state associated with an occasion of resistance to variance, in which various neurodynamical and biomechanical forces act in opposite direction in order to compensate for a state of disequilibrium. It can also be referred to as a state of systemic internal pressure. Tension accompanies grappling, and is characterized by a state of *controlled over-excitation*. This is required for vigilance, reactivity and sensitivity, and can place the system in a situation close to loss of control.

4. Hypothesis

Our hypothesis is that the core of subjectivity and feeling is a dynamics of resistance to variance. To be a 'feeling subject' consists in a behaviour of monitoring and control characterized by a process of resistance to variance through which an embodied neurocognitive system grapples with the inertia of the functional perturbations that its brain and body-proper continuously and inevitably undergo during the process of cognition and emotion. The phenomenology of the process of resistance to variance identifies with basic subjective states. It is shaped by the system's need to engage in intentional behaviours, attend, preserve sensorimotor coherence, control affective upheaval, and decide. It is related to the need to respect the hierarchy of the various influences which affect its internal dynamics and organization, in the context of a real biological system subjected to inertia. The central attention-related profile of this process delineates the dynamic locus of an internal state of affectedness. This state is underlined by conflicting forces of pressure and tension, operating through mechanisms of controlled over-excitation, expressed in vigilance and arousal.

The involvement of this dynamics in subjectivity and feeling can be deduced from general phenomenological, biological and neurocognitive considerations. This general dynamics and its subjective counterpart can be understood in the framework of monitoring and control, which has long been hypothesized to lie at the core of the functionality of consciousness. As we shall see, using it as a principle of organization, the notion of resistance to variance might illuminate a great deal of classical findings in neurophysiology and cognitive neuroscience of emotion, attention and consciousness; and provide a unifying framework to predict and understand the involvement of different anatomic-functional entities in subjectivity and feeling.

2: From the Notion of Affect to the Mechanics of Subjectivity

One way to introduce this theory is to start from the folk psychology notion of 'affect', from which many basic statements about the biology of feeling and subjectivity can be derived (Panksepp, 2004).

All felt states have a common feature: they involve affections by some internal change (Russell & Barrett, 1999). For instance, a core feeling of joy, sorrow or fear invades the mental space, with diffuse corporeal impressions of muscular tension, tingling in the skin, variation in the amplitude of respiration or the working of the heart. This feeling transiently dominates the mental foreground, more or less softly, pleasantly or unpleasantly as the case may be, capturing our mental time, through variations of vigilance and attentiveness. But, whatever the specific orchestration of the change shaping this state of affectedness is, we are affected. Understanding what affectedness means and implies for the brain and organism is crucial in understanding feeling and subjectivity.

At a very basic and general level, the notion of affect suggests that, objectively, the system is perturbed, 'affected' by part of its own internal transformations, i.e. it undergoes its own variance. We know that during emotions and feeling multiple levels of neurophysiologic and psychophysiological perturbations are involved in creating an emotional upheaval, which can in turn affect the system as a whole through functional connectivity.

But this source of perturbing variance is only one side of what the notion of affect really encompasses, perhaps the most easy to grasp. The other side of the notion concerns the question of what is precisely affected in the system by such a variance. As we already suggested, anybody would spontaneously answer: 'me, as a subject'.

Rather than trying to characterize from introspection this phenomenon so difficult to grasp and isolate, the very statement of the problem of 'what is affected in the system' somehow seems to indicate the direction of its solution: a way to search for the biological embodiment of the 'feeling subject' (i.e. to explain what the 'feeling subject' is as a biological entity) is to look for what, objectively, is affected in the system during emotion and feeling. This is in itself a full program of research. It requires understanding and isolating the levels of organization, the types of mechanisms, and the anatomo-functional substrate which constitute the affected 'interface' in the process. As a first step, general statements about the nature of this 'interface' can be reasonably derived using basic rationale.

As revealed by any intense emotion, a central aspect of the phenomenology of being affected is that this is more or less explicitly overwhelming for the subject. We are overwhelmed by affective phenomena, and some aspects of our intellectual faculties no longer function normally. This condition is often accompanied by a psychological and behavioural loss of control. The now dominant sensations impede our efforts to concentrate on other objects, even if we try to do so; a significant effort must be made in order to suppress these perturbing sensations. It is interesting to note that we usually feel these perturbations precisely during our effort to resist them until suppression is achieved. As everyone has experienced in situations of extreme stress or anxiety, intense pain or even pleasure, it may happen that the more we try to escape and resist the invasion of sensations, the more they become intense. Interestingly, in the case of emotions, the level at which our ability to realize incompatible cognitive tasks is overridden is strongly related to the intensity of the emotion. Thus it can be said that affects generally exert a force of pressure on cognition and behaviour, modify them and require adaptation in order to endeavour in current routines and tasks, shift to other states, or simply face them. This pressure or tension itself is a central component of what we feel (Thayer, 1989; 1996; Ben-Ze'ev, 2000). Such a setting suggests that the state of affectedness in the system is grounded in a conflictive organization: a disequilibrium is faced, which possesses a form of force of inertia, as indicated by how this costly confrontation monopolizes our resources and energy.

Basic principles regarding the general properties of biological systems as dynamical systems might help us to precise the nature of this conflictive organization. Biological systems are organizationally closed physical systems (Varela, 1979) continuously endeavouring to maintain their integrity and their identity. Such a dynamics takes place in an unstable equilibrium, which involves physiological stresses threatening the normal operation and eventually the survival of the system. The closure of the organism ensures its autonomy, but at the same time places the organism at the frequent risk of uncontrollable 'resonance', because of the interdependence of its constituents. At each instant, every part of the organism possesses a 'potential of influence' on every other part, defining a field of autoperturbations. In higher organisms, these autoperturbations are related to various biomechanical constraints of the brain-body system, slow and fast physiological adjustments, affective changes often related to memory, conflictive motivational tendencies, fluctuation of vigilance, instability of attention, and are sustained by the activity of the system itself. They are propagated at different speeds in the recursive structure of the organism, introducing delays in the autoperturbing process and making biological systems, including human beings, *recursive, delayed, auto-perturbing systems*. These delays increase the complexity, unpredictability and non linearity of the response of the system to its own activity.

Because of their implementation in real biological systems, these phenomena naturally possess inertia. They constitute sources of internal impediments that the organism has to *grapple* with in the unfolding of its behaviour as an intentional machine.

In this framework, living systems are continuously reacting to changes that occur within their structure and to the constraints that such a structure imposes to their behaviour. They do so through mechanisms of compensation and control which operate at several levels of their organization, e.g., metabolic regulation, immune responses, reflexes, humoral and neural signaling acting on endocrine glands as well as smooth and striated muscles, drives and motivation, pain and pleasure behaviours, attention, intentionality and cognition. In general, the reactions, their magnitude, rate and direction, are coupled to the dynamics of perturbation itself, with variable delays. Because this conflictive dynamics is ongoing and because a viable control of perturbations requires anticipatory strategies, the compensatory reactions often begin, at least in part, before the actual perturbations do.

Such a setting creates the condition of a dynamics of confrontation of the system with itself. Because of the inertia of the process, for the system it is as 'walking against the wind internally', which is to say, walking against itself.

Based on these considerations, it is thus likely that the affected interface that we are trying to characterize is not something static, but rather something active in the system. It is likely to be continuously built and rebuilt, as a steady-state regime, far from equilibrium, which reacts to the incoming or ongoing variance. We may think about it as a dynamical structure which becomes affected through the very reactions to what perturbs it. The idea of the involvement of a dynamical structure is supported by the fact that consciousness and subjectivity depend on specific states of oscillations in the brain. Consciousness and subjectivity can be suspended anytime, as a result of injury, anoxia, intoxication and dreamless sleep. Within the limits of certain conditions of the organism's integrity, they can also be restarted very quickly, for instance by injecting atropine in response to a loss of consciousness due to a vasovagal syncope, or spontaneously every morning when we wake up from dreamless sleep.

The conflictive pattern implied by the notion of affect and the overwhelming subjective pressure exerted in states of affectedness suggest that the type of reaction that the system opposes to its own variance might be a form of resistance. Thus what we would have to consider is a system with a general dynamical organization in which something resists, attempts to control its own transformations, in an eventually very complex patterned way. Consequently, as a first approximation, an essential aspect of the biology of subjectivity could be sought in the form of a dynamical regime of resistance to variance.

The notions of biological resistance and conflict are attractive in a discussion of feeling and subjectivity because it can be said that, at any given moment or in any occasion of being, the living organism who feels is actually defined in a setting of conflict. A full specification and detailed description of an individual subject would require the description of the ongoing conflict between a large range of automated and intended actions of the organism, and the automated and intended reactions with which the organism resists those same actions. Just as it is certainly the case that a living organism is shaped and kept alive as a result of such ongoing action and reactions, it is conceivable that a subject or self is shaped and maintained only as a result of ongoing actions and reactions. Without the dynamics that lead to conflict between a level of control and a level of perturbation, the body could not be animated. And there is evidence suggesting that without proper operation and control of such basic dynamics the individual organism cannot survive autonomously and the self and consciousness dissolve. Coma, vegetative states, and akinetic mutism are extreme illustrations of the consequences on subjectivity and consciousness of the breakdown in the integral conflictive dynamics of action and reaction which makes a wakeful, vigilant, attentive, and emoting individual. Maintaining life implies a struggle and cognition is yet another set of mechanisms for that struggle.

It must be noted that the biomechanical and neurocognitive constraints that are imposed on the system by its own structure can themselves be seen as auto-perturbations in relation to the system's current endeavour. Although it is possible to make a distinction, important from a phenomenological point of view, between resistance to variance (inertial auto-perturbations) and resistance to relative invariance (the inertia of the biomechanical constraints), these two situations can be considered altogether in the general framework of resistance to variance.

3: The Neurocognitive Foundations of the Hypothesis

The notion of resistance to variance has the advantage of being objective enough to be amenable to rigorous theoretical reflections and eventually mathematization and modelling. However the notion is generic, and the functional levels of organization at which such a putative biological mechanism is relevant for feeling need to be specified. In order to be explanatory of the phenomena of subjectivity and feeling, this mechanism should be shown to operate at the core of basic cognitive phenomena known to be central in feeling and consciousness, such as vigilance, arousal and attention.

1. Vigilance and Arousal as a Dynamics of Resistance to Variance

Vigilance and arousal are necessary and central phenomena in the process of feeling, and in consciousness in general. They may be understood or reinterpreted in the framework of a central process of preparation to resist or of actual resistance to variance. Vigilance, both from a behavioural and neurophysiologic standpoint, is literally an ongoing state of increased reactivity, and arousal reflects a modulation of this state. They reflect an overall process of sensorimotor integration and control, based on the interplay between massive sensory processing, including notably bodily monitoring (which can be seen as related to an autoperturbing process), and adaptive attentional and executive mechanisms of control maintaining focus and coherence. They involve simultaneously an increase in central excitability, an increase in peripheral tone, and a coupled increase of inhibitory mechanisms of control of potential endogenous overflow. This setting implements a central state of controlled (over-)excitation. Both from an objective and a subjective point of view, such a setting creates a characteristic state of tension.

The latent conflictive nature of the dynamical organization reflected by vigilance and arousal, and the intimate relationships between states of controlled over-excitation and feeling, are revealed in paroxystic states like anxiety and obsessive compulsive disorders. In these states, dramatically increased arousal is associated with an obvious failure of executive processes, normally operating in the background, to control over-excitation. The individual tries to cope with its overwhelming emotional state by developing compensatory cognitive and behavioural strategies: a state of tension and struggle is visible, and what the subject feels is precisely what he is fighting against, his physiological stress or compulsions, often all the more as he or she tries to resist them. In normal conditions, there is a pronounced correlation between cortical activation, psychophysiological arousal (i.e. visceral tone) and subjective arousal, i.e., the self-reported intensity of the subjective experience during the feeling of pleasant or unpleasant emotions (Lang et al., 1993).

2. Attention and Controlled Over-Excitation

This dynamics is not only operating at the level of the general central state of reactivity. It can also be seen to operate, both from a cognitive and neurophysiologic point of views, at highly integrated cognitive levels, including the organization of the attentional focus.

At a basic level, attention can be seen as implementing an integrated dynamics of resistance to variance as it constitutes a 'traffic bottleneck' in the flow of information. It has to do with resisting and controlling perturbations, such as resisting distractors forcing their access to consciousness in order to specify the information being processed, or the fading of the object to be maintained in focus. Resisting fading or maintaining a mental representation is generally effortful. It is interesting to note that distractors are indeed felt when explicitly resisted: by definition they become distractors as they catch the focus of attention while they compete with the targets of attention.

The idea that attention has to do with resistance to variance does not imply that only resisted distractors would be perceived. The target of the attentional focus is in itself a source of variance to be maintained under control.

Thus a remarkable feature of the neural bases of attention vis-à-vis the general organization of resistance to variance in the system is that attention, in correlation with arousal and wakefulness, reflects the implementation of a basic biophysical conflictive setting of controlled over-excitation, creating an unavoidable situation of tension. On the one hand, when attention is increased, the potential of influence of incoming perturbations of interest is enhanced. This is directly visible in the enhancement of related brain signals. On the other, this situation of increased excitation requires precise strategies of control in order to maintain the overflow in adaptive limits, and reduce the risk of divergence.

This is rather evident in a general phenomenon like the orientation reaction. The orientation reaction is a typical attentional behaviour which involves an obvious tension between enhanced arousal, expressed in electroencephalographic changes and in the modulation of musculo-skeletal and visceral tone, and inhibitory mechanisms attempting to control initiation of explicit motor behaviours. The control is often expressed in an explicit behavioural freezing, in the framework of a process of decision making.

More generally, attentional behaviours involve highly integrated neurodynamical processes with the ability to establish spontaneously, dynamically, and plastically, specific functional relations or couplings between the brain's neurocognitive resources and various structures or 'objects' which become the focus of processing. These couplings must be constantly readjusted because of perturbations, or disengaged when they are no longer needed.

3. Intentionality and Resistance

The dynamics of motivation, in interaction with memory, controls the orientation of attention, shapes goal directed behaviours and intentional cognitive routines. As such it is at the centre of the intentional dimension of subjectivity. Like vigilance, arousal and attention, the dynamics of motivation also implies the organization of a process of resistance to variance (or invariance). Such a process is implied because, as already noted, endeavouring in selected cognitive routines and planned behaviours, or building processes of decision making, oblige real biological systems to cope with the inertia of the variance (or invariance) imposed to them by their own dynamical structure. This variance has to be resisted in order to achieve these tasks. Decision making for instance is based on an integration of large amount of information, which requires suspension of immediate possible responses. It is intriguing to think that cognition itself can have an inertia, and this might have been overlooked. Such a resistance against inertia in the framework of cognition is reflected for instance in concentration and in effortful cognition, the subjective intensity of which is all the more important as the effort is strong.

Interestingly, the organization of the intentional dimension participating in the creation of a given subjective state can be assumed to be outside the scope of current subjective experience, i.e., beyond consciousness. It can be assumed to be in the general neurocognitive and motivational infrastructure of the system, and so needs not per se to be accounted for by the theory. This is important because it makes the theory not circular, so that we are not facing anything like a homunculus problem: neither resistance nor variance requires presupposition of subjectivity. It is the dynamical structure that their interplay generates, the affected interface, which putatively corresponds to the core of subjectivity.

This is not incompatible with the fact that, as a dynamical level of integration of information coupled with sensory processing and attention (and thus, *de facto*, with memory encoding and retrieval), this affected interface is cognitive. It can also be seen as exerting a causal role in respect to the future behaviour of the system, notably by the selections it contributes to operate. As a level of resistance to immediate chains of reflex behaviours, this interface is a fundamental level of organization of high-order decision making, allowing integration and learning. The complex sequencing of these behaviours of intentional coupling reflects the presence of an adaptive functional hierarchy within the system, dealing with the management of its priorities. The interaction between these levels of organization of the dynamics of resistance to variance imbues the system with agency and leads it to assume a position in confrontation with the world and with itself.

4. Consciousness, Monitoring and Control

At a very general level, this dynamics of resistance to variance can be assimilated to a homeostatic-like system of compensation that enables the system to adaptively grapple with its own disequilibrium at the very level of cognition. The dynamics of resistance to variance can be seen as related to a general function of self-monitoring and control. This functional dimension can be emphasized as a supplementary indirect argument in favour of its link with consciousness.

From a functional, cognitive and evolutionary perspective, subjectivity, feelings and consciousness are only intelligible in connection with a framework of monitoring and control. The existence of a monitoring and control function is at the heart of cognition as an integrative phenomenon. Such a function grew in complexity and integration in the course of evolution, and came to reduce the impact of fast automatic reflexes on the appraisal and execution of action, favouring slower, controlled, multifaceted cognitive processes. Also, there is certainly no subjective experience without a minimal focus of attention, which is in itself a form of monitoring and control, and can be related to resistance to variance. Moreover, monitoring and controlling systemic internal variance, including variance from the body proper, imply the existence of a process of somatosensing, which is known to be essential in feeling, and conversely.

Consciousness has been associated with the concepts of monitoring and control for a long time. But these concepts, taken as examples of 'high-level' cognitive functions, have typically been construed in a very abstract and functionalist way, and the emphasis has been on disambiguation, error correction, complex decision making, and the optimization of the system's predictions about the behaviour of objects in its environment (see Mayr, 2004). This approach provides little insight about how the operation of such a function could involve subjective experience *per se*.

4: Subjectivity and Feelings: Elements of Neuroanatomy and Neurodynamics

1. The Brain in the Organization of Resistance

The brain is central in the process. First of all, it is interesting to remark that, at every level, in particular at the level of its highest functions, the brain naturally operates on the basis of a process of resistance to variance.

From a general biophysical standpoint, the brain exhibits an unstable oscillatory dynamics, involving a competition between excitatory signals and active inhibitory mechanisms, which results from its local and large-scale organization. From a functional standpoint, the recurrent organization of the brain, as well as that of the organism in general, requires inhibitory mechanisms able to adaptively impede the risk of phenomena of resonance that could lead to destructive divergence. In certain pathological circumstances, in which the mechanisms of control fail, local activations can influence the rest of the system in a way that leads the brain into a major synchronization of its electrical activity — the sort of electrical storm of which seizures are a dramatic illustration.

Information processing by the brain does not escape the necessity of organizing control of overflow. There is a strong relationship between information processing and the propagation of energy during cognitive processes. When the brain engages an informational process, energy flows through connected networks and the activity of specific local networks generally increases, enhancing their potential of influence on the rest of the system. Such an increase of energy is reflected in the increase of the magnitude of certain electrophysiological signals, in the rate of spike volleys, in global changes in cortical arousal, as well as in metabolic adjustments. This typically shows up in functional brain imaging studies of subjects performing cognitive tasks. Overall, these indicate that high-level conscious processes are associated with more energy consumption than automated low-level ones. The relationship between information flow and energy flow reinforces the notion that the organism in general and the brain in particular must deal with the intrinsic risk of 'overflow' and control auto-perturbations during sensory and cognitive processing. This is all the more true for organisms with complex, highly connected and recurrent nervous systems required for complex cognition.

No less importantly, the variance, resistance and conflict inherent in the neural processes that subserve cognition are played out continuously in the body-proper, through the modulation of the autonomic tonus notably. Auto-perturbations within the neural space are accompanied by auto-perturbations in the theatre of the body which, in turn, may entail further auto-perturbations in neural space.

One of the remarkable properties of the brain, which is certainly essential in the richness of the phenomenology of subjectivity, is its ability to control and create the conditions of its own perturbation. For instance, no perturbation from the body can affect the brain unless the sensory interfaces are 'open' to receive the appropriate signals. Sensory interfaces (or brain maps), involving excitatory-inhibitory mechanisms under the control of higher-order structures, work to channel, format, and modulate the gain of incoming signals. This allows an extraordinarily rich and varied orchestration of the process of auto-perturbation and resistance.

2. Critical Neuroanatomical Nodes

The functional nodes which are critically involved in creating an integrated front of resistance to variance cannot be reduced to a single part of the brain or even to a collection of brain regions. In normal conditions, part of the conflict occurs also in the theatre of the body-proper, in musculo-skeletal striated and visceral smooth muscles, and in the endocrine system. However, predictions can be made based on this theory, concerning the involvement of specific critical brain structures in subjectivity and feeling.

Critical nodes regarding the process of auto-perturbation and variance monitoring include somatosensing regions in the brainstem (e.g. the nucleus tractus solitarius and the parabrachial nucleus), the hypothalamus, the posterior cingulate and retrosplenial cortices, and the somatosensory cortices (the insula, SII, SI, Brodmann area 5), as well as arousing-activating systems, including nuclei of the reticular formation which modulate the system's excitability. The structures essential for the control and modulation of perturbations include, at the lower levels, the periaqueductal gray, the reticular nuclei, parts of the thalamus (e.g. anterior and intralaminar nuclei), and the hypothalamus; at a higher level, these structures involve the frontal cortices, and in particular the anterior cingulate cortex (ACC)., The basal ganglia and amygdala are important as motivational and attentional structures.

3. Elements of Validation and Discussion

Many of these structures are known to be essential for emotion, feeling and consciousness. The structures that we see as involved in somatosensory related variance, in arousal activation, and in the control of resistance, are highly interconnected and interactive, showing clear increased activation during feeling states (Mesulam & Mufson, 1982b; Mesulam & Mufson, 1982a; Mufson & Mesulam, 1982; Friedman et al., 1986; Vogt & Pandya, 1987; Jones et al., 1991;

Talbot *et al.*, 1991; Coghill *et al.*, 1994; Rainville *et al.*, 1997; Critchley *et al.*, 2002). They are also activated during conflict between external information and internal states (Critchley *et al.*, 2002), exercise and mental stress (Critchley *et al.*, 2000). It is apparent that a number of 'somatosensing' structures in the brainstem, hypothalamus, cingulate cortex and somatosensory cortex, including the insula, are involved in feeling a wide range of emotions. These same structures are prominently engaged during feelings of pain, heat, cold, narcotic highs and narcotic withdrawals, as well as the consumption of pleasurable foods or the hearing of thrilling pieces of music (see Craig, 2002; Damasio, 2003).

In the hierarchy of this system, the anterior cingulate cortex (ACC) occupies a central place and its functions are particularly relevant for our proposal. The ACC is known to play an essential role in attentional, motivational and emotional control (see Bush *et al.*, 2000). It is also crucial for tasks involving mental effort (in effortful tasks there is a correlation between ACC activation and the difficulty of the task) and appears to be a key structure for conflict monitoring and awareness (see Mayr, 2004). In neurological patients, lesions of the ACC cause apathy, inattention, dysregulation of autonomic functions, emotional instability, and impairment of the sense of self (see Damasio, 1994; Damasio, 1999). Functional brain imaging and lesions studies clearly suggest its involvement in feeling (Foltz & White, 1962; Hurt & Ballantine, 1974; Lane *et al.*, 1997; Reiman *et al.*, 1997; Lane *et al.*, 1998; Stoleru *et al.*, 1999; Redoute *et al.*, 2000; Sawamoto *et al.*, 2000; Rolls *et al.*, 2003). It appears to be an essential structure in the interaction between emotion and attention (Mesulam, 1981; Mayberg, 1997; Yamasaki *et al.*, 2002; Fichtenholtz *et al.*, 2004; Phan *et al.*, 2004). Along with the ventromedial prefrontal cortex, it appears to serve as a top-down modulator of both intense emotional responses and autonomic arousal during effortful cognitive and motor behaviour (Critchley *et al.*, 2003; Phan *et al.*, 2004). It appears strongly involved in voluntary repression of emotions in fMRI (Beauregard *et al.*, 2001).

Our framework might provide some clues as to why the ACC appears as a fundamental structure for, on the one hand, feeling, attention, and awareness and, on the other, effortful monitoring and control of conflicts. Beyond the empirical findings, the usual explanation for its role in both conflict monitoring and awareness is of a somehow abstract functionalist type (Dehaene *et al.*, 2003). In this approach, consciousness is considered through its putative information processing related function: when simple automatic decisions cannot be made in the framework of a complex world with potentially conflictive information, more controlled operations must be brought into play in order to perform adequate decisions. Such a requirement justifies the emergence of consciousness in regard to evolution. Consciousness is then hypothesized as the cognitive instance specialized in solving such informational conflicts, when the ability of more automatic systems to cope with a given situation is overcome. In order to support this idea, it is important to demonstrate that executive conflict resolution requires awareness and that there are brain structures responding only when coping with executive conflict implies some degree of awareness. It has indeed been recently supported that consciousness of conflict is a necessary boundary condition for the ACC-related control network to come into play, and that intact control in response to conscious conflict requires an intact ACC-prefrontal network (Dehaene *et al.*, 2003).

We tend to agree with this functional view, compatible with our framework although adopting a completely different standpoint. However, in addition to providing indirect functional criteria to define consciousness based on information processing rationale, our framework also provides a way to approach the biophysics of consciousness in a more concrete and causal manner, potentially accounting for phenomenological aspects of subjective experience. Our neuro-anatomical hypotheses are directly derived from phenomenological rationale: if being a feeling subject is a steady-state of conflict between sources of variance and motivational resistance operating at the level of our attentional behaviours, structures involved in conflict monitoring and control should participate in such a dynamics. This might explain why the ACC is involved in awareness at a level of subjective experience.

4. Further Neurodynamical Considerations

Further neurodynamical considerations can be brought to the fore. Let us consider the case of dreamless sleep which is interesting because it exhibits reduced sensory processing and reduced reactivity to perturbation. In dreamless sleep, basic low-level vegetative regulatory processes seem to operate in a way which involves homeostatic responses. The latter might perhaps implement a form of resistance to variance, but not at a level relevant for the class of phenomena which interest us. From a neurophysiological standpoint, as evidenced by classical EEG observations, the central nervous system exhibits general synchronization between local oscillations of low frequency and high amplitude. It is interesting to note that this is also the type of dynamical regime that is generally observed in absence epilepsy, in which seizures are associated with transient loss of consciousness. These dynamical regimes seem to favour low reactivity to changes, both in term of response speed (low frequency of oscillations) and signal-to-noise-ratio (high amplitude of the synchronous background). In this condition, the potential sources of perturbation are not as potent as in other electrophysiological conditions. They are less likely to provoke large-scale cascades of responses and phase transitions in the central nervous system. On the contrary, the latter operate at high rate and with high sensitivity during vigilance. Moreover, in the states of synchronization observed in dreamless sleep and absence, poor internal differentiation of activity occurs. This absence of differentiation is incompatible with the type of internal dynamical conflicts we consider as essential for core consciousness. Activity at every point in the brain can be predicted from any other point: there is no information to acquire and adaptation to produce as a result of unpredictable mutual perturbations or divergence of the dynamics to a different phase. The potential external perturbations are immediately damped, so that the type of inertial neurocognitive changes and adaptation that we bring to the fore in our theory cannot occur.

Now, it is interesting to consider the behavioural and electrophysiological phenomena associated with dreamless sleep as well as absence epilepsy as instances of what the brain basis of consciousness is not likely to be. This suggests, at a very general level, the types of changes in the state of the central nervous system which might be expected to trigger or enable the appearance of conscious feelings. These changes should be compatible with reactivity of the system, intensive processing, and differentiation of internal activities. Thus it is plausible to expect at baseline: (1) low amplitude, endogenous local responses, enhancing the signal-to-noise ratio for incoming perturbations; (2) high frequency oscillatory behaviours, increasing the speed of processing and possible rate of reactivity of the system to perturbations; and (3) relative asynchrony at the large-scale, making differentiated and conflictive dynamics in the system possible, although transient large-scale synchrony can also appear reflecting synergetic coordination between distant systems (Tononi & Edelman, 2000). These dynamical features are typically what is observed during REM sleep and wakefulness.

Based on these simple considerations, the following neural features should be expected to be important in the generation of subjectivity and feeling in the system. (1) The type of distributed interactions and oscillatory behaviours described above, important for the implementation of a dynamics of resistance to variance connected to subjectivity in the central nervous system. (2) An underlying architecture including massive, recursive, multistep, multi-scale, convergent-divergent parallel interconnections between local units. Such architecture would favour mass effects necessary for the emergence of inertia in the conflict; emergence of inertia which is at the core of our explanatory framework. Indeed, from a dynamical system standpoint, in the context of the brain and body, mass effects of global waves of distributed changes propagating in the functional architecture of the system that cannot be controlled immediately by simple local mechanisms, can be understood as a form of inertia. (1) and (2) are precisely the type of dynamics and functional architecture associated with the reticulo-thalamo-cortical system. This system, thus must provide an essential level of organization of subjectivity and feeling.

5: A Principle of Interaction?

We have tried to characterize in some detail the phenomenological, functional, and neurocognitive levels at which a dynamics of resistance to variance could be seen as generating basic subjectivity and feeling. Hypotheses regarding general dynamical and energetic properties can also be formulated based on our framework.

Feeling is hypothesized to reflect the level of internal conflict between inertial sensorimotor perturbations and resisting strategies of control. This suggests that the state of tension which defines the intensity of feeling might be governed by a principle of interaction between the level of resistance and the intensity of variance (the strength of the perturbations). To a first approximation, it might be that feeling intensity or tension V could be a simple function of the resistance R and the perturbation influx I, such as $V = RI$. Such a formula, which amusingly reminds us of a famous law of electricity, must only be seen as a simple and quite limited heuristic tool that can potentially help us to explore the phenomena that we try to understand.

At first glance this relation may appear paradoxical. If one considers that resistance certainly involves the recruitment of inhibitory processes, and/or the recruitment of behaviours opposing perturbations in the system, increased resistance should result in the reduction of I. This might lead to the prediction that reducing or cancelling the intensity of the perturbations by increasing the resistance, would increase the intensity of feeling, which is counterintuitive. But it must be noted that, according to the suggested relation, feeling only occurs when neither of the two terms R and I are null. Feeling occurs during the operation of compensation, when no complete suppression or cancellation has been achieved. Moreover, in itself, the relation $V = RI$ does not say anything about the functional relationships between R and I, which could involve, in certain circumstances, feedback loops that create the conditions for 'explosive' resonance, or the kind of controlled over-excitation we referred to several times in this article. It does not say anything either regarding the time constants governing the interactions between R and I, which must be thought in the framework of an inertial system with limited internal power, and therefore can be rather long. Moreover, in a cognitive perspective the perturbations are information, so that, from an adaptive standpoint, the system should not 'wish' to neutralize them completely. On the contrary, the system should simply maintain the perturbations under control; this is the steady-state that we see as characteristic of vigilance. Accordingly, most of the time what is achieved during a cognitive processes is a steady state of controlled over-excitation, such that V is not 0, but stays within reasonable and adaptive limits (these limits are compatible, for instance, with recognition or learning processes). Locally, the variations of the levels of resistance and variance putatively involved in the modulation of arousal — as in an emotional response — would modulate V. According to our hypotheses, the interval during which such a dynamical tension V occurs is the interval during which one becomes explicitly a feeling subject. If we interpret the tension V as directly related to a term of energy, this predicts that the intensity of feeling is directly proportional to the increase of expenditure of energy in the system, related to such a conflictive dynamics between R and I. At a first approximation, this relationship seems to be true: there is a linear relationship between subjective arousal (feeling intensity) and the magnitude of related evoked potentials in EEG (Bradley & Lang, 2000). Many of the functional brain imaging studies mentioned in the previous section demonstrated linear relationships between the intensity of emotional experience and the levels of activation in the region of interest.

6: Discussion

1. Presence of the Pattern in Basic Emotions

In order to support the phenomenological plausibility of our hypothesis, it is important to determine whether a conflict between variance and resistance can be found among the most basic emotions and feelings. Such a dynamics is rather easily noticeable at the root of unpleasant emotional feelings like fear, disgust, and anger. These emotional behaviours are characterized from a subjective point of view by an intense conflict between the urge to enact certain behaviours (flying, vomiting, or fighting), the various visceral sensations which accompany the emotional upheaval, and the inhibition of these actual behaviours. Action tendency has for a long time been considered as an important content of emotional feelings (Arnold, 1960). Feelings also include highly conflictive cognitive and attentional patterns, generally associated with pain or pleasure, and the anticipation of distress or relief.

In sadness it also appears to us that there is a dimension of resistance to overwhelming perturbations related to body sensations. We invite the reader to consider that the moments of sadness may be more intense when the tendency to cry is resisted than when crying itself is enacted. Very intense moments of distress also occur when anguish is faced frontally. This involves the attempt to exert a certain cognitive control on a growing sensory perturbation, and leads to a strong feeling of tension.

For pleasant emotions the generative relation between resistance to variance and feeling might at first appear less obvious, although we believe it also holds. A paradigmatic example is sexual pleasure, where a most intense moment of feeling coincides with the greatest conflict between overwhelming sensory influx and whole body tension. Feelings of joy also incorporate intensified bodily sensations which invade the scope of our attention and incorporate facial expressions which transform our facial mask and accordingly its sensory representation. Although joy often presents itself as a decrease of certain types of unpleasant tension, still it causes tensions which capture our attentional resources and involve bodily perturbations. It too possesses an aspect of confrontation between internal changes and integrated monitoring as well as control strategies. The dimension of resistance to its overwhelming power becomes more explicit as joy morphs into ecstasy.

A careful examination of weak and harmonious feelings also suggests that a dimension of conflictive dynamics between variance and resistance is at least implicitly present. The sensation of well-being that can occur at rest in a quiet environment incorporates pleasant bodily sensations whose perturbing power is small. Their perturbing power is easily controlled and mastered, and this possibly accounts for part of their pleasantness. The point remains, however, that those 'sensations' are felt when some attention is paid to them — that is to say, when a certain degree of monitoring, however slight, is exerted on them. Again, such monitoring involves arousal and control and, based on our neurodynamical rationale, should imply an increase of resistance to variance.

Considering these facts, and as a prediction of our theory, we suggest the possibility that we *begin* to feel when physiological changes, like muscular tension, and their sensory impact *begin* to be resisted as they reach a certain threshold.

2. Size Matters

As it should be clear, we are not suggesting that the generic and abstract scheme of resistance to variance alone is sufficient to generate subjectivity and feeling. In our view it becomes sufficient when certain structural and dynamical parameters are otherwise implemented. For instance, as we have suggested, the relationships between subjectivity and a dynamics of resistance to variance emerges through the implementation of such a dynamics at the level of specific neurocognitive mechanisms, e.g. vigilance, arousal, emotion, attention and intentionality.

The general mechanism must be considered in the frame of specific embodied morphodynamic properties, drawing on a particular biophysical phenomenology (the rich and varied repertory of emotional behaviours for instance). According to this theory, we feel emotions as such because, as a biological dynamical system, we resist particular embodied inertial transformations in a specific way which is not reducible to a generic and abstract scheme. It is the phenomenology of the resistance to variance which makes the phenomenology of the subjective experience, and the phenomenology of the resistance to variance is totally dependent upon the biological phenomenology of the system. The differentiation among felt states would thus depends on the dynamical orchestration of the attentional, emotive and bodily changes and of the ensuing resistance. At some point, the specific structure and rhythm of our field of transformations and reactions, the modalities of self-grappling and resistance to variance or invariance, should match the phenomenology of our experience and be sufficient to define what we experience from within. This is what an experimental approach should attempt to demonstrate.[2]

Thus, to be applicable, our hypothesis presupposes certain general and specific conditions in entities capable of feeling.

First, feeling entities must be capable of certain kinds of behaviours, namely intentional and emotional behaviours; these are behaviours through which feeling entities connect with objects and situations in the internal or external environment and that involve regulatory reactions related to the maintenance of the condition of viability of the entity.

Second, feeling entities must have a certain size and a certain degree of complexity. Size is generally correlated with complexity of internal structure and with multi-componentiality. Small sizes are less compatible with the sort of inertial delayed auto-perturbing processes we envision. This putative relationship between size and the ability to feel might be seen by drawing upon the heuristic

---

[2] This framework could perhaps be extended to perception in general, which can be seen as a more or less progressive phenomenon of the enslavement of our internal activity by an emerging structure, i.e. the form or the object we are perceiving.

relation we proposed in section 5. Higher animals include increased inertia and complexity in processing related to distributed mass processing of bigger brain and organisms. In such animals, the time constants of the triggering and operation of R (the process of resistance), as well as the inertia of I (the auto-perturbation influx), must be considered as much bigger than in simpler systems. Consequently, V (the tension hypothesized to constitute feeling) cannot be reduced instantaneously, predicting a more likely development of feeling in bigger systems.

Third, as a consequence of the two first conditions, a complex, multi-componential nervous system is required for the management of size, structural complexity, and behavioural complexity. Some specific conditions of the nervous system also must be met — namely, the presence of neural sheaths capable of mapping sensory and motor events, and allowing for functional discrimination and binding of signals as well as sophisticated bioregulatory and motor systems.

3. The Meaning of Control in the Theory

We want to make clear that our approach departs from a classical general information processing framework in dealing with problems of control, such as theory of control, which uses concepts like 'efference copy' and 'feedback' to account for error minimization in servomechanisms. We believe that such classical cybernetic models do not address the brain and body dynamic features we regard as essential for the emergence of subjectivity and feeling, and which are related to the specificity of biological systems. Our view questions the phenomenological consequences of divergence and control of divergence in highly chaotic, sparse, parallel, interconnected and highly excitable biological systems, dominated by the inertia of their embodiment. We do not mean to say that classical control mechanisms and noise reduction operations can not be implemented in the brain. But they do have to face the slowness, complexity, and inefficiency of biological systems, their highly conflictive internal dynamics, all of which lead to delayed periods of decision for perception or action, mistakes, 'improvisations,' and the sort of disequilibria of which emotions are an example. What we wish to stress is that the brain appears unable to 'filter error', anticipate deviations and control them in an optimal manner. Our notion of control, then, is based on different considerations from those of models which assume the existence of optimal solutions. What we stress is the concrete physical problem that a system which operates close to overflow must face. However, we are not using the concepts of 'conflict' and 'resistance' with a negative connotation to imply dysfunction; conflict and resistance are an integrated part of the organism's condition and represent physiological and informational aspects of its behaviour.

4. The Unexplained Phenomenology

Our hypothesis has at least one important limitation in its ability to account for subjective experience. There is a fundamental and striking phenomenon at the core of subjective experience that it cannot explain: the intrinsic 'spatialization' of our subjectivity space. We feel in a projective way. The feeling of our own body is a feeling of a body in space, with interoceptive and proprioceptive sensations grossly localized in our extremities and our face. In normal conditions, the 'origin' of the subjective point of view itself feels located or concentrated in our head and perhaps along the main vertical axis of our body. There is really an auto-perceptive structure in which a subjective point of view confronts a set of body states, including itself, in a concrete geometrical space. Such spatialization is a fundamental aspect of the way we build a representation of our body.

In our view, this spatial structure is more difficult to account for than the temporal dynamics which characterizes the phenomenology of subjective experience. From a theoretical point of view, the temporal dynamics can be more easily assimilated, in an isomorphic framework, to the objective temporal dynamics of the system itself, which is quite nonlinear though.

The spatialization of subjective experience is a supramodal phenomenon, and it is partially independent from our current interaction with the environment. When we close our eyes in a silent room and stop moving we can feel it. There is something 'virtual' in such a representation that a satisfactory theory of consciousness should explain. Indeed, it is not simply the immediate consequence of the fact that our body is a three dimensional structure in an approximately Euclidian space. It is not a pure direct experience of the extension of our body. This is evidenced by pathological conditions in which this representation is deformed, altered or missing, in spite of an intact body — as in dystonia or under certain narcotic states. In other conditions this representation remains in spite of destruction of the corresponding part of the body — as with ghost limbs (see Ramachandran & Blakeslee, 1998). We believe that this phenomenon might be perfectly compatible with our framework but requires supplementary developments.

5. Toward an Experimental Assessment of the Theory

The issue of introducing concrete experimental proposals for assessing this theory is certainly central. We are not sure to be able to address this problem at this stage. The theory would need more specifications, developments and formal modeling. In this article, part of our response to the objective of searching for 'what is affected' in the system, which we regard as a general 'research program', has been to suggest looking for the existence of dynamical phenomena of resistance to variance. If, as proposed by the theory, such phenomena are central for subjectivity and feeling, they should strongly be correlated with subjective reports of feeling. The problem is that we have not yet found satisfying criteria of operationalization for the concept of resistance to variance, in a way that would define simple experimental targets or dependent variables.

As a first approximation, the search for what is affected in the system might benefit from studying the effect of outputs of local sensory regions on global neurodynamical behaviours in the brain. An important question is to know if there is any response of the brain that would suggest the coupling between cascades of perturbations resulting from sensory flows and cascades of compensations damping the former. If relevant order parameters describing collective behaviours related to the post-sensory cascades could be isolated, predictions could perhaps be made regarding how the time course of such parameters should be damped if a process of resistance would take place. Described in an adequate phase space, the trajectory of the dynamical behaviour associated with cascades of perturbations might exhibit a divergence in relation to baseline, which might be proportional to the intensity of the resistance. If we consider that inertia plays an important role in the process, then the time constants of the damping itself or the power decay related to the energy spent in the damping, might be interesting measures of the level of resistance to variance. Also, if resistance and variance are coupled so that, often, resistance increases as variance does and variance decays as resistance increases, specific patterns of oscillations might be predicted. Provided that we possessed such measures, the prediction is that the intensity of subjective feeling would be proportional to these putative time constants and rate of divergence and would be correlated with the time course of the predicted oscillations. Various time sensitive electrophysiological methods might be used in order to measure these phenomena, such as EEG and MEG. The definition of relevant order parameters might benefit from attempts to model the class of phenomena of interest (phenomena of delayed processes of damping in autoperturbing systems) using arrays of oscillators. At this point these research cues are still ill-defined, but the problem is not simple.

Thus the complexity of the processes makes it unlikely that we will be able to soon reach the goal of finely describing matching between subjective experience and specific 'orchestrations' of phenomena of resistance to variance in the brain (see section 6.2). This will require dramatic progresses in our understanding of how, in detail, large-scale computation and physics are related in the brain and brain-body system; this depends in great part on our ability to model the dynamics of these systems. It is also likely that more advanced technologies of functional brain imaging, allowing the quantification of various physiological parameters with high spatial and temporal resolutions, will be required. Also, psychological techniques of detailed quantification, or 'imaging' of subjective experience itself, will have to be developed so that matching between subjective experience parameters and phenomena of interest in the brain could be objectively determined. These techniques should notably provide measurements of the temporal dynamics of subjective experience.

7: Conclusion

As a heuristic to define a class of mechanisms of interest for subjectivity and feeling, among all the mechanisms operating in the organism, we tried to demonstrate that the very notion of affect phenomenologically implies a certain type of dynamical configuration: resistance to variance. We tried to show that such a dynamics is operating in the organism at most levels of organization that are known to be associated with subjectivity and consciousness, like vigilance, arousal, attention and feeling. From this we concluded that the physical core of subjectivity and feeling might be a dynamics of resistance to variance.

In what sense could we say that this theory, beyond proposing putative empirical relationships, reduces the explanatory gap? If science tries to account for phenomena by modeling them accurately, our task was then to model the phenomenon of being a feeling subject accurately, by reference only to the mechanics of the biological entity in which it is observed. An adequate and complete model would show that this phenomenon is a biophysical phenomenon. Rigorously, this would require an equation (or a system of equations), with on one side some variable satisfactorily describing the phenomenology of subjectivity as a spatiotemporal object and on the other some function of known physical quantities. At this point, both sides of these equations are largely missing, and this indicates that the theory is incomplete. What we have proposed is at best a heuristic qualitative gross approximation of part of this theoretical object. The only reduction of the explanatory gap that this theory could claim to have achieved, for the moment, is qualitative. Essentially, it can only be 'validated' on the basis of phenomenological intuitions, which are subjective, and as such subject to controversy, or empirical considerations which might be considered as too correlational.

In the introduction of this article, we stated that an explanatory model of subjectivity and feeling should make 'visible' these phenomena in the isolated biological mechanisms. In other words, we wanted a model, including a type of pattern in space and time, delineating a subject of sensory experiences. More generally, what we wanted was to be intuitively inclined to think that there is something that it is like to be such a physical system. (Perhaps as one would have the intuition of how a machine behaves by looking at a (very) simplified schematic diagram of its mechanics).

Let us draw such a simplified schematic diagram regarding the objective dynamics of being. It can be said, based on objective biological and neurodynamical considerations, that the class of physical systems and biological entities we belong to is characterized by the self-organized endeavour of an internal dynamical structure of resistance to variance. In this mechanics, a physical, organizationally closed, intentional machine confronts itself (literally and not only metaphorically). The system intensely grapples with the inertia of an internal ebb and flow of auto-perturbing patterns, directly linked to the operation of cognition. The phenomenology of this grappling is shaped by the need of the system to engage in intentional behaviours, attend, preserve coherence, and cope with divergent cognitive, emotional and motivational tendencies. It is shaped by the need to control behaviour, to cope with delayed auto-perturbations of the brain-body system — which implies sensory monitoring - and to delay possible responses in order to make adaptive decisions in the context of a mass of competing information. As an ongoing endeavour, it reflects how the system adjusts to respect the hierarchy of the various influences which affect its internal dynamics and organization through functional connectivity. Such an integrated dynamical framework generates internal states of controlled over-excitation, underlying vigilance and arousal. It creates a systemic tension dynamically coupled with various sources of sensory motor constraints, notably while the system copes with its own affective reactions. Moreover, it is rooted in the history of the system, and patterned by its personality, i.e. the set of its modes of reactivity.

Does such a purely mechanical model delineate satisfactorily something like a subjectivity and a process of feeling? Does it feel something to be such a pattern in space and time? Do we have here an entity which, although purely physical, is something more than a selfless and insensitive zombie? We think so, at least at a certain level of abstraction and approximation. In this sense, this theory might provide the beginning of an explanation of why and how we are feeling subjects.

Acknowledgements

We want to thank Francisco Varela, inspiring colleague, who read and discussed at length a former formulation of this theory. Kenneth Williford for his major help on this text; Evan Thompson, for all the illuminating discussions throughout the multiple versions of the paper; Jean Petitot, Patricia Churchland, Ralph Adolphs, and Paul Bourgine, for helpful readings of other versions of the text.

This work has been supported by a grant from the Mathers foundation to Antonio Damasio.

References

Arnold, M.B. (1960), *Emotion and Personality* (New York: Columbia University Press).

Beauregard, M., Levesque, J. & Bourgouin, P. (2001), 'Neural correlates of conscious self-regulation of emotion', *J Neurosci*, **21**(18), pp. RC165.

Ben-Ze'ev, A. (2000), *The Subtlety of Emotions* (Cambridge: MA: MIT Press).

Bradley, M.M. & Lang, P.J. (2000), 'Measuring emotion: behavior, feeling, and physiology', in *The Cognitive Neuroscience of Emotion*, ed. R. Lane, L. Nadel, G. Ahern, J. Allen, A. Kaszniak, S. Rapscak & G. Schwartz (New York: Oxford University Press).

Bush, G., Luu, P. & Posner, M. I. (2000), 'Cognitive and emotional influences in anterior cingulate cortex', *Trends Cogn Sci*, **4** (6), pp. 215–22.

Coghill, R.C., Talbot, J.D., Evans, A.C., Meyer, E., Gjedde, A., Bushnell, M.C. & Duncan, G.H. (1994), 'Distributed processing of pain and vibration by the human brain', *J Neurosci*, **14** (7), pp. 4095–108.

Craig, A.D. (2002), 'How do you feel? Interoception: the sense of the physiological condition of the body', *Nature Reviews Neuroscience*, **3** (8), pp. 655–66.

Crick, F. & Koch, C. (2003), 'A framework for consciousness', *Nat Neurosci*, **6** (2), pp. 119–26.

Critchley, H.D., Corfield, D.R., Chandler, M.P., Mathias, C.J. & Dolan, R.J. (2000), 'Cerebral correlates of autonomic cardiovascular arousal: a functional neuroimaging investigation in humans', *J Physiol*, **523 Pt 1**, pp. 259–70.

Critchley, H.D., Mathias, C.J., Josephs, O., O'Doherty, J., Zanini, S., Dewar, B.K., Cipolotti, L., Shallice, T. & Dolan, R.J. (2003), 'Human cingulate cortex and autonomic control: converging neuroimaging and clinical evidence', *Brain*, **126**(Pt 10), pp. 2139–52.

Critchley, H.D., Melmed, R.N., Featherstone, E., Mathias, C.J. & Dolan, R.J. (2002), 'Volitional control of autonomic arousal: a functional magnetic resonance study', *Neuroimage*, **16**(4), pp. 909–19.

Damasio, A. (2003), *Looking for Spinoza: Joy, Sorrow and the Feeling Brain* (New York: Harcourt).

Damasio, A.R. (1994), *Descartes' Error: Emotion, Reason, and the Human Brain* (New York: Grosset/Putnam).

Damasio, A.R. (1999), *The Feeling of What Happens: Body and Emotion in the Making of Consciousness* (New York: Harcourt).

Dehaene, S., Artiges, E., Naccache, L., Martelli, C., Viard, A., Schurhoff, F., Recasens, C., Martinot, M.L., Leboyer, M. & Martinot, J.L. (2003), 'Conscious and subliminal conflicts in normal subjects and patients with schizophrenia: the role of the anterior cingulate', *Proc Natl Acad Sci USA*, **100** (23), pp. 13722–7.

Dehaene, S. & Naccache, L. (2001), 'Towards a cognitive neuroscience of consciousness: basic evidence and a workspace framework', *Cognition*, **79** (1-2), pp. 1–37.

Edelman, G.M. (1989), *The Remembered Present: A Biological Theory of Consciousness* (New York: Basic Books).

Fichtenholtz, H.M., Dean, H.L., Dillon, D.G., Yamasaki, H., McCarthy, G. & LaBar, K.S. (2004), 'Emotion-attention network interactions during a visual oddball task', *Brain Res Cogn Brain Res*, **20** (1), pp. 67–80.

Foltz, E.L. & White, L.E., Jr. (1962), 'Pain "relief" by frontal cingulumotomy', *J Neurosurg*, **19**, pp. 89–100.

Friedman, D.P., Murray, E.A., O'Neill, J.B. & Mishkin, M. (1986), 'Cortical connections of the somatosensory fields of the lateral sulcus of macaques: evidence for a corticolimbic pathway for touch', *J Comp Neurol*, **252** (3), pp. 323–47.

Hurt, R.W. & Ballantine, H.T., Jr. (1974), 'Stereotactic anterior cingulate lesions for persistent pain: a report on 68 cases', *Clin Neurosurg*, **21**, pp. 334–51.

Jones, A.K., Brown, W.D., Friston, K.J., Qi, L. Y. & Frackowiak, R.S. (1991), 'Cortical and subcortical localization of response to pain in man using positron emission tomography', *Proc R Soc Lond B Biol Sci*, **244** (1309), pp. 39–44.

Lane, R.D., Reiman, E.M., Axelrod, B., Yun, L.S., Holmes, A. & Schwartz, G.E. (1998), 'Neural correlates of levels of emotional awareness. Evidence of an interaction between emotion and attention in the anterior cingulate cortex.' **10** (4), pp. 525–35.

Lane, R.D., Reiman, E.M., Bradley, M.M., Lang, P.J., Ahern, G.L., Davidson, R.J. & Schwartz, G.E. (1997), 'Neuroanatomical correlates of pleasant and unpleasant emotion.' *Neuropsychologia*, **35** (11), pp. 1437–44.

Lang, P.J., Greenwald, M.K., Bradley, M.M. & Hamm, A.O. (1993), 'Looking at pictures: affective, facial, visceral, and behavioral reactions', *Psychophysiology*, **30** (3), pp. 261–73.

Logothetis, N. (1998), 'Object vision and visual awareness', *Curr Opin Neurobiol*, **8**(4), pp. 536–44.

Mayberg, H.S. (1997), 'Limbic-cortical dysregulation: a proposed model of depression', *J Neuropsychiatry Clin Neurosci*, **9** (3), pp. 471–81.

Mayr, U. (2004), 'Conflict, consciousness, and control', *Trends Cogn Sci*, **8**(4), pp. 145-8.

Mesulam, M. M. (1981), 'A cortical network for directed attention and unilateral neglect', *Ann Neurol*, **10** (4), pp. 309–25.

Mesulam, M.M. & Mufson, E.J. (1982a), 'Insula of the old world monkey. I. Architectonics in the insulo-orbito-temporal component of the paralimbic brain', *J Comp Neurol*, **212** (1), pp. 1–22.

Mesulam, M.M. & Mufson, E.J. (1982b), 'Insula of the old world monkey. III: Efferent cortical output and comments on function', *J Comp Neurol*, **212** (1), pp. 38–52.

Mufson, E.J. & Mesulam, M.M. (1982), 'Insula of the old world monkey. II: Afferent cortical input and comments on the claustrum', *J Comp Neurol*, **212** (1), pp. 23–37.

Panksepp, J. (2004), 'Basic affects and the instinctual emotional systems of the brain. The primordial sources of sadness, joy, seeking', in *Feelings and Emotions. The Amsterdam symposium.*, eds. S.R. Manstead, N. Fridja & A. Fischer (Cambridge: Cambridge University Press).

Phan, K.L., Wager, T.D., Taylor, S.F. & Liberzon, I. (2004), 'Functional neuroimaging studies of human emotions', *CNS Spectr*, **9** (4), pp. 258–66.

Rainville, P., Duncan, G.H., Price, D.D., Carrier, B. & Bushnell, M.C. (1997), 'Pain affect encoded in human anterior cingulate but not somatosensory cortex', *Science*, **277**(5328), pp. 968–71.

Ramachandran, V.S. & Blakeslee, S. (1998), *Phantoms in the Brain: Probing the mysteries of the human mind* (New York: HarperCollins).

Redoute, J., Stoleru, S., Gregoire, M.C., Costes, N., Cinotti, L., Lavenne, F., Le Bars, D., Forest, M.G. & Pujol, J.F. (2000), 'Brain processing of visual sexual stimuli in human males', *Hum Brain Mapp*, **11** (3), pp. 162–77.

Reiman, E.M., Lane, R.D., Ahern, G.L., Schwartz, G.E., Davidson, R.J., Friston, K.J., Yun, L.S. & Chen, K. (1997), 'Neuroanatomical correlates of externally and internally generated human emotion.' *American J of Psychiatry*, **154** (7), pp. 918–25.

Rolls, E.T., O'Doherty, J., Kringelbach, M.L., Francis, S., Bowtell, R. & McGlone, F. (2003), 'Representations of pleasant and painful touch in the human orbitofrontal and cingulate cortices', *Cereb Cortex*, **13** (3), pp. 308–17.

Rudrauf, D. & Damasio, A. (2005), 'The biological basis of subjectivity: A hypothesis', in *Consciousness and Self-Reference*, ed. U. Kriegel & K. Williford: forthcoming (MIT Press/Bradford Books).

Russell, J.A. & Barrett, L.F. (1999), 'Core affect, prototypical emotional episodes, and other things called emotion: dissecting the elephant', *J Pers Soc Psychol*, **76** (5), pp. 805–19.

Sawamoto, N., Honda, M., Okada, T., Hanakawa, T., Kanda, M., Fukuyama, H., Konishi, J. & Shibasaki, H. (2000), 'Expectation of pain enhances responses to nonpainful somatosensory stimulation in the anterior cingulate cortex and parietal operculum/posterior insula: an event-related functional magnetic resonance imaging study', *J Neurosci*, **20** (19), pp. 7438–45.

Stoleru, S., Gregoire, M.C., Gerard, D., Decety, J., Lafarge, E., Cinotti, L., Lavenne, F., Le Bars, D., Vernet-Maury, E., Rada, H., Collet, C., Mazoyer, B., Forest, M.G., Magnin, F., Spira, A. & Comar, D. (1999), 'Neuroanatomical correlates of visually evoked sexual arousal in human males', *Arch Sex Behav*, **28** (1), pp. 1–21.

Talbot, J.D., Marrett, S., Evans, A.C., Meyer, E., Bushnell, M.C. & Duncan, G.H. (1991), 'Multiple representations of pain in human cerebral cortex', *Science*, **251** (4999), pp. 1355–8.

Thayer, R.E. (1989), *The Biopsychology of Mood and Activation* (New York: Oxford University Press).

Thayer, R.E. (1996), *The Origin of Everyday Moods: Managing Energy, Tension, and Stress* (New York: Oxford University Press).

Tononi, G. & Edelman, G. M. (2000), 'Schizophrenia and the mechanisms of conscious integration.' *Brain Research. Brain Research Reviews*, **31** (2–3), pp. 391–400.

Varela, F.J. (1979), *Principles of Biological Autonomy* (New York: Elsevier/North-Holland).

Varela, F.J. (1995), 'Resonant cell assemblies: a new approach to cognitive functions and neuronal synchrony.' *Biological Research*, **28** (1), pp. 81–95.

Varela, F.J. (1996), 'Neurophenomenology: a methodological remedy to the hard problem', *J Consc Studies*, **3** (4), pp. 330–50.

Vogt, B.A. & Pandya, D.N. (1987), 'Cingulate cortex of the rhesus monkey: II. Cortical afferents', *J Comp Neurol*, **262** (2), pp. 271–89.

Yamasaki, H., LaBar, K.S. & McCarthy, G. (2002), 'Dissociable prefrontal brain systems for attention and emotion', *Proc Natl Acad Sci U S A*, **99** (17), pp. 11447–51.

Zeki, S. & Bartels, A. (1999), 'Toward a theory of visual consciousness', *Conscious Cogn*, **8** (2), pp. 225–59.

JCS SUBSCRIPTION ORDER FORM

secure web ordering: www.imprint-academic.com/jcs

Name . . . .

Address * . . . .

. . . .

Home phone no . . . . Email . . . .
Credit card customers must supply cardholder registered address

ANNUAL SUBSCRIPTION RATES: Volume 12 (2005)

Twelve monthly issues. Prices include accelerated delivery (UK & USA), rest of world surface.

Individuals: $115/£62   Libraries: $385/£203   Students: $84/£46.50*
*(full-time student status evidence & course completion date required)
New for 2005: If you have a UK bank account you may like to consider subscribing by
Bankers' Direct Debit for only £15.00 per quarter. Contact sandra@imprint.co.uk for details.

☐ Please enter my library/individual/student subscription for Vol.12 ☐Airmail extra: $52/£26

Free with new subscription. Choose one of the following special back issues:
☐ *Trusting the Subject, Part 1* (10, No.9-10), ed. Jack & Roepstorff
☐ *Psi Wars: Getting to grips with the paranormal* (10, No.6-7), ed. J. Alcock *et al.*
☐ *Is the Visual World a Grand Illusion?* (9, No.5-6), ed. Alva Noë
☐ *The Varieties of Religious Experience: Centenary Essays* (9, No.9-10), ed. M. Ferrari
☐ *The View from Within: first person approaches* (6, No.2-3), ed. F.J.Varela & J.Shear
☐ *Reclaiming Cognition: action, intention & emotion* (6, No.11-12), ed. Freeman & Núñez
☐ *Between Ourselves: second-person approaches* (8, No.5-7), ed. Evan Thompson

Back Volumes Special Offer

The full set of back volumes 1–11 (1994–2004) @ *70% discount*. Includes all special issues.
Individuals and Students: $380/£205; Institutions: $1,270/£670.

☐ Please enter my Individual/Student/Institutional discount back volume order.

Payment Details

☐ Check — pay 'Imprint Academic' — $US (drawn on US bank or £ Sterling, drawn on UK)

☐ VISA ☐MASTERCARD ☐AMEX ☐SWITCH ☐DELTA ☐JCB

Card No . . . .

Expiry date . . . . . Signed . . . .
Credit cards (except US Amex) charged in £ Sterling and converted to local currency by card issuer

☐ **10% introductory discount on Volume 12 for CCDD (credit card direct debit)**,
whereby you authorise us to charge your card at annual subscription renewal time. We will notify you
by post in advance to give you plenty of time to cancel the transaction and your consumer rights are
fully protected by your card issuer. *I authorise Imprint Academic to recharge my card on the annual
subscription renewal date. Signed* . . . .

ORDER OFFICES:

US: Consciousness Studies, Dept. of Psychology, University of Arizona, Tucson AZ 85721
Rest of World: Imprint Academic, PO Box 200, Exeter EX5 5YX, UK
Tel: +44 (0)1392 841600   Fax: +44 (0)1392 841478   sandra@imprint.co.uk

Executive Editors

Joseph A. Goguen (Editor in Chief). Department of Computer Science University of California at San Diego, La Jolla, CA 92093-0114, USA. Phone: (858) 534-4197. Fax: (858) 534-7029. Email: goguen@cs.ucsd.edu

Robert K.C. Forman, Director, The Forge Institute, 383 Broadway, Hastings on Hudson, NY 10706, USA. Tel/Fax: (914) 478 7802. Email: Forman@TheForge.org

Keith Sutherland (Publisher). Imprint Academic, PO Box 200, Exeter EX5 5YX, UK. Tel: +44 1392 841600 Email: keith@imprint.co.uk

Managing Editor *(address for manuscript submissions and books for review)*
Anthony Freeman, Imprint Academic, PO Box 200, Exeter EX5 5YX, UK. Tel: +44 1392 841600. Email: anthony@imprint.co.uk

Associate Editors

Jean *Burns*, 1525 – 153rd Avenue, San Leandro, CA 94578, USA. Tel: (510) 481 7507. Email: jeanbur@earthlink.net
Ivo Mosley (Poetry), Imprint Academic, PO Box 200, Exeter EX5 5YX, UK. Tel: +44 1392 841600. Email: ivomosley@aol.com
Chris Nunn (Book Reviews), Imprint Academic, PO Box 200, Exeter EX5 5YX, UK. Tel: +44 1392 841600. Email: cmhnunn@btinternet.com
Jonathan Shear, Department of Philosophy, Virginia Commonwealth University, Richmond, VA 23284-2025, USA. Tel/Fax: (804) 282 2119. Email: jcs@infionline.net

Annual Subscription Rates (for 12 monthly issues)
Individuals: $115/£62
Institutions: $385/£203
Includes accelerated delivery (UK & USA), surface mail rest of world.
Orders to : Imprint Academic, PO Box 200, Exeter EX5 5YX, UK.
Tel: +44 1392 841600; Fax: 841478; Email: sandra@imprint.co.uk.
Cheques (£ or $US 'Imprint Academic'); VISA/AMEX/MASTERCARD

STYLE SHEET AND GUIDE TO AUTHORS

JCS is aimed at an educated multi-disciplinary readership. Authors should not assume prior knowledge in a subject speciality and should provide background information for their research. The use of technical terms should be avoided or made explicit. Where technical details are essential (for example in laboratory experiments), include them in footnotes or appendices, leaving the text accessible to the non-specialist reader. The same principle should also apply to non-essential mathematics.

Articles should not normally exceed 9,000 words (including footnotes). A short 150 word summary should accompany each submission. In general authors should adhere to the usages and conventions in Fowler's *Modern English Usage* which should be consulted for all questions not covered in these notes.

Footnote numbering should be consecutive superscript throughout the article. References to books and articles should be by way of author (date) or (author, date). Multiple publications from the same year should be labelled (Skinner, 1966a, b, c . . .). A single bibliography at the end should be compiled alphabetically observing the following conventions:

1 References to complete books should take the following form:
Dennett, D.C. (1998), *Brainchildren* (Cambridge, MA: MIT Press).

2 References to chapters in books should take the following form:
Wilkes, K. (1995), 'Losing consciousness', in *Conscious Experience*, ed. T. Metzinger (Paderborn: Schöningh).

3 References to articles should take the following form:
Humphrey, N. (2000), 'How to solve the mind–body problem', *Journal of Consciousness Studies*, **7** (4), pp. 5–20.

SUBMISSION OF MANUSCRIPTS BY EMAIL

Authors are encouraged to email their wordprocessor files (retaining italics, accents, superscripts, footnotes etc.) or PDF files. We cannot currently review LaTex files. Send all submissions to **anthony@imprint.co.uk**.

Where it is necessary to send contributions by normal mail, they should be clearly typed in double spacing. One hard copy should be submitted, plus a copy of the article on disk. This will enable us to email it to editors and reviewers and speed up the review process. Please state what machine and wordprocessing program was used to prepare the text.